Varia Folklorica

World Anthropology

MOUTON PUBLISHERS · THE HAGUE · PARIS

Varia Folklorica

Editor

ALAN DUNDES

MOUTON PUBLISHERS · THE HAGUE · PARIS

ISBN 90–279–7720–8 (Mouton)
0–202–90066–5 (AVC Inc.)
Jacket photo by Cas Oorthuys
Cover and jacket design by Jurriaan Schrofer
Indexes by Society of Indexers, Great Britian
Printed in Great Britain

General Editor's Preface

Reviewers of books emanating from conferences often disparage "edited" books as less than those by a single author; and in many cases they are justified. There are at least two kinds of exceptions. The most obvious is when the book consists of interdependent parts: a new subject in science is created by specialists brought into combination by a hitherto unasked question which may be "in the air" but still has to be revised and answered. The editor orchestrates the result; and if it is excellently done deserves the praise given to the composer and/or interpreter of a symphony. The present book represents a different exception, and in some ways a more difficult challenge. It chooses from some hundreds of papers submitted to a Congress, a minimum number of high quality to show precisely the variety of ways in which the general subject of folklore is being internationally pursued. The challenge was the greater because many of the best Congress papers were destined instead for books designed to develop special themes. But all became possible in a Congress which had uniquely written into its plans both variety and quality.

Like most contemporary sciences, anthropology is a product of the European tradition. Some argue that it is a product of colonialism, with one small and self-interested part of the species dominating the study of the whole. If we are to understand the species, our science needs substantial input from scholars who represent a variety of the world's cultures. It was a deliberate purpose of the IXth International Congress of Anthropological and Ethnological Sciences to provide impetus in this direction. The *World Anthropology* volumes, therefore, offer a first glimpse of a human science in which members from all societies have played an active role. Each of the books is designed to be self-contained; each is an attempt to update its particular sector of scientific knowledge and is written by specialists from all parts of the world. Each volume should be read and reviewed individually as a separate volume on its own given subject. The set as a whole will indicate what changes are in store for anthropology as scholars from the developing countries join in studying the species of which we are a part.

The IXth Congress was planned from the beginning not only to include as many of the scholars from every part of the world as possible, but also with a view toward the eventual publication of the papers in high-quality volumes. At previous Congresses scholars were invited to bring papers which were then read out loud. They were necessarily limited in length; many were only summarized; there was little time for discussion; and the sparse discussion could only be in one language. The IXth Congress was an experiment aimed at changing this. Papers were written with the intention of exchanging them before the Congress, particularly in extensive pre-Congress sessions; they were not intended to be read aloud at the Congress, that time being devoted to discussions — discussions which were simultaneously and professionally translated into five languages. The method for eliciting the papers was structured to make as representative a sample as was allowable when scholarly creativity — hence self-selection — was critically important. Scholars were asked both to propose papers of their own and to suggest topics for sessions of the Congress which they might edit into volumes. All were then informed of the suggestions and encouraged to rethink their own papers and the topics. The process, therefore, was a continuous one of feedback and exchange and it has continued to be so even after the Congress. The some two thousand papers comprising *World Anthropology* certainly then offer a substantial sample of world anthropology. It has been said that anthropology is at a turning point; if this is so, these volumes will be the historical direction-markers.

As might have been foreseen in the first post-colonial generation, the large majority of the Congress papers (82 percent) are the work of scholars identified with the industrialized world which fathered our traditional discipline and the institution of the Congress itself: Eastern Europe (15 percent); Western Europe (16 percent); North America (47 percent); Japan, South Africe, Australia, and New Zealand (4 percent). Only 18 percent of the papers are from developing areas: Africa (4 percent); Asia-Oceania (9 percent); Latin America (5 percent). Aside from the substantial representation from the U.S.S.R. and the nations of Eastern Europe, a significant difference between this corpus of written material and that of other Congresses is the addition of the large proportions of contributions from Africa, Asia, and Latin America. "Only 18 percent" is two to four times as great a proportion as that of other Congresses; moreover, 18 percent of 2,000 papers is 360 papers, 10 times the number of "Third World" papers presented at previous Congresses. In fact, these 360 papers are more than the total of *all* papers published after the last International Congress of Anthropological and Ethnological Sciences which was held in the United States (Philadelphia, 1956).

The significance of the increase is not simply quantitative. The input of scholars from areas which have until recently been no more than subject matter for anthropology represents both feedback and also long-awaited theoretical contributions from the perspectives of very different cultural, social, and historical traditions. Many who attended the IXth Congress were convinced that anthropology would not be the same in the future. The fact that the next Congress (India, 1978) will be our first in the "Third World" may be symbolic of the change. Meanwhile, sober considerations of the present set of books will show how much, and just where and how, our discipline is being revolutionized.

The present book is one of very many in the series on the human experience, substantively, and the ways in which scholars and scientists deal with it. Languages, cultures, peoples in their common elements and as they differ through time, and geographically, are the subjects of most of the volumes in *World Anthropology*; and folklore and the arts of at least a dozen.

Chicago, Illinois
August 4, 1978

SOL TAX

Preface

The eleven essays which make up *Varia folklorica* treat folklore from many different parts of the world. Africa, Asia, Europe, and North America are all represented, as well they should be, for the study of folklore is nothing if it is not an international discipline. Yet the essays share no common theme. Nor is there a common methodology or approach to folklore. A number of the papers are concerned to some extent with structural analysis, but this is certainly not true of the discussion of Latvian dance or the bibliographical survey of folklore research in India.

The variation in subject matter is matched by the differences in sophistication in folkloristics. Several of the papers, e.g., the essay by the late Professor Francis Utley, both demonstrate and assume great expertise in folklore theory and method. Others appear to have been written in almost total ignorance of the formal field of folklore. On the other hand, some of these studies by nonfolklorists contain fresh and exciting insights. I believe each of the papers has something important to say about some aspect of folklore.

I should like to thank the authors for allowing me to include their valuable essays in *Varia folklorica*. I wish also to express my gratitude to Professor Richard M. Dorson and to Professor Linda Dégh for their encouragement and counsel. Finally, I must indicate my debt to Marsha Siefert, former Mouton editor, whose personal interest in folklore helped *Varia folklorica* find its way into print.

Berkeley, California ALAN DUNDES

Table of Contents

The Folktale: Life History vs. Structuralism

FRANCIS LEE UTLEY†

One powerful argument for the compulsion toward polarities and binary oppositions that Claude Lévi-Strauss and Roman Jakobson find in man's languages, oral and written literatures, and societies is the almost instinctive way in which its rich insights have seemed — to the disciples, at least, if not to the masters — to be set in opposition to those of historical linguistics, the historical study of the folktale, and ethnohistory. Thus "structuralism" seems to be at war even with the threefold distinctions that Dumézil (Littleton 1966), the folktale triad, the linguistic patterning of front, central, and back in both vowels and consonants, and our own rhetorical instincts tell us are also basic.

As we know, this is the century of configurations, of models: for the atom and the universe; for the corporation — industrial, academic, and governmental; for society and kinship; and for the structures of language, whether they be the once highly favored phonemic systems or the currently favored phrase structures, "trees," and ordered rules. The centuries themselves are binary, for the nineteenth was the century of origins: of organic (biology) and inorganic (geology) evolution; of dialectical materialism, with its three neat stages and the historical replacement of one by the other; of stages of society — patriarchal and matriarchal, hunting and fishing, agricultural-rural and industrial-urban; and of the spread of Indo-European languages from a center somewhere in eastern Europe to their present wide distribution. In the study of the folktale, the search for origins of the historical-geographic school has of late been severely criticized as outmoded, and, in addition to acquiring the great wisdom which has added to the picture studies of context and process, we have been tempted more and more toward structural charts and mathematical formulae which bring light out of the nineteenth-century darkness.

Not only the triads, but also the binaries, have been always with us. They are basic abstractive devices. As Kenneth Burke — an American protostructuralist too often neglected by the modern controversialists — has argued, man abstracts both by binaries or polarities and by categories (Burke 1966:28). Whatever the dual systems mean to the more competent, more brilliant scholars of the subject, for the mediocre student they often reduce themselves to a simple clash between two arduous pursuits, one of which — theory and the gathering of data — it is very pleasant to abandon. Are we not back to the basic conflict between Aristotle and his teacher Plato (both of whom, of course, transcended their own temperamental prejudices), the only difference being that now the student leans to the theoretical and the teacher to the factual? The particular and the universal, the nominal and the real — this is the history of man's thinking, and there will always be exponents of both, whatever the fashion of the moment (Steiner 1972:15–34).

It is understandable that, as the "facts" grow more massive in number and variety, more taxonomized yet still adamant and difficult to use, young people nowadays fly to "theory," to universals. They live in an age which, having sabotaged such certainties as social trust, inner direction, religious faith, and even the belief in the dominant ego, cries out for simple methods or theories, taught from without, which may be applied without searching through the Gargantuan mass of data which the latest centuries have bestowed upon them. Some of the conflict is not merely generational, but temperamental: some philosophers and scientists wish at once to solve the problems of the ghetto and the compulsion to war; others might seek to go more directly to the nature of life and of wisdom in the hope that such humane pursuits might lead to wider understanding that could, in turn, help solve other problems. Our basic binary perhaps gives way to a triad, adding to Platonism and Aristotelianism the Deweyan "application," a kind of problem-solving that came before the philosophers — with the Greek geometers who could ultimately lead to a Timaeus, the very practical alchemists and astrologers who preceded and gave more than is generally admitted to the now respectable sciences of chemistry and astronomy, the teachers of grammar who led to a Saussure, a Dumézil, a Lévi-Strauss, and a Jakobson. The question still remains whether the problem is to be solved by the scientist *qua* scientist or *qua* intelligent humanist informed by science, for in recent years sharp cries of "mandarinism" have made us all afraid of our shadows whenever we have tried to find data without some kind of prejudice. Of course we are prejudiced, for we are human; but some over the ages have thought that there were ways of at least reducing the prejudices and that one was to gather accurate fact and the other to use rigorous theory and philosophical critique. So the binary may still remain an ideal, at least: some scholars — ambitious enough not to take one road in solitude — might gather both facts and advance theories of great importance, temporal and seminal and sometimes verging on universals. We might cite, for instance, Darwin, or Boas, or even Pike and Hockett.

Surely there was virtue both in Platonism, in which one began with a theory of universal ideas and worked them out in Socratic discussion (in the earlier dialogues at least), and in Aristotelianism, in which one studied political systems and poetics and ethics and came out both with valuable data and with reasonably satisfactory theoretical taxonomies that have lived on with us, instructed us, moved us forward, and sometimes chained us. It is a paradox that today the youth are the "theorists," for once it was the older scholars who, after long experience with continually fresh new data and series of careful hypotheses, arrived tentatively at theories which even some of the most "reductionist" among them advanced with caution, as qualifications in footnotes. The long work justified a Frazer, a Freud, or even a Marx in some final claims of theoretical consistency, yet a careful search of their work will usually reveal that the sciences of man, or any of the sciences, can never be codified without killing them. Here, indeed, is the time for the formulation of theory — about the time of life that Socrates was ready to drink the hemlock. In earlier days — not such dull days after all when one really takes a close historical look at them — the younger man, more vigorous and active with his legs, arms, and muscles, and even his eyes and ears, was expected to be the accurate fact-gatherer, the worker in the field. It was his task to learn new methods, to plunge into the unstudied oral and written literatures, to seek out hard-to-find and difficult-to-penetrate societies. If he generally began with some theory, it was only to get his fieldwork off the ground. He was expected to modify his hypotheses as, in the course of his work, he found new and contradictory facts. Thus Carl Voegelin used to insist that one should start out with a phonemic structure in mind as one sought the language in need of further study, but should begin to modify the structure when in the field one discovered new contrastive features and gaps in the "pattern." As Kurath (1967:20) has shown, the selective "theories" that described English as a single set of phonemic contrasts, as one composite pattern, became simplistic when one really paid attention to the data of linguistic geography. These examples merely show that the problems of particular and universal, nominalism and realism are themselves ultimate binaries.

For the folklorist, the major polarity of recent years is contained in the methodologies proposed by the Finnish historical-geographic school and the structural-formalistic school or schools. Recently there has been much criticism of the first of these schools; this is natural, because it is the older. Jason (1970), herself a highly competent practitioner of archival study and the life history of the folktale as well as of structural analysis, has conveniently summed up the major Russian charges against the Finnish school: (1) the material is limited to oral literature and ignores the importance of written; (2) the concept of the tale type as a stable entity is erroneous; (3) there is too much emphasis on an artificial abstract entity at the expense of the living, fleshed-out tale; (4) there are many theoretical inconsistencies in the Aarne indexing scheme; (5) there is overemphasis on monogenesis and on *Urform*; (6) there is a tendency, derived from *Urform*ism, to assume that later tales are in decay if they differ from the theoretical construct; (7) the use of a mechanistic theory of diffusion ignores the importance of cultural adaptation; (8) the belief in a *Normalform* of the tale is based on statistical tables, themselves based on the strikingly different chances of collecting in depth or shallowness; (9) there is a lack of explanation in the mechanically collected tale-monographs; and (10) abstraction, rather than true history, rules. It would be impossible to answer all of these points in order to defend what still is a profitable method, but there is nothing necessary or sufficient about these excesses and errors of the school. Written material (the chapbook, for instance) could easily be included among the data (Dégh 1969:146–163; Bettridge and Utley 1971); stability must be studied along with variability and juncture with other "types"; despite costs of printing, we *must* include as much as possible of the fleshed-out tale in its living reality (something that all abstractors except life historians are careless about); the theoretical inconsistencies of the classification can either be removed by a brilliant and energetic collaborative effort or retained for the time because of their simple convenience for reference and communication among archivists (might we not compare the chaos of library classifications, which persists in spite of all the rationales that have been applied to them at, say, Harvard, the Library of Congress, the British Museum, and the Bibliothèque nationale?); emphasis on the *Urform* is giving way to the study of distribution, migratory patterns, and subtypes — really to simple common sense; common sense likewise demands that we find both rise and fall, improvement and decay, in the folktale, especially as we recognize the relative roles of improvisation and memory, continued creativity and the *Urform* borrowed from literary textual reconstructors, and the relativity of "best" as we study the differing functions of a tale or ballad in its different stages of existence; cultural adaptation and milieu become more and more the center of our interest in comparative folktale study (Dégh 1969); the dangers of shallow collecting are more and more recognized as collecting becomes less shallow and more extensive, with even a sense of time-depth included; the monographs certainly need to be improved in explanatory factors as well as statistical tables, but this, though it also involves a war with the printer, is as easy as fleshing out the tale; and, finally, abstraction, selectivity rather than exhaustiveness, is the danger of all methods — the place where the corrective has to be applied by the serious student as opposed to the dilettante. I offer these remarks only as responses to the Russian charges (which are sound despite some debt to ideology and to the massiveness of the effort that would be required to index the rich Russian archives more successfully than they have been so far by the international methods). The indexing will come without question, because, despite the criticism, the values of the Aarne-Thompson numbers are already duly recognized and can be used in communication with those who correspond with Moscow and Leningrad and speak with heartfelt warmth with their folklorist peers at world congresses. The critique I have just offered should be evidence that the study of folktale history and geography still has a vigorous life before it and that none of the forms of "structuralism," taken by itself, is a substitute for this major academic discipline.

But the newer disciplines also must not be neglected, even by the fact-gatherer/analyst. The Finns themselves move farther and farther away from a doctrinaire "school," though they do, of course, honor Antti Aarne, Julius and Kaarle Krohn, and their many active successors both in Scandinavia and elsewhere in the world, including America. The FF Communications publish more and more in-depth studies of folk life and material culture, and they have also published Dundes' provocative *Morphology of North American Indian folktales* (1964), one of the most influential of the new structural documents. By an odd paradox, "structure" became a magic word in folklore and anthropology at just about the same time as it became a derogatory word in linguistics, a field in which the structuralism of Saussure and Bloomfield enlightened us all until in the late 1950's it fell to the onslaughts of Noam Chomsky. But the paradox is merely a semantic one, however it may delude the unwary, for the Finnish school has migrated to the America of Stith Thompson and Archer Taylor, to the Ireland of James Delargy and Sean O'Sullivan, to the Scandinavia of a host of remarkable scholars including the late Reidar Christiansen, and to the Germany of Kurt Ranke and a multitude of careful workers in both the East and the West. Poland, Hungary, Rumania, Czechoslovakia, Greece, France, and Italy are all beginning to show valuable results of international classification and migratory study; even the Middle East, the Far East, and Africa are joining the cosmopolitan venture, as witness the publication *Fabula* and the congresses of the International Society for Folk Narrative Research. Even in linguistics the paradox is only apparent, for most mature transformationalists will admit that one has to be a good structuralist before one can be a good transformationalist. We may borrow the dictum and assert that one has to be a good life historian, an avid student of folktale data both in libraries and in the field, before one can be a good structuralist. Conversely, a life historian who makes no use of the immense and exciting open-ended discoveries of structuralism — a word which brings together a number of disciplines and covers many theoretical conflicts — is scarcely at the center of modern folklore research.

What is happening, indeed, is that the sciences of man, especially those dealing with oral and written literature, are discovering so many new and valuable approaches that they need constant interchange of ideas, constant mutual critiques, and constant new field research for the testing of hypotheses. By eschewing the important data of linguistic geography, generative grammarians have often created empty abstractions. By going wild over classifications based on an unthinking use of the Thompson indexes, folklorists have been in danger of losing both the essence and the existence of the folktale — the beauty of the tale as told by the skilled, active tradition bearer. By trying to quantify language or society or folktales with statistical demonstrations alone, we have produced impressive pieces of paper, often mile-high computer printouts, which say little or nothing to the avid student. The computer is our tool, a most valuable defense against drudgery, but it is not yet, or should not be yet, our master.

Perhaps it is the glorification of the particulars a computer can handle that has brought us back so strikingly to the problem of universals. Greenberg and Chomsky have shown us to our amazement how many things, products of the psyche of *Homo sapiens*, the world's seemingly so diversified languages have in common: the noun phrase and its indissoluble bond with the verb phrase, articulation, a limited set of distinctive phonetic features, nominalization and embedding, deep as well as surface structures. Thus the emphasis has shifted from Bloomfieldian linguistics, which often aimed at showing how many varied structures, how many varied features and devices we could find in the world's languages. Yet structural linguistics, which gave priority in teaching and rigor to phonology and morphology and left syntax and semantics very much to the future, was more selective and more abstractive than the modern open-ended generative grammars. No science of man will ever describe everything, which I suppose is what is meant by the axiom "All grammars leak." The new emphases are therefore of the highest value, and the rapid advances of linguistics in the sixties and seventies demonstrate the fact that the plumbing, though continually needed, tends to repair the damages of each generation's special faults and virtues. Most notably, to bring our linguistic analogies a little closer to folklore and anthropology, we can welcome the abandonment of a flaccid, behavioristic psychology for a generative psycholinguistics that offers us hope of gaining a closer understanding of the human mind.

In dealing with folktales, the problems of selectivity, exhaustiveness, particularity, and abstraction are similar. The historical-geographic school (emended as I have suggested above) can work from hundreds of classifiable folktales, which show both a striking stability of features and fascinating variability. The stable factors are structural, but they are very real. They are based on a fundamental and coherent logic of narrative, of poetry — a logic not quite the same as that practiced by Hume or Quine, but a logic nonetheless. In "Cinderella" (Type 510A), for example, we find, in hundreds of versions the world over, five stable episodes (Roman numbers in Aarne 1961): Persecuted heroine, Magic help, Meeting with the prince (and Separation), Recognition, and Marriage. These consistent elements are quite coherent, so much so that they might even be used to support a universalism of psyche instead of the historical-geographic hypothesis of diffusion from a center (by this remark I am not deserting my own "Finnish" position). Because the heroine is persecuted, she can scarcely take action as do normal, unfrustrated or humanly favored girls (the stepsisters); she needs some kind of supernatural help or magic (in a modern office-girl romance, derived from the Cinderella theme, that type of help would take the form of coincidence, a lucky meeting with an unpredatory "angel," for instance). The help, which puts her on a par with or above her rivals, can only be for one logical purpose — a triumphal success at a ball, which means dancing with the prince (or the boss or the boss's son). Peripety demands some continuation of the story, and so the girl escapes (an episode bound in most versions with something like the coming of midnight, when magic loses its power). Continuity demands some way for the prince to find the girl again, and the nature of fairy-tale logic — that is, of human empathy and wish — demands a happy marriage at the end. The variability lies in the style which differs strikingly from country to country and region to region, and in the motifs which flesh out the abstracted episodes. Thus the persecution may come from a vain, incestuous, or love-greedy father (as in Love like salt, a common additonal episode), a stepmother, a concubine, or a common-law wife; the cinders so remarkably common (though not exactly universal) in the type are symbolic, indicating that the persecuted girl does all the dirty work and lives in the least attractive part of the dwelling. In short, we have an essential coherence among versions, a fairy-tale logic within the folktale entity (abstract) and its many versions (particular), a logic that is the very basis of the functional entertainment characteristic of the *Märchen*, with all that that means for human wish reinforcement and the glimmerings of social or at least of poetic justice.

As evidence that the bridges of structuralism can involve written literature as well as oral, I might cite two rather different approaches. One is that of Dorfman (1969; see Utley 1971), who applies the term *narreme* to certain basic, essential, and coherent elements in the early medieval epics of France and Spain, such as the *Chanson de Roland* and the *Cid*. No matter what the rest of the narrative may include, there seems to be in these poems and some of their early congeners, including even the Arthurian romances of Chrétien de Troyes, a fundamental structure of linked episodes or narremes: a family quarrel (such as that between Ganelon and his stepson Roland), an insult (Roland's charge of cowardice in Ganelon's engineering of a mission to the Saracens), an act of treachery or of prowess (Ganelon's plotting with the enemy for an ambush against Roland), and punishment or reward (the trial and execution of Ganelon). Romance scholars have perhaps not been too receptive to this kind of "structuring" of their favorite epics, and the usual danger of reductionism is certainly present here, as always in the seeking of a formula; but I have found in Dorfman's hypothesis a certain element that may be appealing to historically minded anthropologists, or culturally minded historians. That element is the way in which the logical narreme coherences can be coordinated with the feudal age — the importance of dynasty, the significant tensions within dynasty which lead to insult in an age when "honor" is the very essence of sensibility, the inevitability of strong action (treachery or prowess) when a feudal noble's honor is impugned, and the rigid nature of justice in a system in which the King's justice is the only thing that will keep peace among arrogant semi-autonomous nobles. So long as the narreme approach is taken, not as the essence of complex medieval epics, but merely as one useful method of analysis, it may provide some of the fresh understanding which both literary and anthropological study needs.

Literary critics have long considered themselves free to make their own interpretations of structure because they make no pretensions to the exact sciences. Yet they too enjoy their searches into form. Burke, for example, in his *Language as symbolic action* (1966:201), provides us with a delightful "Dramatistic" and Hegelian view of that mysteriously attractive "fragment" *Kubla Khan*:

> Stanza One (Thesis) amplifies the theme of the beatific vision.
> Stanza Two (Antithesis) introduces and develops the sinister, turbulent counter-theme (plus, at the close, a notably modified recall of the contrasting dirt theme). And the Third Stanza fuses the two motives in terms of a beatific vision (the "damsel with a dulcimer") seen by a poetic "I," the mention of whom, despite the euphoria, leads to the cry, "Beware! Beware!" and to talk of a "dread" that, however "holy," in a sinister fashion is felt to befit the idealistic building of this particular air-castle.

Of course no literary critic would leave it at this, with so few words, but I offer the analysis as a remarkably appealing statement of why this "fragment," attributed to an opium dream, has become one of the world's favorite poems.

The literary critic and the literary folklorist both write on one level of abstraction, reasonably full of detail; they may even seek another level and move to a close reading that reveals delicate touches of style; they will, following the kind of analysis I have suggested for "Cinderella," concern themselves deeply with the variations in motifs chosen to fit the stable episodes. We have seen that Persecution may come from an incestuous or tyrannical father or from some substitute for the girl's mother like a stepmother or second wife, where polygamy is permitted. Magic help may be offered by the ubiquitous, but not inevitable, fairy godmother or by the spirit of the real mother which often, more coherently or more symbolically, acts through a tree or animal in which the dead mother's spirit rests. Such choices clearly reflect the stages of animism which the originating or preserving culture command. Since we deal with supernatural powers, a taboo is usual — the girl must be home by a certain hour. Now finely dressed, in striking contrast to her usual garb of ashes, she goes to the ball or feast or wedding or potlatch. In the closely related tale, "Cap o' Rushes" (Type 510B), the form of dress becomes the central motif. Initially the girl wears ugly or idiosyncratic clothes; the appearance of her cap or dress is implied in the name of the Norse heroine Katie Woodencloak. Magic help creates for her a marvelous dress of gold, silver, and stars. In such a universally appealing tale, there can be no question that the prince will fall in love with the girl, her beauty enhanced by fine clothes, but the midnight taboo works and the girl rushes home; the prince must now find her. In some versions he merely sees her in passing; the taboo is absent. In the version of Charles Perrault, the one we know best, the Recognition is by a slipper — *verre* [a glass slipper] by an odd homonymic substitution for *vair* [a fur slipper] — but it can just as well be by a ring or some other token baked in a cake or thrown into the prince's soup, or by the capacity to pluck an apple from a tree (a task akin to the test of Arthur and the sword in the stone), or by the reappearance of the magnificent dress of gold, silver, and stars. Marriage with the prince, the *summum bonum* of a modest, although perhaps not a modern, girl's life, inevitably follows. The changes in motifs are historical, but the stable center and the folktale logic are structural for a study of a similar kind of logic in riddles, see Köngäs Maranda 1971:195).

Our error in too sharply contrasting historicism and structuralism is probably a binary error; models can also be constructed on Dumézilian triads or on continua like the physical spectrum. Folklore permits many levels of abstraction, each heuristic in its own fashion. Careful study and the notable motif of the dress in the latter have led scholars to separate "Cinderella" and "Cap o' Rushes" into Types 510A and 510B. Each has its own migratory history and represents a rather broad kind of oikotype or local variation. The regional oikotype has proved a valuable methodological concept: it indicates sub migrations, as when a Swedish variant turns up in Finland or even in Africa (where the missionary who brought it there is identifiable); it forms the basis for the study of special culture traits (as when the American version of the ballad "The demon lover" "rationalizes" out the demonic element and changes the title to

"The house carpenter"); and, very practically for the teacher, it allows the breakdown of immense collections of versions from all over the world into a limited set for a local region, with an easily controllable number of tales and a more native knowledge of the culture on the part of the student. This does not mean the oikotypal method is better than and should be substituted for the original historical-geographic method; it only means that there is some convenience in modifying the latter method for practical and immediate ends. One can call "Cap o' Rushes" and "Cinderella" two tales or one, depending on what one wishes to talk about. Or one can follow Propp (1968) and, for a number of what the Aarne-Thompsonian would call separate tale types, compose an analytical formula which is archetypical. The method is appealing because it places emphasis on the communality of interest among audiences and tale tellers; the folk poet becomes a momentarily useful abstraction like the economic man. Basically, magic in a tale is a kind of wish fulfillment, corresponding to such actualities as psychosomatic factors, lucky coincidence, or instructive traditional, if not systematic, knowledge; and the fairy tale, meant for entertainment (that is, pleasure and empathy), thrives on wish fulfillment or, paradoxically, on its frustration. Because the genre is not without overlap, the fairy tale may also involve didactic elements, so that the evil one is frustrated, as in "The fisher and his wife" (Type 555) or the various tales of "Poor and rich" (Type 1535) or "Kind and unkind" (Type 480). Valuable as the functional distinction between tales told for entertainment and tales told for didactic purposes may be, the history of both oral and written literature gives evidence that the two cannot be rigidly separated. For instance, we enjoy the identification and the punishment of the villain even as we rejoice in the cunning of the trickster (a very ambiguous figure) and in the ultimate successes of the persecuted heroine, the neglected younger son, or the scorned fool. Even a saint's legend or a *Sage* of witch or ghost can entertain, despite the fact that its major purpose is instructional. The Proppian formula, therefore, is useful in that it allows for a convenient simplification, a broad and general clue to the complex "fairy tales" which interest men in Russia, and we need not object too much to extrapolating the formula beyond a section of Afanasiev. Some of us find that kind of abstraction of the greatest interest. Others may find it self-defeating because its appearance of finality robs it of interest for those scholars who enjoy the particulars. Many of us owe ultimate allegiance to the tale itself, the individual artifact, with all its fascinating relationships to broad genres, archetypes, and Aarne-Thompson tale types. "Interest" or "significance" is a matter of personal temperament, and the "science" or "discipline" is what it is because scholars of many temperaments are enthusiastic about the ongoing results of their curiosity. Cassirer and Panofsky have emphasized these temperamental oppositions and the help they provide for each other, the profound values of analysis on various levels of abstraction (Białostocki 1970). One might exclude from this generalization the catatonic temper, but hardly any other which has had the opportunity to discover the riches of the world of man and nature.

Though Dundes was deeply influenced by Propp, in his choice of a new subject matter, the American Indian folktale, he provided an important shift of evidence and showed that we need not be limited by Afanasievan fairy tales. Dundes (1971:171) quite clearly identifies his work with the Proppian school:

> Generally speaking, there seem to be two basic types of analysis of folklore, both of which claim to be "structural." In one (Propp, Dundes), an attempt is made to discover linear or sequential structure. In folk tales, this would be plot structure. In the other type of analysis (Lévi-Strauss, Köngäs and Maranda), the given folkloric data (*given* in the sense of coming from an informant) is rearranged by the analyst. The rearranged data inevitably falls conveniently into an a priori abstract formula which is largely based on the premise that folk narrative consists of a series of binary oppositions which are mediated with varying degrees of success.

Dundes' view has proved of special value for the American Indian tale. Despite all the careful work done by scholars like Boas, Swanton, and Lowie, there is something about the "logic" of these tales that remains difficult to understand; they are not satisfying to the Indo-Europeanists who may easily accept the kind of fairy-tale logic or coherence I have been discussing. Indian tales, studied in psychological depth by Jacobs (1958–1959, 1959, 1960) and Hymes (Maranda and Köngäs Maranda 1971:52), can be shown to have a wealth of texture, psychological penetration, and cultural and societal reinforcement. Yet one has to know this one culture in depth to accomplish what Jacobs accomplished, and international folklorists need approaches, akin to those of life history, which they can apply to cultures that they know less certainly. It is just such an approach that Dundes seeks to provide.

Using Saussurean principles to coin the term *motifeme* to cover something that is a little larger than the episode found in the stable Aarne-Thompson type (for a discussion of "episode," see Krohn 1971:30–31) and at the same time a higher-level that will contain many stable episodes and variable motifs, Dundes establishes several rigid logical sequences. One of these is a nuclear one, which can of course be expanded: Lack/Lack Liquidated. Though we get progressively farther away from the *Ding an Sich*, we can apply this formula with some accuracy; it will cover the lacks of the Persecuted Heroine and the liquidation of the Magic Help in "Cinderella," and it might even apply to the prince's loss and recovery (Escape and Recognition) of the transformed girl. A more complicated sequence is Interdiction/Violation/Consequence/Attempted Escape from the Consequence, an abstraction which will contain a taboo or the Irish *geasa* and the inevitability of a violation, followed by the story that results from these beginnings. In "Cinderella" and in "Griselda" (Type 887), the taboo is not violated; in "Bluebeard" (Type 312) it is, with many consequences, including at last the death of the Monster Glutton who kills wives and hides the evidence in a forbidden chamber. Deceit/Deception perhaps fits well the broad category in Indo-European jests of Biter/Bit — the trickster tales, with their many ambiguities of tone and function, tales of Br'er Rabbit, Renard, Anansi, and the human counterparts in the "Brave little tailor" (Type 1640) and "Dr. Know-All" (Type 1641). Given these simple structural abstractions, these essential coherences, Dundes applies them to more extended tales in which the story line is much harder for us to follow, among them "Lodge boy and thrown-away," a widespread American Indian complex.

In a sense Dundes' method has a parallel in that used by Jackson (1961; see Utley 1964), who analyses a number of complex Welsh tales from the *Mabinogion* and shows them to be vastly more coherent and clear when they are considered as conglomerations of Aarne-Thompson types. Similarly, Dégh, in her *Folktales of Hungary* (1965), makes a point of choosing, not merely the conventional tale types, properly stable like the "Cinderella" I have described and found in every collection from Grimm to Afanasiev to Briggs (1970–1971), but tales which once would have been called "contaminations" and now would be called a mixture of types. The mixture naturally creates confused motivations as conflicting motifs cross one another; yet many of them may be more representative of the country from which they come even as they are less "universal."

Perhaps the most significant structuralist "hero" of them all (or at least the best-known and most frequently cited for controversy and for discipleship), Claude Lévi-Strauss, has combined his "structural" demonstrations of the relationships between South American myth and tale not only with striking musical analogies (the essence of established "forms") and binaries like the "raw" and the "cooked," but also with a large body of new raw data in an area previously little studied. The tales he discusses are linked together through motifs rather than representing coherent Aarne-Thompson structures, and thereby they make us wary because they resemble the work of nineteenth-century students like Clouston (1887). Lévi-Strauss and his followers come closer to success, however, because their point is not migration, as Clouston's was, but the demonstration of essential polarities common to remote and familiar cultures. The casual methods of Clouston, based on insufficient data, brought a good deal of discredit to the profession of folklorist; but Lévi-Strauss, working brilliantly in the field as well as in the library and with a disciplined group of fellow professionals (some enthusiastic, some very skeptical, and others capable of balanced critiques), succeeds in advancing the science. Even the contrast with the historical method, which would seem to be partly appropriate for Dumézil, cannot be charged in any absolutist fashion against Lévi-Strauss, though perhaps it pertains to his less well-informed disciples (Lane 1970:158, 171; Donato 1967:564).

My contrast between the newer structuralism and the older but improvable historicism is not one of those too common ones that set up a new theory by arguing that all prior theories are erroneous. Dundes, for instance, despite his fondness for Propp and for depth psychologies, has a very keen sense of culture contrast, including contrast in history as well as in synchronic societies (Dundes 1971:183). The approach that rests on the destruction of prior theories (better labeled hypotheses) probably owes something to the pedagogy (though not the method) of the sciences, in which one too easily ridiculed past ages by simply mentioning the philosopher's stone, epicycles, or phlogiston. The errors of the approach may in part account for youth's present flight to the occult: "We keep an open mind," they say. Of course the mind has to be logical as well as open, but there is no doubt that prior pedagogy justifies a good deal of questioning as well as a call for some solid answering.

In the folklore field, we used to begin with the Grimms, who, in spite of their practical invention of the field of folklore and their classic collection of the tales themselves from authentic sources, were shown to be "guilty" of some rewriting and "literation" of the tales and, even worse, of advancing extensive theories about how folktales were myths at base — what we would now call a serious confusion of function. (A good example of this approach can be found in Thompson [1951:367–370], though the somewhat parodistic tone of the account I am providing is more that of the unfledged student than that of the master.) The Grimms (1880–1888: vol. 1, pp. 265–272) thus find Frau Holle or Holda, a kind of weather-goddess, to be the generating center of Type 480, "The spinning women by the spring," rather than, as we should say today, a chance use of a famous name, once that of a goddess, in a tale of destiny which exists with quite different characters all over the world. Today, instead of finding Greek myths in folktales, we are more likely to find the folktales preserved in mythical surroundings and hence erroneously labeled myths (with their notable functions of cultural and personal reinforcement); examples are the tales of Polyphemus, Nausicaä, and even Circe in the *Odyssey* and "Cupid and Psyche" (Type 425) in Apuleius. This is not to rule out relationships between myth and folktale, because it is an axiom that genres overlap in both oral and written literature, whatever they may do in science (even there, what about the duck-billed platypus?). What our criticism should amount to is simply that we can learn more by treating Types 480 and 425 as international popular tales with a traceable history and countless versions than we can by tying them rigidly to a Teutonic or even an Indo-European myth, whatever adventures they may have shared with that myth as they developed through the folklore process.

In any event, unless we wish to include Vico, the Grimms are the first of those generally cited as having drawn up a reductionist view of the folktale. Their successors emulated them. The greatest sinner was Max Müller, who not only derived most stories from myth, but concentrated on one myth, the solar one. It was congenial to his special field, Hindu mythology and language, and in his hands it looked as though every god and hero was on the way to becoming a sun-god. What is more, he combined it with another congenial notion, that myths were the pathology, the distortion, of language — puns, mistakes, and misunderstandings. Because he had wit and great learning, he could argue with skill, and his work was extraordinarily popular, the more so because he wrote for both Germans and Englishmen. Yet, with the special help of Andrew Lang (himself something of a reductionist in his theory of the evolutionary concept of an originally Supreme Deity in all cultures and in his over emphasis on the survivals of savage myth in modern folklore), we have come to consider Müller as a facetious, if not a demonic, figure, so much so that as young students we would flee from a book if it had a solar god in it. Yet, having recently run out of books to read and also having had a wish to clear my shelves, I have been reading *Chips from a German workshop* (Müller 1880–1888), and I must say that there is much more good sense in Müller than nonsense (though there is plenty of that too — he is human). The inspirer of the great collection of *Sacred books of the East* cannot have been merely an empty theorist. The next culprit is Theodor Benfey, who, like Müller, was enamored of Sanskrit and its derivatives and at one stage of his work (which was overstressed by his disciple Emmanuel Cosquin) tended to follow the Indo-European philologists in deriving everything, including folktales, from India. Yet Benfey was his own best critic, and his edition of the *Panchatantra* (1966) is a book of great value. Müller's solar myth generated a host of lunar and stellar mythologists, each passionately defending his own new gods of nature. The most famous was Sir James George Frazer, who brought nature back to earth from the skies and stressed the fertility deities, the dying and resurrected god, the *hieros gamos*. Obviously his own theory, though richly defended in twenty learned volumes, involved reductionism and special pleading. He himself admitted that the Golden Bough of Nemi worked better for the Middle East than for Rome, and Fontenrose (1966) has shown that, as a library folklorist, Frazer attributed a god-king combat to the Shilluk and other African tribes, when in the field it was constantly cited merely as a legend.

Next in order as reductionist theorists of folktale origin are Freud and Jung, who, despite their differences, seek the origins of myth and other story material in the universal human psyche; they and their disciples are their best mutual critics. Though their contributions to a unified science of man are of the greatest importance, their stress on universals is a classic example of how one needs always new accessions of facts. Obviously an international tale type may be influenced in some measure by Oedipal or Great Mother concepts: "Oedipus" itself is an international type (931). But the emphasis placed by the careful collector upon the biography of the singer or teller is ignored at one's peril; it is perfectly certain that, depending on whether the teller is a man or a woman or, more particularly, a man who lives with his mother and has never married, the Oedipal "universalities" may be strikingly modified in a fashion of the greatest interest to any true student of psychology. (For a good summary of the historical student's insistence on gathering as much information about the informant as possible, see Gower 1973.)

The historical-geographic school, like these others, rests on certain assumptions, e.g., the stability and variation of single tale entities, the migration of tales, and their solid documentation all over the world. (This documentation needs much greater extension [Utley 1974], better archiving, especially for the non-European continents, including the Americas, a much more sophisticated history demonstrating culture contrast and shifts of function and genre, and better contact with the structural search for universals.) Diffusion remains a part of the theoretical pattern, one less doubtful because of the present factual richness and accuracy of collection. The old debate between evolutionism and diffusionism should be over; as a brilliant series of lectures at the Harvard Tercentenary in the late 1930's indicated, the problem has shifted to independence, convergence, and borrowing in art and culture. Finally, we are aided by the new configurational approaches, which are vastly open-ended and keep controversy alive among themselves. Edmund Leach, for instance, is one of Lévi-Strauss's biographers and also one of his most profitable critics (Hayes and Hayes 1970:127; Hippler 1972).

The pedagogical drama of historical theoretical errors must surely be abandoned, along with the temptation to make that drama into a real "history" of the science of man. It is very tempting to be an antireductionist — to take one's authority as a scholar from the confutation of another scholar, the more famous the better. I myself have sought all my life to provide a critique for reductionism, especially that reductionism which is not the inevitable result of an attempt to present an honest case but seems at times a quite conscious closing of one's eyes to clear evidence that might confute one's position. Yet I sometimes wonder whether I may not have to make retribution, in the medieval sense, with a deathbed repentance (Utley 1964, 1965a, 1965b, 1967). Surely there was justice in pointing out in the work of many of these earlier folklorists errors in fact, the abuse of polemic, fuzzy argument, too much extrapolation from too little evidence, obstinate unwillingness to see the virtues in, or even to notice, one's opponents. Folklore today bases itself on very solid ground, rather than on theoretical reconstruction; it now has at its disposal hundreds of versions of one tale type like "The love of three oranges" Type 408, (Walter Anderson's life work, still needing posthumous completion), increasingly better-recorded oral versions extending even to videotape, and vastly better contextual knowledge of milieu and of the single informant and his antecedents (Dégh 1969; Gower 1973). Yet we are still in danger, as we contemplate all these riches, of repeating the old pedagogical error of the history of error and forgetting the positive values of our predecessors.

Although the Grimm *Hausmärchen* are not myths, some of them had striking connections with myths. Müller overstressed the sun-god and philology, but there were plenty of sun-gods, and philology lies at the center of some of the best modern theoretical reconstruction (Littleton 1966:6), such as that of Dumézil. Whether Loki was a spider or a spirit of flame may never be settled, but what we do know about this mysterious trickster-god will always have something to do with language, which can never, as Cassirer (1946, 1953–1957) has shown us, be disassociated from myth and metaphor. Frazer still haunts us, perhaps too much, with his attractive theories, his probes into the sources of life and creativity, and his skillful prose; but whoever studies a Greek drama or a Celtic myth or the *Aeneid* or the *Gilgamesh* epic without consulting Frazer might just as well turn in his credentials as mythographer or folklorist. Freud may have been a bit naive about folklore and anthropology; his purpose, however, was not to explain oral or written literature, but to seek clues to the psychological motive and the therapy for man's psychic illnesses in the tales that have entertained men and in those despised phenomena the dream and the jest. An amateur Freudian (and most of us are that) can be too readily lured by the Oedipal theory. In the ballad, for instance, it is not merely the mother who is the principle of evil ("Edward" and "The cruel mother"), but the sweetheart ("Lord Randall" and "Pearl Bryan") and the envious sibling ("The two sisters" and "The two brothers") as well, and the center of villainy will shift with the individual singer. Yet all of these enemies of the hero or heroine belong to the domestic complex, and it may be very difficult to separate the strands of motivation of the different kinds of kinship (Burke 1966:31). Jung has made himself more responsible for the literary aspects of myth; some of his disciples have been either too arrogant or too casual, but none of us can deny the power of his concept of the dark and light goddesses, virgin and mother, his mastery of traditional symbolism, and his discoveries in alchemy, which may not make sense to us but made considerable sense in an age in which the male-female cosmic principle was basic.

So too it seems that if Lévi-Strauss goes too far with his "raw" and "cooked," forcing the facts of life and of literature into polarities that are heavily subjective, we must still thank him for his vigorous fieldwork and for his role in forcing us to take a careful look at the binary conflicts which are as real in the world's chaos as the triadic concepts are in the world's search for order. The best of his disciples concern themselves as much with data as he does, or as the Finnish school has done (Lane 1970:294). Dundes and Propp, in turn, work with levels of abstraction which may not always be our favorite ones, yet when we study the various dragon-slaying stories, or the persecuted wives and maidens, or the trickster tales and ogre stories, we may wish at times to avail ourselves of a higher level of abstraction than that involved in the study of one "Cinderella" or one "Dr. Know-All" entity, in spite of the lure of their individual styles and individual motif variables (Utley 1971:196–198).

The progress of science, including the sciences of man, involves many reductions. Indeed, it may be impossible for a theory to be advanced without reduction because (1) we must make our case in the limited space allowed by a publisher or editor, (2) we must make it against the last fashionable case and therefore select the best evidence in our own favor, and (3) we must argue with some force, or even with wit and polemic, against the assumptions of the last fashionable case or cases. Paraphrase, analysis, and synthesis of data are always categorical in literature and can never be holistic. The drama of scholarship, the joys of controversy and the clash of mind against mind, should not be turned into a mere defense of one's latest favorite stance. Structural anthropology and the transformational linguistics that is so closely related to it are full of trees and arrows and graphs — well, perhaps we are all more McLuhanesque than we should like to believe ourselves, and in our last phases of work we may find some consolation in outlines and models and statistical tables because the treasured data, however alluring, cannot be held in the mind or transferred to the mind of another *in toto*. If graphic or even mathematical representations help to shed some light on the polarities of culture, art, and humanity, and if they work as models and then are abandoned when better models come forward (as in the physical sciences — see Nutini 1970:76–107; Macksey and Donato 1972:70–71), they may be of the highest value, even when one wishes to modify them or criticize them (for some useful graphs of the kind, see Hayes and Hayes 1970:57; Lane 1970:313, 367–407). But if such representations become fetishes which destroy the power of words, of language, and of myth, they are as guilty of error as many of these other abandoned schools of thought I have been discussing.

Therefore, though each competent scholar and school cannot avoid some reductionism, we must insist that each contributes something new to the science, and the great synthesizers (Mircea Eliade comes to mind among the present students of myth and religion) realize that we can have myth in folktales, solar gods, fertility deities, shamans, psychic patterns, social patterns, structures, and migratory patterns.

A common charge against structuralists in anthropology and in linguistics is that they cannot make up their minds; we find Propp against Lévi-Strauss, Barthes against the field, and a host of minor and major disagreements everywhere. This is no calumny, but praise, for it shows that the field is open-ended and that younger and older scholars are all finding inspiration in one or more of the major controversialists. We may remember how in linguistics the neogrammarians knocked down the earlier historical linguists, Jespersen attacked the neogrammarians, Bloomfield abandoned Jespersen, Chomsky excommunicated Bloomfield, and now many younger scholars are showing their independence of the rigidities of the earlier Chomskyan positions. Yet the more one looks into the deep structures of the history of linguistics, the more one discovers that controversies ultimately lead to agreements and to a gradual strengthening of the field as a whole. Of course it remains controversial, and therefore alive. Linguistics, stylistics, anthropological and folkloristic historicism and structuralism must have rigor, because rigor is heuristic; but rigor, after its heuristic phases, is often a form of refrigeration, even of embalmment. The history of scholarship is not the history of error, but the history of many partial attempts which slowly establish knowledge, proffer critiques for the last formulation, and build new constructions on the old. The explanation of everything (or rather of the facts one wishes to select without new excursions into the field — itself a never ending process) by one formula is reductionism, but the play of many formulae against one another and their reconciliation, cleared of earlier errors, is science.

Scholars still can talk to one another if they are willing to master many of the disciplines of the sciences of man, even though they sometimes may grow a little complicated in their jargon, forget those in related disciplines, or just baffle intelligent men and women who would like to get the picture. The mixture of disciplines is by this time a necessity, even when our academic departmentalization does everything it can to defeat it. The most important contribution of those various schools that are called structural is their linking of anthropology, folklore, literature, linguistics, mythology, and psychology (Leach 1967:88–89).

Anthropology and folklore, thank goodness, are disciplines in which men deal with simple ideas and simple cultures as well as with complex ones, and the human element in all that they study can, if we stay close to it, keep us lucid. Nietzsche (1960) has a couple of useful remarks for us here, but we must as always beware of his special irony: "He is a thinker: that is to say, he knows how to take things more simply than they are" (p. 194). "Mystical explanations are regarded as profound; the truth is that they do not even go the length of being superficial" (p. 169).

Wishing to retain something of the lucidity and simplicity to which we all are reduced for common understanding, I have not considered here some of the tough problems of structuralism and historicism. I still believe that the migration of folktales, more and more traceable as we develop increasingly better collecting and archiving techniques and a better study of folklore context, is a valid and exciting method of approach (Utley 1974). It is not an easy method because it demands extensive tracking down and translation of what has already been collected and what needs to be collected, which involves constant correspondence with the generous scholars in archives abroad, difficult modes of interpretation, and massive bodies of tales to reproduce, classify, analyze, and bring to new life. My own pleasure lies most in coming back to the tales themselves, away from the over-abstracting studies which merely tell us that there are ten subtypes with certain locales and leave it at that. The style, form, function, and credibility status of the tale, the subtlety of the changes of motifs between one version and another, the cultural modifications and "rationalizations," the creative combinations with other tale types, and, above all, the coherence of the stable structure as it appears with its motival variety are all the potentially rich fruit of the study of the single folktale entity, the Aarne-Thompson type. Perhaps, as the inventors of the system believed, by putting many of these studies together we may rise to a higher level of abstraction and learn something more about the world history of tale making and dissemination and about the forces in the psyche which cause some tales to be created, some to live long lives, and some to die prematurely. Continuity, retention, survival, and refunctioning are all phenomena which the study of stable tale types can illuminate (Herskovits 1966:45, 52; Ward 1972:108–121). As we accumulate our data and work with them, we come close to the basis of human creativity in oral literature and in its written derivatives, and we may find that the logical structures of Dundes and the dynamic structures of Lévi-Strauss are at the very center of our ultimate results. But if we shrug our shoulders and say that all the important data are collected, that one can find all the syntax in Jespersen, all the lexicon in the *Oxford English Dictionary* and its derivatives, all the motifs in Thompson and the types either there or in some other collection; if we give up the task of the fieldworker and the historian, which is not merely to collect but to discover what to do with what we collect; if we say as one young undergraduate, influenced by Norman O. Brown, once said to me, "Facts are obsolete," we are not likely to have a living science of man and of his poetry or to reveal anything very important about human culture now or in the very relevant past.

REFERENCES

AARNE, A.

1961 *The types of the folktale* (second revision). Translated and enlarged by Stith Thompson. FF Communications 184.

BENFEY, THEODOR
1966 *Panchatantra*, two volumes. Hildesheim: George Olms. (Originally published 1859.)

BETTRIDGE, W. A., F. L. UTLEY
1971 New light on the origin of the Griselda story. *Texas Studies in Literature and Language* 13:153–208.

BIAŁOSTOCKI, JAN
1970 Erwin Panofsky (1892–1968): Thinker, historian, human being. *Siniolus* 4:68–69.

BRIGGS, KATHARINE M.
1970–1971 *A dictionary of British folk-tales*, four volumes. Bloomington: Indiana University Press.

BURKE, KENNETH
1966 Language as symbolic action. Berkeley: University of California Press.

CASSIRER, ERNST
1946 *Language and myth*. Translated by Suzanne Langer. New York: Harper.
1953–1957 *Philosophy of symbolic forms*. Translated by R. Manheim and C. W. Henfel. New Haven: Yale University Press.

CLOUSTON, W. A.
1887 *Popular tales and fictions: their migrations and transformations*, two volumes. Edinburgh: William Blackwood.

DÉGH, LINDA
1965 *Folktales of Hungary*. Chicago: University of Chicago Press.
1969 *Folktales and society: story telling in a Hungarian peasant community*. Bloomington: Indiana University Press.

DONATO, EUGENIO
1967 Of structuralism and literature. *Modern Language Notes* 82:549–572.

DORFMAN, EUGENE
1969 *The narreme in the medieval romance epic*. Toronto: University of Toronto Press.

DUNDES, ALAN
1964 *The morphology of North American Indian folktales*. FF Communications 195.
1971 "The making and breaking of friendship as a structural frame in African folk tales," in *Structural analysis of oral tradition*. Edited by Pierre Maranda and Elli Köngäs Maranda, 171–185. Philadelphia: University of Pennsylvania Press.

FONTENROSE, JOSEPH
1966 *The ritual theory of myth*. Folklore Studies 18. Berkeley: University of California Press.

GOWER, HERSCHEL
1973 Wanted: the singer's autobiography and critical reflections. *Tennessee Folklore Society Bulletin* 29:1–17.

GRIMM, JACOB
1880–1888 *Teutonic mythology*. Translated by James S. Stallybrass. London: Swan Sonnenschein and Allen.

HAYES, E. NELSON, TANYA HAYES, *editors*
1970 *Claude Lévi-Strauss: the anthropologist as hero*. Cambridge: M.I.T. Press.

HERSKOVITS, MELVILLE
1966 *The New World Negro*. Edited by F. S. Herskovits. Bloomington: Indiana University Press.

HIPPLER, ARTHUR E.
1972 Is "raw" or "cooked" a useful analytical tool? *American Anthropologist* 74:1319–1320.

JACKSON, KENNETH
1961 *The international popular tale and early Welsh tradition*. Cardiff: University of Wales Press.

JACOBS, MELVILLE
1958–1959 *Clackamas Chinook texts*, two volumes. International Journal of American Linguistics 24(2), part two; 25(2), part two.
1959 *The content and style of an oral literature*. Viking Fund Publications in Anthropology 26.
1960 *The people are coming soon*. Seattle: University of Washington Press.

JASON, HEDA
1970 The Russian criticism of the "Finnish school" in folktale scholarship. *Norweg: Folkelivsgranskning* 14:215–294

KÖNGÄS MARANDA, ELLI
1971 "The logic of riddles," in *Structural analysis of oral tradition*. Edited by Pierre Maranda and Elli Köngäs Maranda, 189–232. Philadelphia: University of Pennsylvania Press.

KROHN, KAARLE
1971 *Folklore methodology*. Translated by Roger L. Welsch. Publications of the American Folklore Society, Bibliographical and Special Series 21.

KURATH, HANS
1967 *A phonology and prosody of modern English*. Ann Arbor: University of Michigan Press.

LANE, MICHAEL
1970 *Structuralism: a reader*. London: Jonathan Cape.

LEACH, EDMUND
1967 *The structural study of myth and totemism*. London: Tavistock.

LITTLETON, C. SCOTT
1966 *The new comparative mythology: an anthropological assessment of the theories of Georges Dumézil*. Berkeley: University of California Press.

MACKSEY, RICHARD, EUGENIO DONATO
1972 *The structuralist controversy: the languages of criticism and the sciences of man*. Baltimore: Johns Hopkins University Press.

MARANDA, PIERRE, ELLI KÖNGÄS MARANDA, *editors*
1971 *Structural analysis of oral tradition*. Philadelphia: University of Pennsylvania Press.

MÜLLER, F MAX
1880–1888 *Chips from a German workshop*, four volumes. London: Longman's, Green.

NIETZSCHE, FRIEDRICH
1960 *Joyful wisdom*. Translated by Thomas Common. New York: Frederick Ungar. (Originally published 1882–1886.)

NUTINI, HUGO G.
1970 "Some considerations on the nature of social structure and model

building: a critique of Claude Lévi-Strauss and Edmund Leach," in *Claude Lévi-Strauss: the anthropologist as hero*. Edited by E. Nelson Hayes and Tanya Hayes, 70–107. Cambridge: M.I.T. Press.

PROPP, VLADIMIR

1968 *Morphology of the folktale* (second edition, revised by Louis A. Wagner). Austin: University of Texas Press.

STEINER, GEORGE

1972 Whorf, Chomsky, and the student of literature. *New Literary History* 4:15–34.

THOMPSON, STITH

1951 *The folktale*. New York: Dryden Press.

UTLEY, F. L.

1964 Arthurian romance and structural folktale method. *Romance Philology* 17:596–607.

1965a Robertsonianism redivivus. *Romance Philology* 19:250–260.

1965b *Lincoln wasn't there, or Lord Raglan's hero*. Washington, D.C.: College English Association.

1967 Anglicanism and anthropology: C. S. Lewis and John Speirs. *Southern Folklore Quarterly* 31:1–11.

1971 Review of: *The narreme in the medieval romance epic*, by Eugene Dorfman (Toronto: University of Toronto Press, 1969). *Language* 47:247–250.

1974 The migration of folktales: four channels to the Americas. *Current Anthropology* 15:5–13.

WARD, D.

1972 The fiddler and the beast: modern evidence of an ancient theme. *Fabula* 13:108–121.

The Structural Schemes of a Fairy-Tale Repertoire: A Structural Analysis of Marina Takalo's Fairy Tales

JUHA PENTIKÄINEN and SATU APO

PRINCIPLES OF PROPP'S STRUCTURAL ANALYSIS

Vladimir Propp's is one of the oldest and most widely known schemes for depicting the syntagmatic structure of narrative. *Morphology of the folktale (Morfologija skazki)* was published in 1928, as was the article, "The transformations of the magical tale" ("Transformatsiy volshebnykh skazok"), that supplemented it (see Propp 1970, 1971). It did not, however, begin to influence structural studies of narrative at the international level until its appearance in English in 1958.

Propp constructed two models for depicting the structure of fairy tales: a syntagmatic scheme linked to the chronology of the narrative and an achronic model of the dramatis personae whose basis is the division of functions among the characters appearing in the narrative. The syntagmatic scheme consists of thirty-one functions, basic units furthering the progression of the narrative. These units have been "isolated" by comparing plots with attention to the events that constitute them. The functions — the invariants recurring in the series of events making up each fairy tale — assume differing forms. Propp attempted to classify these; e.g., Function *D* (the first function of the donor) has specific realizations definable as a test (D^1), greeting and interrogation (D^2), etc. He used the terms "forms of functions" and "aspects of functions" for units of this level. A further level of abstraction in his analysis is "concrete realizations" (Fischer 1963:288).

We would like to express our indebtedness to Matti Kuusi, Pentti Leino, Heikki Paunonen, and Pirkko-Liisa Rausmaa, who read our article in manuscript and offered many valuable suggestions. We would also like to thank Eugene Holman and Robert Goebel for the translation into English.

Propp condensed the results of his syntagmatic analysis of the structure of fairy tales into four theses (1958:20–21):

1. Functions of characters serve as stable, constant elements in a tale, independent of how and by whom they are fulfilled. They constitute the fundamental components of a table.
2. The number of functions known to the fairy tale is limited.
3. The sequence of functions is always identical.
4. All fairy tales are of one type in regard to their structure.

If each basic unit is given a letter index, the pattern of any folktale can be written as follows (p. 95):

$$\mathrm{ABC}\uparrow\mathrm{DEFG}\frac{\mathrm{HJIK}\downarrow\mathrm{Pr\text{-}Rs\ o\ L}}{\mathrm{LMJNK}\downarrow\mathrm{Pr\text{-}Rs}}\mathrm{Q\ Ex\ TUW^{*}}$$

According to Propp, all fairy tales can be reduced to this invariant thematic scheme. Only some of the thirty-one units of the pattern appear at any given time, but the fact that some functions are left out does not change the order of the remaining ones. Only Function *A* (villainy) or its alternative *a* (lack) is obligatory. This function and the basic events following it form a kind of macrosegment, a move. A fairy tale may consist of one or several moves. In defining functions, the assimilation of the means by which they are fulfilled must be taken into account. The system of functions and their manifestations is so flexible that the same unit of content may be the realization of more than one function. Which function is represented by a given case depends on the position of the unit within the narrative as a whole (pp. 60–63).

Propp's analysis of fairy tales has been further developed by Dundes (1964), among others. In place of Propp's function, Dundes uses the motifeme, which he relates to Pike's behavioreme (see Dundes 1964:58–59). Lévi-Strauss (1960) has suggested that Propp's thirty-one–component pattern could be considerably reduced by defining certain functions as variants of the same basic unit or as opposites of one another. Greimas (1966:203) has offered the following reduction of Propp's pattern:

$$\bar{\mathrm{p}}\ \bar{\mathrm{A}}\ \bar{\mathrm{C}}_1\ \bar{\mathrm{C}}_2\ \bar{\mathrm{C}}_3\ \mathrm{p}\ \mathrm{A}_1\bar{\mathrm{p}}_1\ (\mathrm{A}_2 + \mathrm{F}_2 + \mathrm{non\ c})\ \mathrm{d}\ \overline{\mathrm{non\ p}}_1\ (\mathrm{F}_1 + \mathrm{c}_1 + \mathrm{non\ c}_3)\ \mathrm{non\ p}_1\ \mathrm{d}\ \mathrm{F}_1\ \mathrm{p}_1\ (\mathrm{A}_3 + \mathrm{F}_3 + \mathrm{non\ c}_1)\ \mathrm{C}_2\ \mathrm{C}_3\ \mathrm{A}\ (\mathrm{non\ c}_3)$$

Here *A* stands for agreement (order, acceptance), *F* for struggle (attack, victory), *C* for communication (sending, receiving), *p* for presence, and *d* for rapid movement. The different types of test situation are the most important components of Greima's structural scheme (p. 206): the preliminary test (*l'épreuve qualifiante*), or acquisition of magical agents, the main test (*l'épreuve principale*), by means of which a situation of equilibrium is restored through a battle or the accomplishment of a difficult task, and the additional test (*l'épreuve glorifiante*), by means of which the hero is recognized.

In addition to these tests, Melentinskiy (1969) defines the series of events leading to a catastrophe occurring at the beginning of a fairy tale as a test yielding a negative result. Meletinskiy indicates the preliminary test by the symbol ε and the main test by the symbol E.The additional test is indicated by E' and the preliminary phase leading to a catastrophe by $\bar{E}$. The results of the tests are correspondingly labeled λ (the result of the preliminary test, magical agent, advice, etc.), l (the result of the main test, removal of lack, reestablishment of equilibrium), l' (the result of the additional test, recognition), and $\bar{e}$ (the negative results, catastrophe, lack). Thus his scheme takes the following form (pp. 26–27):

$\bar{E}\bar{l} \ldots \varepsilon\lambda \ldots El \ldots E'l'$,

in which $E = f(\lambda)$ and $E' = f(l)$.

The level of abstraction of Greimas's and Meletinskiy's schemes is much higher than that of Propp's. In fact, Greimas was not so much interested in the depiction of actual folklore material as in the description of Propp's scheme, especially from the standpoint of the logical and semantic relationships to be found in it. His structural model is so abstract that it can be utilized for the depiction of other forms of narrative besides fairy tales. Similarly, Brémond's (1964) three-phase scheme or elementary sequence (opportunity, the use of it, and the result) and the binary division of an extended series of events into amelioration and deterioration of the situation are part of the general study of narrative structures.

MARINA TAKALO'S REPERTOIRE OF FAIRY TALES

In the following we shall study the possibility of applying Propp's theses and structural scheme to the fairy tales of Marina Takalo, a White Sea (or Viena) Karelian tradition bearer (Plate 1). Takalo was selected because her entire repertoire of fairy tales has been taped, some variants several times. Additionally, there exists a holistic study of her as a religious personality and a tradition bearer (Pentikäinen 1971) with which the results of a structural analysis can be compared. An investigation of the correlation between the variables that influence the performance of narratives is also possible because we have a rhythmic analysis of Takalo's narrative technique from a phonetico-musicological standpoint (Pentikäinen 1974).

Marina Takalo was born in Russian Karelia in 1890 and died in Finland in 1970. Her stories, like most of her tradition, stem from the part of Karelia bordering on the White Sea (Figure 1), where she spent the first thirty-two years of her life (1890–1922). Since she was illiterate, oral communication was her sole means of transmission of information. Her repertoire — amounting to about a hundred hours of taped material — includes all the genres of Karelian and Finnish tradition.

Plate 1. Marina Takalo, a White Sea Karelian tradition bearer

Approximately a third of Takalo's repertoire — thirteen of thirty-four tales — is fairy tales. She seemed to enjoy many of them, if we may judge from her active desire to tell them, her admiring comments following each tale, and her remarks accompanying the actual performance. Knowledge of fairy tales seems to have enhanced her prestige as a raconteuse in both her own and her associates' opinion. Knowledge of a complex fairy tale was a challenge to the memory that, as a tradition bearer unable to read or write, she was always pleased to tackle.

Marina Takalo was a person deeply interested in folklore; she seems to have collected her extensive repertoire over a long period of time from many different people. She seems especially to have actively sought the company of people with knowledge of and interest in oral tradition. For this reason, it is not unusual that her thirteen fairy tales were collected from eight different sources. All of her informants seem to have been residents of Oulanka, her home parish. With one exception, all of her fairy tales were collected during the first twenty-five years of her life. The most significant source was her father's aunt, from whom she learned at least four; for some of these she has furnished us with the first Finnish-

Figure 1. Russian Karelia and eastern Finland, showing Marina Takalo's home parish, Oulanka, ⊗ , and the various regions with whose fairy tales her repertoire is here compared

Karelian version. Eight of the fairy tales were learned from members of her own family.

In her study of the Hungarian village of Kakasd, Dégh (1962) has demonstrated that the internal narrative events of the village were usually secondary from the standpoint of the narrators: most tales were learned in situations in which the narrators found themselves working outside the village. The same seems to be indicated by Takalo's repertoire of tales and her description of the situations in which tales were told in Oulanka. Telling tales within the family circle was rare, occurring only when there were guests in the house. Within the community, tales were told when visiting, on Sundays and holidays — especially during Lent, when many kinds of work were forbidden. Men usually functioned as storytellers more frequently than women, although the latter often knew tales better than the former. Most tales were learned and transmitted in work situations, usually of a seasonal nature and taking place outside the village (for example, logging). At home, women told tales to their children to entertain them or to make them go to sleep. Parents made use of tales for instructional purposes within the family circle. Children also related tales to one another, but this type of situation cannot be regarded as of much significance from the standpoint of acquiring a repertoire of tales.

Marina Takalo herself appears as a teller of tales in three different types of situation: to her playmates and peers as a child and young adult, to her fellow workers in the logging camps, and to her children at home. She did not usually assume the role of storyteller on her own initiative if a storyteller better known or older than she happened to be present. After she moved to Finland in 1922, she was encouraged to tell tales by interested friends, especially in Kuusamo from 1922 to 1925. A return to Oulanka of two years' duration (1942–1944) ended a twenty-year latent period in her storytelling. The old memories inspired by the sight of her native district caused her to recall its oral tradition. Her reproduction of tales had advanced to such a degree by the time of her evacuation in 1944 that she made public appearances as a storyteller on her return to Kuusamo and was highly regarded as a master of the art. During her evacuation journey, the telling of tales was a scene repeated everyplace she spent the night: "An evening tale was a pastime for tired travelers." In the 1950's, when she was living at Kuusamo, she was the central figure in the homes of the village of Heikkilä at evening get-togethers. Her following included not only the children of the house, but also the adults.

In this fashion took shape the repertoire which Takalo spontaneously perfomed for the collectors of oral tradition who came to interview her from 1959 onward (Plates 2, 3). During the decade of fieldwork, her repertoire increased substantially. When in 1960 she was asked to recount those stories which she remembered spontaneously and enjoyed telling, her repertoire only contained six tales. A systematic interview in 1962 demonstrated that she remembered elements of twenty-five tales, but many of them were fragmentary and did not yet form a part of her repertoire; at this point her active repertoire was twelve tales. During the following four years, inspired to intense recollection by the interviewers' questions, she increased the number of tales, including fragmentary ones, to thirty-four, and six of the stories that she had known only as fragments entered her active repertorie to bring the total to eighteen. During the course of a long period of interviewing, Takalo would occasionally stay awake all night, and by the following morning she had sometimes remembered a tale which she had not been able to recall the previous day. The repertoire was also supplemented by her active participation within the family as a story teller (Pentikäinen 1971, 1978a, 1978b).

Plate 2. Takalo's cottage at Kuusamo

Plate 3. Takalo and Pentikäinen at Kuusamo in 1960, when the gathering of her tales began

An examination of Takalo's repertoire of tales throws light on many problems, of which only a few can be given thorough treatment within the confines of this article. We have concentrated primarily on clarification of the following questions: What were the structural schemes she knew and used? How does the structure of her fairy tales relate to the models constructed by folklorists (e.g., Propp)? Can clear stereotyped structures be found in her repertoire? What is the relationship between levels of structure and plot? A certain amount of attention has also been devoted to other variables appearing in the narration of tales, among them content, style, language, rhythm, and function. An interesting question is that of the possibilities of the narrator in relating tales: Is the telling of tales primarily a matter of artistic creation, or is it a process of memorization and reproduction? In order to assess the contribution made by Takalo as an individual, we have compared the structural features of her repertoire with those of other tales from White Sea Karelia. Since Takalo had a period of over twenty years in which she did not perform as a storyteller, a study of the relationship between the characteristics of her repertoire and those of both the corpus of White Sea Karelian oral tradition and the general narrative style of fairy tales is not without interest. For the entire period of Takalo's activity as a teller of tales, she functioned almost completely uncontrolled, lacking an audience steeped in the same cultural tradition. For this reason, speculation is in order as to the degree to which lack of this type of social control has led to personal patterns of dealing with problems, for example, on the level of plot structure. It would also be of interest to study the possibility for the tradition bearer, given competence in the stylistic, rhythmic, structural, and content norms used in the narration of tales, of composing (transforming) tales or reproducing fluent narrative units from the fragmentary material in her memory.

THE STRUCTURAL SCHEMES OF TAKALO'S FAIRY TALES

Propp's structural scheme has not hitherto been used to depict a single storyteller's repertoire of fairy tales. In analyzing Takalo's tales, we have devoted special attention to two aspects: the structural characteristics of the tales and the instrumental value of models such as Propp's for the description of fairy tales. The decision to use the models constructed by Propp was reached for several different reasons. Propp's functional scheme and model of the dramatis personae are specific and detailed, one of their express purposes being to make it possible to distinguish and classify individual fairy tales on the basis of their structural characteristics (Propp 1958:89–93). A comparison of the concrete level of content with the abstract structure seems to have more intrinsic interest than a similar comparison using models characterized by a high degree of abstraction (e.g., Greimas's and Meletinskiy's reductions of the Propp scheme). Additionally, it seemed probable that Propp's scheme, which is based on Russian fairy tales, could be rather easily adapted for use in depicting the structure of White Sea Karelian fairy tales: these show many similarities to Russian fairy tales, and many of them have been demonstrated to be of Russian origin, having been acquired by the Karelian population through tradition.

In carrying out the structural analysis of Takalo's fairy tales, we first determined the structure of each tale. In this connection, notes were also made concerning assimilation and exceptional ordering of the functions. The schemes thus obtained were arranged in a chart following Propp's basic scheme and using his symbols. From the chart it could be seen that some of the tales bore a greater structural resemblance to one another than they did to others. The structural schemes were divided into four types in terms of their relationship both to Propp's basic scheme and to that of the other tales of the repertoire.

In the quantitative description of the tales, primary attention was given to the functions inherent in the tales, the number of episodes, the repetition of structural units, and the length of the tales. Analysis of the structures was often rendered difficult by the assimilation mentioned above. Determining the "unclear" units of Takalo's tales called for particular attention to the distribution of these units, a factor which may be regarded as having increased the level of abstraction inherent in the analysis to the level of generalization used by Greimas and Meletinskiy. The Takalo material seems to indicate that assimilation is by no means to be regarded as exceptional: in more than a half of the tales investigated (eight out of thirteen), one or more cases of assimilation occur.

We shall show one scheme for each structural type identified and summarize each of the tales representing that type. Symbols in accordance with Propp's scheme have been included in the summaries. At the end of each summary will be found comments on the relationship of Takalo's version to the overall body of eastern Finnish tales. Material for comparison with Takalo's tales may be found in, for example, the taped corpus of White Sea Karelian tales published by Virtaranta (1971).

The thirteen fairy tales told by Marina Takalo, numbered in accordance with the Aarne-Thompson tale-type system, are as follows: 301D + 318, "The dragon-slayer" + "The faithless wife"; 311, "Rescue by the sister"; 315 + 302, "The faithless sister" + "The ogre's heart in the egg"; 400, "The man on a quest for his lost wife"; 402, "The frog as bride"; 403A, "The wishes"; 471, "The bridge to the other world"; 480, "The spinning women by the spring"; 510A, "Cinderella"; 533, "The speaking horsehead"; 550, "Search for the golden bird"; 613, "The two travelers"; and 707, "The three golden sons."

Structural Type 1: Proppian Adventure Tales

Tales of the first structural type (301D + 318, 315 + 302, 550) are quite close to the archetypal tale constructed by Propp. The sample scheme is a slightly simplified version of the structure of 315 + 302:

$\beta \uparrow$ DEF [A]BC $\uparrow$ HIKW

The tales of this type are journeys of adventure (beginning with ↑, departure). In the first episode of each, functions *A, D, E, F, H, I,* and *K* occur in addition to ↑. The decisive event is a confrontation ending in a loss for the villain and not merely the completion of a difficult task. Propp uses this criterion for separating structural types, and his scheme is well suited to the depiction of the structure of tales of this type, at least after cases of assimilation have been clarified. Use of the scheme is also facilitated by the fact that most of the variants of functions appearing in these tales are mentioned in Propp's list of forms of functions and their realizations. For this reason, interpretation is not needed.

On the level of plot, and particularly from the standpoint of the nature of the characters occupying the standard roles, tales of this type also have characteristic features in common. In these tales we find only one main character, whose action is followed throughout. In other structural types (3 and 4) there occur tales with plots that are not as straightforward. The hero is always a man (which is not the case in tales of Structural Types 3 and 4). His opponents (villains, false heroes) are in most cases men. The tales of this first type are so-called heroic tales (*Heldenmärchen*) (Meletinskiy 1969:29–30).

Two of Takalo's longest tales, 301D + 318 and 315 + 302, are to be found in this group; 301D + 318 is the only one of Takalo's fairy tales with three episodes (moves).

301D + 318: A queen gives birth to a girl about whom the prediction has been made that an evil spirit will abduct her on her fifteenth birthday (γ). The girl is kept underground. She asks to be released and is given permission (δ). An evil spirit abducts her (*A*). The czar begins to search for someone to rescue her (*B*). Portteipraaporššik, the hero, promises to go (*C*). He sails to a foreign country with his men (↑). They arrive at an empty hut and leave one of the men behind in it to cook their food. An old man with one eye arrives and asks for some soup. Upon receiving a negative answer, he causes the cook to become dizzy, eats the soup, and leaves. When it is P.'s turn to cook, he offers the old man soup (*DE*). He gives the old man liquor to drink, but he does not drink anything himself. Then he kills the old man (*HI*). He finds a golden key in the old man's pocket (*F*). He finds a boulder (*G*) that can be opened with the key. The princess he has been searching for is found inside the boulder (*K*). She gives P. a ring (*J*). On the morning of their departure, P. forgets the ring and returns to search for it (β). In the meantime, P.'s men leave, taking the princess with them (*A*). P. goes for a walk (↑) and arrives at a house whose owner asks him to take care of three larders. He is forbidden to open the last larder. He opens it despite the order not to (*DE*). The owner gives P. the magical agents nevertheless (*F*). P. tries out the magical agents and arrives with the speed of thought in the city he had left (↓). The boat carrying the princess arrives, but P. does not let himself be seen (*o*). One of the boatsmen claims to be the person who found the princess (*L*). At the wedding of the boatsman and the princess, P. puts the ring given to him by the princess into her drinking glass and is recognized (*Q*). The boatsman is revealed (*Ex*). P. marries the princess (*W*).

P.'s wife falls in love with the son of the enemy chief. P.'s rival starts a war, but P. is able to defeat him repeatedly by means of his magic sword. His wife finds out about P.'s secret ($\varepsilon\zeta$) and steals the sword (*A*). P. returns to the donor of the magical agents (‖↑) and receives the ability to change into any form he desires (*DEF*). Then he returns (↓). He changes himself into a stallion and is taken to his former wife and her lover (*o*). His wife recognizes him and commands that he be killed. A series of metamorphoses follows (stallion, park, duck) which ends in P.'s victory and the destruction of the wicked pair (*HI*). P. marries a servant girl who has aided him (*W*).

Neither the structure nor the units of content of this tale show any significant difference from a version recorded in Ingria in 1900 by Viljo Tarkiainen. In the Ingrian version, the preliminary episode leading up to a catastrophe (Functions $\gamma\,\delta$) is absent. Otherwise, the tales have identical structures.

315 + 302: After the deaths of their mother and father (β), a girl and a boy go out into the world (↑). The boy catches a pike in his shoe at a pond, but when the fish asks him to release it the boy does so. The pike promises to help the boy later (*DEF*). The boy also releases an eagle who has gotten entangled in some branches (*DEF*). The girl's fiancé hates the boy and blinds him (*A*). The boy walks around blind (↑). A titmouse heals the boy's eyes (*K*). The boy hears that an evil spirit has carried a princess off to a glass mountain (*AB*). He sets off for the glass mountain (*C*↑). He finds the princess, and she hides him under her bed. The evil spirit arrives and reveals where his spirit is hidden (*DE*?). The boy sets off to look for the egg containing the spirit (*G*). He is able to acquire possession of the egg with the help of the eagle and the pike (F or *M–N*?). The boy returns and begins a battle against the evil spirit. The egg breaks and the evil spirit dies (*HI*). The boy takes the princess away (*K*), and they marry (*W*).

In Takalo's variant of this tale, we see a highly original combination of plots, one not to be found in the White Sea Karelian fairy tales in the folklore archives of the Finnish Literature Society. The preliminary episode of the tale (Functions β–*K*) corresponds to the beginning of a version of 315 collected in Ladoga Karelia in 1939. The final episode (Functions *A–W*) corresponds to an episode of 302 as told by the White Sea Karelian Mari Kyyrönen. The only difference is that in Takalo's version there are remnants of Karelian 315 versions of the villain episode: The sister and brother wind up in a den of thieves. The brother kills all the thieves but one, who manages to entice the sister over to his side. The brother is blinded but regains his sight later.

550: Three brothers go out into the world one after another (β). The two older boys come to a fork in the road and take a wrong turn. The road they take leads them to a girl who entices them into bed ($\eta\ \theta$) and drops them into a grave (*A*). Cinders choose the right road when he comes to the fork. He meets a hungry wolf who asks him for his horse (*DE*). C. gives it to him and the wolf allows him to ride on his back (*F*). They gallop away (*G*). The wolf tells C. to get a fine steed (*M*). C. tries, but, in spite of orders not to, he touches the horse's bridle and therefore cannot have the horse ($\overline{NK}$) unless he first brings a golden bird, whose cage he is not allowed to touch (*M*). The wolf and C. go off to get the bird. C. touches the cage, and thus cannot have the bird ($\overline{NK}$) unless he brings the czar's daughter (*M*). Transition. Aided by the wolf, C. succeeds in getting the girl (*NK*). Transition. C. gives up the wolf to acquire the cage and the bird (*NK*). Transition. Then he gives the wolf, which has returned to him, to acquire the horse (*NK*). The wolf returns again, and he and C. go off to save C.'s brothers (↓). The girl tries to tempt C. (η), but he throws her into the grave (*HI*). The brothers are saved (*K*), and the oldest one takes the wicked girl as his wife (*W*). The brothers kill C. and steal his property (*A*). The wolf brings C. back to life (*K*). C. returns home (↓). The brothers and the wicked girl die (*U*). C. goes to live on a farm with his wife (*W*).

This version corresponds to one recorded on tape by the White Sea Karelian Outi Lipkinä only in its overall features (the acquisition of three objects, Functions *M–NK*). The preliminary episodes are quite different: in Lipkinä's version, villainy appears in the form of the destruction of a harvest. Nor does Lipkinä have the "treacherous brothers" in the final episode.

Structural Type 2: The Accomplishment of a Difficult Task

The second structural type to be found in Takalo's fairy tales is of an extremely homogeneous nature. Tales 471, 480, and 613 are representatives of this type. The sample below depicts the structure of 480:

$\eta\ \theta$ A↑ M–N K|$\eta\ \theta$ A↑ M–$\bar{\text{N}}$ $\bar{\text{K}}$ U

The tales of this type have almost identical structures: villainy (*A*), represented in 471 by lack (*a*); a departure (↑); a meeting with a person who presents a difficult task and the accomplishment of the task ($M\bar{N}$); and the reestablishment of equilibrium (*K*). This last-mentioned feature is connected with the punishment of a villain (*U*) in 480 and in the second episode of 613. Thus a conclusion is reached after accomplishment of the difficult task rather than as a result of a direct conflict between the villain and the hero. In these tales, the most common form of happy ending — *W* (a wedding and accession to a throne) — does not appear. This feature distinguishes tales of this type from Takalo's other tales.

Applying Propp's scheme demands a certain degree of interpretation, since Propp did not list and classify the innumerable variant types of difficult tasks which form the decisive points of all the tales in this group. The decisive point of tale 613 demands the most interpretation: the sequence in which the poor brother climbs into a tree and sees the people of the sea arriving with their treasure, reacts in the "appropriate" manner, and gets their treasure has been classified as *M–N* (a main test). Mention should also be made of the fact that in 471 and 480 the person demanding that the difficult task be performed has some features in common with the arranger of the preliminary test (the donor). This appears to be a further example of assimilation.

If the oppositions of the characters are observed, we notice that in 480 and 613 destruction of the villain is caused not by the hero (as in the tales of Structural Type 1), but by the person presenting the difficult task, the donor (the old woman, the people of the sea). In 471 there is no actual villain figure. Rather, the hero and the donor are opposed to one another. The donor rewards the hero for behaving in the correct manner. The structure is reminiscent of the sequence of events found in certain religious tales told by Takalo (750B, 751A).

The tales of this type are on the average shorter than others, approximately forty lines (the average length being sixty lines).

471: A rich farmstead needs a shepherd. If the shepherd is able to do his job he will receive "eternal goodness" as a reward. Two brothers go to try out as shepherds (↑), and the owner of the farm directs them to bring water from the pond that the cows drink from (*M*). Confronted there by a fiery waterfall, they bring the farmer water from the river instead. Whey they are not able to tell what they saw at the pond, they lose their jobs ($\bar{N}$). Cinders goes (↑), gets the job (*M*), and follows the cows over the waterfall to the pond. There he sees a pair of swans fighting, a pair of waterbirds cooing, an axe lodged in the head of an old man, and entrails strewn about all over the yard. He brings water from the pond and tells the farmer what he has seen (*N*). The farmer explains the meanings of the visions, and in this way C. receives useful advice about life (*K*).

The structure of the version of this tale told by Mari Kyyrönen corresponds completely with that of Takalo's version (for a full account of the latter, see Pentikäinen 1974). As concerns content, the degree of similarity is almost as great.

480: A demonic woman sends the daughter of an old man and woman along with her own daughter to a grave to spin. She gives her own daughter silk to spin, but the daughter of the old man and woman is given beard moss (η). When the girl's thread breaks (θ), the demonic woman kicks her into the grave (*A*). The girl walks off (↑) and meets an old woman who gives her work. The girl is supposed to carry water to the sauna in a sieve and bathe the old woman's lizards and frogs (*M*). She carries out these tasks well (*N*). The old woman gives her a chest full of gold (*K*). After the girl returns home (↓) with her treasures, the demonic woman sends the daughter off again to spin. This time she gives her own daughter beard moss to spin (η) and kicks her into the grave when the thread breaks (*XA*). The daughter walks away ($\uparrow$), meets the old woman, is assigned the tasks (M), and carries them out badly ($\overline{N}$). The old woman gives her a chest full of fire and tar ($\overline{K}$). She and her mother open the chest and are burned to death (U).

Mari Kyyrönen's recorded version corresponds to this one in both structure and content. The version told by another White Sea Karelian, Tatyana Huotarinen, differs from Takalo's only in that it also includes an introduction leading to a catastrophe (an old man takes a demonic woman as his wife, Functions η θ).

613: A rich brother tries to kill his poor brother but does not succeed. Eventually the rich brother takes his brother to an island ($\eta\theta$) and leaves him there (A). The poor brother walks off ($\uparrow$) and climbs up into a tree to have a look around. He sees people coming from the sea bringing goods with them to the shore. He shouts "Boo!" from the tree, and the people disappear into the sea. He is able to get the treasures left on the beach for himself (M–NK). The rich brother comes to see if the poor brother has died yet. The poor brother tells the rich one how he has obtained his treasure. The rich brother remains on the island and climbs up into the tree. He sees the people of the sea coming and bellows out: "Are you coming here again to make noise?" The people of the sea take their things away (M–$\tilde{N}\bar{K}$), cut down the tree, and split the rich brother in half (U).

The version of this tale recorded in 1891 at Ylikiiminki, northern Ostrobotnia, corresponds to this one in both structure and, for the most part, content.

Structural Type 3: Being Released from a Spell

This type is rather heterogeneous. All of these tales (400, 402, 403A, 510A) have the common feature on the structural level that they seem to diverge rather greatly from Propp's basic scheme. The following scheme is for 403A:

a C$\uparrow$ η θ A W o? M–N? L$\uparrow$ Ex D E F? K U W

The sequence of the functions in tales belonging to this group differs from that demanded by the basic scheme more often than in tales of the first and second structural types. The content units of the decisive event are most often such that they can only be assigned to functions through interpretation. For example, Cinderella's arrival at the feast (510A) is preceded by her acquisition of a magical agent (F) and is connected with the revelation of a sign which ultimately leads to her recognition and a wedding. From the standpoint of distribution, the episode is located in the story at the point of the main test — but is it any test situation? The same difficulty can be seen in 402 and 403A: it is not easy to distinguish which event leading to a final decision could be considered an actual main test. In 402, a decision takes place *ex machina*: a chance passerby kicks a frog into a river and the spell is broken. Interpretation of the events leading to a final decision in 403A seems equally forced if we interpret them as some kind of test.

If the plots of tales of this structural type are examined, we notice that the stories tell of girls who are being haunted, have been transformed by magical means into a different form, or have been forced to hide their true identity (Cinderella). Their opponents are in all cases women of demonic nature, sometimes a stepmother, sometimes a false bride. Determining the actual main character of the story is often rendered difficult because the plot follows the action of both the hero and the heroine. In some stories there is a place in which the girl is active in functions actually belonging to the realm of the hero. Outside of this structural type, this phenomenon can only be observed in one story, a representative of Structural Type 4 (707).

The length of these stories ranges from thirty-five to one hundred fifteen lines.

This third type includes tales which are rather difficult to relate to the metaplot constructed by Propp. In fact, the divergence begins to assume such magnitude that it would be possible to speak of them as "non-Proppian fairy tales."

400: (Villainy [*A*] is revealed only during the course of the tale.) A man wanders and arrives at a house (↑). The master of the house offers him work: a farmhand has to watch the soup pot and make sure that the fire underneath it does not go out (*M*). The man does the job (*N*), receives gold from the master of the house (*K*), and leaves for the city. On the way, he sees a girl who has risen little by little out of the stump of a tree (*K*). The girl asks the man to cook for one year more so that she will be able to get out of the stump. In the city the man is not allowed to go into the stores because he is so dirty (*X*). When he returns from the city for the third time, he is met by the girl who came out of the stump (*K*). She tells him to ask for what he has been cooking for the last three years as his salary, and he is given the egg by the master of the house. When the girl, a princess, hits the egg with a stone, her brother appears from it (*K*). She and her brother set off for their own kingdom and promise to come to get the man who has saved them later (β?). While he is waiting, he enters an accordion-playing contest and wins it (*M*–*N*). The prize is another princess and half of the kingdom (*K*). Nevertheless, the man goes to wait for the first princess and her brother, who have promised to come and get him at a pier. An evil spirit puts sleeping needles under his head, and he does not wake up when his bride's ship arrives (M–$\bar{N}$ or *A*?). The princess sends a letter in which she says that she will come for him again (*M*?). After winning the accordion-playing contest for the third time, he almost has to marry the princess who has been the prize (*X*). Just at that moment, the first princess comes to rescue him and takes him away with her (*W*).

A version recorded in Ladoga Karelia in 1901 corresponds to this tale in both structure and content, at least in its main features.

402: (Villainy [*A*] is revealed only during the course of the tale.) An old man and woman have three sons who compete in a shooting contest in order to win a bride (*a, M–N*). The oldest boy wins the czar's daughter and the middle one a minister's daughter, but Cinders gets a frog (*K*). He goes to get the frog from the swamp, but he cannot take it with him (*X*). Nevertheless, he finally takes the frog home to be his wife (*W*). A sewing bee is organized. The frog wins it (*M–N*). C. and the frog go to the celebration connected with the competition ($\uparrow$), the frog on a sleigh pulled by a mouse. At the bridge, a man comes up to them and kicks the frog into the river. A beautiful girl, freed from the magic spell, comes up out of the river (*K*).

In this tale, the same functions appear as in most of the eastern Finnish versions contained in the folklore archives of the Society for Finnish versions. There are more divergences in the content.

403A: A czar's son wants the sister of the son of Ivan the merchant as his wife (*a*). Her brother goes to fetch her ($c\uparrow$). While rowing back, they hear a demonic woman shouting to them to let her into their boat (η). The girl at first refuses to take her along ($\bar{\theta}$), but the third time she calls the demonic woman is let into the boat (θ). She makes the girl deaf so that she cannot understand her brother's speech. The third time the girl hears her brother's jokingly meant request to jump into the sea, she obeys it, and changes into a duck. The demonic woman appears as the czar's son's bride in her place. The girl, now duck, goes to an old widow's house in the evenings to do needlework (*o*?). She makes a mattress, a pillow, and a quilt, which a dog takes to the czar's son one at a time (*M–N* or *B*?). The demonic woman tells the csar's son that she has sewn the bedclothes herself (*L*). The czar's son goes to ask the old widow where the bedclothes have come from ($\uparrow$). She tells him how things really are (*Ex*) and how he might catch the girl (*DEF*? or *M*?). The czar's son catches the girl (*N*?, *K*). The demonic woman is burned in an iron sauna (*U*). The czar's son and the girl marry (*W*).

An eastern Finnish version corresponding completely to Takalo's is represented by a tale recorded in Liperi, Savo, in 1895. Another version recorded on tape from Tatyana Huotarinen in 1968 diverges from Takalo's only slightly in terms of structure, adding an extra episode of villainy (the placing of the sleeping needles).

510A: A demonic woman has cast a spell over an old woman, turning her into a black sheep (*A*). The demonic woman decides to kill the sheep (*A*), and the enchanted woman's daughter goes to inform her mother. The mother requests her daughter to take her bones to the base of a certain tree. The girl complies (*DE*). A feast is arranged at the czar's palace. The girl goes to cry over her mother's bones because she has no clothes (*a*). She receives clothes and a horse (*F*) and goes off to the feast (*G*). She sits at the best table while the demonic woman's daughter has to be satisfied with leftovers (*M–N*). On the way home, the daughter of the old woman kicks the demonic woman's daughter, thus breaking her leg (*U*?). When a feast is arranged for the third time, the czar's son tars the floor, and the girl's shoe gets caught in it (*J*). A search for the girl is begun ($aC\uparrow$?), but she has taken the fine clothes and the horse to the grave (*o*). The shoe is tried on all the girls of the kingdom. The demonic woman files down her daughter's foot, but the shoe will not fit her (*L*). The daughter of the old woman is presented, and the shoe fits her foot (*Q*). She and the czar's son marry (*K* + *W*).

The versions told by the White Sea Karelians Tatyana Torvinen and Irina Ahonen correspond in their main features to Takalo's, but her version lacks the introduction ending in a catastrophe (an old man takes a demonic woman as his wife — Functions η θ). Additionally, Torvinen and Ahonen add a continuation episode: Torvinen 409 and Ahonen 707.

Structural Type 4: "Non-Proppian" Fairy Tales

The fourth structural type includes 311, 533, and 707. These tales contain features that make it especially difficult to describe them in terms of Propp's scheme. The scheme that follows describes the structure of 533:

$\beta\ \eta\ \beta\ \eta\ \theta$ A Q + Ex K U

This tale, as Takalo tells it, is constructed solely in terms of a crime and its punishment. The same plot features occur in certain religious tales (cf. 780–789, "Truth comes to light"). It is difficult to conceive of the decisive moment in this tale (the girl's complaint) as fitting into any test situation, the dénouement typical of "Proppian" fairy tales.

In 311, the final part of the narrative (which is more than a third of the tale in length) describes how the heroine outsmarts the dim-witted rogue in two different ways. Units corresponding to this sequence are not to be found in Propp's scheme — unless such an extensive and many-phased series of events is to be interpreted as the realization of a single function (in this case *K*). The final sequence recalls the theme of certain animal tales and of stories about the stupid ogre: the weak but clever hero outwits the strong and simpleminded antagonist. (Takalo herself classifies this fairy tale with animal tales; according to her, it is a tale about the slow-witted bear.)

The most questionable of all, 707, is reminiscent of those romantic tales of the wife driven out on the basis of a false accusation (cf. 870–879, "The heroine marries the prince," and 880–899, "Fidelity and innocence").

Summing up the tales of this structural type, we can say that they are far removed from Propp's scheme. The features of their plots also bear a resemblance to other genres of folktales.

311: An old man goes out to get some reels for his wife's spinning wheel (β). A bear comes along and threatens to eat him if he does not give him his daughter in marriage (*A*). The old man acquiesces and, on returning home, following the bear's instructions, he says that he forgot the reels behind the fence (η). The eldest of his three daughters goes to fetch them (θ), and the bear carries her off to his abode (*A*). When leaving in the morning, the bear forbids the girl to go into the third larder. She nonetheless sticks her finger into the keyhole of the forbidden larder and it becomes golden ($\gamma\delta$). When the bear sees the finger he chops off the girl's head (A). The bear carries off her two sisters, too. The youngest succeeds in opening the door of the larder and revives her sisters (M–N,K?). The girl hides one of her sisters in a chest and asks the bear to take it unopened to their house as a visitor's gift (X). On the way, the bear wants to check to find out what is making the chest so heavy, but the hidden sister forbids him to have a look. The bear wonders at his wife's good vision, thinking that she is watching him from home (X). The bear flings the chest in the girls' yard (K?). The third time this journey is repeated the youngest sister gets into the chest herself after having placed a spinning wheel on the roof of the cottage and having fashioned from clothing the effigy of a spinner (X). En route, the bear is again about to have a look inside the chest, but the girl gives a forbidding shout. The bear guesses that the girl who is spinning on the roof has a good view of him (X). After he has brought the last girl back to her parents (K?), he returns home and discovers how he has been tricked.

A variant from the White Sea region which fully corresponds to this one in terms of structure is a tale that Tatyana Huotarinen recorded on tape. There is nevertheless some degree of divergence in the content of the introduction which sets forth the crisis ($\eta\theta$). The variant of another storyteller from the White Sea region, Iro Remsu, includes only parts of the tale. Remsu's description is confined to the deception of the slow-witted bear (the transporting of the girls and the trap laid for the bear) and leaves out the test situation (the bear forbids the girls to go into the third larder).

533: Three brothers leave home while their mother is expecting a baby (β). They send a white ptarmigan to look for a prearranged sign: if there is a spinning reel above the door, the child is a girl; if there is an axe, it is a boy. A girl is born, but a demonic woman changes the sign (η). When the girl has grown up, she sets out to meet her brothers (β). The demonic woman meets the girl and coaxes her to go swimming; when the girl refuses, the demonic woman slashes to pieces the dog the girl has with her ($\eta\theta A$). On the sixth time, the girl goes swimming, and the demonic woman steals her clothes in order to be able to impersonate her before her brothers ($\eta\theta A$). The girl is forced to become a shepherdess. While watching over her beasts, she intones a lament which the brothers hear (Q, Ex). When they find out how things really stand, they heat up the sauna and burn the demonic woman to death (K, U).

A variant written down in Ilomantsi, northern Karelia, in 1845 corresponds to this version. The realization of the villainy function of the Ilomantsi version (and of the K function which corresponds to it) differs slightly from Takalo's: the demonic woman robs the heroine of her mind and tongue and the heroine gets them back.

707: An old man and woman have three daughters. One evening, while they are sewing, the czar's son listens to what they are saying at the window. The girls are talking about what they would do if they were to get a czar's son as their husband. The youngest girl promises to bear three golden boys in the course of one year (M–N?). The czar's son chooses her to be his wife (W). When she gives birth to the children, a demonic woman exchanges all but the last of them for magpie chicks (*A*). The demonic woman persuades the czar's son to chase his wife away (*A*). The girl is put into a barrel along with the son that she has saved. The sea carries the barrel away (↑). The child prays to God for help, and God fulfills his request. The barrel breaks along the stones lining the shore, and the girl and the child receive food, a castle, and a bridge which leads to dry land (*DEF*?). The mother takes milk from her breasts and make unleavened bread. She sends her son to take this bread to his brothers (*M,J* or B?). The boy arrives and hides under the table when his brothers arrive to taste the bread (*o*?). Then he reveals himself (*Q*) and takes his brothers to their mother (*N*?). A search for the boys is begun (*aC*). The czar's son arrives at the castle, which is located on an island, and finds his family. His wife reveals the plot of the demonic woman, and the czar's son takes her back (*ExK*). The demonic woman is burned in an iron sauna (*U*).

The version recorded on tape from the White Sea Karelian Mari Remsu corresponds in its essentials to Takalo's in both structure and content. Remsu's story contains an introduction ending in a catastrophe, lacking in Takalo's, in which the demonic woman is taken as a midwife (Functions $\eta\theta$), as well as an episode in which some beggar women describe to the czar the wonders of the heroine's castle.

PROPP'S MODEL OF THE DRAMATIS PERSONAE AND TAKALO'S CHARACTERS

Constant roles are the striking feature of Propp's model of the dramatis personae. Each role has its own sphere of action, consisting of those functions whose fulfillment the bearer of that role dominates. According to Propp's system (1958:72–75), there are seven constant roles: the villain, the donor, the helper, the dispatcher, the object of search, the hero, and the false hero.

In none of Takalo's tales do bearers of all seven roles appear. In the longest of the tales, 301D + 318, there are six roles — only the helper is missing. In seven of the thirteen there are three or four roles. In 480, for example, the villain is the demonic woman, the donor is the old woman, the hero is the daughter of the old man and woman, and the false hero is the daughter of the demonic woman.

The relationships existing among the characters and the constant roles in Takalo's tales are arranged in the manner formulated by Propp. The simplest case is the one in which one role is played by a single character, as in 480. The same role may be distributed among several different characters: for example, in the cases of the son of Ivan the merchant (403A) and the three golden boys (707), it is difficult to decide which of the several characters is the hero. The same character can also function in more than one constant role. Quite commonly, the same character functions first as the donor (initiator of the preliminary test) and then as a helper in connection with the main test (the pike and the eagle in 315 + 302, the wolf in 550).

If we make a closer study of the way in which the constant roles are filled, it can be seen that in eight of the thirteen tales the villain is a person having some association with the supernatural (an ogre, a demonic woman, or an evil spirit, also called the devil by Takalo). This feature may be explainable within the context of the collective tradition of the White Sea area. Additionally, Takalo seemed, even in the role of a storyteller, to be a person who enjoyed searching for supernatural interpretations of stories and relating stories to her own view of the world, personality, and personal history. Close relatives make up a second group of villains: an unfaithful wife, a sister's husband, a brother or brothers. These two most widespread groups of villains — supernatural opponents and evil close relatives — partially overlap: the demonic woman may be a stepmother.

Women are strongly represented: in six tales, the hero is a woman. In the cast of characters as a whole, the part played by women is considerable; besides functioning as heroes, women are also the main and subsidiary villains (demonic woman, daughter of a demonic woman) and donors (the old woman in 480, the mother in 510A). The repertoire of a male storyteller would probably diverge considerably from Takalo's in this respect. Notice should be taken of the fact that in the plots of almost half of Takalo's stories there is a girl who has got into trouble. Only three of Takalo's fairy tales can be regarded as heroic tales.

Thus it can be seen that Takalo observes the world from a woman's point of view in her fairy tales, allowing her personal interests to be reflected in the characteristics and fates of the heroes. On the basis of a quantitative analysis of the content of these tales, the same kind of conclusion can be drawn as resulted from Azadovskiy's (1926) study of the details of the content, especially from the standpoint of descriptions of milieu and people, of the tales told by his informant Natalia Vinokurova. Azadovskiy concluded that Vinokurova was a realist in her role as storyteller, her viewpoints and descriptions colored by a woman's perspective.

SUMMARY: THE APPLICATION OF PROPP'S SCHEME TO TAKALO'S REPERTOIRE

On the basis of a structural analysis of Takalo's fairy tales, it seems possible to conclude that Propp's scheme is most easily applied to heroic tales, e.g., 300–303, 550–551 (Meletinskiy 1969:29). In contrast, the stories about girls under a spell and about false brides are so far from the metaplot constructed by Propp that relating their structure to it often seems forced.

Of the tales of Takalo's repertoire, a considerable number are of such a nature that they can be fitted into Propp's scheme only with difficulty or not at all: some of the tales of the third type and all of those of the fourth — that is approximately half of the examples here analyzed (six out of thirteen). In any case, it is clear that the degree of divergence of different types from the metaplot constructed by Propp varies. Some of Propp's prerequisites may have had some influence in the matter. In spite of his formalistic method, Propp was an evolutionist as an investigator of tradition and explainer of the historical genetic relationships existing in oral tradition. He was especially interested in the connections between fairy tales and myths. (Propp 1958:96; 1971:101–105). The purpose of *Morphology of the folktale* is to demonstrate that all Russian fairy tales can be derived from a single archetype whose structure is depicted by the basis scheme "discovered" by Propp (1958:93; Brémond 1964:25). During the course of the analysis, however, the basic scheme has acquired such a form that it can be used to depict not only the structure of fairy tales, but also that of certain myths. Propp had in mind myths reminiscent of the so-called heroic tales. He even suggested that the term "fairy tales" could be replaced by the term "mythical folktales" in the case of this type (Propp 1958:90, 96). Analysis of the Takalo material seems to indicate that the more the plots of fairy tales diverge from those of tales with mythological features, the more difficult the depiction of the structure of the tales in terms of Propp's scheme becomes.

It can hardly be overemphasized that the instructions given in *Morphology of the folktale* quite often leave room for interpretation. The phenomenon of assimilation, "the double morphological meaning of a single function," and a sequence of the units that diverges from Propp's scheme make it possible for analyses of tales to result in more than one solution. Propp's theses have also been strongly criticized; some of them have been shown to be badly formulated and some of them erroneous. The third thesis and the fourth thesis derived from it have been the subject of the most severe criticism. It has often been pointed out that the third thesis ("The sequence of functions is always identical") is incorrect even for the examples that Propp himself analyzed: in the structural schemes of forty-five tales found at the end of *Morphology of the folktale* there are more than thirty exceptions to the sequence required. In the opinion of his critics, the methodologically weakest point is the fact that the third thesis is sometimes realized by definition. When an analyst sets out to determine what function a particular content unit represents, his decision will depend upon the location of the unit in the series formed by all of the units making up the tale. When a unit is out of place, it changes in nature. Thus, if *E* occurs between *O* and *Q*, then it is no longer *E*, but *P* (Brémond 1964:11–18).[1]

[1] Propp proposed logical necessity as the basis of his third thesis: "Theft cannot take place

In our structural analysis of Takalo's fairy tales, the objections raised by various critics proved correct. In the ten stories that followed Propp's scheme to at least some extent, there were eleven exceptions to the order of functions presupposed by Propp. The numerous cases of assimilation mentioned above also indicate that the criticism of Bremond and others has some justification.

Propp regarded his structural analysis as one method of constructing a basis for the classification of different types of folktales. The taxonomic nature of his analysis is supported to a certain extent by the observation made above that the tales of Structural Type 4, which diverged from Propp's basic scheme to the greatest extent, contained features typical of other genres of folktales. The relationships between the Aarne-Thompson folktale types and Propp's scheme have, nevertheless, not yet been clarified.[2] Investigating the structures present in even such a small body of data as that presented by Marian Takalo's repertoire of fairy tales raises many questions. How many of the fairy-tale plots in the Aarne-Thompson index are actually constructed in the manner required by Propp's scheme? Which types of folktale can be related to the basic scheme only after interpretation (an increase in the level of abstraction of the analysis)? What does an investigation of this type reveal about the Aarne-Thompson index? What does it reveal about Propp's scheme?

Finally, there is reason to consider the question as to how many of the plots occurring in genres of folktales other than fairy tales may be depicted utilizing the Proppian scheme. Are all narratives relatable to the scheme in some way or another "Proppian folktales," "folktales subject to the seven-character scheme," or "mythical folktales"? It must be remembered that the number of functions identified by Propp is so great, and some of them are so abstract (villainy, lack, liquidation of a loss or harm), that the depiction in terms of them of narrative types demonstrating a considerable divergence from the fairy tale is possible. As examples of this we might mention Dundes's motifeme sequences of North American Indian narratives and Beneš's (1966–1967) analysis of legends. In Beneš's opinion, Propp's functions cover eleven of the fifteen segments present in the legends he investigated.

In this article only the structure of fairy tales has been considered, and consequently Propp's analysis has been applied only to them. A depiction

before the lock is broken." Brémond has shown that the order of functions is only partially determined by logic: the order of the so-called elementary sequence (e.g., paired functions) is fixed, but the manner in which elementary sequences of different types are connected is often determined by the conventions of storytelling, which can be disregarded.

[2] Drobin (1973:9–10) discusses the taxonomic nature of Propp's analysis and concludes: "Propp's system is by no means final. . . . Much remains to be done before Propp's model can be used operatively. Several substantial suggestions have been made by E. Meletinskiy, and it seems possible to improve Propp's system so that it can be used as a complement to Aarne-Thompson's type system and, in the future, to Thompson's motif index as well."

of other genres of narrative (myths, sacred tales, legends, and memorates) would require the use of new schemes based on the syntagmatic structures typical of those genres. Their investigation is a part of a holistic investigation of Takalo's oral tradition repertoire (Pentikäinen 1978b: ch. 36–38).

STRUCTURAL PATTERNS AND NARRATIVE TECHNIQUE

Examination of plot structures carried out only in the manner suggested by Propp gives an exceedingly superficial picture of the features of any individual tale. This is, of course, attributable to the fact that the main purpose of Propp's analysis was to clarify the structural characteristics of an entire genre. If, on the other hand, information is sought in the texts concerning the individual characteristics of different narrators, attention should also be drawn to the details of the content of the tales, the narrative technique, and the style, all of which are clearer vehicles for the expression of individual differences than are features of the structual level.

The social functions of storytelling make certain narrative, technical, and stylistic features more easily comprehensible. The situation in which a tale is told should be regarded as a social, communicative event in which several people usually participate. Such a situation has an analogue in the communication pattern of the "circle" (Bavelas 1960): it is a leader-centered, directed situation in which the other participants contribute only in the form of short comments and occasional remarks.[3] The storyteller directing the situation is in the central position. The most highly respected storyteller speaks and the others remain silent, even though they may know the content of the story being told as well as the storyteller. Many of Takalo's stories are pedagogical in nature. The central function of storytelling is nevertheless that of a pastime. The storyteller is a source of recreation for the community, providing a means of spending leisure time. This is also one explanation for the abundance of detail and wasteful repetition characteristic of folktales.

If the main function of fairy tales and the communicational situation typical of storytelling are both taken into account, it is easy to understand the relative length of fairy tales as opposed to other genres of oral tradition. Storytellers have been shown to try constantly to lengthen their tales; according to Dégh (1962:88–90), the ability to extend tales is

[3] The polyphonic narrative technique of the legends discussed by Dégh and Vászonyi (1971) seems impossible to apply to the telling of fairy tales. Information on different types of communication situations may be found in Pentikäinen (1971). In clarifying the structural and narrative features typical of a particular genre, the communication situation typical of it must be taken into consideration.

considered one of the most important criteria of narrative ability. In connection with the structural analysis of Takalo's fairy tales, consideration was also given to the factors influencing the length of the tale (see Fischer 1963:249–252).

The first method of lengthening a tale is to increase the number of separate basic events (functions). For example, a tale may include several different types of test situation. In the first two episodes of Takalo's longest fairy tale (301D + 318), all four of the tests listed by Meletinskiy appear: (1) an introduction resulting in a negative conclusion (it is impossible to prevent the abduction of the princess), (2) a preliminary test (Portteipraaporššik, the hero, receives the magical agents from the donor), (3) the main test (the hero kills the abductor of the princess), and (4) an additional test (the hero drops a ring into the bride's drinking glass and thus obtains a "victory" over the false hero). The length of this tale has also been increased by inclusion of the episode of the "treacherous wife" (318). The lengthening of a story by combining different plots offers the narrator the possibility of individual choices (Dégh 1962:177–180). Several combinations of plots are traditional; for example, this one is widespread (Rausmaa 1972:123). The final episode consists of test situations again. This time there are three of them, the last of which is a main test.

Combination of plots causes repetition which can be observed only on the level of abstract structure and large syntagmatic units (test situations). Tales may also be lengthened by telling episodes whose identity is apparent. The identity of the repeated episode is not total in every case. For example, in Takalo's 550, the hero has to go and fetch a different object each time. The repeated episodes also diverge from each other in that the accomplishments of the hero and his competitors (brothers, half-sisters) and their results are opposite: The hero acts correctly and the competitors incorrectly; the hero is rewarded and the others are not, or are punished.[4]

The repetition of a group of functions in Takalo's tales is considerably more common than the repetition of a single function. This indicates that the groups of functions are structural units in the consciousness of the narrator (cf. Propp's paired functions and Bremond's elementary sequences).

As an example of the extensive repetition appearing in Takalo's fairy tales, her 533 might be mentioned. In this tale, the group of functions $\eta\theta A$ (a demonic woman entices a girl to swim, the girl will not go, the evil woman chops the dog to pieces) is repeated five consecutive times. Repetition also occurs within the repeated sequences on the level of

[4] The rules identified by Meletinskiy as to the behavior of the characters in a folktale admit of exceptions: Takalo's tales contain examples of a hero achieving his goal (acquiring the magical agents or defeating the villain) even though behaving inappropriately. The logic of storytellers appears to be more flexible than that of their investigators.

sentences and their components. The number of repetitions varies from one tale (or episode) to another. It is most frequent in the story just mentioned, in which repetition of sequences of functions accounts for forty-two percent of the volume of the tale (twenty-two out of fifty-five lines). On the other hand, the repetitions in 301D + 318 account for twenty-nine percent of the first episode (twenty-three out of seventy-eight lines.)

The extent of the repeated sequence also varies, and this influences the rhythm arising from the progression of the story. In 533, an extremely short sequence is continually repeated: the extent of the sequence accounts for only one-tenth of the material relevant for the story (that is the material necessary for the advancement of the plot), and the repetition seems to be dense, choppy. A more extensive, broader repetition can be found at the beginning of 400, in which the repeated material accounts for one-third of the relevant material in the episode.

In addition to the presentation of as many different functions as possible, the use of repetition, and the addition of new episodes, a tale may also be lengthened by extending one of the basic events through enumeration of several successive variants of it. In 471, the units *M–N* (a difficult task) is complex in structure: the hero must (1) bring water from the pond that the cows drink from and (2) tell what he saw at the pond. The "visions" form a series: (1) the fighting pair of swans, (2) the cooing pair of water birds, (3) the axe lodged in the head of the old man, (4) the entrails strewn about all over the yard. Takalo's tales contain several examples of recurring variants (400, 403A, 471). In this case, too, we may be said to have an example of repetition. In some tales (400, 471) these may be regarded as free variants; their order may change, and they may be deleted from the story without changing it. The components of the extended basic event can nevertheless be connected to one another according to a certain logical order. For example, the villainy unit of 403A takes the following form: (1) a demonic woman makes the heroine deaf (Propp's A,^{6} maiming, mutilation). For this reason she understands her brother's speech incorrectly and jumps into the sea and (2) changes into a duck (A,^{11} the casting of a spell, transformation), at which time (3) the demonic woman may appear in her place as the bride (A,^{12} substitution). The structure is also climactic — initially, only a small example of villainy is presented, and only after that does an actual catastrophe occur.[5]

A story can also be lengthened by describing its basic events, or at least some of them, in extreme detail. According to Dégh (1969:178–179), this method is used by the best Hungarian storytellers and by Azadovs-

[5] The climactic effect is also emphasized on the rhythmic level, as has been demonstrated by the phonetic analysis of the fundamental frequency of folktale narration (see Pentikäinen 1974).

kiy's informant Natalia Vinokurova. In Takalo's fairy tales, detailed descriptions of milieu or people do not appear. Takalo's most frequently used method of lengthening fairy tales is the simplest of all—repetition.

In examining the common features of Takalo's fairy tale repertoire, it was possible to observe, in addition to similarities in structure, identity on the level of variants. A "difficult task" often takes the form of a competition in these tales. A "punishment" is usually burning; an "interdiction and its violation" is represented by three larders both in 301D + 318 and in 311. Inquiries and answers formulated in the same words are found in 301D + 318 and 315 + 302. Constant roles also take on the same manifestations in different tales: a demonic woman often plays the role of villain. A feature familiar in folk epics may be observed in these tales, namely, that identical units may be used in different structural wholes and even in different structural functions (the same inquiry and answer is the realization of different functions in 301D + 318 and 315 + 302; cf. Propp's conception of assimilation).

TAKALO'S FAIRY TALES AND THE FOLKTALE CORPUS OF WHITE SEA KARELIA

Most of Takalo's fairy tales are in quite good accord with the fairy-tale tradition of White Sea Karelia. The White Sea variants of most of the types of fairy tales told by Takalo are in line with her variants in terms of both structure and content.

Different narrators exhibit divergences in that their tales include varying numbers of functions. Tatyana Torvinen's version of 510 differs from Takalo's in that it includes an additional test situation; a series of events is related which leads to misfortune (Meletinskiy's $\overline{El}$); the upshot of these events is that the heroine's mother turns into a black sheep. A similar situation occurs in 707, where Takalo's variant lacks a test which ends in a negative result — an aspect included by Mari Remsu, who describes how the demonic woman inveigles the czar's son into taking her as a midwife (Propp's Functions $\eta\theta$).

The narrators also differ from each other in the way they combine plots and episodes (moves). Okahvie Mäkelä links 403 and 409, and Tatyana Torvinen combines 510 and 409, while Takalo provides no continuation whatever for 403 or 510A. On the other hand, Takalo adds a "treacherous brothers" episode to 550 while Outi Lipkinä does not.

Differences also show up in the way narrators make use of repetition. In many cases, repetition is a function of plot type (in plots based on the theme "good girl and bad girl", certain passages are repeated twice; in others, three brothers, in turn, figure in the action three times), but the narrators also have wide latitude for individual selection. In 301D + 318,

Takalo relates Functions *C* (the hero promises to go in search of the princess) and *DE* (the hero has to take care of three larders) three times each. In the Ingrian variant written down by Viljo Tarkiainen, these passages are not repeated. Certain series of events are related three times by Takalo in 403A (the conversation in the boat, the dog's bringing bedclothes to the czar's son). Tatyana Huotarinen relates the corresponding passages twice.

When two narrators relate the same type of fairy tale, the greatest number of differences turn up in the details of the content. In Takalo's 471 it is the "master" who sets the test, whereas in Mari Kyyrönen's variant it is the "czar." Takalo's hero herds cows, but Kyyrönen's keeps watch over a single ox. One shepherd performs his task by grabbing hold of the bull's tail and swimming across the river, the other by jumping onto the ox's back and flying across the sea. These two narrators also give different accounts of what is seen in the other world. Takalo mentions a pair of swans, a pair of water birds, an axe lodged in the old man's head, and entrails strewn all over the yard. Kyyrönen's list is considerably shorter: lizards and frogs jumping about on the floor of the cottage and an old man with an axe sticking in his head.

The most striking difference between Takalo's fairy tales and the White Sea variants used as comparative material is their length. In 510 it takes Tatyana Torvinen two hundred lines to tell a section which corresponds to Takalo's fifty-five lines. As told by Mari Remsu, 707 is three hundred forty lines long, whereas Takalo's version has sixty lines.

The concise format of Takalo's fairy tales in most cases is not due to phenomena that are perceptible at the level of structure, i.e., to a reduction of functions or moves. It is part of Takalo's narrative style — how elaborately or dramatically she describes the events. The following excerpts from 510A give a picture of two different styles of narration:

Marina Takalo: And when that evil woman feeds the sheep she always tells the old man in a wheezing voice that he should slaughter that black sheep because it neither eats nor drinks. The old man starts to sharpen his knife and the girl runs crying to her mother. She said, "They're going to kill you." "Well, when they kill me," she said, "they'll cook my flesh and my headbone, so take them to the foot of such and such a tree. Bury everything and put all the bones together in one place." Well, she did what she was supposed to do.

Tatyana Torvinen: The evil old woman notices, that hag, that she doesn't want the sheep to talk. "Go ahead, old man, and kill that sheep," she says, "we haven't got any use for it."

When the girl hears this she goes to the sheep, throws her arms round its neck and cries: "Oh, mother, now they're going to kill you," she says, "whatever is going to become of me?" "Easy, now," she says, "if they kill me, then so much the better. Then I'll be freed from this curse, and you'll be better off. Let them kill me," she says. "I'll tell you what to do, deary," she says. "When they kill me, don't eat of my flesh and don't drink any of the broth," she says. "When they make lamb soup and put some in your bowl, then put in all the pieces of meat," she says, "and gather together all the bones and take everything away. Say: 'I'm taking this' and make like you're going out into the yard to eat," she says. "And take these victuals to the fodder field, out to the white meadow, and place them under the big rock. Go out with your soup and take them there and place them there, the bones I mean, all of them, and count them as you put them there and wet them with the soup and dump the water you use to do the dishes on the ground and wet my bones with it."

Well, then, they go ahead and kill the sheep. The poor girl weeps, the poor girl weeps when they kill it, but she daren't say a thing. They make meat soup. "What's wrong with you?" shouts the old hag, "What's wrong with you?"

The girl is filled with fear as she eats and she says: "I'd rather eat out in the yard."

Comparing the styles of Takalo and Torvinen, we see that the latter is a narrator who feels the spirit of the tale: she is lively and dramatic. Takalo's variant lacks Torvinen's true-to-life dialogues and detailed explanatory descriptions.

Marina Takalo does not creatively reshape the tales she narrates. Her variants of the same tale recorded in different years are nearly identical. Virtually no differences can be observed in their structures. There are probably several reasons that Takalo's tales are succinct and schematic. It is not a matter of lack of imagination or creative ability. Proof of this is offered by the allegorical narrative poems she composed about her own life. The nature of her fairy-tale narration was most likely influenced by the fact that her ties with White Sea Karelian masters of the genre were severed quite early (at the age of thirty-two, when she was a passive storyteller). In trying to recall her repertoire of fairy tales, she was unable to fall back on examples offered by other Karelian narrators, and she also lacked the social control that they might have exercised on her style of narration.

TAKALO'S FAIRY TALES AND THE "EPIC LAWS" OF FOLK NARRATIVE

A scholar who focused particular attention on the question of the regularities of folk narrative was Axel Olrik, who in 1908 advanced his theory of the so-called epic laws of folk narrative (Olrik 1921). In his opinion, the entire folk narrative tradition — in this connection he departs from present-day terminology and employs the concept of *Sagenwelt* — adheres to rules that are above time and culture. Olrik agrees that particular national traits exist but considers them more on the order of dialect differences. Olrik (1965:131) states: "We call these principles 'laws' because they limit the freedom of composition of oral literature in a much different and more rigid way than in our written literature."

The way in which Olrik sets forth his laws indicates that he considers them to be universally true, irrespective of time, nationality, or culture. To use the terminology of cultural anthropology, what is involved here is the notion of *superorganic* structures of culture. According to this notion, in addition to the organic level controlled by man, there is a superorganic level which is above man (Dundes 1964:129–130); man is dependent on it, and it renders his behavior consistent. Olrik deems that the epic laws somehow control individual narrators and are above them: the narrator obeys them blindly. Carried to the extreme, this view of the significance of epic laws might lead one to underestimate the individual and social components in the narrative cycle. In this respect we need merely consider the lack of interest which diffusionists show in the study of individual tradition bearers. In their opinion, storytellers are more or less verbal automatons who carry a narrative from place to place. This view is reflected in Krohn's (1922) notion of "automigration," which envisions a folktale as migrating of its own accord. A similar hypothesis is Anderson's (1923) law of self-correction (*das Gesetz der Selbst-Berechtigung*), according to which folktales seem to correct themselves and retain their integrity, immune to the lapses of memory or the errors of the folk narrator.

Are epic laws, in the last analysis, superorganic? In any case, there seems to exist a danger of overlooking the useful question of how they function in the process of communication. On what levels can these rules be studied analytically? Do all narrative genres obey the same laws, as Olrik assumed? Are the tradition bearers aware of these epic laws or not? Are their functions manifest or latent? To what extent are creation, transformation, and reproduction cognitive processes and to what extent do they escape the awareness of the narrator? Many such questions might well be answered by studying the individuals who transmit a genre as well as the communication process itself.

For example, do the epic laws apply to all the genres of narrative? On the basis of a study of Takalo's repertoire, a negative answer seems to be indicated. It is more likely that each genre has its own rules, which differ to a greater or lesser degree from those of other genres. Takalo, who was familiar with all the narrative genres of the White Sea Karelia region, seemed to recongize the different meanings and uses of different narrative genres. She categorized the stories using her own "natural" terminology and seemed quite aware of when she was telling a folktale ("tale," "story that has no truth in it," "amusing account") and when a saint's legend ("story of a holy man"), a legend ("story," "hearsay," "event"), or a memorate ("experienced event," "close event"). She also had a feeling for the meaning, function, and use of different stories and, in the course of telling them, would select the code appropriate to the genre from among the possible alternatives. This meant a choice in each case between different norms governing content, form, style, texture, and structure. In distinct contrast to what Olrik supposes, most "epic laws" do not seem, at least on the basis of Takalo's material, to apply to all narrative genres, though many fairy tales do seem to follow them.

Olrik's first law, the Law of Opening and the Law of Closing, deals with the beginning and conclusion of a fairy tale: the tale neither begins nor ends suddenly; the climax comes after a leisurely beginning, but the narration continues after the climax, tapering off at the end. Thus, every one of Takalo's fairy tales begins with an existential sentence which briefly introduces the protagonists and at the same time transports both the narrator and those listening beyond the world of everyday reality: "In olden days there lived an old man and woman, and they had three sons." No other genre besides the fairy tale and a few legends begins with this formula. It is thus one of the distinguishing characteristics of the fairy tale, and when listeners hear it they know what to expect. Equally common is the concluding formula: "And that is the long and short of it," or "This tale is indeed true because the last person to tell it is still alive." The action fits in between the beginning and concluding formulas in the manner described by Olrik; this seems to be a rule to which some narrative genres do not adhere.

The second law is the Law of Repetition: the gist of the tale is underscored and the excitement compressed by repeating the important details, usually three times. This repetition, which occurs at several levels — not only that of episodes, but also that of dialogues, sentences, and individual words — enhances the narration and gives it a particular rhythm. At the same time, it fills out the narration. There is no need for the narrator to know a lot of details in order for him to be able to transform the tale. The Law of Three is connected with this: there are three tasks, or a task is performed in the course of three days. It is interesting that triple repetition occurs in Takalo's narration somewhat regularly, even at the lexical level: "swam, swam, swam," "walked, walked, walked," "asked, asked, asked."

The following laws — the Law of Two to a Scene, the Law of Contrast — posit the polarity of the tale, a kind of dualism and contrast. There are only two persons on the stage at a time. Their conversation takes the form of a dialogue. The narrator thus in general identifies himself with only two roles at a time. After the dialogue, the shift to periodic narration means a change in tempo. The fairy tale represents an interplay of contrasts: hero and villain, good and bad, rich and poor. Olrik considers the appearance and comparison of twins to be so central that he speaks of the Law of Twins. A law which is nevertheless more pertinent and common is a kind of bow-and-stern emphasis (the Importance of Initial and Final Position). The most important person, the strongest, appears first, but it is the last person to appear who decides the issue. He often represents the weaker party. This trait points to the significance of the fairy tale for the community of listeners. It gives them an opportunity to identify with the underdog who comes out on top and thus furnishes a way to compensate for deprivation, a way to transcend everyday reality and its monotonous routines.

Though Olrik considers the above-mentioned seven laws to cover the entire universe of folk narrative, they are in fact mainly distinguishing characteristics of fairy tales. Scholars should try to clarify just what are the unwritten rules of communication for each particular genre.

In addition to the above, Olrik also advances a number of other laws which he considers more general. The principle of *action* means that characters are described not in terms of a series of adjectives, but in terms of deeds and events whose content indicates their characteristics concretely. The principle of *patterning* means that persons or situations of the same sort are not as different as possible, but as similar as possible. The principle of the *single strand* means that the threads of the plot are not woven together, the narrator choosing instead to follow a single main plot line. Background information, for instance, may thus be given in the dialogue. The principle of the *use of tableaux* means that tales have a kind of sculpture-like quality; the characters in an episode are placed side by side, inviting comparison. The principle of the *logic* of the *Sage* means that tales have their own rigorous consistency, which does not always conform to the laws of everyday reality but which enhances their credibility and emotional impact at the thematic level. The principle of *unity of plot* means that each event in the tale foreshadows the next. The principle of *concentration on a leading character* refers to the tendency to associate the action and its details with the protagonist.

Olrik's aim was clearly to give the outlines of "laws" that are above the narrator and control him. He wished in particular to stress the difference between folktales and other types of literature. Many of his observations are doubtless of considerable value and should be tested. Could we indeed show in detail whether the difference Olrik saw between folktales and other types of literature really exists? As far as oral communication is concerned, Olrik's "laws" should be studied as hypotheses, taking into account both the differences between genres and the communication process as a whole, both as an individual and as a social phenomenon. The evidence here suggests that most of Olrik's laws deal with fairy tales and the level of style, though they obviously depend also on other levels of the deep structure of the genre, such as its content, form, structure, and language. It should also be emphasized that Olrik's hypothesis is based on a study of texts and not on a holistic examination of the communication process. What is needed in folkloristics today is holistic, process-oriented studies of "epic laws" in the transmission of different genres: the generic grammar of folklore.

REFERENCES

ANDERSON, WALTER
1923 *Kaiser und Abt*. FF Communications 42.

AZADOVSKIY, MARK
1926 *Eine sibirische Märchenerzählerin*. FF Communications 68.

BAVELAS, ALEX
1960 "Communication patterns in task-oriented groups," in *Group dynamics* (second edition). Edited by Dorwin Cartwright and Alvin Zander, 669–682. Evanston: Row, Peterson.

BENEŠ, BOHUSLAV
1966–1967 *Lidové vypráveni na Moravských Kopanicich: pokus o morfologickon analijzu pověrečných povidek podle systému V. Proppa*. Slovácko 8–9

BRÉMOND, CLAUDE
1964 *Le message narratif*. Communications 4.

DÉGH, LINDA
1962 *Märchen, Erzähler und Erzählgemeinschaft dargestellt an der ungarischen Volksüberlieferung*. Berlin: Deutsche Akademie der Wissenschaften zu Berlin, Veröffentlichungen des Instituts für deutsche Volkskunde.
1969 *Folktales and society: storytelling in a Hungarian peasant community*. Bloomington: Indiana University Press.

DÉGH, LINDA, ANDREW VÁSZONYI
1971 Legend and belief. *Genre* 4:281–304.

DROBIN, ULF
1973 The need for a complement to Aarne-Thompson's type system and Thompson's motif index. *NIF Newsletter* 1 (3):7–11.

DUNDES, ALAN
1964 *The morphology of North American Indian folktales*. FF Communications 195.

FISCHER, J. L.
1963 The sociopsychological analysis of folktales. *Current Anthropology* 4:235–273.

GREIMAS, A. J.
1966 *Sémantique structurale*. Paris: Larousse.

KROHN, KAARLE
1922 *Skandinavisk mytologi*. Helsinki: Holger Schildts.

LÉVI-STRAUSS, CLAUDE
1960 *L'analyse morphologique des contes russes*. International Journal of Slavic Linguistics and Poetics 3.

MELETINSKIY, ELEASAR
1969 Zur strukturell-typologischen Erforschung des Volksmärchens (Strukturno-tipologicheskoye izucheniye skazki). *Deutsches Jahrbuch für Volkskunde* 15:1–30.

NATHHORST, BERTEL
1969 *Formal or structural studies of traditional tales: The usefulness of some methodological proposals advanced by Vladimir Propp, Alan Dundes, Claude Lévi-Strauss, and Edmund Leach*. Stockholm.

OLRIK, AXEL
1921 *Nogle grundsætninger for sagnforsning*. Copenhagen.
1965 "Epic laws of folk narrative," in *The study of folklore*. Edited by Alan Dundes, 131–141. Englewood Cliffs: Prentice-Hall.

PENTIKÄINEN, JUHA

1971 *Marina Takalon uskonto: uskontoantropologinen tutkimus*. Forssa: Suomalaisen Kirjallisuuden Seura.

1974 *On rhythm in storytelling*. Studia Fennica 17.

1978a "Oral transmission of knowledge," in *The anthropological study of education*. Edited by Craig J. Calhoun and Francis A. J. Ianni. The Hague: Mouton.

1978b (in press) *Oral repertoire and world view*. FF Communications.

PROPP, VLADIMIR

1958 *Morphology of the folktale*. Bloomington: American Folklore Society.

1968 *Morphology of the folktale* (second edition revised by Louis A. Wagner). Austin: University of Texas Press.

1970 *Les transformations des contes merveilleux*. Paris: Editions du Seuil.

1971 "Undersagans transformationer," in *Form och struktur*. Edited by Kurt Aspelin and Bengt A. Lundberg. Stockholm: PAN/Norstedts.

RAUSMAA, PIRKKO-LIISA, *editor*

1972 *Suomalaiset kansansadut. I. Ihmesadut*. Forssa: Suomalaisen Kirjallisuuden Seura.

VIRTARANTA, PERTTI

1971 *Kultarengas korvaan*. Vammala: Suomalaisen Kirjallisuuden Seura.

The Big-Bellied Cat

BENGT HOLBEK

In this paper I shall analyze the Danish records of Aarne-Thompson Type 2027, "The big-bellied cat," the tale of a cat who gets so hungry that he eats everything at home and then marches out into the wide world, swallowing all the animals and people that he meets until finally he is killed and his victims escape. The aim of the paper is to get a clear picture of the life of this tale in Danish tradition. For this purpose, a kind of simple structural analysis is used along with other analytical methods.

The most peculiar and, at the same time, the most interesting version of this tale was recorded in West Sjælland in 1912. It was told by an old woman, born in 1844, who in turn had heard it from her mother, also in this area.

The old woman was going out, so she cooked meal-pudding and herring for herself and for her cat. She put her own meal-pudding and herring on the stove. The cat's meal-pudding and herring she put on the floor. "Now be a good Puss and eat your meal-pudding and herring, but you must not touch my meal-pudding and herring."

"Mew," said the cat, and then the old woman went out. But Puss was hungry right away. He ate his meal-pudding and his herring. Then he waited and waited, but the old woman didn't appear. Then he thought that he had better go out and look for her, for now he was hungry again. "Mew," said Puss. And then he ate all the old woman's meal-pudding and all her herring. Then he went out to look for her again. But then she came.

"Well, my little Pussy-Cat, are you there, have you eaten your meal-pudding and your herring? Now I'm going to have mine."

"Mew," said Puss.

But alas! when the old woman came, her meal-pudding and her herring had been eaten. "Where is my meal-pudding and my herring, Puss?" Now she was angry. "If you have dared eat it, I'll give you a beating."

"Mew," said Puss. Then, when the old woman came with the stick, Puss swallowed both her and the stick, the pot and the ladle, and then he marched along the road. Then he met a man who was plowing.

Then the man said, "But where are you going, little Pussy-Cat, since your belly is so big?"

"No wonder my belly is big, I have eaten my meal-pudding and my herring, the old woman's meal-pudding and the old woman's herring, the old woman and her stick, the pot and the ladle. If you do not shut up, I'll swallow you too."

"Indeed," said the man, "I rather think you don't swallow such big mouthfuls."

"*Hap*!" [spoken while breathing inward — onomatopoeia] said Puss, and then he swallowed the man, and the plow and horses as well. Then Puss marched off again. He then came to a man who was harrowing.

Then this man said, "Where are you going, my little Pussy-Cat, since your belly is so big?"

"No wonder my belly is so big, I have eaten my meal-pudding and my herring, the old woman's meal-pudding and the old woman's herring, the old woman and her stick, the pot and the ladle, a man who was plowing and his horses. If you do not shut up, I'll swallow you, too."

"I don't think so," said the man.

But Puss swallowed the man, and the harrow and horses as well. He then came to a man who was rolling his land.

"Where are you going, my little Pussy-Cat, since your belly is so big?"

"No wonder my belly is big, I have eaten my meal-pudding and my herring, the old woman's meal-pudding and the old woman's herring, the old woman and her stick, the pot and the ladle, a man who was plowing and his horses, a man who was harrowing and his horses. If you do not shut up, I'll swallow you too."

"Indeed," said the man.

But the cat swallowed the man, and the roller and horses as well. He then came to man who was sowing.

This man said to him, "Where are you going, my little Pussy-Cat, since your belly is so big?"

"No wonder my belly is big, I have eaten my meal-pudding and my herring, the old woman's meal-pudding and the old woman's herring, the old woman and her stick, the pot and the ladle, a man who was plowing and his horses, a man who was harrowing and his horses, a man who was rolling and his horses. If you do not shut up, I'll swallow you, too." He then swallowed the man and his bag right away. He now went on and came to some men who were mowing a meadow.

Then they said to him: "But where are you going, my little Pussy-Cat, since your belly is so big?"

"No wonder my belly is so big,I have eaten my meal-pudding and my herring, the old woman's meal-pudding and the old woman's herring, the old woman and her stick, the pot and the ladle, a man who was plowing and his horses, a man who was harrowing and his horses, a man who was rolling and his horses, and a man who was sowing and his bag. If you do not shut up, I'll swallow you, too."

"No, wait a bit, my little Pussy-Cat, this won't do at all." And one of them cut Puss's head off. Then came the man and his bag, the man and his roller, the man and his harrow, the man and his plow, and all the horses kicked. There came the old woman and the stick, the pot and the ladle, the old woman got her meal-pudding and her herring again. Then she put Puss's head back on and took him home. She now cooked a new portion of meal-pudding and herring for Puss, for now she knew that nobody had such a Puss as she had. And there they were living together the last time I went past, and no doubt they still do today.

The text was copied in 1923 by Lars Andersen, who sent it to the Danish

Folklore Archives (DFS 1906/14). It has not been published until now. Neither this text nor the type in general has been the subject of any investigation.

The tale belongs to the group of cumulative tales first classified by Taylor (1933). Such tales are quite common in popular tradition. After a brief prose introduction, a jingle is recited as part of a dialogue. The jingle grows with each new episode until it finally bursts. Seidelin (1970) has observed that the reciting of these tales depends on the breath rhythm of the storyteller: the jingle, which is usually rhythmic, has to be recited in one breath or it will fall apart. When it reaches the bursting point, the tale must be brought to a close.

"The big-bellied cat" is clearly an instance of the rhythmic *Märchen*-style described by Berge (1915–1933). His general conclusion, however, that tales told in this style date back to something like the Viking period, is probably not correct in this case. I hope to demonstrate that the text just quoted is a rather recent innovation, although based on an older, more widespread tradition.

An interpretation of this tale must be based upon its form. It is divisible into eight episodes of similar content, only the first and the last differing from the usual pattern (Table 1). The dialogue, including the cumulative

Table 1. Episodes of "The big-bellied cat"

Episode	Object	Resistance	Result
1	the cat's own meal-pudding and herring	—	cat eats
2	the old woman's meal-pudding and herring	"You must not touch my meal-pudding and herring."	cat eats
3	the old woman and her stick, the pot and the ladle	"If you have dared eat it, I'll give you a beating."	cat eats
4	a man who was plowing and his horses	"Indeed, I rather think you don't swallow such big mouthfuls."	cat eats
5	a man who was harrowing and his horses	"I don't think so."	cat eats
6	a man who was rolling and his horses	"Indeed."	cat eats
7	a man who was sowing and his bag	—	cat eats
8	some men who were mowing a meadow	"No, wait a bit, my little Pussy-Cat, this won't do at all."	cat's head is cut off, everything eaten returns

jingle, does not appear until the fourth episode. Each episode has three units of action: (1) the cat wishes to eat something, (2) it has to overcome resistance (lacking in the first and seventh), and (3) the encounter results in a meal (except in the last, where the cat loses all that he has swallowed in episodes 2–7). The elements of the three columns of table 1 exhibit differing patterns. That of the "Result" column is the simplest: up to the last episode, the cat swallows everything in sight; then all he has swallowed is freed, so that the original order is restored. The cat even gets his head put back on and has another portion of the precious meal-pudding and herring.

The development of the "Resistance" column is of particular interest. In the first episode there is no resistance; the cat eats his own food. In the second episode, however, the main conflict of the tale arises: on the one side is the cat's growing hunger, on the other a strict prohibition supported by a threat of punishment. The cat waits for a long time, but he gets increasingly hungry, and, finally, the order breaks down on his violation of the prohibition. It is like the bursting of a dam: once it has started, more and more is pulled down. The old woman is the first victim. She is angry, she has a stick, but she has come too late to maintain order and therefore she succumbs. The pot and ladle that creep into the jingle at this point are remnants of earlier forms of the tale, in which the cat had to cook porridge while the old woman was away; in those versions, the cat ate the porridge and went on to eat the pot and ladle.

The cat now leaves home and, marching along the road, swallows one person after another. Their remarks indicate a steadily declining resistance; the last man to be swallowed has nothing to say at all. Obviously, this is not a coincidence. In all the other cases, the recurring dialogue is fully reproduced, to the point of boredom (though one must bear in mind that when the tale is told to a child, the effect is far from boring). We are justified in assuming that the storyteller has a specific intention in this progressive weakening. The trend of the tale is abruptly reversed in the last dialogue. The mowers, far from being intimidated by the threats of the cat, behead it, thereby liberating its victims. The cat's violation of the old woman's prohibition in the second episode is exactly matched by the men's violation of the cat's order to shut up in the eighth episode.

The "Object" column exhibits yet another pattern, beginning with the fourth episode. In Denmark, plowing is customarily done in the autumn. Harrowing, rolling, and sowing are done in the spring, and the meadows are mowed in the summer. Perhaps the meal-pudding and the herring indicate the abundance of harvest-time — but even if this is too sophistic, the cat has obviously marched most of the year round.

How are these patterns to be interpreted? Do they, considered together, constitute a structure?

The second and third columns are easily combined. The conflict between the cat's hunger and the old woman's prohibition first results in the violation of a norm; this is advantageous to the cat but disastrous for everybody else. Then order is restored, and the cat loses his unlawful gains. He is reintegrated into society after punishment. Were the tale to be interpreted on the basis of these facts alone, it would be, like so many others in oral tradition, a tale of violation and reintegration and nothing more. What is interesting here, however, is the combination of this traditional pattern with the annual sequence of agricultural tasks. The cat's hunger grows beyond its natural limits in the autumn, the resistance to it weakens during winter and spring, and order is restored in summer. What does this mean?

New facts are needed here. Our structural analysis will carry us no farther. The investigation must go from text to context.

As I have said, the narrator lived in a rural district in West Sjælland. She had learned the story when she was a child, i.e., in the middle of the nineteenth century. The obvious question is: did her milieu contain any feature which could be connected with the main themes of the tale, hunger and the annual sequence of agricultural tasks? It did. Modern people do not experience any marked nutritional rhythm, apart from seasonal price fluctuations and the changing supplies of fresh vegetables and fruits; therefore, the problem is not immediately understandable to us. The peasants of old, however, had a strongly marked nutritional rhythm. In the autumn the crop was harvested; before Christmas, those animals that were not to live through the winter were butchered; then one had to subsist through the winter and spring on the food thus stored. This was possible only in a strict household economy. If the harvest had been bad, severe measures were necessary from the very outset, and still the spring might see empty storehouses.

The stores were administered by the housewives. This becomes especially significant when bearing in mind that our narrator, and her mother before her, were housewives. They knew from their own experience the necessity of a strict household economy. The following interpretation of the tale lies close at hand: In the autumn, there is plenty of food, but the housewife, the "old woman" of the tale, gives the cat no more than his due. The cat is not satisfied. He takes the old woman's share, and the well-ordered household economy breaks down. During winter and spring a famine ensues, illustrated by the farmers' weakening resistance. Only in the middle of the summer, when food is again plentiful, can anyone gather the strength necessary to reduce the cat to order. The risk of a new outbreak remains, however: the cat is revived and lives on in the old woman's house.

The tale, then, tells of the conditions of the household economy through the changing seasons. The cat does not symbolize hunger, or winter, since there is no reason to treat the tale as an allegory. Rather, it resembles the dream of Pharaoh in the Old Testament (Gen. 41 : 16–24) of the seven fat cows that were swallowed by the seven lean cows and the seven full and good ears of corn that were swallowed by the seven withered ears. Joseph explained the dream as a portent of plenty and hunger to come, and the tale of the cat may be interpreted in a similar way. In the mind of the farmer, nothing looms larger than the uncertainty of the crop. He does everything in his power to secure it, and it is natural for him to visualize famine and crop failure in the form of an omnivorous monster. The dream and the folktale originate in the same vivid imagination, not in the narrow paths of allegorical thought. The tale is intimately connected with the daily life of narrator and listener. The little girl has undoubtedly seen the cat jump onto the kitchen table to steal, and she has seen her mother administer the stores of the house and her father work in the field. The lesson of the tale, that it is disastrous to eat more than one's due, is quite clear to her.

Is this interpretation of the tale correct? Unfortunately, we cannot ask the narrator; she died long ago, and we know next to nothing about her. Her tale comes down to us only in the form of a written record, which resembles the tale itself in the same way as a photograph may resemble a long-dead person. In folktale research, however, another method is available: comparison with parallel material. Almost all folktales exist in several records, and at least in theory we may expect a structure discernible in one record to exist in other records as well.

In Denmark, we have recorded twenty versions of Type 2027. A list of these is given in Appendix 1. The numbers below refer to that list. Some of these versions are presented in Appendix 2.

The main actor is a cat in all versions except Nos. 14 and 17. In No. 14, the voracious animal is a wolf. He comes to a shepherd and begs for some food. When the boy refuses to give him anything, the wolf eats the boy and his food, and afterwards the sequence of animals and people that is usual in the Jutland versions (without the wolf, however). We may assume, in this case, contamination by Type 2028 (conversely, a cat sometimes appears in that type). In No. 17, the main actor is a boy who is coming home to visit his mother. On his way he eats various people; no reason is given. Finally, a little goosegirl hits him on his stomach so that it bursts, "and there all of it lies in a big heap." Obviously, this version is rather garbled. It is not contaminated by any other tale type, and the events appear to be inexplicable.

In No. 6, the cat is a transformed princess. An old hag has kidnapped her and transformed her into a cat. One day she leaves home after ordering the cat to cook a pot of porridge. The cat eats the porridge and leaves home. She eats various people until a prince beats her with his stick. She is then transformed into a princess again, the prince marries her, and nothing more is heard of the unfortunate victims of her hunger. Probably this tale arises out of contamination by Type 313–314, the flight from the ogre being replaced by the sequence from 2027. Characteristically, the number of victims is reduced to three; this is the typical number of events in the flight from the ogre, whereas the typical number of events in Type 2027 is between five and seven.

The beginning of the tale has two main forms: In Nos. 1, 2, 4, 5, 6, 7, 10, 11, 12, 15, 16, 18, and 20 (the text quoted above), the cat eats the porridge or meal-pudding, and when the old woman is about to punish him, he eats her, too. Then he marches off. The motif is somewhat weakened in No. 6, as mentioned above; in No. 18, where the old woman appears only at the end of the tale, as the one who kills the cat; and in No. 12, where the cat begins by eating a couple of boys who are digging clay and only afterwards eats an old woman who is stirring her porridge. In Nos. 3, 8, 9, 13, and 19, we only hear that the cat eats a prodigious amount of food before leaving home, still driven by hunger. The introductions to Nos. 14 and 17 are, as we have seen, atypical and need not be considered here.

The main part of the tale is the story of the cat's hunger march. In every case the cat enumerates his victims in a cumulative jingle, the most conspicuous feature of tales of this type. There is, however, no instance apart from No. 20 exhibiting the features on which my analysis is based: the annual agricultural cycle and the weakening resistance. This means that my interpretation, valid though it may be for No. 20, does not apply to the type as a whole. A dual question arises: how should the other texts be interpreted, and how are they related to No. 20?

The explanation should be looked for in the same place as before, in the sequence of episodes. In all the texts, all the encounters except the last are successful for the cat. He eats various kinds of animals and people until somebody cuts his belly open and liberates his victims. The cat is not revived in most cases, the exceptions being No. 6, where the cat is a transformed princess, and No. 20. In terms of Table 1, the "Result" column is the same in all cases; the "Resistance" column does not exist as a significant factor in Nos. 1–19. In the "Object" column, we find the following:

Bornholm

18: hen, duck, cow, old woman with a stick

8: hen, duck, goose, foal, man with a cartload of thorns and briars, ram

19: as 8

Jutland

9: hare, magpie, fox, wolf, old man with a cartload of wood, little boy with a sword

13: magpie, hare, wolf, fox, two farmhands with two pairs of oxen, little boy with a sword

14: shepherd, magpie, hare, fox, man with twelve pairs of oxen, soldier with a sword

3: magpie, hare, fox, twelve farmhands, twelve pairs of oxen, twelve cartloads of wadmal, twelve quill-drivers, one of them with an axe

Møn

4: magpie, horse, seven birds in a flock, seven girls in a wood, man who was plowing, another cat

Sjælland and Samsø

11: goose, fox, three girls, four girls, farmhand with a cartload, parson with a crooked staff, sexton with a tall hat, dog

1: Skohottentot, Skolinkenlot, five birds in a flock, seven girls in a dance, lady with a white trained dress, parson with a crooked staff, woodcutter with an axe

5: Skoggerenlat, Skallingentat, otherwise as 1

7: Skahottentot, Skalinkenlot, five birds in a flock, seven children in a dance, lady in a white trained dress, parson with a crooked staff, woodcutter with an axe

15: as 7

16: as 1

10: man with a wheelbarrow, farmhand with a cartload of thorns and briars, congregation, parson, sexton, herd of bellowing cows, ram

2: man with a cartload of thorns and briars, five farmhands digging in a clay pit, girl with a dog

6: four farmhands digging in a clay pit, three girls coming from church, sexton in a white dress-coat, prince

12: two boys digging in a sand pit, old woman with porridge and ladle, foal, farmer with a cartload of thorns and briars, congregation, sexton, parson, ram

17: man who was plowing, girl who was harrowing, five men sitting on a fence, four dancing girls, goosegirl

20: man who was plowing and his horses, man who was harrowing and his horses, man who was rolling and his horses, man who was sowing and his bag, mowers

Text No. 1, which comes from East Sjælland, was printed in 1861 and later reprinted in a widely distributed collection of popular folktales. It has evidently influenced versions Nos. 5, 7, 15, and 16, which were recorded in Jutland but because of their dependence on No. 1 have been listed here with the versions from Sjælland. The characters Skohottentot and Skolinkenlot are undoubtedly small animals or birds, although the Jutland versions speak of "a man named Skahottentot" and the like. The names are garbled versions of the pet names usual in this type. *Sko-* being *skade* [magpie], *-hotten-* being *hoppen* [hopping], *-linken-* being a dialect word for "limping," and *-tot* being *-tå* [toe], these names should be rendered approximately as "Magpie-hopping-toe" and "Magpie-limping-toe."

In No. 14, as was mentioned above, the shepherd appears as a result of contamination by Type 2028 and may be disregarded in the analysis.

In No. 3, the twelve farmhands, twelve pairs of oxen, and twelve cartloads of wadmal appear on the scene separately. We may, however, safely count them together as one item, since this is the case in closely related forms of the tale.

The lady in a white trained dress seems to be a person of some social importance; no peasant woman would have occasion to wear such a dress. The crooked staff of the parson seems to indicate that he was a bishop in earlier versions of the tale.

At first glance, the victims of the voracious cat seem a haphazard collection of animals and people, changing from one version to the next without rhyme or reason. On closer inspection, however, a strict order emerges. It is discernible in the first fifteen texts and if we disregard the two clay-digging boys and begin with the old woman and her porridge, as is usual in the type — also in No. 12. The victims are small animals or birds, larger animals or a flock of birds, groups of girls or children, one or several men at work, a lady — or, curiously, a congregation — and one or several men of distinction. The quill-drivers in No. 3, being men of letters, are more distinguished than the farmhands who precede them. This can be illustrated as in Table 2, with the numbers indicating the position in the

Table 2. Sequence of the cat's victims in sixteen versions of "The big-bellied cat"

Version number	Small animals or birds	Larger animals or flock of birds	Girls or children	Men at work	Lady or congregation	Men of distinction
18	1, 2	3				
8	1, 2, 3	4		5		
19	1, 2, 3	4		5		
9	1, 2	3, 4		5		
13	1, 2	3, 4		5		
14	2, 3	4		5		6
3	1, 2	3		4		5
4	1	2, 3	4	5		
11	1	2	3, 4	5		6, 7
1	1, 2	3	4		5	6
5	1, 2	3	4		5	6
7	1, 2	3	4		5	6
15	1, 2	3	4		5	6
16	1, 2	3	4		5	6
10				1, 2	3	4, 5
12		3		4	5	6, 7

sequence of the cat's victims. In No. 10, a herd of bellowing cows is swallowed last, after the congregation, the parson, and the sexton. This does not affect the general picture: it is evident that the cat's career is one of mounting ambition. Beginning with small animals or birds, he goes on to swallow larger animals, then persons of low status, and finally the most distinguished persons visible from the point of view of the narrators. At that point, his career is logically interrupted.

The versions from Jutland, Bornholm, and Møn usually end with a man or men at work. When the cat comes across a ram or a man with a sword, i.e., dangerous beings, he is killed. In the tales from Sjælland, several people appear, and the animals more or less disappear from the scene. In No. 1, the man at work is placed at the end, as the monster killer and liberator. The identity of the monster killer seems to be unimportant. Any being that can cut or tear will do. From this it may be concluded that attention should be concentrated on the function expressed in this episode, not on the actor in any particular version; in a sense, the cat is the only actor in the tale.

A combination of these observations may be expressed in the following way: In Jutland and on the islands of Bornholm and Møn, "The big-bellied cat" exhibits a clear pattern of *mounting ambition and abrupt downfall*. This is the traditional pattern of the tale. It is comparable to "The fisherman's wife" (Grimm No. 19, Type 555). In both, a lowly being gets the opportunity to better his (or her) position, only to be carried off by ambition to a tragic end. Most of the versions from Sjælland exhibit the same pattern, even though the introduction of several categories of humans obscures it to some extent. In the versions from West Sjælland and the adjacent island of Samsø (Nos. 2, 6, 17, and 20), this pattern is lost. The tale quoted at the beginning of this paper arose out of that confusion. We may imagine how a narrator, acquainted with one or several versions of the tale and dissatisfied with its lack of perspicuity, decided to do away with most of the beings of the tale and created instead, on the basis of the plowman, a wholly new version of the tale with a new message. Thus version No. 20 came into being.

From this we may conclude that narrative structure is not necessarily identical with the structure of meaning.

APPENDIX 1: VERSIONS EXAMINED

1. *Katten*. From Stevns, East Sjælland. Printed in Grundtvig (1861:77–78, no. 42); reprinted most recently in Seidelin (1970:85–87).
2. *Katten*. From a place near Slagelse, West Sjælland. Printed in Arne (1862:83–84).
3. *Den slugne Kat.* Recorded by Lovise Hansen in Hurup, Thisted, northwestern Jutland. Printed in *Skattegraveren* VII (1887) 183–84/786.
4. *Den slugne Kat*. Recorded by N. E. Hansen, Borre, Møn. Printed in *Skattegraveren* VII (1887) 193–94/791.

5. *Den grådige Kat*. Recorded by Maren Bonde, Vedersø, West Jutland. Printed in *Skattegraveren* XI (1889) 187–88/552.

6. *Den forheksede Kat.* Recorded by Mikkel Sørensen, Besser, Samsø. Printed in Kristensen (1896:59–61, no. 119).

7. *Den slugne Kat*. Recorded by Evald Tang Kristensen from Mads Kr. Mortensen, Ørre, West Jutland, Printed in Kristensen (1896:61–62, no. 120).

8. *Sandsage om Mœtte-Bugekat*. Recorded by Evald Tang Kristensen from Kr. Skovmand, Bornholm. Printed in Kristensen (1896:62–63, no. 121).

9. *Katté*. Recorded by Evald Tang Kristensen from Andr. Beiter, Tarm, West Jutland. Printed in Kristensen (1896:63–64, no. 122).

10. *Den brøsige Kat*. Recorded by Evald Tang Kristensen from Mads Jepsen, Kongsted, South Sjælland. Printed in Kristensen (1896:64–65, no. 123).

11. *Den tykke Kat*. Recorded by Evald Tang Kristensen from Kristian Pedersen, Gørlev, West Sjælland. Printed in Kristensen (1896:65–66, no. 123 [a mistake in numbering]).

12. *Katten, der revnede*. Recorded by Evald Tang Kristensen from Hans Larsen, Hørsholm, North Sjælland. Printed in Kristensen (1896:66, no. 124).

13. *Per Kåkhålms Kat*. Recorded by Evald Tang Kristensen from Mikkel Andersen, Vindum, East Jutland. Manuscript in Dansk Folkemindesamling: Evald Tang Kristensens eventyr, afskriftsrække, no. 53b. Printed in Kristensen (1896:66–67, no. 125).

14. *Ulven*. Recorded by Evald Tang Kristensen from Povlsen, Grimstrup, West Jutland. Printed in Kristensen (1896:67–68, no. 126).

15. *Katten, der aad*. Recorded by Evald Tang Kristensen from Else Jakobsen Nørregaard, Gjellerup, West Jutland. Manuscript in Dansk Folkemindesamling: Evald Tang Kristensen's diaries, p. 1721b; eventyr, afskriftsrække, no. 827.

16. (No title). Recorded by Anker Hårup in 1908. Learned from his mother, Karoline Møller, Øster Alling, East Jutland, about 1893. Manuscript in Dansk Folkemindesamling: DFS 1906/14.

17. *Den tykke Dreng*. Recorded by Johan Rasmussen from Ane Kristine Pedersdatter, Egebjerg, Northwest Sjælland. Copy sent to Dansk Folkemindesamling in 1923: DFS 1906/16.

18. (No title). Recorded by Johs. Chr. Jensen in 1935 from Ellen Folkmann, Klemensker, Bornholm. Manuscript in Dansk Folkemindesamling: DFS 1906/14.

19. *Mette byggekat*. Recorded on tape by Iørn Piø in 1956 from Ingegerd Skovmand, Bornholm. Tape in Dansk Folkemindesamling: mgt GD 1956/02.

20. *Den Bugede Kat*. Recorded by Lars Andersen in 1912 from Kristiane Rasmusdatter, Højby, West Sjælland, who had heard it from her mother as a child. Copied in 1923. Manuscript in Dansk Folkemindesamling: DFS 1906/14.

APPENDIX 2: SELECTED TEXTS

[No. 1]
Once there was an old woman, she was cooking porridge. Then she wanted to leave for a moment to visit a woman in the neighbourhood, and then she asked the cat to look after the porridge in the meantime.

"I shall do so," said the cat. But when the old woman had left, the porridge smelled so good that the cat ate both it and the pot as well.

Then when the old woman came back, she said to the cat: "Now, but where is the porridge?"

"Well," said the cat, "I have eaten both the porridge and the pot, and now I'll eat you, too." And then he ate the old woman. Then he ran out the door, and on his way he met Skohottentot.

Then Skohottentot said to him, "What have you eaten, my little cat, you are so stout?"

Then the cat said, "I have eaten both the porridge and the pot and the old woman, and now I'll eat you, too." Then he ate Skohottentot. After that he met Skolinkenlot.

Then Skolinkenlot said, "What have you eaten, my little cat, you are so stout?"

"I have eaten both the porridge and the pot and the old woman as well and Skohottentot," said the cat, "and now I'll eat you, too." Then he ate Skolinkenlot.

Now he met five birds in a flock, and they said to him, "But what have you eaten, my little cat, you are so stout?"

"I have eaten both the porridge and the pot and the old woman as well and Skohottentot and Skolinkenlot, and now I'll eat you, too," said the cat, and then he ate the five birds in a flock.

Then he met seven girls in a dance, and they also said to him, "My, my, but what have you eaten, my little cat, you are so stout?"

And then the cat said, "I have eaten both the porridge and the pot and the old woman as well, and Skohottentot and Skolinkenlot, and five birds in a flock, and now I'll eat you, too." And then he also ate the seven girls in a dance.

When he had gone somewhat farther, he met the lady in her white trained dress, and she also said to him, "My, but what have you eaten, my little cat, you are so stout?"

"Well," said the cat, "I have eaten both the porridge and the pot and the old woman as well, and Skohottentot and Skolinkenlot, and five birds in a flock and seven girls in a dance, and now I'll eat you, too." And then he also ate the lady in her white trained dress.

A little later he met the parson with his crooked staff, and he said the same as the others: "My, but what have you eaten, my little cat, you are so stout?"

"Well," said the cat, "I have eaten both the porridge and the pot and the old woman as well, and Skohottentot and Skolinkenlot, and five birds in a flock and seven girls in a dance, and the lady in her white trained dress, and now I'll eat you, too." And then the cat also ate the parson with his crooked staff.

Then at last he met the woodcutter with his axe. Then the woodcutter said, "But what have you eaten, my little cat, since you are so stout?"

"I have eaten both the porridge and the pot and the old woman as well, and Skohottentot and Skolinkenlot, and five birds in a flock and seven girls in a dance, and the lady in her white trained dress and the parson with his crooked staff, and now I'll eat you, too," said the cat.

"No, indeed you won't, my little cat!" said the woodcutter, and then he took his axe and hewed him in two. And out jumped the parson with his crooked staff and the lady in her white trained dress and the seven girls in a dance and the five birds in a flock and Skolinkenlot and Skohottentot, and the old woman took her pot and her porridge and ran home with it.

[No. 8][1]

Once there was a couple, they had to go out, and then their cat should look after the house while they were away. Then they put seven loaves and seven pails of

[1] The tradition represented by this version and No. 19 still exists. The grandson of the woman who told it has passed it on to his own children. The informant, a professor of history, recently told me that he saw Hitler's career in the light of the career of the big-bellied cat.

milk on the table, in order that he should have something to feed on in the meantime. No sooner had they gone than the cat jumped up and ate all of it at once. Then he went into the ktchen. There a hen was clucking. When she saw the cat, she said, "Good morning, Full-Belly-Cat, where have you been today, you are so stout?"

"I have good reason to be stout," said the cat, "I have eaten seven loaves and seven pails of milk, and now I'll eat you, too, you Hen-Scratching-Foot." Then he swallowed the hen, and then the cat went on.

Then a duck was quacking: "Good morning, Full-Belly-Cat!" said the duck, "but where have you been today, you are so stout?"

"I have good reason to be stout," said the cat, "I have eaten seven loaves, seven pails of milk, Hen-Scratching-Foot, and now I'll eat you, too, Duck-Quacking-Beak!" Then he swallowed the duck.

Then he went on and met a goose, she said, "Good morning, Full-Belly-Cat, but where have you been today, you are so stout?"

"I have good reason to be stout," said the cat, "I have eaten seven loaves, seven pails of milk, Hen-Scratching-Foot, Duck-Quacking-Beak, and now I"ll eat you, too, Goose-Waddling!" Then he swallowed the goose.

Then he went on. Outside a foal was dancing; it came over immediately and said, "Good morning, Full-Belly-Cat, but where have you been today, you are so stout?"

"I have good reason to be stout," said the cat, "I have eaten seven loaves, seven pails of milk, Hen-Scratching-Foot, Duck-Quacking-Beak, Goose-Waddling, and now I"ll eat you, too, you Foal-Straddling-Leg!" Then he swallowed the foal.

Then he went on and met a man who came driving with a cartload of thorns and briars and with two big horses. Then the man said, "Good morning, Full-Belly-Cat! Where have you been today, you are so stout?"

"I have good reason to be stout," said the cat, "I have eaten seven loaves, seven pails of milk, Hen-Scratching-Foot, Duck-Quacking-Beak, Goose-Waddling, Foal-Straddling-Leg, and now I'll eat you, too, you Man with Thorncart and Horses!" Then he swallowed the man with his cartload of thorns and briars and the cart and the horses.

Then he went on and came to a ram that was standing on a hill. Then the ram said, "Good morning, Full-Belly-Cat! Where have you been today, you are so stout?"

"I have good reason to be stout," said the cat, "I have eaten seven loaves, seven pails of milk, Hen-Scratching-Foot, Duck-Quacking-Beak, Goose-Waddling, Foal-Straddling-Leg, a Man with Thorncart and Horses, and now I'll swallow you, too, you Ram with your Crooked Horns!"

"No, wait a bit," said the ram, "let us have a contest," and then the cat should stand in the valley and the ram on the hill, and then the ram took a running leap and butted the cat and made a hole in his side, so that the man drove out and hurried home, the foal came out dancing, the goose cackling, the duck quacking, the hen clucking, but the cat lay there and could do no more. Snip, snap, snout, my tale is out. Tip, tap, tin, now you may begin.

[No. 9]

Once upon a time there was a big cat; he got for breakfast every morning seven pails of milk and seven mice. Then he went out one morning, and met a hare. "Good morning, Hare-Romping Toe!" said the cat.

"God be with you, cat!" said the hare. "What have you had for breakfast today?"

"I have had seven pails of milk and seven mice, and I might as well take you, too!" And then the cat rushed upon the poor hare and swallowed it. A little later the cat met a magpie. "Good morning, Magpie-Chirping-Toe!"

"God be with you, cat! What have you had for breakfast today?"

"I have had seven pails of milk and seven mice and a hare, and I might as well take you, too!" Then he swallowed the magpie. Now the cat came to a fox. "Good morning, Fox-Shaking-Tail!"

"God be with you, cat! What have you have had for breakfast today?"

"I have had seven pails of milk, seven mice, a hare, and a magpie, and I might as well take you, too!" He now swallowed the fox and then met a wolf. "Good morning, Wolf-*Vejselænd*!"[2]

"God be with you, cat! What have you had for breakfast today?"

"I have had seven pails of milk, seven mice, a hare, a magpie, and a fox, and I might as well eat you, too!" Now when he had put an end to the wolf, he walked for a while, and then he came to an old man with a cartload of wood. "Good morning, you old man with your cartload."

"God be with you, cat! What have you had for breakfast today?"

"I have had seven pails of milk, seven mice, a hare, a magpie, a fox, and a wolf, and I might as well eat you, too!" Finally the cat met a little boy with a sword at his side. "Good morning, you little boy with your sword," he said.

"God be with you, cat! What have you had for breakfast today?"

"I have eaten seven pails of milk, seven mice, a hare, a magpie, a fox, a wolf, and an old man with a cartload of wood, and I might as well eat you, too!"

"No, God forbid!" said the little boy, and then he took his sword and hit the cat so that he fell dead. Then he cut open the belly of the voracious animal, and the seven pails of milk, the seven mice, Hare-Romping-Toe, Magpie-Chirping-Toe, Fox-Shaking-Tail, Wolf-*Vejselænd*, and the old man with his cartload of wood came out again, and all of them were happy that the little boy had set them free.

REFERENCES

ARNE (pseud.)

1862 *Nogle Fortællinger, Sagn og Æventyr, indsamlede i Slagelse-Egnen*. Slagelse.

BERGE, RIKARD

1915–1933 Norsk eventyrstil. *Norsk Folkekultur* 1:12–21; 3:145–150; 4:49–79; 5:156–172; 7:64–68; 12:64–72; 16:118–122; 19:41–65.

GRUNDTVIG, SVEND

1861 *Gamle danske Minder i Folkemunde*, volume three. Copenhagen.

KRISTENSEN, EVALD TANG

1896 *Danske Dyrefabler og Kjæderemser*. Århus.

SEIDELIN, ANNA SOPHIE

1970 *Folkeeventyr og remser*. Copenhagen: Thaning og Appel.

TAYLOR, ARCHER

1933 A classification of formula tales. *Journal of American Folklore* 46:77–88.

[2] This name is unintelligible. *Vej-* means "road-"; probably the wolf is being characterized as one who runs far and wide.

Oral Narrative Process and the Use of Models

HAROLD SCHEUB

The performer of oral narrative elicits emotions from the members of her audience, then patterns those emotions — shapes and gives them form. The first of these operations is achieved primarily through the images that the artist evokes. The result is a variegated flow of emotions which is then patterned by the rhythm of the performance, through repetition in its several forms.

Images, the basic material of oral-narrative art forms, are taken from two sources, reflecting activities from the contemporary world and those which are artistic. The former are realistic, always immediately comprehensible; those from the art tradition are probably quite old, and are often fantastic. Images from other contexts and derived from other cultural institutions and experiences are introduced into an artistic world, a narrow, neat world in which such alien images are placed into new environments, often strange, and are hence newly experienced by members of the audience, who have been encountering them in different ways in their daily routines. Once introduced into the work of art, these images begin to obey new laws.

Images are felt actions or sets of actions evoked in the imaginations of the members of an audience by verbal and nonverbal elements arranged and controlled by the performer, requiring a common experience by both artist and audience. Many such images are extreme, fantastic, vivid, even violent; others call forth warmer emotions, feelings of the hearth, familiar and serene. The former are most frequently derived from the art tradition, the latter from the real, contemporary world.

The artist blends these images through the rhythm of the performance. They are organized into repeated segments. Thus, in a Russian narrative (Afanas'ev 1945:425–427), a sister murders her brother, who returns in the form of a reed, singing of the crime:

An earlier version of this paper appeared in *New Literary History* 6 (1974–1975):353–377.

Gently, gently, shepherd, blow,
Else my heart's blood you will shed.
My treacherous sister murdered me
For juicy berries, slippers red.

The song organizes the images of the narrative and also controls the emotional responses of the members of the audience, simultaneously evoking and shaping those responses. In the repetition, tension is created, manipulated, heightened until release occurs at the confrontation with the murderer herself.

The special nature of rhythm in oral narrative traps the images from the real world, working them into a system which parallels and mixes them with images from the art tradition. The images from the contemporary world are worked into patterns and are thus aligned with other images that are not recognizable as being a part of the routine. Humans, who are familiar, are paired with witches, who are not. The objects of everyday life often behave oddly in this new world: in Hausa narrative, for example, food talks, gives directions, and has an effect on the fate of certain of the characters.

The combination of real-world and artistic images during a performance links the members of an audience with the art tradition in a deeply emotional way, and past and present are brought together in the process. The sense of order achieved in the performance through patterning is an emotional sense that establishes the relationship between present and past. Homilies and cultural data, often a part of the process, are no more than complex sets of images, their chief function also being to evoke emotional responses. The designs of image sequences through patterning result in the organization of images, the fragmented world depicted in the narrative now being put back together both as story and formally. Resolution means the reconfiguration of the fragmented world, and the sense of order that results brings with it many emotions that have been trapped in the separate images. The final sense of order is the form of the narrative performance, form composed of images from the real world, worked into unique designs by the patterns, and images from the artistic tradition. Music and movement, as well as ancient images, surround real-world images, giving them form.

Words do not have the malleability that sound has in music, color in painting, stone in sculpture. Experiences cling to words; their sounds, moreover, cannot be altered in any dramatic way without a consequent loss of sense. It is not the combination of words that composes the material to be shaped by the performance; rather, it is the audience's experience of a variety of images. Words are among the vehicles that call up and control the image-experiences created by the performance, the means whereby images are evoked, arranged, and manipulated. When the artist objectifies such images, the audience gives them life in deep and colorful ways; it not only brings the surface narrative to life, but introduces into the performance its many experiences with that narrative in scores of varied contexts. Thus, each new performance evokes the actions of countless earlier ones, actions which have been provided with many shades of meaning by many artists in their separate efforts to bring the audiences into harmony with their artistic visions. The performer thus seeks to harmonize the random experiences of the members of the audience. She evokes from the audience a flow of emotions, then patterns the emotions, leading the members of the audience to an identical, harmonious experience.

The sounds of the words and the connotations of the images make it impossible for word and image to be twisted into fantastic shapes. Still, the artist must attempt to channel and govern the audience's experiences of the images. This imposes upon the artist a special aesthetic method; to manipulate the word into image, and to liberate the image from its many connotations at the same time that those connotations are exploited, the oral performer must bring that image into contact with yet other images, altering the effect of the first by means of others. She cannot substantially change the images simply by evoking them, and she cannot diminish the values that the members of the audience bring to them. The narrative images are not altered; it is the audience's experiences of the images that are progressively narrowed and sharpened by the artist.

The tools involved in this performance are developed at an early age. In southern African societies, all members of the community seek to perform narratives. There is no formal apprenticeship (see Scheub 1975: 17–43) whereby the complex aesthetic tradition is mastered. Children learn by their membership in audiences, and they slowly build a repertory of images and patterns, the two elements essential to the evocation and control of emotions. The child witnesses performances of narratives frequently, becoming intimately familiar with them and their variations. She becomes aware of the possibilities of manipulating images for more complex purposes. She learns the plotting of story units, experiments with them, is caught up in them during their performance, and discovers the potential grouping of them into seemingly endless combinations.

Most narratives involve the disruption of social harmony by some villainous being; the resolution usually brings the villain into confrontation with a heroic character who diminishes its destructive nature. Images are organized by means of a song, chant, or action that can be repeated any number of times to form an expansible image (Scheub 1970). Repetition of the basic image sequence moves the narrative toward its resolution. In a Xhosa narrative (Scheub 1975:196–201), some girls have gone to dig for red clay, which is used to dye garments and as a cosmetic. One of the girls leaves a piece of clothing behind, and when she asks the others to return with her, they refuse. Each time she asks and each time there is a refusal, a song is sung:

Cikizo, my cousin!
Cikizo, my cousin!
We went to dig clay, my cousin!
We went to dig clay, my cousin!
I'm Mvondwana's sister!
I'm Mvondwana's sister!

With each repetition of the song, the plight of the child is deepened, her alienation from the group is heightened, her gathering aloneness is slowly and persistently revealed. Finally, she is indeed alone, and must return by herself to confront the fearful demon who stands over her clothing.

In a Mbundu narrative (Chatelain 1894:126–129), two brothers go hunting. When the younger kills all the game, the jealous elder brother kills him. He disembowels his brother and attempts to feed the entrails to the dogs, but they refuse to eat them. Instead, the dogs sing:

Ndala the elder
And Ndala the younger,
They went into the world
To destroy others.
We praise
Mutelembe and Ngunga,
To whom were thrown the bowels;
They refused to eat them.

The elder brother kills one of the dogs, but the dog returns from the dead and again sings the accusing song. Then he kills both of the dogs and buries them, but they return and sing the song once more. Each time the song is sung, he is closer to the village and to his destiny. His guilt deepens with each repetition. Thus, the repeated verses not only move the narrative toward its climax, but develop the culprit's fear-ridden conscience as well.

The child thus develops a repertory of repeatable image sequences and, at this early stage, a single pattern: the repetition of the sequence as frequently as necessary to develop a conflict. This expansible image requires little more than repetition to move it toward resolution. The child will learn that this pattern can become more complex. For example, as her repertory of images grows, she will bring two full expansible-image sequences into parallel relationship, so that they have the illusion of unity, the one seeming to flow logically into the other. Each, at this stage of the child's development as a storyteller, is developed by means of the simple pattern. The child has at this point all the material she needs — the repertory of images and the basic pattern for their organization — to develop into an accomplished artist.

In many cases, the final repetition of the image sequence is altered so that the resolution can take place. In a Xhosa narrative (Scheub 1975: 406–411), a young wife receives scarce firewood from a mountain bird on several occasions, the bird insisting each time that she not inform those at home:

You look as if you've told the people at home,
That you saw an important little bird
Which had gathered and stacked some wood.
This bird took the bundle over there,
A stack of wood — I *could* follow you!

The girl responds:

No, I haven't told the people at home,
That I saw an important little bird
Which had gathered and stacked some wood.
This bird took the bundle over there,
A stack of wood — it *could* follow me!

On each occasion that the girl returns home, the people there urge her to inform them of the location of this treasure of wood. She stubbornly refuses to disclose her source, but each time the song exchange takes place the bird's suspicion deepens as the girl's protestations of innocence increase. Finally, she does tell her family where the bird is, and during the final singing of the song the usual details which surround it are altered in a dramatic way: the bird is destroyed by the girl's relatives. The singing of the song itself results in no alteration of narrative movement, but the details surrounding the song do.

In a Chaga narrative (Radin 1964:237–242), the oldest of three sons, Mrile, digs up a bulb which is "as handsome as my little brother." He hides the bulb and nourishes it, and a child develops from it. When his mother discovers this, she destroys the child. Then the saddened Mrile rises into the air on a chair, and his family sings the following song to him:

Mrile return,
Return my child,
Return!

Mrile responds:

I shall return no more,
I shall return no more,
Mother, ah, I,

I shall return no more,
I shall return no more.

His younger brother, his father, his age-mates, his uncle then sing the song, and all receive the same response. With each repetition of the song, Mrile moves farther and farther away in his airborne chair, and finally, as his uncle sings, he disappears. Again, the expansible image both organizes the images and moves the narrative to its resolution.

A man in a Bena Mukuni narrative (Radin 1964:186–189) kills his pregnant wife because of a dispute regarding food, but "the child that was in the womb rushed out of it, dragging its umbilical cord." The child sings:

Father, wait for me,
Father, wait for me,
The little wombless.
Who is it that has eaten my mother?
The little wombless. . . !
How swollen are those eyes!
Wait till the little wombless comes.

Then the frenzied father kills the child, but its bones gather themselves together and it again sings the song. The father destroys the child once more, then hurries to the kraal of his dead wife's mother. When his in-laws wonder where his wife is, he tells them that she is still at his home. Meanwhile, the child has squeezed itself out of the hole where it had been put; it comes closer and closer, singing the song, as the in-laws wonder about these strange events. The man is afraid: "Everyone is staring. They said, 'There comes a little red thing. It still has the umbilical cord hanging on.'" In a final haunting scene, all is silent within the house. "Meanwhile the child was coming on feet and buttocks with its mouth wide open, but still at a distance from its grandmother's house," again singing the song. When the child reaches the grandmother's house, it leaps onto the bed and sings again. The truth is then revealed, and the murderer is punished.

In a brief and powerful Xhosa narrative (Scheub 1975:182–185), a woman hurries across the vast and lonely veld with her two children. A cloud of dust in the distance slowly whirls toward them; it is a monster, which keeps repeating mysterious words, "Rwebethe! Rwebethe!" (or, in some versions, "Qwebethe!"). The mother cries,

Rwebethe, Rwebethe, what is it?
I am leaving my child behind on the veld,
I am leaving him behind on the veld,
I am leaving him behind.

And she takes one of the children and throws it to the threatening monster. She goes on, and the same fearful details are recounted, and again the song, and again a child is thrown to the beast, and now she is alone. The narrative ends, "The woman went on her way, she travelled alone now. She arrived at her home, and she arrived now without those children."

The expansible image can thus be used for a variety of purposes: for the heightening of tension, the simple movement of the narrative to its resolution, the organization of divers images. Whatever the narrative design, the repeated image sequence remains the element around which the performance is constructed. It has other, more complex, purposes, but these are developments of this central patterned image configuration.

The artist who creates such performances, then, works within a tradition which imposes upon her certain patterns and image sets. These materials provide links with the past at the same time that they supply the artist with the essentials of her craft. The performer has a repertory of images that are preconstructed; much of the plotting of these images is predictable. The audience has the same repertory; its aesthetic and intellectual expectations therefore go beyond the development of conflicts and resolutions. The system becomes a complex interweaving of patterns and images which produces messages understandable only to those familiar with the tradition, who have many experiences of images and patterns.

From the fundamental expansible-image pattern, other, more complex, narrative designs develop. A key to the narrative system is the transformation of images into models and the artistic manipulation of models to reveal the form of the work of art. Through repetition, image sequences become a part of the audience's experience, and so become predictable. The experience of the narrative is both linear and nonlinear, an emotional involvement in which the story units and the narrative that they unfold and the nontemporal categories that this activity provokes are blended. There is a relationship between the repeated images, forming the rhythmic pattern or grid of the production, and the surface narrative, which flows easily across the grid, developing out of the repeated images but in no way inhibited by their circular movements. Against this regular rhythmic background of repeated image sequence, corresponding models are altered; seemingly unlike images are experienced as identical. This experience is a revelation of form. Because the audience, wholly caught up in the production because of the images and patterns and because of the verbal and nonverbal devices employed by the artist, is by now an emotional part of the images, because through repetition the model has been fully experienced and is intimately known, any alteration is keenly felt, so that message is conveyed by any sensory dislocation, by the sensing of identical patterns organizing different image sets.

The repeated performance of a single sequence of images to move the narrative toward a resolution becomes more complex when image sets are more fully detailed. The expansible image is altered in two ways: first, it is limited in its repetition, usually to two evocations of the model; and second, each of these evocations is fully detailed and may itself be composed of an expansible-image sequence. In one variation, two expansible-image sets come into contact with one another, but the two sequences are identical in important respects so that they can be seen as evocations of the same model. A pattern is established in the imaginations of the members of the audience similar to that established by the expansible image. Predictability and expectation take over as the audience, having experienced the first set of images, anticipates that the second set will duplicate the first. That is, the audience expects the second image sequence to respond to a model (which has been established by the first image set).

A mother-in-law in a Lamba narrative (Doke 1927:216–221) tells her son-in-law where a great herd of animals can be found. The son-in-law warns her, "Speak with certainty, a lie returns." She insists that she has indeed seen the herd, so he goes to the place and shoots his arrow. It pierces each of the animals, moving in circles until all the animals have been killed; then it returns to the son-in-law. The pattern has been established; the members of the audience are now presumably involved in the narrative, and the artist repeats the opening set of images to fix it in their minds. The next day, a man tells the son-in-law about a large herd of animals that he has seen, and the son-in-law again sounds the warning: "Speak with certainty, a lie returns." The man insists, so the son-in-law goes off to seek the game. Again he shoots the arrow, again it takes the circuitous route, killing all the creatures; then it returns to him. The second evocation of the image set insures that the audience is fully in control of the pattern, and it also prepares the way for the final performance of the model.

The audience in an oral society is prepared for the repeated image sets; it is conditioned through much experience to accept the initial construction as the model and the subsequent repetitions as insuring its proper reception. As with all expansible images, repetition of this kind could go on for a long time, but in this Lamba narrative, two repetitions are sufficient. One message has, of course, already been communicated: "Speak with certainty, a lie returns." The repeated sequences, along with the formal experience, which is less intellectual than emotional, will convey this theme.

After a time, food runs out, and the mother-in-law seeks a way to get her son-in-law back on to the plains to hunt more game. She claims that she has again seen a great herd of animals. The son-in-law's warning has by now become a cliché: "A lie returns." He argues that he must not be blamed for what will happen if she is not telling the truth. And she is indeed lying in this case. The son-in-law looks for the creatures, but finds none: he shoots the arrow anyway. It goes around and around, seeking its quarry. While he awaits the return of the arrow, the son-in-law climbs a tree and watches it making its rounds. Finally, it reaches the mother-in-law and pierces her breast. Then it returns to him. The people of the village want to punish him, but he is forgiven when he reminds them of his series of warnings.

The composition of this narrative is straightforward: three repetitions of a cliché which is a partial statement of theme ("A lie returns"). Patterned image sequences of this kind seem especially, though by no means exclusively, to be associated with trickster narratives. The bungling-host narratives of native American cultures provide excellent illustrations of such constructions. In an Ojibwa performance (Henry 1914:14–15; cf. Dorsey 1906:439–445; Teit 1898:vi, 40; Thompson 1966:71–73), Nenebojo pays visits to a series of friends, seeking food:

After a while, when Nenebojo was hungry again, he thought he would pay a visit to his younger brother, the duck. When he arrived at the duck's lodge, the latter was just cooking some wild rice. Then the duck defecated in the pail and boiled this together with the wild rice. After the wild rice was cooked, he was given some to eat. In leaving he said to the duck, "Whenever you are hungry, come over to visit me."

The pattern has been set, and it is now up to Nenebojo to duplicate the actions of the duck. It is a model which depends for its effect on repetition; the humor of the episode is to be found in the flawed replication of the model:

After a while, the duck went over to Nenebojo's lodge to pay him a visit. Then Nenebojo told his wife to clean a kettle, so that he could prepare something with which to feed his visitor. So he defecated into the pail, but he merely soiled it, and the pail had to be cleaned again.

It is now left to the duck to reestablish the model:

Then the duck defecated into the pail and there was a large quantity of wild rice. Then Nenebojo ate and so once again he was fed by the duck.

Such patterning is frequently repeated a number of times:

After a while Nenebojo was hungry again, so he decided to visit another of his brothers, the woodpecker. When he arrived at the woodpecker's lodge, he said, "So this is where you live." Then the woodpecker said to his wife, "We have nothing with which to feed our visitor." Then he jumped on a tree and cried, "Kwe, kwe, kwe!" He pecked at the tree and made a hole in it, and soon he threw down a raccoon. This was boiled to feed Nenebojo. After he had eaten, he thanked the host for giving him such a good meal, when he was hungry. "Whenever you are hungry, come over to my lodge," he said in leaving.

Again, the pattern is established, and again Nenebojo will seek unsuccessfully to duplicate it. The flawed pattern has now become a new design, the flaw having been worked into the pattern:

After a while the woodpecker thought he would go and visit his older brother, Nenebojo. When he arrived at Nénebojo's lodge, he said, "So this is where you live," and Nenebojo answered, "Yes, this is where I live." Then Nenebojo climbed the tree, just as he had seen the woodpecker do. But instead of sticking the stick he carried into the tree, he stuck it into his face and he fell from the tree. "Indeed, you are very foolish," he was told by the woodpecker. "Someday you will kill yourself through your foolishness."

Patterned image sets are put to humorous use in a Kordofan narrative (Frobenius 1971:46–56), in which a bridegroom is told in a dream that he must make a pilgrimage to Mecca. He leaves his young bride behind, and a canny muezzin, with the assistance of a crone, convinces the woman that she has within her an unfinished baby. The old woman tells the bride that her husband was called away before he had finished making the baby:

It was only its body he completed. If the baby is born as it now is it will have neither head nor limbs. He went away leaving his work undone, and it is you who will have to bear the humiliation of giving birth to a cripple.

Fortunately, the old woman says, she knows a muezzin who can help her. As for the muezzin, he tells the young woman that he will "put all my strength into the work at once," and it takes many sessions to form the child properly — its mouth, its nose, its toes. When the husband finally returns home, the young wife angrily turns on him for having left her with an unfinished baby, and she praises the muezzin for saving the child.

The pattern has thus been established, and the effect of the narrative is achieved by repetition, by the evocation of images which respond to the model that has now been created. This time, the muezzin is the dupe of the groom. The model builds anticipation and predictability into the dramatic performance, and the audience thus becomes crucial to the development of narrative. The groom shrewdly becomes close friends with the muezzin, not revealing that he has learned what had occurred during his absence. The muezzin finally trusts the groom to accompany his own wife home from a distant town. Along the way, they sleep on the side of the road, and while the muezzin's wife is sleeping, the groom steals her jewelry. She is frantic when she discovers that she has been robbed, and she begs the groom to help her to find the gems. "You know," the groom explains,

that as between men and women there is a difference. . . . Well, now, in many women the difference is thievish and much given to stealing. Theft is a natural characteristic of the female difference. Generally, however, a woman's difference steals only from men. But if for any length of time it has not been able to steal from men, it may well steal something from its own mistress.

Having convinced the woman that she has been stealing from herself, the groom reveals to her how she can recover the jewels:

> It cannot be accomplished by a woman alone. A man has to introduce his difference slowly and carefully into hers in order to search it. It must be done, however, soon after the theft and in addition, slowly and with care, for otherwise the booty will disappear further and further inside and, as you know, it can then only come out again in the form of a child. Otherwise, your difference will turn the jewelry into a stone baby.

Horrified, the muezzin's wife urges the young man to begin the search, and so he slowly recovers all of the woman's jewelry in the same way that the muezzin had originally finished the work on the other woman's unborn child. When they finally get home, the woman informs her husband of her good fortune in encountering this good man. But the latter is humble: "How else could I have repaid you," he says to the chagrined muezzin, "for the way you came to my assistance on an earlier occasion?"

This model represents a step toward complexity; the way is being paved for more intricate models with more involved messages. These will be based on the same expansible images that are found in simpler narratives.

Fantasy is the material that ties present-day images to the past, that makes possible the working of contemporary images into a form that is emotionally apprehended by members of an audience. Fantastic images are frequently highly concentrated realistic experiences. Such images have proved so useful to generations of artists and audiences that they have been incorporated into the artistic repertory. Audiences are brought to a recognition of their relationship to contemporary images in the alignment with the fantastic sequences. While the artist may separate contemporary and fantastic imagery by space, that distance collapses under the influence of patterned relationships; and because the members of the audience are emotionally caught up in those patterns, they are led to a realization of the identical natures of the separate image categories. It is this process that creates form, and form is the message; past and present are combined, experienced as the same thing. The critical relationship between narrative surfaces and repeated patterns moves the audience into an experience of form, but this process would be impossible without fantasy.

The elementary forms are manipulated into more complex narratives. In another Lamba narrative (Doke 1927:44–51), a chief has a number of daughters, all of them married except the youngest. She refuses to marry, saying, "I want a man who can pass through a hole in the tree with a ball." The chief calls his people, all try, but no one succeeds in passing through the hole in the tree. The child adamantly refuses to marry; the chief becomes despondent, the child thin. This is the opening set of images, repeated as various suitors strive to win the girl's hand by participating in the unique competition. A grid is established, the rhythm set up and fixed in the minds of the members of the audience through repetition. Then this opening image set is interrupted by a second; the first set will be recalled and repeated at the end of the narrative.

In a remote land, two brothers and their brother-in-law decide to try to win the princess. A younger brother wants to go along with the three suitors, but they refuse to allow him to do so. They threaten to beat the child if he follows, but he persists. Finally, because he is so small and "is not responsible," they agree that he can accompany them, but he must carry a basket of meal. When a huge bird comes along, he throws it some meal. When he encounters some black ants, he gives them some of the meal. And when he comes to a stream, he gives some of the meal to a fish. This image set (common in African oral narrative traditions) enables the boy to satisfy three of the elements, air, water, and earth.

When they get to the house of the princess, the first image set is again evoked. The second will be recalled later; it is patterned, and only the first part, the model, has so far been established. The first image set details the contest; each of the three new suitors attempts and fails. When the youngest brother tries, he succeeds. Everyone is happy except the three, who vow to kill him. They gain the assistance of their mother-in-law, persuading her to set certain impossible tasks for the young groom. She first insists that he produce a baby. The youth is upset, but the bird he helped earlier comes along and brings him an infant. Next, the mother-in-law, again at the prompting of the brothers, throws some seed on the ground and asks the youth to pick it up. The ants he once assisted now come to his aid and perform the task. The mother-in-law concludes that her son-in-law is indeed wise, but the brothers prevail upon her once again. This time, she takes a basket of beads and pours them into a stream; the fish the youth once fed assists him in gathering the beads. The brothers are punished, and the young man lives with his wife in her village.

Two image sequences make up this narrative. First, everyone tries to pass through the hole in the tree and fails. This is the repeated action, and the alteration in the pattern occurs with the success of the final suitor. The second image set is also patterned: the youth helps the bird, the ants, and the fish, and when he is in trouble they return to assist him. The two simple narrative strands are brought together and worked into a unified performance. The second sequence is locked into the first — the first is interrupted by the second, then the second by the first — and is crucial to its successful completion. Narratives may become more complex, but the system remains the same. This narrative, more intricate in its construction than the simple expansible-image narrative, is nevertheless a logical development of the simpler form. It is, in fact, a combining and an interweaving of two simple expansible images.

The essence of patterning is the breaking of the pattern. This is central to the aesthetics system of oral narrative. In the breaking of the pattern, the model remains constant, but the character working through the model fails or refuses to complete it. One of the most common of these patterns is the good girl/bad girl narrative: A good girl has a series of encounters, all of which she responds to courteously and with a good heart; she is rewarded. Her sister has the same experiences (the basic model is unchanged), but she responds in precisely the opposite way (the pattern is broken), is evil-minded and petty; she is punished (Scheub 1975: 366–373). In a German narrative (Grimm and Grimm 1944:290–311), a youth sits under a tree with some creatures. A witch is in the tree, cold, and frightened of the animals. She asks the youth to touch these animals with her wand, so that they will not harm her when she comes down. He does this, and they are turned into stone. When the witch descends from the tree, she touches the youth with the wand also, and he too is turned to stone. That is the model. His twin brother comes along later, and the identical experience is encountered, but this brother breaks the pattern by refusing to touch the animals with the wand. He subdues the witch, then brings his brother back to life.

The original expansible image has given rise to a major organizing model of oral narrative. This is a duality, a patterning in which the model is established by one character, then repeated by another, but in the repetition the model is somehow not followed. The model retains its integrity; the character is flawed. This kind of duality is composed, obviously, of polarities — a good girl and a bad girl; a brother who is killed, a brother who brings life. In each case, the model is itself neutral; the witch becomes ambiguous, reflecting the characters who come into contact with her. This is, in fact, the nature of villainy in many oral performances.

A central image in such narratives is the swallowing antagonist: the monster or dragon or cannibal who swallows a human or humans and is then ripped open by a hero or heroine who releases those held captive inside. The villain thus has both destructive and creative potentials, and the hero is defined as the one who confronts this character, tames its destructive capabilities, and releases the creative. This is a basic set of images, a duality grounded in the expansible image, and it has many uses in oral tradition.

In a Xhosa narrative, a child, Siswana Sibomvana (Little Red Stomach), is swallowed by a monster; her mother seeks her and causes herself to be swallowed also. She then cuts the monster open from the inside, releasing her daughter, herself, and others. The monster is destructive in obvious ways, but it is also creative, in the sense that it provides life. This creature as both death-dealer and life-giver becomes ambiguous and works effectively between the fantastic and realistic imagery of the narrative. In the epic of Mwindo (Rureke 1969), this dual quality of the villain is made a major theme in the discussion Mwindo has with the god

Nkuba after the hero has destroyed a dragon (see Scheub 1976). In another Xhosa narrative (Zenani 1972:528–561), Sikhuluma's sister confronts a water monster, taunting it, "Come out and eat me!" and thus leading it slowly back to Sikhuluma's home, where it is killed. This water monster is evil, destructive; it eats people. But it also has a life-giving quality: it is skinned, and a cape is made of its hide. Sikhuluma takes the cape with him when he goes to get a bride from the dangerous land of the terrible villain Mangangedolo. When Mangangedolo sends a creature to kill Sikhuluma, the hero puts on the cape, and the water monster comes to life, destroying the creature. The water monster has both positive and negative possibilities. In the same narrative, the bride's father, Mangangedolo, is pure evil, and he finally succeeds in killing Sikhuluma with his magic. But his daughter, an extension of the father and the creative part of him, uses the same magic to restore Sikhuluma to life.

Two brothers quarrel in a Kongo narrative (Dennett 1894:65–68), and the younger takes his wife and leaves the village. He goes to another place, where he asks a stranger if he can settle there with him. The stranger agrees. They build a pit to trap animals, and it is agreed that the young man will get all male animals caught there, the stranger all female animals. During the first days, many animals are trapped, all of them males. The young man keeps them all, sharing none with the stranger. Then one day, his wife, having gone to gather wood, fails to return. The husband and the stranger look for her and discover that she has fallen into the pit. She now belongs to the stranger, who refuses to release her, reminding the other "of his agreement, and how he had given him nothing of all the meat he had entrapped." The elder brother, hunting, comes to this place and sees what is happening. He behaves in a cold manner to his brother, and when the stranger asks the elder brother to mediate the matter, the elder answers that the female in the trap belongs to the stranger "and that he had better go in and kill her." The stranger pushes the younger brother aside and leaps into the pit to claim his quarry. Then the elder brother says to his younger, "See, now, that male in your trap; he is yours by agreement, even as your wife is his. Spare his life, and perhaps he will give you back your wife." (In an interesting variant of this narrative, a snake plays the role of the stranger. There is a Xhosa version; for an Italian one, see Thompson [1974:2–3].)

The duality is more complex here; the two brothers form a part of a whole, first divided by an argument, further by wisdom, and then by space as the younger brother moves to a new home. That brother then agrees to a new duality, an arrangment with the stranger. The original balance is established when the elder brother returns.

Another Kongo narrative (Dennett 1894:60–64) concerns twin brothers, Mavungu (the first-born) and Luemba. At the time Mavungu sets out on his travels, the daughter of Nzambi is ready for marriage. She refuses to marry various animals that come to her, and Mavungu determines to marry her. With the help of his charms, he gets the materials needed for the journey. When Nzambi's daughter sees Mavungu, she wants to marry him. The happy couple goes to stay in a house which has many mirrors, all of them covered. Mavungu uncovers one and sees the reflection of his home village. In another mirror, another village is reflected, and so on. Nzambi's daughter will not allow her husband to see one of the mirrors, "because that is the picture of the town whence no man that wanders there returns." Mavungu insists that he see the town, and his wife finally relents. But when he wants to go to this terrible place, she begs him not to. "My charm will protect me," Mavungu says. He sets out, and along the way he asks an old woman for fire to light his pipe. She agrees, but kills him.

In the meantime, Luemba wonders about his brother and decides to follow him. He also has a charm which provides him with all the materials he requires for the journey, and he arrives at Nzambi's village, where he is mistaken for his twin brother. A feast is held, and he is to sleep that night with his brother's wife. His charm keeps the two separated during the night. Luemba is also curious about the mirrors, also insists that he see the forbidden one, also determines to go to that town "whence no man returns." He too comes to the old woman and asks her for fire, but he kills her instead. He gathers the bones of his brother and touches them with his charm, and Mavungu comes to life. Then they join the bones of hundreds of people and bring them to life. On the return journey to Nzambi's village, the brothers quarrel about their followers, and Mavunga kills Luemba. But Luemba's horse, with the charm, brings Luemba to life, and Luemba then kills Mavungu.

There is a German version (Grimm and Grimm 1944:290–311) which is much longer than the Kongo narrative but which has as its central organizing structure the dual relationship between brothers. This device is also used in a fine Lamba narrative, "The Story of Mr. Cow-child and Mr. Lion-child" (Doke 1927:14–23). The three narratives contain similar elements — each has two characters who are very close, each involves the death of at least one of these characters and his resurrection by the other, and each involves the obtaining of a wife by at least one of the brothers. All three narratives depict a move away from the home, each tracing the activities of one of the brothers. When that brother dies, the other brother pursues him and gives him life. In each of the narratives, we reach a false resolution, in which the character whose activities we are following marries and seemingly achieves his ends. Thus, the Kongo brother settles down with his wife, Lion-child marries and becomes a chief, the German youth kills the dragon and gets the princess. But in all cases, there is further movement; the narrative shifts back to conflict — the Kongo twin insists on going to the forbidden village, the Cow-child continues his journey to the land of God, and the German youth pursues a snow-white hind into a vast forest. We shall examine one of these narratives in detail.

In the Lamba narrative, a series of image sequences is evoked, each connected with the next by a journey of five nights and five days. The number in itself is not significant, but it provides a neat demarcation between the various sequences that make up the narrative. In the opening set, Lioness attempts to become friends with a human chieftainess, but she is turned down: "Not I, I won't make friends with a lion!" So Lioness and Cow cross countless rivers and travel five days and nights, eventually building a homestead in the wilderness. Lioness gives birth to a man-child, and so does Cow. Cow fears that Lioness will destroy her, and she warns her child of this. Cow is indeed killed by Lioness, and Cow-child ties the mother's entrails into a bundle. Then Cow-child tells Lion-child what has happened. "Mate," Lion-child responds, "my mother is fierce, she has eaten your mother, and what is more, we two are alike, we have the scent of people, indeed she will come and eat us also." So they take their axes and cut off Lioness's head. Then they cross five rivers and travel five days and nights, and they build a new homestead.

Several important details are established in this opening set of images: the human chieftainess refuses to have anything to do with a lion, Lioness and Cow bear children who are men, Lioness destroys Cow, and Lion-child joins with Cow-child to kill Lioness. The repeated elements in this sequence are two: each creature gives birth to a man-child, and both Cow and Lioness are destroyed.

The second sequence begins when Cow-child and Lion-child reach a village and ask the people there for water. They learn that the inhabitants do not drink water. "The chief's son," they are told, "will carry a man to the water tomorrow, in the evening he will return; then when another five days pass, they will go again to draw water." In the morning, when the people take the chief's son to draw water, Cow-child and Lion-child follow. At a great lake, they discover that the people have come to sacrifice a man in the water — as they apparently do every five days. They watch as eight "creatures with long white beards" float on the water and gaze about. Cow-child and Lion-child cut off their heads, and from that day the people are able to drink water without human sacrifice. The chief then presents the elder of the two, Lion-child, with his daughter. Cow-child conjures with some porridge, and says, "I am going far five nights and five days, so if my charm dries, you will know that Cow-child is dead." That is the end of the second image sequence, and the performer now narrates its companion sequence, this one involving the exploits of Cow-child, who climbs a ladder which reaches into the clouds.

He arrives at a small house, where he finds the daughter of God. Now, he says, I too will marry. But the child of God tells her slave to tell her father, "An enemy at your child." Soldiers arrive. With his knife, Cow-child kills all the soldiers but one; he cuts that man's arm off and sends him back to God. The next morning, the pattern is repeated, but this time, when all have died, Cow-child hears some dogs eating the stomach and intestines of his mother, Cow. "Ah," he laments, "today I die!" And the next morning, when the pattern is repeated, the enemy takes two sticks and kills Cow-child.

Lion-child knows that Cow-child is dead, because of the porridge, so he travels five days and five nights to find him. After searching through all the corpses, he finds his friend. He strikes Cow-child with an animal's tail and brings him to life. "Now we have become two," Lion-child says. The child of God sends her slave to her father, according to the pattern already established. Next morning, the two kill all of the soldiers except one, sending him back to God. Others soldiers arrive the next day, and they meet the same end. Finally, God abdicates, giving his daughter to Cow-child; he also gives Cow-child his kingdom.

In this performance, the artist is manipulating the most complex of oral structures, image sets that are parallel (Scheub 1971*a*, 1971*b*, 1972). Unlike the patterning that occurs in simple expansible-image designs, in which sequences are the same, the patterning here involves juxtaposing unlike sets. The parallel nature of the final two image sets in this narrative should be clear. In the second set, the two heroes kill all the old creatures (ambiguous, in the sense that they are both destructive and creative: they kill people, but they possess life-giving water). In the third sequence, the repeated elements consist of God's actions when he has been informed that an enemy has approached his child and the destruction of the soldiers first by Cow-child and later by the two heroes together.

The opening image set is tied to the second and third. In the second and third sequences, the heroes perform services to mankind. In the second, they eradicate the superstition that has kept the people from life-sustaining water and periodically robbed them of life through human sacrifice. In the third, they force God, who sends soldiers to destroy anyone who dares approach him, to abdicate his throne. Justice is absent in both the secular world and the celestial kingdom, and there is a definite progression from the activities of the terrestrial village to the activities in the heavenly realm. But there is a further progression, and this is the purpose of the first image set — the purpose, actually, of the entire narrative.

It is only when the full narrative has been experienced that the opening set of images can be seen as paralleling the second and third. The first image set is the model for the second and third. The tyrannical lioness, who destroys the cow, must herself be destroyed. The heroes move from this animal world into the human world and thence into the heavenly world, and along the way they change things. The chieftainess ousts Lioness from her human village at the very beginning: there can be no relationship between the animal and human worlds, and this establishes a major theme in the performance. Cow-child and Lion-child kill Lioness, thereby destroying that element within them which would keep them in a state of animalism. The wanton destruction of Cow by Lioness is paralleled by the destruction of sacrificial victims by the eight old men, and this in turn is paralleled by the efforts of God to destroy those who would come to him. Cow-child and Lion-child are ambiguous characters, as their names indicate — they are both animal and human, and the narrative shows their movement away from an animal existence to full humanity. The old order is passing in a more general sense, too, and the heroes are Cow-child and Lion-child, enemies in the old dispensation (the performance graphically underscores this by having Lion destroy Cow). Cow-child learns in the end that his mother's intestines have been devoured; the final contact with the past is destroyed by the dogs, and it is at this melancholy moment that he allows himself to be killed. This death is necessary, for Lion-child, whose mother killed Cow in the opening image set and who, if he follows the pattern set by his mother, must destroy Cow-child, now demonstrates through resurrecting Cow-child that change has occurred. Lion-child, more effectively than most such characters, reveals the dual quality of the hero, for the hero (like the villain) also possesses both destructive and creative potential. Precisely the same struggle goes on within the character of Mwindo, in the Nyanga epic, as two other characters, one positive and one negative, strive for ascendancy, and Mwindo in subduing the negative character tames the destructive element within himself. The villain's duality, which is in essence a unity, is frequently matched in oral narrative by the duality of the hero.

As Cow-child and Lion-child bring humaneness to the animal, human, and godly realms, they are simultaneously ridding themselves of their animal origins and destructive instincts, which persist as well in the worlds of man and God. They thus reduce their own destructive potentials and release their creative energies by doing the same to the worlds they inhabit. The final purging is revealed by the destruction of Cow's intestines and by Lion-child's life-giving act. Each part of the performance develops images against a rhythmic background of life and death. This complex narrative, building on a model composed of expansible images, and dependent upon a duality revealed in its two central characters, is a development of the same system that produced the simplest oral narrative consisting of a single expansible image.

REFERENCES

AFANAS'EV, ALEKSANDR
1945 *Russian fairy tales*. Translated by Norbert Guterman. New York: Pantheon Books.

CHATELAIN, HELI
1894 "Mutelembe and Ngunga," in *Folk-tales of Angola*. New York: Houghton Mifflin.

DENNETT, RICHARD EDWARD
1898 *Notes on the folklore of the Fjort (French Congo)*. London: The Folk-Lore Society.

DOKE, CLEMENT M.
1927 *Lamba folk-lore*. New York: G. E. Stechert.

DORSEY, G. A.
1906 *The Pawnee mythology*, volume one. Washington, D.C.: Carnegie Institution of Washington.

FROBENIUS, LEO
1971 *African nights*. New York: Herder and Herder.

GRIMM, JACOB, WILHELM GRIMM
1944 *The complete Grimm's fairy tales*. New York: Pantheon Books.

HENRY, JOHN
1914 "Nenebojo goes visiting," in *Some myths and tales of the Ojibwa of southeastern Ontario*. Edited by Paul Radin. Ottawa: Government Printing Bureau.

RADIN, PAUL
1964 *African folktales and sculpture*. New York: Pantheon Books.

RUREKE, SHE-KARISI CANDI
1969 *The Mwindo epic, from the Banyanga (Congo Republic)*. Edited and translated by Daniel Biebuyck and Kahombo C. Mateene. Berkeley: University of California Press.

SCHEUB, HAROLD
1970 The technique of the expansible image in Xhosa *Ntsomi*-performances. *Research in African Literatures* 1(2):119–146.
1971a Parallel image-sets in African oral narrative-performances. *Review of National Literatures* 2:206–223.
1971b Translation of African oral narrative-performances to the written word. *Yearbook of Comparative and General Literature* 20:28–36.
1972 Fixed and nonfixed symbols in Xhosa and Zulu oral narrative traditions. *Journal of American Folklore* 85:267–273.
1975 *The Xhosa Ntsomi*. Oxford: Oxford University Press.
1976 Narrative patterning in oral performances. *Ba Shiru* 7(2):10–30.

TEIT, JAMES A.
1898 *Traditions of the Thompson River Indians*. Boston: Houghton Mifflin.

THOMPSON, STITH
1966 *Tales of the North American Indians*. Bloomington: Indiana University Press.
1974 *One hundred favorite folktales*. Bloomington: Indiana University Press.

ZENANI, NONGENILE MASITHATHU
1972 "Sikhuluma," in *African folklore*. Edited by Richard M. Dorson. Garden City: Anchor Books.

Tales in the Night: Toward an Anthropology of the Imaginary

SORY CAMARA

The purpose of this paper is to present some idea of a vast research program which took place over a number of years with regard to the Mandingo of West Africa. The project was concerned with determining the conceptions these people held of society, of the life of the individual within it, and of man's relations with his natural environment and his past.[1]

Ethnographers have already attempted to do all this with some degree of success. Some have started from the observation of behavior in everyday life, embellished with thoughts expressed by the subjects studied. They have used an inductive method to describe representations the people studied are *supposed* to have of life, death, marriage, etc. These attempts have certainly contributed to the progress of ethnography. The drawback of this method however, is that it approaches the psyche, the "mentality" of a people, through outward appearances.

It is possible to justify this approach by saying that questioning of natives on such subjects produces very unsatisfactory replies: "It is the custom," "The ancestors always acted in this manner," and so on. This would amount to saying that they hardly ever ask any questions and that they live according to rites whose effectiveness depends on something other than theoretical justifications. It is true that for modern ethnography, using only the techniques of the interview and questionnaire, the Mandingo may be very unsatisfactory subjects, because all knowledge of any importance here is secret (*gbȗdũ*). Proverbs proliferate, and their roundabout way of expressing an idea touches upon the Mandingo spirit.

[1] These investigations relate essentially to the Mandingo of eastern Senegal. They were conducted over a period of years with the assistance of the Centre de Recherches Anthropologiques, Musée de l'Homme and the Université de Bordeaux II.

The imperative of discretion is opposed to any ill-considered diffusion of knowledge: the Mandingo saying is *básí tó bɔ̀dɔ́ dɔ́ kà à sɔ̀*, "[one] contributes to the fetish by leaving it in the bag." *Kuma*, "words" uttered exclusively during the night (myths, legends, tales), constitute aspects of the disguised expression of a knowledge which is at once sociological and psychological. They are aspects of a folk wisdom which is revealed only on privileged occasions.

Through these "words," however, what we are most interested in learning about is the man, the Mandingo. For this reason, it was necessary to accord as much importance to the manner of collecting the texts as to the texts themselves. Thus, when I was dealing with chronicles, I took careful note of the social status of the griot (poet or musician) who related them. For other *kuma*, tales (*tali*) in particular, I had to pay even closer attention to the context. The social and domestic status of the narrator, as well as his personality, are eminently important. Thinking along the same lines, one may wonder if there are not favored subjects for particular social categories. Here precise ethnographic observations concerning differences in status according to age, primogeniture, initiation, and caste are very valuable. I also tried to vary narrative situations: I recorded tales both in domestic enclosures and at night on the village square, where everyone could intervene. In one village, for a week I called upon women to speak, to the exclusion of men; the following week I reversed the situation. Finally, I recorded the performances of well-known "storytellers," "experts" who go from village to village practicing their art.

From this it appeared that not just anyone may tell any tale. Within the family, each person has a monopoly on a group of tales, and no one else tells them. They constitute the expression of his own imaginary world. This world is in keeping with the narrative worlds of others. At the village (100–300 inhabitants) level, the theme of incest shows the following distribution: Women tell tales in which a father wants to marry his daughter. Men tell tales in which a mother wants to have incestuous relations with her son. Both men and women tell of incestuous adventures between brother and sister. These latter subjects are by far the most common; this seems to me to be one characteristic of the Mandingo's psychology.

Beyond this, psychological investigation is required to determine more precisely the relation between the narrator and his narrative. To this end, it was necessary to group and analyze all the tales told by the same person and then compare the results of this analysis with those of a sort of test of imagination which I developed. I asked an African artist[2] to draw the situations of the best-known tales. Then I presented the drawings to each narrator and asked him three questions: What are these persons doing?

[2] Pierre Louisin, to whom I express full gratitude.

How do they happen to be there? How will this story end? For example, Figure 1 is inspired by a tale summed up as follows:

A young man has fallen in love with one of his sisters. He is a ferryman who spends the whole day on the riverbank. His sisters bring him his meals in turn. One day he decides that he will no longer eat the meal prepared by Indigo, the sister with whom he is in love. After all the others, Indigo arrives; she enters the canoe with her brother. Having reached the middle of the river, the two throw themselves together into the waves. The sister is transformed into a female hippopotamus, the brother into a male hippopotamus.

In this type of incestuous tale, the incest remains symbolic. There is another type in which it actually takes place — brother and sister cross the river, marry, and settle on the other side. When Figure 1 is presented to persons who relate this type of incestuous tale, they have no difficulty in imagining a love story with a happy ending: The man proposes to the woman that she enter his canoe; they cross the river; they marry on the other bank.[3] Others imagine a monster threatening to capsize the canoe. Among the countless narratives of the folk tradition, *each thus appears to choose those which express his personal problems*: "Tell me your tales, I will tell you who you are."

In all cases I made a phonetic transcription of the Mandingo texts as well as a French translation, for if one wishes to understand the mentality of a people one must begin by respecting the expression of this mentality. Often, a pretense is made of forgetting this. Unfortunately, it has not been posssible to present the documents in this form.

Finally, it was necessary to study the contents of the narratives and to devise an adequate method of analysis. In speaking of my own civilization and people to another civilization to whose influence I am subject, my constant concern is not to betray the Mandingo. I am also basically guided by their instructions as to how their tales should be told. Using "The Marriage of the Young Girl" as an example, I shall attempt to describe this method in detail. In particular, I shall show how it permits the resolution of certain problems.

Each narrator gives his own interpretation of narratives which have been transmitted to him and which he has only to report. Since the text of the tale is not fixed, what remains of the original message after the long chain of tradition to which it has been submitted? Is this message transformed to the point of actually becoming another? Or do particular narratives have relatively stable outlines? If the latter is the case, it should be easy to distinguish in the narrative what is picked up from the collective imagination and what comes from individual imaginations, for nothing can survive as tradition that does not reflect the consensus of the

[3] It is interesting that no subject ever recognized the tales by which the illustrations were inspired — happily, for if this had not been the case my experiment would have failed.

Figure 1. Drawing by Pierre Louisin, inspired by tale of Indigo and the ferryman

successive interpreters who have transmitted it. While these outlines are independent of the persons who interpret them, do they not vary with the theme? Do not these transformations correspond to the particular psychological processes of the central personages of these tales? It should therefore be possible to establish a psychological typology of individual development for each sex and thus to sketch an "anthropology of the imaginary." Transformations on another level would bring us back to the narrator's art and his psychology.

To understand the tales from the point of view of the Mandingo themselves, it is necessary first to focus attention on the songs and the formulas which open and close the narratives.[4] Analysis of these has established that:

1. The adventures related by Mandingo tales do not record reality, but neither are they pure fantasy.

2. They are often set in the beginning of time, but it is also said of them: "You will find that that still occurs today."

3. The tales are announced as the recitation of a personal experience. However, this experience cannot be localized anywhere. Furthermore, it is in no way the privilege of age. In this area, the child may teach his parents.

In short, the Mandingo tale relates a drama which comes to a head on this side of the reality of the event. It is not a past which is definitively completed: it is an impending drama. It may burst out at any time and anywhere. It is a movement which is indefinitely contained, a psychic reality.

4. Although its narration has a beginning and an end, an introductory chant says: "A tale has no end/A unique tale has no end." It is not an accomplished fact with regard to meaning. Therefore it will be necessary to group narratives in order to analyze them.

5. Like the soothsayer, the Mandingo narrator describes a spectacle which he alone is supposed to have seen. But unlike the soothsayer, the narrator wants to have us discover his mysterious universe: he wants to bring us to see it. Thus, one has only to listen to him to see. But what must one see? Everything he describes? Not for the moment, for above all it is a matter of apprehending collective representations. As I have said, tales are the subject of oral tradition, and each text must be regarded as a particular interpretation of something the narrator has not invented. It is precisely this "something" which one must see first, and which analysis must separate from individual interpretations.

It is also necessary to represent the tale in the form of a drama, in time and space — a silent drama stripped to its bare essentials, for we are in the realm of pure imagination, as analysis of the narrator's art would reveal it: beings and things must be reduced to their essential features, for these

[4] These formulas are analyzed in a 300-page report filed at the University of Chicago.

alone are capable of being transmitted from mouth to ear, from generation to generation, without alteration. All words, all individual descriptions, last only as long as it takes for each particular narration. No one would dream of preserving the entire text of a tale. The same narrator generally never repeats himself exactly. Thus one has to simplify the tale by making it undergo an essential thinning out. However, this thinning out must not be irreversible: starting from the outline thus obtained, one should once again tell the same tale.

Now, what one "sees," then, are beings in movement in relation to others in the space of the tale, beings whose changes in location are ordered in time. I shall attempt to test this rule of essential thinning out by applying it to an analysis of some tales.

Long association with the texts (at the time of recording, drawing up index cards, phonetic transcription, and translation) has given me the feeling that Mandingo tales are grouped by "families" in some way. At the time of narration, this grouping takes place quite naturally. The narrator, after the introductory formulas, immediately announces the subject: "There was a girl. She did not wish to marry." When encouraged to do so, the narrators who told this tale endeavored to give other variants of the same subject. It was discovered that rejection of marriage forms the subject of a considerable number of Mandingo tales. Now, one may wonder whether this grouping rests on a similar organization of the narratives in question. Do they develop in accordance with a similar schema? To answer this, I shall begin by showing that Mandingo tales are always organized within a particular time and space. The following tale bears the registration number CMM.25-A.3:

> A marabout has married a girl, but she refuses to cross the conjugal threshold. She is accustomed to play all alone in the evening on the edge of the bush. She sings: "Solitary games, solitary games, I play all alone." One night the young disciples of the marabout go to look for the girl who has run off. One of them finds her at the edge of the bush. He sings a song. The girl becomes afraid. She flees toward the village. But all the doors are closed, except for that of the marabout. Pursued by the song of the small boy, she enters the hut of her husband and remains there.

The principal persons of this tale are grouped in two camps. This distinction is determined by the attitude of the girl, who does not wish to abandon her parents' home for the husband's hut. The girl and her parents are in one camp and the fiancé of the girl and his disciples are in the other. The heroine's action even brings about a differentiation of the microcosm of the tale. Rejecting the village norm of marriage, she flees to the bush. This may be outlined as shown in Figure 2.

This is the initial situation. In terms of the narrative, the girl changes her attitude; she develops. This development is signified in the spatial

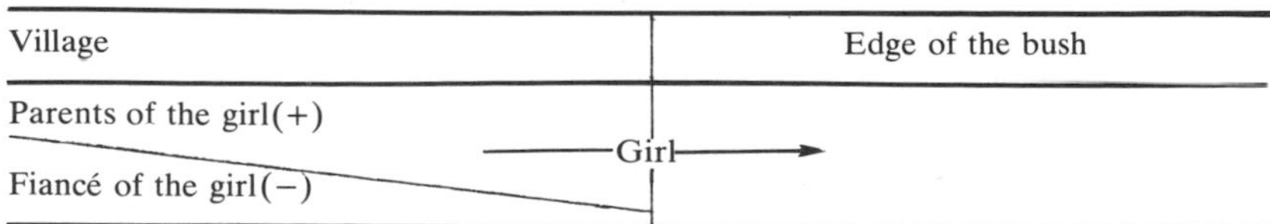

Figure 2. The initial situation of Tale CMM.25-A.3

language of the tale by a change of position (Figure 3). This naturally assumes a duration, which is also concretely expressed in terms of movements. The movements effected by the girl and other persons between the initial situation and the final situation will be considered to explain her development: (1) flight of the girl every night to the edge of the bush (repetition expressing duration); (2) appearance of the young male disciples of the fiancé; (3) scattering of the boys; (4) discovery of the girl by one of the boys, and his singing; (5) flight of the girl to the village, followed by the boy; (6) arrival of the girl and the boy at the fiancé's door; (7) entrance of the girl into the hut; (8) disappearance of the boy.

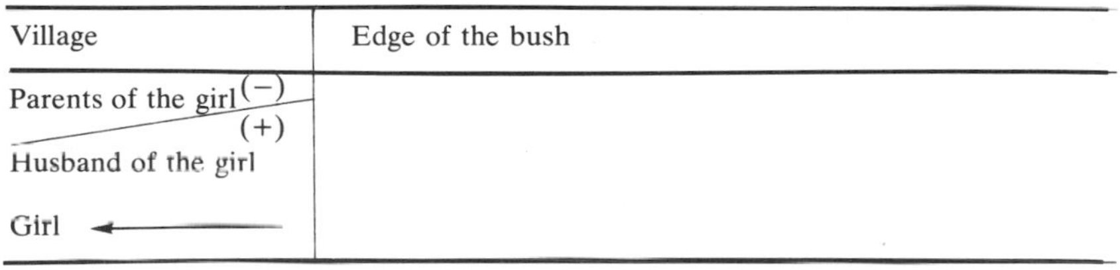

Village | Edge of the bush
Parents of the girl (−)
(+)
Husband of the girl
Girl ←

Figure 3. Development in Tale CMM.25-A.3

One may distinguish three phases in this development: (1) movement of the girl back and forth between the village and the bush; (2) movement of a new person from the village to the bush; (3) movement in the reverse direction (toward the village) of the girl and the boy.

To simplify things, let us say that two criteria permit us to distinguish these phases: In the first place, one counts as a phase each time a new person passes from one zone to another (these zones being constituted by the village and the bush). In the second place, one counts as a phase each time the direction of movement is reversed, even if the person who moves is the same. Thus these phases are characterized by the movements of the protagonists with regard to each other within the differentiated microcosm of the tale. I call them *movements*. The sum total of these movements constitute *the schema* (in a philosophical sense) of the tale. Figure 4 illustrates the outline of Tale CMM.25-A.3.

This schema undoubtedly constitutes a thinning out of the narrative. It is still possible, however, to reconstitute it from such an outline. The new text will not be identical with the initial one, but that does not much matter, for, as I have said, the Mandingo tale is transmitted from mouth to ear, and the narrator never seeks to preserve the original text. His recitation is a recreation, an interpretation. What he interprets in this manner is in fact a schema, one which is relatively constant with relation to an eminently variable text.

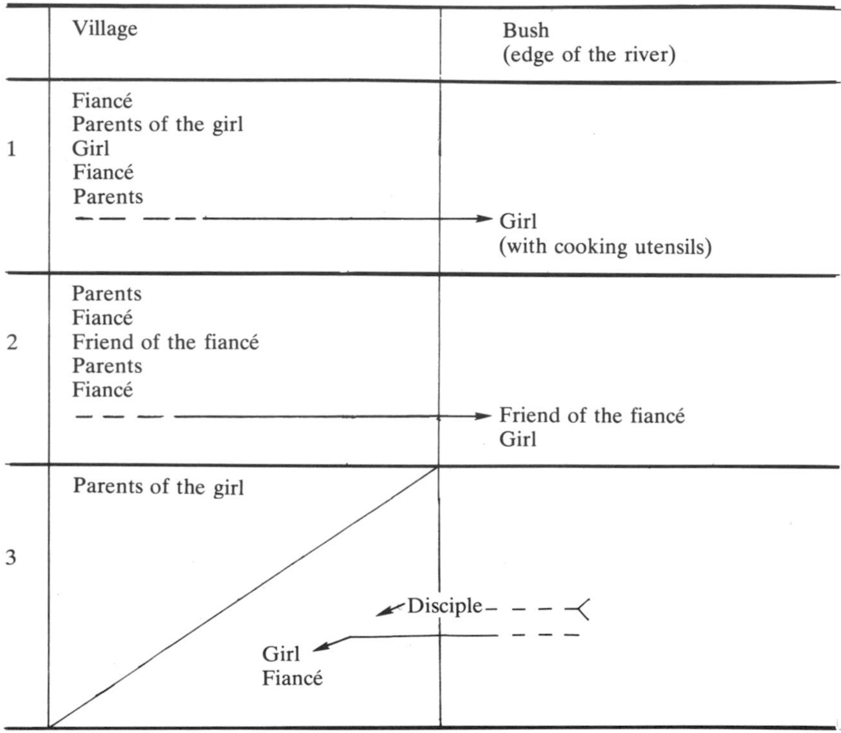

Figure 4. Outline of Tale CMM.25-A.3

The movements of the schema just developed raise many questions. First, what do the repeated flights of the girl and her solitary games mean? Placing them in context may clarify them somewhat. The flight from the village is contemporary with the refusal to marry; it is as if the former were a consequence of the latter. The rejection of the village's norm is accompanied by periodic new flights by the heroine to the edge of the bush. However, marriage is not only a village rule; it is simply a recognition of a natural function. It appears that the girl is not refusing to carry out this function, but only rejecting the village form of it. If this is indeed the case, then she will have to substitute another form for it. Now, the flight and solitary games take place at the very moment of conjugal relations. May they not be compensation for these? If so, the former will have the same meaning as the latter: a sexual meaning. But these hypotheses will have to be confirmed by the study of other tales.

Yet another question arises: what do the small boys represent? Another question is linked to this: how is one to explain the flight of the girl toward the village when she hears one of them? Here again, it is only possible for the moment to formulate hypotheses for later investigations to confirm or invalidate. The role of the young disciple is limited to a simple mediation between the village and the edge of the bush, between the fiancé and the girl in flight: he appears when the latter flees from the village; he disappears when she returns there. He remains near her and, apparently, rouses her as long as she is far from her fiancé. As soon as she enters the conjugal bed, he ceases to trouble her and disappears. How is it, however, that his song alone can suffice to interrupt her games and make her flee? The disciple is in himself quite inoffensive, and his song has nothing disturbing in it, but the girl is intrigued by it and perhaps frightened: a fright which the tale translates by a flight toward the village and which seems out of all proportion to its cause.

Perhaps the following tale (CN.16-A.4) will enable us to solve this problem:

> At the moment of departure for the conjugal residence, the girl flees to the bush, to the edge of a river, with all her cooking utensils. She settles there and feeds herself. Her husband's friend goes to the edge of the river and plays the *sībīŋo* (a stringed musical instrument) while singing. On hearing this sound, without seeing anyone, the girl flees to the village. She asks her parents and grandparents for refuge. Her grandmother, jostling her a bit, takes her to her husband's house. The latter's friend follows her there. When she goes into the conjugal hut, the husband's friend turns back.

The outline of this tale is summed up in Figure 5. Taken as a whole, this outline is similar to the first: between the initial situation and the final situation there is in both cases a total reversal. After having rejected marriage and fled the city of men and its norms, the girl returns there and crosses the conjugal threshold. The development which is thus accomplished is accounted for by a movement of mediation: an inhabitant of the village intervenes with the girl. As in the first case, the male mediator is an associate of the fiancé: his friend. Finally, the direction of the three movements is identical. Thus we may consider the two outlines similar.

The variations which I shall note now will be regarded as secondary and as not signifiying any change of subject. They must, however, be taken into consideration at another level, which I shall define later. Therefore it will be helpful to pause here for a moment.

In the first place, a nuance will be observed in the organization of space. The differentiation between the two zones here is more marked: the first might be called the *city of men*, the second the *woodland world* or the *domain of the wild*. All the adventures of the heroes unfold within this framework, and their fate is played out there.

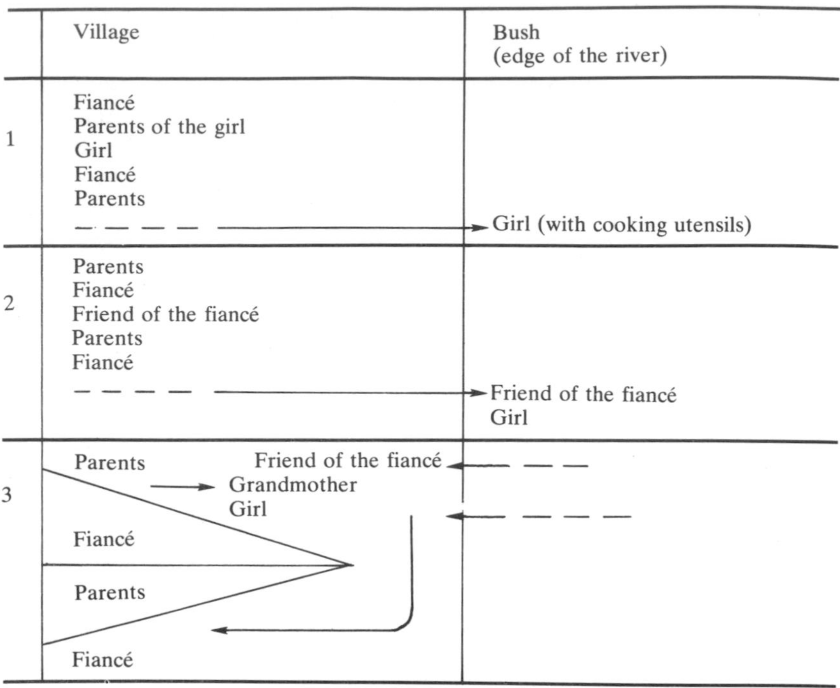

Figure 5. Outline of Tale CN.16-A.4

As in the second tale, the heroine flees from the village. Here, however, her flight is not one of many attempts at escape; it has a lasting character: she settles in the bush. This time she no longer plays; instead, she eats. For a girl of an age to start housekeeping, one cannot help but be surprised. To understand this point, it is necessary to refer to everyday life. With the Mandingo, cooking is, for a woman, associated with sharing the marital bed. Thus the heroine's culinary activity evokes sexuality. But she does not cook for any man: she feeds no one but herself. Her behavior is like an appeal for sexual exchange, but an appeal which is smothered and consequently has no echo. It is as if the refusal to marry condemned her to give herself up to actions whose completion is only possible in marriage. This aborted appeal is found once again in another action. The flight ends at the edge of the river. Now, the road which leads there is favorable to furtive meetings with young men. It is the road on which juvenile loves are formed. It is also the one used for adultery. The village road is not favorable to such meetings. Thus the choice of the river evokes sexuality, but a sexuality which has not yet been "socialized," or has already eluded the norms. Thus one may legitimately put forward the theory that the meaning of the culinary concerns of the young girl in flight is of a sexual nature — which confirms the hypothesis offered apropos of the preceding tale. It is important to note, however, the slight difference at the level of the action's representation.

Another variation appears in the course of the second movement: the mediator is no longer a reduced representation, a younger version, of the fiancé; rather, he represents the fiancé with all the traits of an adult man. This is a development which must be related to the girl's withdrawal into the bush and her settlement there; the mediator's intervention must therefore be all the more effective. The man is characterized by a new attribute, the *sībīŋo*, a musical instrument with seven strings played by griots who sing of their hunting exploits. Thus the music evokes hunting. Here the flight of the girl may be understood better than in the first tale: in the present context it seems as if she were in the position of the "game." After all, she lives in the bush. Thinking of it in these terms, she is another wild creature, and she is pursued up to her husband's threshold. This point is important to note; we shall return to it in order to clarify its meaning.

It should also be noted that the man who pursues the girl is at no time seen by her. Though she hears the noises he makes, she is unable to connect them with a man. The anxiety she feels is none the less for this. In the first case, the heroine who heard the song could think of a person, another human being; here there is nothing of this nature, nothing but an apprehension.

The last variation is introduced by the intervention of the grandmother, who in a way constitutes a redoubling of the mediation. She intervenes only in the village, completing the task undertaken by the other in the bush. She differs from the latter, however, by sex and origin, since she is a woman and belongs to the family of the girl while the other is male and linked to the fiancé. We shall have to seek the significance of this familial mediation.

What I have just noted is a group of variations with relation to the outline, which, for its part, remains constant. This distinction does not imply that only the outline, because it is constant, is significant and the rest, because it depends on contingencies, is arbitrary. On the contrary, we are dealing here with two levels of significance. In order to be in a position to lay the foundations for this hypothesis, however, one must first establish the constant character of the outline by analysis of a large number of narratives.

Tale CN.19-B.2, the inspiration for Figure 6, is as follows:

The girl does not wish to marry. She goes regularly to bathe in the river. There she removes her breasts, washes them, and places them on a white loincloth, in the

Figure 6. Drawing by Pierre Louisin, inspired by Tale CN.19-B.2

sun. One day her fiancé's friend changes into a sparrow hawk, carries off the girl's breasts, and brings them to the fiancé. The girl, stripped and in distress, returns to the village to look for her breasts, but no one in her family is able to help her except her grandmother. The latter takes her to her husband's door. He responds to her song by playing the *sībīŋo*. She finds her breasts in the conjugal bed.

On the whole, the schema of this tale (Figure 7) is similar to the two

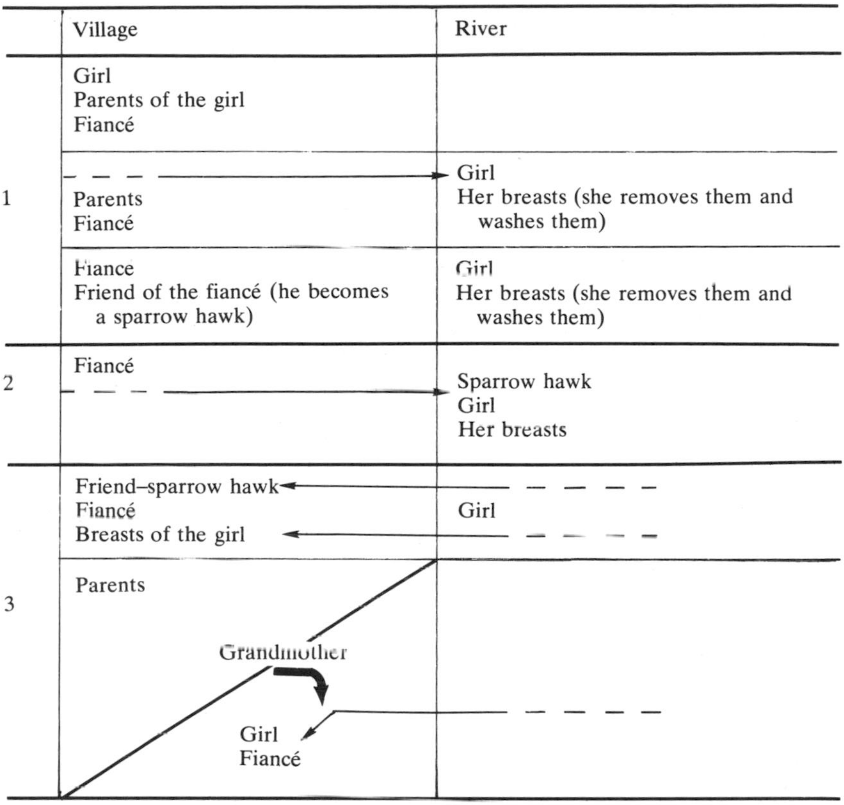

	Village	River
	Girl Parents of the girl Fiancé	
1	Parents Fiancé	Girl Her breasts (she removes them and washes them)
	Fiancé Friend of the fiancé (he becomes a sparrow hawk)	Girl Her breasts (she removes them and washes them)
2	Fiancé	Sparrow hawk Girl Her breasts
	Friend–sparrow hawk Fiancé Breasts of the girl	Girl
3	Parents Grandmother Girl Fiancé	

Figure 7. Outline of Tale CN.19–B.2

preceding ones; the movements of the persons and the directions of these movements are identical, and the number of movements is the same. In comparison with the culinary activities, the game with the breasts constitutes a secondary variaton. The chest is regarded by the Mandingo as an erotic part of the body. The griots know formulas for a particularly suggestive rhythm depicting the dance of the breasts while walking. In young men's huts, games are oriented toward the touching of breasts. Thus the heroine's gesture clearly has a sexual significance. By concentrating her attention on her breasts, she guides our attention toward them. By exposing them, she gives herself up to predatory action: like the foolhardy chick that strays from under the protective wing of its mother, the breasts are carried away by the sparrow hawk. The hunting symbolism slightly suggested in the first narrative is obvious here. Is the sparrow hawk not the best-known wild hunter in the village? Does it not threaten the farmyard daily? Thus the hunting relation returns to sexuality: on the one hand, the prey is the object of sexual desire; on the other hand, this hunt constitutes a prelude to the conjugal act.

In fact, having thus been stripped of her femininity, the girl cannot long remain in the bush. It is no longer anxiety which chases her from the bush, but the actual inadequacy of the state in which she has placed herself by rejecting marriage. Outside the village, the need which is represented by this institution remains unsatisfied: it is necessary to return. Finally, moved by her own desire to rediscover her femininity, the girl enters the conjugal hut, and she appears less oblivious of her own steps than the first two girls, who were fleeing out of pure panic. If at the beginning she was not fully aware of the possible consequences of exhibiting her body, she is now fully aware of the purpose of her flight: to rediscover her full femininity, of which her rejection of man had robbed her. In addition, she rediscovers it only at the moment when she shares her husband's bed.

For the first time, the latter is represented by an animal (a bird of prey): the friend is thus transformed before revealing his presence in the bush. This phenomenon is not completely new. In the preceding narrative, the fiancé's friend has to provide himself with a musical instrument before penetrating the bush. This is a form of transfiguration, for it made the sounds by which he announced his presence strange and unrecognizable. The inability of the girl to identify them confirms that the transfiguration was equivalent to a metamorphosis. The effects produced on the girl in the two cases are identical.[5] After all, the girl does not meet the animal any more than she met the man who was playing the *sībīŋo*; there is only the impression of a presence.

Thus, the mediator between the wild girl and her future sexual partner from the village appears successively in the form of a child whose voice only is heard, an adult man who manifests himself by strange sounds, and finally an animal. These variations in the features of the agents accomplishing the identical function are not arbitrary: they reveal a meaning which none of the features by itself could establish at all definitively. We have already seen that the person of the mediator is a representation of the husband. The analysis of this latest tale now reveals that he also constitutes a representation of the need experienced by the girl in flight. Now it is possible to detect slight differences in the person of the

[5] However, it is necessary to remember that the animal appears for the first time in the wild area in which the heroine has taken refuge and that he exhibits himself as a representation of the sexual partner.

mediator. The latter cannot be defined as an image of the husband, who, in the actual matrimonial state, does not conjure up anything seductive for the girl. He is only the one for whom her parents have intended her, generally without asking her opinion. Often he does not correspond to her expectations. In the last tale, the person of the mediator becomes the incarnation of the girl's own desire: what he represents no longer proceeds only from outside, but also echoes the heroine's own feelings. One should therefore speak of the representation of *the sexual partner* and not of the husband. This nuance is important: it signifies that the image of the sexual partner may possibly not correspond to that of the husband recognized by the law of the village — that is to say, the one the parents have chosen. It is true that in the last narrative this image develops toward the representation of the husband, but will this always be the case? Will the sparrow hawk always bring back the breasts to the husband as a well-trained dog brings the game back to his master? Nothing could be less certain!

Tale CN.16-B.3 is as follows:

A little girl goes off into the bush with her brothers. She meets some creatures (*gɔɔtɔ*) there playing *wɔ̀li* and begins to play with them; her brothers return to the village without her. They send her younger brother to look for her on the following day, and then on the following days, but in vain. She grows up in the bush. The man who has asked for her hand in marriage grieves. A friend proposes to help him. On his ankles and wrists he wears some cattle-bells which make a strange noise; this is how he is going to surprise the girl in the bush. The latter, on hearing him, takes fright and flees to the village, still followed by the strange noise. At her house she finds the door closed, but her grandmother leads her to her husband. The latter responds to her song by playing the *sībīŋo*. As soon as she lies down in the conjugal bed the strange noise vanishes.

If the two journeys are considered to constitute the same movement, then the schema of this tale (Figure 8) is similar to the others as a whole. The doubling of the mediation scarcely alters the general meaning of the narrative. In fact, one could do away with the intervention of the younger brother without fundamentally changing the meaning of the tale. Thus his intervention is secondary with regard to the outline. The presence of the *gɔɔtɔ* should also be considered in this way, since they could be left out without altering the meaning of the narrative.

These first tales have shown us that there are many ways for a girl to remain in the bush. One may play there all alone, cook, remove one's breasts, and, finally, play there with one's woodland partners. These are variable actions with regard to a relatively stable schema. This means that, though they are not significant at the level of the schema, they may be so at another level. In a way, they permit case studies of different personalities found in similar situations. Contrary to the common situation which has been made concrete by the outline, they acquire significance only through

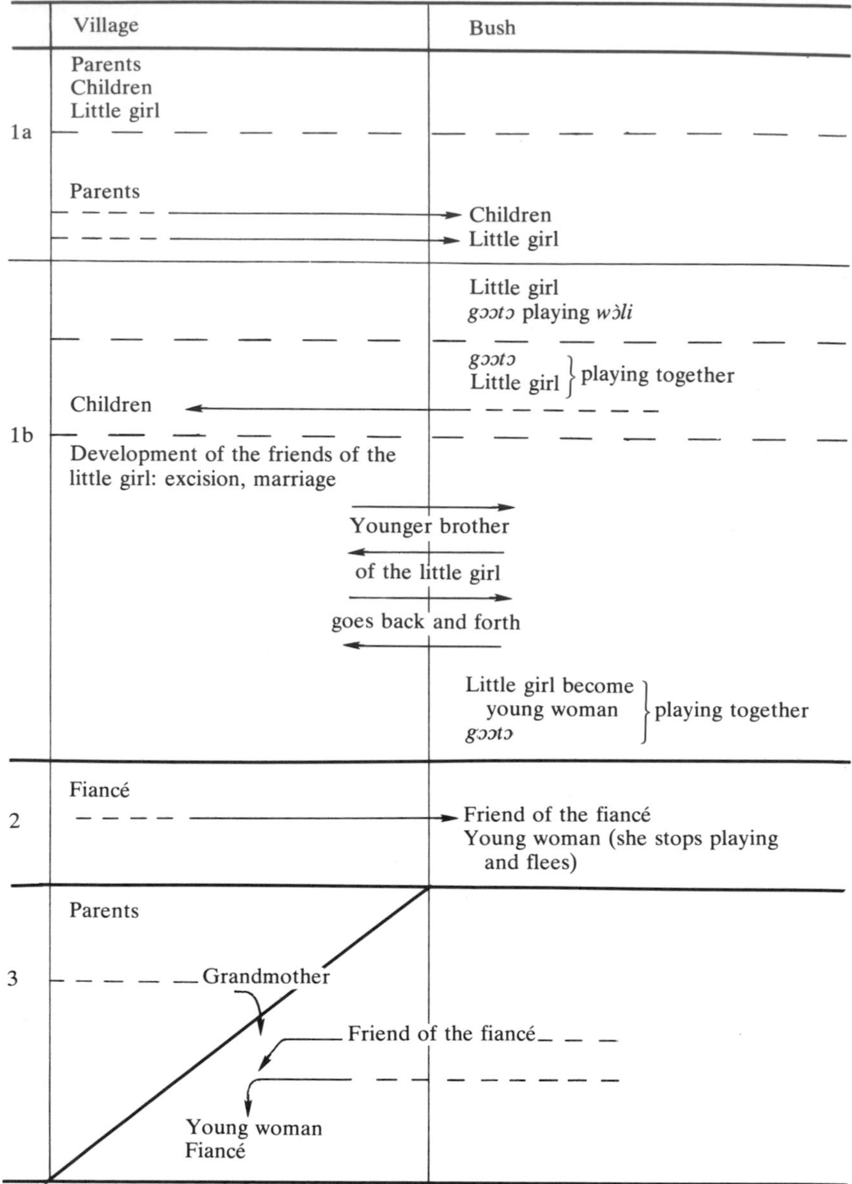

Figure 8. Outline of Tale CN.16-B.3

their very variations; the significance of the outline, in contrast, is linked to its relative stability.

Now, what are the *gɔɔtɔ*? They are small, hairy anthropomorphic beings which are supposed to live in the bush. It is reported that they walk with their heels in front. They are generally represented with masculine features and appear to be endowed with supernatural power. Insofar as they are woodland beings, they call to mind the sparrow hawk of Tale CN.19-B.2. While the latter "chases" the girl and "heads her back" toward the village, however, the *gɔɔtɔ* fascinate her and keep her in the bush. Furthermore, their relationship with her is unusual. *Wɔ̀li (wɔ̀lìtǎγɔ̀)* is an exclusively masculine game. In playing it with "males," the girl is in an uncertain position in relation to her feminine status: she identifies herself with man. She thus denies the conjugal relationship which is her village vocation. The heroine is truly a "wild child": she has lived in the bush for all the important phases of her childhood and her youth. Perhaps this is what explains the difficulty of returning, which necessitates two successive mediators.

In fact, the time which has gone by is that of the period of "maturation," as the psychologists call it. This means that the return to the village marks, not only the efficiency of the mediator, but also the maturity of the girl. Up to now, all the mediators have succeeded, but all the preceding heroines were marriageable at the time of the intervention. This explains why the small boy of the first tale succeeds despite his age.[6] As the others are adults, the problem does not arise.

In the present case the first mediator is young, as was the small boy of the first tale, but he intervenes when the girl has not yet reached marrying age; he fails in his task. When she has become marriageable, she will be sensitive to the intervention of a man, but an adult one. With regard to this point, one may note that the mediators and woodland partners of the girl remain indifferent to each other's presence: nevertheless, they are in the position of adversaries with regard to her. A latent conflicts exists there. If it were to break out, would it jeopardize her emotional development? The very meaning of the tale would then be changed. We must listen to other tales on the same subject to be able to answer this. For example, Tale CMM.26-B.2 is as follows:

> A girl decides that her future spouse must not bear the mark of any scar, which eliminates all suitors (for every Mandingo male must be circumcised). A serpent, having learned of this, transforms himself into a handsome young man and comes to the village to marry the girl. Having been transformed into a fly, the younger brother of the girl goes to visit the most secret parts of his body and in fact does not find any scar. The man-serpent takes the girl off into the bush; the younger brother–fly follows them, and one day he discovers that the husband of his sister is a serpent. He flees with her to the village. A small bird helps them cross a river but drowns the man-serpent. The brother and sister return to their parents' house in the village.

The schema of this tale (Figure 9) inaugurates a basic change with regard to the others, and this is apparent in the direction of the movements. If

[6] This notion of the mediator's youth is quite relative: it must be evaluated in relation to the heroine's age.

	Village	Bush	River	Serpent's home
	Parents Girl Younger brother			Serpent
1	Parents Girl Younger brother become fly Serpent become man ←	....	....	....
2	Parents .... →	Serpent become man Younger brother become fly Girl		
3	Parents	Girl Younger brother ←		.... Serpent ....
	Parents Younger brother Girl ←	.....	Serpent (dead) →	

Figure 9. Outline of Tale CMM.26-B.2

one takes the letter V as the code for village and B as the code for bush, then a movement from the village to the bush may be represented by the code $\overrightarrow{VB}$. Movement in the reverse direction will be indicated by $\overleftarrow{VB}$. The outline for the preceding tales may be represented as follows:

$\overrightarrow{VB}$

$\overrightarrow{VB}$

$\overleftarrow{VB}$

However, to be able to give grounds for the resemblance of the schemas of the first four tales, one must also bear in mind that persons who carry out these movements. Now, in all these examples we are dealing with a girl in the first movement ($\overrightarrow{VB}$: girl), a representation of the fiancé in the second movement ($\overrightarrow{VB}$: friend of the fiancé), and the girl and a man associated with the fiancé in the third ($\overleftarrow{VB}$: girl and friend of the fiancé).

The schema remains the same in each case. This constancy is significant with regard to the ending of the drama. In fact, in all these narratives the girl accedes to a normal sexuality: she marries.

What happens in the present case? In the first place, the movements have changed direction:

←

VB

→

VB

←

VB

Furthermore, the person who carries out the second movement is no longer the same. Instead of a man associated with the fiancé, it is a small boy associated with the girl — a younger brother, we are told. It is true that he has been mentioned in the preceding narratives, but there his interventions have had no effect. For these two reasons it can be said that there has been a change of schema, which corresponds to a change of theme. We are no longer dealing with a girl who does not wish to go to her fiancé's home. This time the heroine imposes an inhuman condition on her suitors. Having done this, she is doing more than eliminating possible partners from the village: her action implies an appeal. Given the organization of the microcosm of the tale, only a woodland partner can respond to it: hence the serpent's invasion of the village.

This intervention by a woodland partner into the girl's adventures is nothing new, but the present narrative introduces a new element in that the relationship with the woodland partner is a perfect conjugal representation: the heroine lives with the husband; she cooks for him. These alterations introduce a change of schema. It may also be expected that this different form of progress will have a different ending: for the first time, the return of the girl to the village takes her to her parents' residence. She does not marry, and this is reflected on the spatial plane by a lack of differentiation of the village. In contrast, the bush is differentiated into two zones separated by a boundary: the river. On the one hand, there is the residence of the man-serpent, on the other, the place of refuge of the girl and her younger brother. These represent the opposing poles of conjugal relations and familial relations. It is as if the bush had just acquired a differentiated organization to the detriment of the village. In addition, the girl's road can no longer lead anywhere but to her parent's home, since she has already crossed the conjugal threshold in the bush. Furthermore, the woodland partner, that is, the exogamous representation of the partner, has perished in the river. This death explains the impossibility for the heroine to accede to normal sexuality; there can be no exogamy if the image of the *partner from another place* vanishes. The woodland tragedy is all the more revealing of the chain of events in that the death of the bush partner is due to the intervention of the person who has come from the family in the village: the younger brother. Here the conflict breaks out which was latent between the younger brother and the *gɔɔtɔ* of Tale CN.16-B.3. While it was latent, it did not prevent the heroine from achieving her normal sexuality; when it is brought into the open, it does.

This conflict is a phenomenon which deserves more thorough analysis. In fact, it reveals that the mediator is not unimportant in the girl's emotional development. Depending on whether he is associated with the familial or the conjugal region of the village, the significance and effect of his intervention vary. The younger brother is intimately linked with the girl: he forms part of her earliest environment. His mediation is directed by this fact; he can only lead her to the family home. On the other hand, the friend of the fiancé, who is basically linked to the latter, leads her to the conjugal home. This fact may be represented symbolically. Each mediator will be designated by m or f, depending on whether he is a man or a woman. A mediator who is a member of the girl's family will be designated m^o or f^o. The parents will be symbolized by PP, the fiancé by Mv, and the girl by F. Any woodland partner of the male sex will be designated Mb. A code with slashes through it will indicate that the person is dead.

This outline of the tale we are analyzing can then be represented as follows:

$$PP + F + m^o$$
$$PP + F + m^o + Mb \ \ldots\ \overleftarrow{VB}$$
$$PP \ \ldots\ldots\ldots\ldots\ldots\ \overrightarrow{VB} \ \ldots\ F + m^o + Mb$$
$$PP + F + m^o \ \ldots\ldots\ldots\ \overleftarrow{VB} \ \ldots\ \not{M}\!\not{b}$$

Following the same procedure, one may represent the outline of Tale CN.16–B.3 as follows:

$$PP + F + m^o$$
$$\overrightarrow{VB} \ \ldots\ (m^o) + F + MbMb$$
$$\underline{m}^o \ \ldots\ldots\ \overset{\rightleftarrows}{VB} \ \ldots\ (\underline{m}^o) + F + MbMb$$
$$Mv + m$$
$$Mv \ \ldots\ldots\ldots\ldots\ldots\ \overrightarrow{VB} \ \ldots\ m + F + MbMb$$
$$PP + F^o + \underline{F} + \underline{m} \ \ldots\ \overleftarrow{VB} \ \ldots\ (MbMb)$$
$$Mv + F + \overline{(f^o m)}$$

Here the doubling of a term means that more than one person is involved; thus, the *gɔɔtɔ*, the woodland partners, are symbolized by $MbMb$. The terms underlined indicate which persons have traveled. A code element placed between parentheses refers to the disappearance from the narrative of the person to whom it corresponds, as in the case of the *gɔɔtɔ* after the heroine's return to the village and the fiancé's friend (m) and the grandmother (f^o) after her entrance into the conjugal hut.

This codification has the advantage of simplifying the outline without thinning it out too much. Thus, comparison becomes all the easier. In this way one notes that the mediator associated with the familial zone of the village does not necessarily alienate the girl from conjugal life. Depending on whether it is a man (m^o), or a woman (f^o), the mediator turns her away from it or leads her to it. At least this is what may be asserted in the present state of affairs. After all, it seems that when the mediator is a woman (f^o), she never intervenes in the bush, but only in the village. That is, she is not the source of the emotion which wrenches the heroine from her infantile, wild games and drives her into the conjugal hut. She is only an advisor, a guide. She does not instigate the movement that takes place, but simply gives notice of it.

On the other hand, in Tale CN.19-B.2, the sparrow hawk carries off the girl's breasts (evoking sexuality through the hunting relationship), and the result is the reunion of the girl and the fiancé. Here the bird carries off the girl in the same manner, but with her younger brother this time, and makes them cross the river. It is as if this action brought together these two persons. The analogy between the two instances places the brother in the position of husband. Moreover, "to cross the river with someone" signifies, for a girl, having sexual relations. In their moonlight singing, girls sometimes sing: "If I did not fear the judgement of the King/I would cross the river with you. . . ." If such is the case, one may wonder whether the position of the brother and sister does not foreshadow an incestuous relationship. The hypothesis is fragile, however, unless one has established the constancy of the intervention of the bird and of the brother in relation to the impossibility of the girl's getting married. The following tale, CN.3-B.3, will help us in this:

The girl says that she will marry the man who has no anus. A serpent transforms himself into a man and comes to the village accompanied by representatives of the bush — pebble, mud, shrub, bamboo — in human form. The younger brother of the girl, having been transformed into a fly, flies under the trousers of the man-serpent and does not find any anus on him. The girl marries him, follows him, accompanied by her younger brother, who is still transformed into a fly. On the way, the representatives of the bush each return to their original appearance. Having arrived in the bush, the younger brother discovers that his brother-in-law is a serpent. He flees with his sister. The serpent pursues them. The younger brother transforms himself into a bird perched on his sister, who has been transformed into a tree stump, to deceive the serpent. This is how he succeeds in bringing his sister back to his parents' home.

In the schema of this tale (Figure 10), one sees at once the constancy of the brother-bird relation with regard to the girl's conjugal failure. This is not, however, the only analogy. The persons and movements are comparable with those of the preceding tale. The hypothesis of a correspondence between subjects of tales and their outlines is thus verified. This is all the

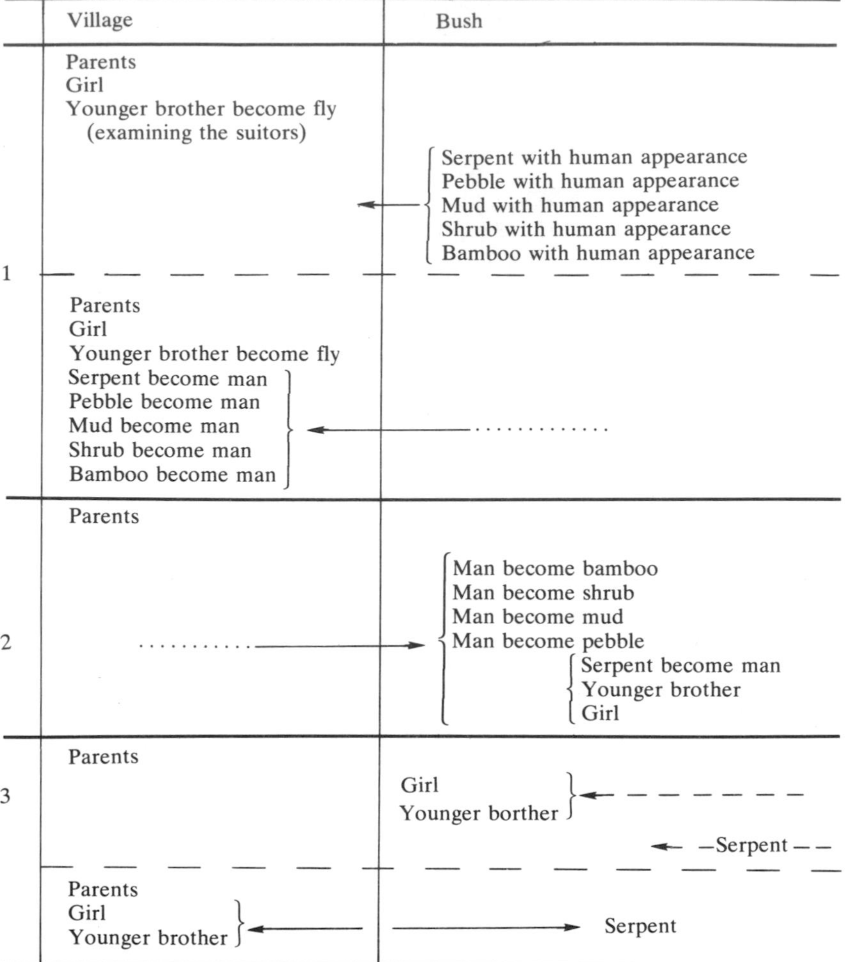

Figure 10. Outline of Tale CN.3-B.3

more significant if each outline is considered as depicting a specific psychic advance, a particular development of a type of Mandingo girl. If it turns out to be possible to prepare a table of all the schemas of narratives relating to the girl's marriage, then it will be possible to draw up an exhaustive typology, the importance of which may be imagined.

At this point, it is useful to note that certain constants underlie the variability of the outlines. In the first place, the flight appears as a necessary movement, an inescapable phase of the heroine's development. The girl must respond to the appeal of the bush before crossing the conjugal threshold. In the second place, the intervention of a male mediator is necessary, for the girl never leaves the bush spontaneously. Female mediators intervene only when she has returned to the village —

when she has been driven there by the man. These two features thus establish a continuity between outlines which in other respects differ: outlines of tales where the girl does not wish to marry in opposition to those in which she imposes inhuman conditions on her possible suitors.

However, the last tale introduces a new detail: multiplicity of companions. Tale CMM.25-A.3 also had a multitude of companions appearing alongside the fiancé, but these were inhabitants of the village who were prepared to invade the woodland area. Only one mediator reached the place of refuge. Here, on the other hand, it is the suitor from the wilds and his whole entourage who invade the girl's residence. Tale CN.16-B.3, with its plurality of woodland partners, appears to bear more resemblance to the one we are now studying. However, there is a difference: while the plurality of partners is irreducible in CN.16-B.3, here unification takes place. One after another, the serpent's companions leave the procession and resume their usual form and place. The wild face of the man-serpent is progressively revealed by these successive returns to woodland origins. Little by little, the illusion fades away. In the end, the younger brother will discover the strange husband without an anus in his true appearance as a serpent. In CN.16-B.3, the development takes place by abrupt changes, by "mutations": the image of multiple small woodland beings is replaced by the single one of a small boy, then that of a mature man.

Contrary to this process, the last two narratives reveal a conflict between two types of masculine representations: the younger brother, the familial representation of man (the man-from-home), neutralizes or eliminates the serpent (the man-from-outside). Having done this, he makes it impossible for marriage to take place with someone from outside the village. These are hypotheses which deserve to be reconsidered in the light of other narratives. Here is another, CMM.25-A.5:

Two inseparable women marry the same man on the same day [the Mandingo are polygamous]. On the same day they give birth, one to a boy and the other to a girl. The two children grow up inseparable. When the girl has to depart for the conjugal residence, she demands that her brother accompany her. The latter spends the night in the nuptial hut with her sister and brother-in-law. On the following morning he is assassinated in the bush by the latter, but his sister brings him back to life, thanks to a medicine which is suggested to her by two serpents. Brother and sister return to the village, where they are married.

The schema of this tale (Figure 11) shows that the spatial organization has an original feature: for the first time, the village of the girl is separate from that of her fiancé. (I did not feel it would serve any purpose to show the space which separates them in the schema, for nothing significant occurs there.) At first sight, this schema seems to return to the first one. In

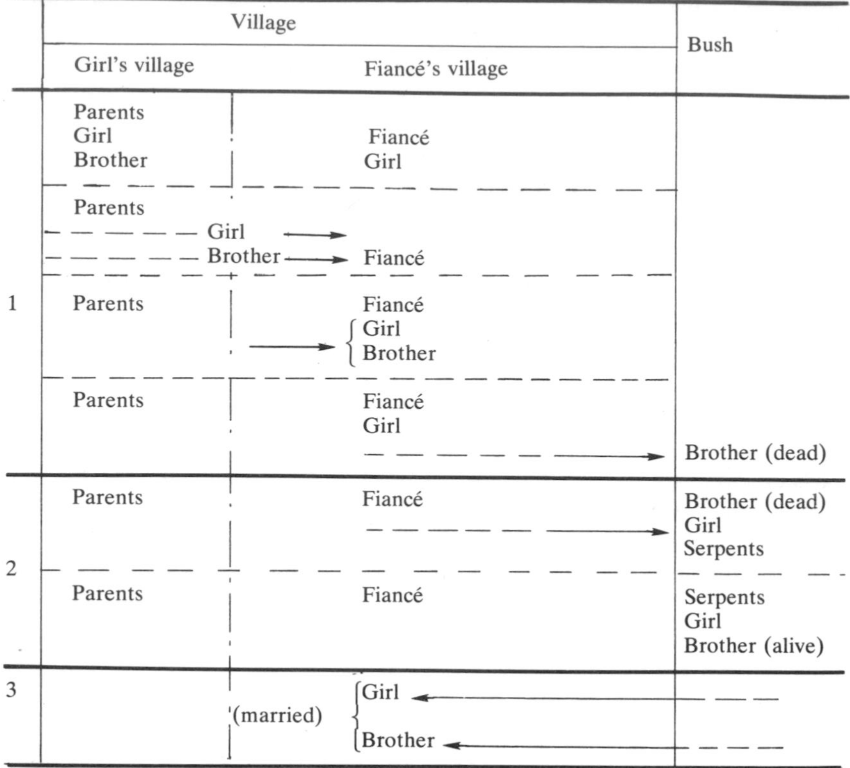

Figure 11. Outline of Tale CMM.25-A.5

fact, if one were to make an abstract representation of the persons involved, the movements would remain the same:

$\rightarrow$
VB
$\rightarrow$
VB
$\leftarrow$
VB

It would be a serious mistake, however, to proceed in this manner, for in this method of analysis persons are at least as important as movements. Now, in Figure 11 the first movement is carried out by the brother, the second by the girl. In relation to the outline shown in Figure 4, there is thus a transposition of persons in these first two movements. Furthermore, the ending is completely different from the one we have seen up to this point: the girl marries her brother. The modification of the schema announces a change in the ending of the imaginary drama.

Of course, it is possible to observe a certain continuity in the relations between the persons involved. One discovers the same triadic relationship between the girl, her brother, and her fiancé in the last three tales. In all three cases, too, the relations of the girl and her sexual partner are disturbed by the antagonism which opposes her fiancé and her brother, the man-from-outside and the man-from-home. The conflict, however, has developed to a considerable extent here. This time, there is a direct confrontation between the brother and the spouse from the village. Parallel with this, the brother is no longer a younger brother. He is the same age as the girl — which corresponds to or approaches more closely the image of the husband in everyday life, in which the man is at least as old as his wife, if not older. In addition, the conflict breaks out scandalously in the full view of the village. No longer is it repressed in the bush. Further, the tragedy does not sacrifice the same victim. Instead of the man-from-outside, it is the man-from-home who dies first: the brother is killed by the husband. Paradoxically, the consequences of this tragedy are the same for the girl; marriage outside the village remains impossible, in spite of the death of the person who has appeared to shackle her. Finally, incest, the tendency toward which has previously been implicitly expressed, now actually takes place.

It is important, however, that the girl is only marrying a phantom. The brother will die first in the bush, for the village cannot shelter with impunity those who violate the fundamental rule of exogamy: the man who is to return to marry his sister has already died with regard to his village existence. He lives out a life which originates in the bush, from the medicine of the serpents. Now, it is his sister who used this medicine. Thus one may say that the incestuous brother is only brought back to life through the "wild" action of his sister. In less concrete language, this may be summed up as follows: although mortally repressed in the bush, the incestuous brother comes to life again in the girl's psyche and prevents her from marrying another man.

Thus the schema delivers a message which must be developed: although the coexistence of the man-from-home (with the brother's features) and the man-from-outside always determines a conflict in the female psyche, it remains true that the two representations are equally necessary for the girl's development. The brutal elimination of either has the same consequence: the failure of marriage and exogamy. What, then, is the solution?

This is suggested by comparing the present schema with that of Tale CN.16-B.3 (Figure 8), where the little girl plays with numerous small woodland creatures. Here the brother, representing the man-from-home, appears only in the girl's childhood. At the moment she reaches the age of marriage, he disappears. Only then does the image of the man-from-outside (with the features of the husband's friend) come into play. Under the influence of the emotional torment which overwhelms her, the girl flees to the village. At her parents' home, she finds the door closed. No man-from-home is able to help her in this case; that is, any male family image has become null and void. By losing his efficiency at the moment when the heroine experiences the first emotions of sexual origin, the man-from-home can no longer oppose the representation of the man-from-outside. Because the two contradictory representations are not of equal force at the moment of their meeting, they confront each other without violence. Now, it is precisely the opposite which occurs here. The brother's influence is exercised with equal regularity and intensity on the girl, even up to the conjugal bed. Everything I have just said implies the archaic nature of the representation of man with the features of the man-from-home. Thus one may say that in all cases in which the heroine accedes to normal sexuality, she preserves a woodland representation of man up to the husband's threshold, having already forgotten the man-from-home. The two types of image do not have the same permanence.

The animal representations develop, changing in significance, from one narrative to another, while the representations of patners with the features of the-man-from-home hopelessly preserve the same meaning: endogamy and incest. On the other hand, the animal representations are not always incompatible with the image of the normal partner. Sometimes they depict a fascinating deer who turns the girl from her village fate, while at other times they appear as a domestic animal (which hunts for the spouse from the village). Finally, in many cases they are only transfigured men. This is the case with the disciples of the husband in CMM.25-A.3, and it is so for two reasons. The first is that the small boys appear under the same conditions as the animals. The girl does not manage to identify them. The second and more important reason is historical: The tale was related to me by a woman who was a practicing Moslem and had made the pilgrimage to Mecca; thus, the narrative carries the imprint of Islam. The protagonists have been replaced by Moslem persons: a marabout and his young disciples. This change results in others. In the place of the *sībīŋo*, the mediator has only his own voice: it is precisely this that makes the transfiguration unnoticeable, that makes him unable to provoke the fear which chases the girl from the bush and drives her to the village. This is why it was not possible to understand the latter's return to the city of men. This historical focus thus explains perfectly the ranging of the small boys alongside the transfigured human as extreme forms of animal representations. Thus the animal representations are eminently malleable. They may develop toward men-from-outside, thus assisting in promoting marriage outside the village, but they may also be associated with endogamous tendencies, appearing as the man-from-home, the brother.

Having reached this point, it becomes possible to present a recapitulation which is necessary for clarifying the method. I have spoken of *representations* and *images* with reference to certain persons, to the exclusion of others. What justifies this distinction? This is an important question: to answer it, we must return to the language of the tale itself. We already know that the Mandingo narrator wishes to make us see. By following his instructions, we have managed to obtain, beyond the sonorous discourse of words and onomatopes, a concrete language of beings and things which move, approach each other, separate, transform themselves, and at times disappear. Their development in space, the microcosm of the tale, and their succession constitute what I have called the outline. Now, in this context the question must be reformulated. In this universe of beings and things in movement, how can one distinguish beings *sui generis* from those which are only representations — which only refer to other realities?

To resolve this problem, I carefully compared a large number of outlines, and from this it developed that certain persons are very stable with regard to their appearance. This is the case, for example, with the girl and her husband. Other persons' appearances, in contrast, are either unstable or ambiguous. They may display (1) metamorphosis (fiancé's friend, younger brother–fly, man–serpent); (2) transfiguration (fiancé's friend); (3) ambiguity (*gɔɔtɔ*); (4) phantom life (resuscitated brother who marries his sister); (5) migration (contrast between a person and his habitat — a human being who lives in the bush for the whole length of the narrative, or an animal that definitely lives in the village); (6) mutation (a person displaying behavior appropriate to a species other than his own, for example, an animal speaking like a man); (7) dream presence (a person who influences the hero or heroine without actually meeting him); or (8) reflection — a last criterion completely different from the others, but one which I cannot examine here in any detail because of lack of space. It determines *self-image* and is defined by reference to everyday reality; it is the case with the grandmother for the girl. These criteria make it possible to distinguish objectively, referring both to the concrete language of the tale and to reality, three categories of beings: persons *sui generis*, representations of the other, and representations of oneself or models of identification.

In fact, analysis very quickly revealed that a tale always contains elements which cannot be fully understood without recourse to several other tales. The comparison of various outlines reveals variations which contribute very important information. At the extreme, one could say that a single tale may only be definitively explained when one has made an inventory of all tales, but if this were so, the goal of analysis would be unattainable.

My method permits a resolution of this difficulty through the establishment of levels of explanation. First, outlines are drawn up and grouped in families. Starting with comparison of some examples of a type, it becomes possible to classify, *a priori*, all the outlines which are theoretically possible. The type of codification adopted for transcribing outlines considerably facilitates this comparison. Table 1 allows us to compare three of them. Each column is to be read from top to bottom. This table includes only the spatial organization of outlines — the directions of

Table 1. Spatial organization of three tale outlines

1	2	3
$\overrightarrow{VB} \ldots F$	$\overrightarrow{VB} \ldots F$	$\overleftarrow{VB}$
$\overrightarrow{\overleftarrow{VB}}$		
$\overrightarrow{VB}$	$\overrightarrow{VB}$	$\overrightarrow{VB} \ldots F$
$F \ldots \overleftarrow{VB}$	$F \ldots \overleftarrow{VB}$	$F \ldots \overleftarrow{VB}$

movements. I have deliberately omitted the persons (with the exception of the girl, for the sake of intelligibility). This will permit varying the persons in the different movements at will. In short, the movements remain constant while the persons change.

In the transformation which takes place in passing from Outline 2 to Outline 1, which I shall call a *Type 1 transformation*, the first and last movements remain identical, but there is a doubling of the second movement. By varying the persons who might carry out these two movements, it is possible to classify all theoretically possible cases:

1. A single person tries to bring back the young girl and eventually succeeds, this person being either (*a*) a man-from-home, (*b*) a man-from-outside, (*c*) a woman-from-home, or (*d*) a woman-from-outside. (I have never encountered an outline in which *c* or *d* appears; a woman never goes into the bush to bring back the young girl in flight. Furthermore, a mediator, once he has failed, is finished.)

2. Two persons intervene; the second succeeds. Several cases are logically foreseeable: (*a*) The first mediator is a man-from-outside; he cannot bring the girl back to the village. The second is a parent of the girl; he succeeds. (I have never encountered this case.)

(*b*) The first mediator is a man-from-home; he fails. The second, a man-from-outside, succeeds (as in Tale CN.16-B.3):

$$\overrightarrow{VB} \ldots \underline{F}$$

$$m^0 \quad \overrightarrow{\overleftarrow{VB}} \ldots \underline{m}^0 + F$$

$$\overrightarrow{VB} \ldots \underline{m} + F$$

$$M + \underline{F} + \underline{m} \ldots \overleftarrow{VB}$$

In what I shall call a *Type 2 transformation*, the transformation from Outline 3 to Outline 2, the number of movements remains the same, but the direction of the movements changes. At the same time, new persons make their appearance. Thus, the woodland partner, who did not move in Tale CN.16-B.3, passes as early as the first movement from the bush to the village. Here one may envisage the following alterations:

1. The seduced girl carried away into the bush gets rid of her woodland partner by her own means, then returns to the village:

$\underline{Mb} \; .. \; \overleftarrow{VB}$

$\qquad \overrightarrow{VB} \; ... \; \underline{F}, \underline{Mb}$

$\underline{F} \; .... \; \overleftarrow{VB} \; ... \; \cancel{Mb}$

2. A man-from-outside accompanies the girl, defends her against the woodland partner, and brings her back to the village:

$\underline{Mb} \; .. \; \overleftarrow{VB}$

$\qquad \overrightarrow{VB} \; ... \; \underline{m}, \underline{F}, \underline{Mb}$

$\underline{m}, \underline{F} \; .. \; \overleftarrow{VB} \; ... \; \cancel{Mb}$

3. A man-from-home accompanies the girl, eliminates the woodland partner, and brings her back to the village:

$\underline{Mb} \; .. \; \overleftarrow{VB}$

$\qquad \overrightarrow{VB} \; ... \; m^0, F, \underline{Mb}$

$\underline{m^0}, \underline{F} \; .. \; \overleftarrow{VB} \; ... \; \cancel{Mb}$

Of these logical possibilities, the only one the Mandingo imagine is the third (CMM.26-B.2). The absence of the second undoubtedly means that at this stage of her development (the woodland stage) the girl has not yet developed an exogamous representation of the woodland partner. Only the man-from-home can save her from the danger of woodland alienation. The absence of the first indicates that the development of the girl does not depend just on her conscious will; rather, the key to her development is the representations of man whose blossoming in her is favored by the environment.

The *Type 3 transformation* concerns Outline 2 alone. First, taking the persons and the direction of movements as invariable, we may reduce the number of the latter:

1. The girl goes off into the bush and remains there forever:

$\overrightarrow{VB} \; .... \; \underline{F}$

2. The girl and the man-from-home flee at the same time into the bush and remain there forever:

$\overrightarrow{VB} \; .... \; \underline{m^0}, \underline{F}$

3. The girl goes off into the bush, a man-from-home joins her there, and they live there forever:

$\overrightarrow{VB} \ldots . \underline{F}$

$\overrightarrow{VB} \ldots . \underline{m^o}, F$

4. Next, we may change the order of the movements:

$\overrightarrow{VB} \ldots . \underline{m^o}$

$\overrightarrow{VB} \ldots . F, \underline{m^o}$

Of all these cases, only the second and fourth are realized in Mandingo tales. Both give rise to tales in which brother and sister have incestuous relations.

There is no need to continue this inventory. These illustrations show that it is perfectly possible to continue it to its end. It appears that the Mandingo have in their tales only a limited number of the outlines which are logically possible. The analysis of relationships between these outlines and those which do not occur in any actual tale should give a relatively precise idea of their psychological conceptions.

Within the imaginary world which has been thus delimited by this choice, certain elements have been asserted to vary while others present a certain constancy. What remains constant in all the tales reported is, first and foremost, the structure of the scene of the drama. Here one distinguishes two different regions: on the one hand, the village, and on the other, the bush. There is also the flight of the girl into the bush. This phase of her development appears to be necessary and inescapable.

If we now consider the persons who intervene in this woodland adventure, we see that for certain girls mediation with the village is guaranteed by the man-from-outside, while for others it is the brother who fulfils this function, and never the father. This being the case, it makes it impossible for the sister to agree to a relationship outside the tribe. That is to say, the crux of the drama of the Mandingo girl is principally constituted by her brother. This is an important fact. I shall analyze it by starting from the hypothesis that the area in which the adventures of the girl unfold represents the person's psychic viewpoint. Thus, every Mandingo girl must, in the course of her development, "plunge into her bush" before agreeing to the fullness of "her village life." This bush, however, is not the same for all types of girls. It is close to the village for some, very far away for others. Sometimes it harbors a threatening animal, but in other cases it only contains small woodland beings with whom one is able to play. These variations permit one to draw up a typology of the girl.

If I had been able to include here tales relating the marriage of the young man, a change of psychic viewpoint would have been apparent; it would then have been differentiated into three zones, two villages separated by the bush: his home village, the bush, and the village of his potential wife. This indicates that deviation through endogamy is avoided by the young man because of the fact of the structure of the area. The village of the woman to be married is separated there from that of the woman-from-home. In contrast, the structure of the feminine psychic field is such that the man-from-outside and the man-from-home inhabit the same village. Thus we understand that in leaving the bush — that is, at the moment of marriage — the girl sometimes returns to her own.

Purpose and Function in Modern Local Legends of Kentucky

WILLIAM HUGH JANSEN

Too many people have struggled too long to define *legend* and *local legend*. I shall not enter the lists at this time. For the purpose of this paper, a legend is a tale that has an air of veracity about it, a narrative in a real setting with real persons as the doers, a tale that is told as the truth and that is heard as the truth. A legend is local if the setting and the real-person characters are known only to the residents of a strictly limited area — a town, a county, a village.

There are local legends which exist in no other form except that involving one set of proper names; and there are localized legends which tell about a specific place and specific local people, a tale which is told in many other places about as many other specific localities and local characters. Examples of the latter are "The ineradicable bloodstain," "The murdered pack peddler" (sometimes combined with the preceding narrative), and various buried-treasure tales. The localized legend is close kin to such folk fictional genres as the tall tale and the realistic tale. Indeed, in performance many folk narrative genres are made by their performers to resemble legends, particularly local legends, in an effort to maintain as long as possible the illusion of veracity.

The forty-one tales used here to represent Kentucky local legends have a kind of unity. Collected by one of my students from her father, they are the stories he tells when reminiscing about his hometown. They are all trivial narratives, completely possible, innocuously realistic. Certainly their teller believes at least most of them, maybe all of them, while their hearers probably believe all of them (although occasionally a hearer may detect a disturbingly familiar detail in one or two). Equally certain, every one of the simple events or sayings could have happened. Indeed, I believe that most of the events narrated did take place, most of the memorable remarks were made, and the speakers, actors, and settings were just as they are specified.

These forty-one narratives are remarkably precise. All are implicitly or explicitly set in the one small community. It is a community which in the last twenty years or so has become a kind of symbol of rural pride, independence, and virtue, its reputation enhanced by local and regional newspaper accounts of its efforts to maintain political and economic identity. Our informant's narratives about his hometown may have received more sympathetic understanding because of the local reputation of that community, but the reputation may also have been reinforced by his narration.

Forty of the tales have as speakers or actors persons who either still live in Williams Corners or still have family members and acquaintances residing there. Forty-four persons are specifically mentioned, some of them frequently and in combination with others. They represent a surprisingly comprehensive sampling of the social structure of Williams Corners or, for that matter, of any small town. Doctor, dentist, cleric, farmer, ne'er-do-well, drunkard, businessman, intruder, old settler are all here. Three named characters are also racially identified.

Some of the tales are quite explicitly set in the Golden Age that the teller knew or had heard of in his youth. It is both natural and reasonable to suppose that all the rest of these tales are implicitly set in this same wonderful period. Such a time setting gives them a faint fictional aura despite the fact that they involve real persons doing real things in a real place.

Brief and slight though they be, the narratives share certain stylistic and structural traits. Most of them convey a sense of formal opening. This sense may depend merely upon the use of real proper names, which of course serve as a kind of documentation for the narrative. It is frequently reinforced by an identification or stereotypic characterization for one or more of those proper names. (Incidentally, this technique of folk narrative is common in poetry, both folk and literary; cf. "Barbara Allen" and some of the poems of Edwin A. Robinson, Robert Frost, and Edgar Lee Masters.) Perhaps more noticeable is the sense of climax in each narrative. While the literary critic might argue that the very word "narrative" implies or includes the concept "climax," in folk aesthetics mere chronology or even the consumption of time may set the structure and confines of narration. Of these forty-one tales, however, thirty lead up to — and abruptly stop with — what some particular person said in a specific situation. The other eleven all exist to tell what a particular person did at a specific moment; having exposed that action, they promptly cease.

In brief, these are oral art forms, however, rudimentary. The tales all have a fairly recognizable, fairly delicate opening formula; they all have clearly recognizable, abrupt climactic endings; their time-setting borders on the romantic; otherwise their content is realistic in the sense that local colorists were and are realists. They are so terse and their content so insignificant that it is tempting to call them seed tales, embryo tales, or tales a-borning.

Most, if not all, of the stories did happen. Little in them is scandalous, but much could be embarrassing. The characters and their families are well known, even sometimes beyond their community and its environs. Therefore, and despite the trusting assurances of the informant himself, I decided after long soul-searching to change every proper noun in the narratives. I have substituted names which I hope have the same national, ethnic, regional, and emotional tones as the originals. I have tried to preserve the values implicit in diminutives and conventional epithets such as "Willy" and "Uncle." Of course, should they be needed for scholarly purposes, the real names have been preserved.

The tales were collected by a folklore student whom I shall call Sarah Fergus. Her father, R. B. Fergus, dictated them in spare moments during the spring vacation of 1965 (March 13 to 21) and on the following weekend (March 26 and 27). Some of the tales he dictated to her directly, but most he recorded on a dictaphone. Miss Fergus transcribed the cylinders. Her father read all the final drafts and suggested a few emendations (names and the like).

As the tales are presented here, they are arranged more or less by content and characters. There seemed to be no significance to the order in which the stories were collected or recollected, other than that there was a wavelike pattern quantitatively. On March 13, Mr. Fergus dictated fourteen stories (1, 2, 3, 4, 5, 6, 13, 18, 19, 25, 31, 32, 37, and 39); on March 14, a Sunday, he told one story about a preacher (29); on March 16, he remembered nine more stories (10, 11, 12, 14, 15, 17, 20, 27, and 38); on March 17, four stories (9, 24, 30, and 36); on March 18, five stories (7, 8, 16, 21, and 22); and, a week later, on March 26, four stories (23, 28, 40, and 41) and on March 27, four more (26, 33, 34, and 35).

Mr. Fergus is a professional man and holds a demanding public position of considerable trust that requires administrative skill. He has a local reputation as a raconteur and as a speaker to service clubs, church groups, and graduating classes. He, of course, no longer lives in Williams Corners, where he is thought of as one of the local boys who moved away to the big city and made good.

Williams Corners is an agrarian community surrounded by good farming land. Its population (about 600) has varied very little since the end of the nineteenth century. At present it has no industry, though once it had a little. County government and school systems and the encroachment of larger towns all threaten its independent existence, so the town has some reason for cherishing tales of the good old days.

Here are the narratives Mr. Fergus dictated for his daughter. Each is accompanied by comment, intended mainly to conjecture its possible purposes (the narrator's intended effects, conscious or unconscious) and functions (the effects upon the auditors, recognized or not).

[1.] The nurseryman, Mr. L. S. Weyermill, whose father was the founder of the Mill House Nursery and the patentnor [*sic*] of the Olympic apple, was considered to be quite an eccentric. He was a very stingy businessman as well as the absent-minded village philosopher, atheist, and socialist politician. Mr. Weyermill, or Looney Lou, as everybody in Williams Corners called him, had rather peculiar qualifications for his employees drawn from the village labor force. He would only use those people who would argue and discuss politics with him even though he required them to be on duty from dawn to dusk. However, he had one exception and that was he would never employ a person who used rawhide shoelaces and rolled his own cigarettes because he figured that the man would spend half his time tying his shoelaces and the other half rolling his cigarettes. Mr. Weyermill's particular obsession against people who rolled their cigarettes stemmed from an incident when Uncle Joe Fisher was driving a team of horses and an orchard spray. Uncle Joe had stopped the spray wagon to roll a cigarette when a bumble-bee stung one of the horses and the team started to running away. Mr. Weyermill claimed that Uncle Joe made a great decision, whether to hold the lines or finish rolling the cigarette, and of course since Uncle Joe's cigarette came first, he threw away the lines and the team destroyed a $2500 spray. Damn. Uncle Joe cost him $2500 immediately, but he taught him a lesson that was worth $100,000 in a lifetime.

Neither entirely coherent nor completely typical, this is the longest of Mr. Fergus's tales. From the pattern of his other tales, we can guess that the last sentence in this story is meant to be a quotation from Mr. Weyermill, a proof of both his oddity and his wisdom.

All of these stories have the purpose of entertaining — obviously they are meant to be in varying degrees amusing. The teller expects them to be interesting, or he wouldn't be a teller. Insofar as he is successful, these tales — like most others — serve the function of entertaining, amusing, interesting the auditors. This is a truism, of course, but it must be said lest the reader think the writer has forgotten it.

Beyond this, this first narrative is intended to glorify the past, to show that the teller and the auditor shared a community that had once been a microcosm, a world of rugged individualism (whether it be Looney Lou's or Uncle Joe's) and of giants — even if eccentricity and a colossal failure to regard consequences are the manifestations of gianthood. Certainly, too, there is the desire to lead into and recreate a ludicrous but exciting incident.

The audience reaction (the function of the narrative) would certainly be satisfaction at having seen a bit of past history that belonged to the audience, satisfaction at seeing the eccentricity of a son of a "great man," and satisfaction with the illustration that for the well-to-do even an eccentric catastrophe turns to profit. It's the way of the world: "Them what has, gets."

[2.] Looney Lou became a follower of Bernard MacFadden, the famous physical culturist. He read all of his publications, followed his diet (he would have a whole wheat flour made by taking wheat to the mill and have it rough cracked). The limit of his interest was reached when he started to taking cold baths every morning as his zeal increased. On the advice of MacFadden, he ran around his house every morning in the nude no matter how cold it was, but Looney Lou's interest in physical culture completely ceased when one morning as he was running around the house just before dawn he stumbled and fell over one of his mole traps and he couldn't wear his shoe the rest of the winter. That was the last of Looney Lou and his Physical Culture.

Of course, the purpose is to present a realistic, plausible anecdote that shows how eccentricity can carry a fad to excess and how ludicrous the local tycoon could be. The specific details of cracking the wheat and falling over a mole trap are remarkably artful means of conveying respectively the general and the specific truth of the narrative. The audience is allowed to compensate for its own economic straits by laughing at the wonderfully burlesque image of that same tycoon, nude, cold, painfully hopping about in the dark, one foot in a mole trap. Just as the faddism is verified by the cracked-wheat statement, the comic image is made realistic by the painful inability to wear a shoe in the winter.

[3.] Looney Lou had one old bachelor, J. D. Jolley, who was a favorite employee, but he lost his trusted service when he and Mr. Weyermill were balanced on a seat-board driving on a wagon (wasn't a spring seat) when Mr. Weyermill suddenly jumped up to emphasize a wild political point and J. D. fell out of the wagon. J. D. jumped up and exclaimed, "It's too damn' dangerous to work!" and thenceforth he was never known to do another lick of work another day for anyone.

This is, on the surface, a humorous *pourquoi* story, a rather effective one, and I suppose part of the purpose is to intrigue by using this subgenre. However, I think the main purpose is not to explain why old J. D. never worked or why he was a bachelor (inviting though it is to see in those two clauses some sort of cause-and-effect relationship), but to show how great was the interest in politics, particularly in our "socialist politician," in the good old days.

The audience would appreciate the subtlety of the form. It would, I think, see the story not primarily as a commentary upon old J.D., but as a piece in the mosaic picture of Weyermill and secondarily as a detail in the saga of the Jolley family, which looms large in the folk annals of Williams Corners.

[4.] Looney Lou was overheard talking to himself one day and somebody asked him why and he replied that he liked to hear a smart man talk.

This compact but effective little anecdote probably represents the localization of a migratory wisecrack. It fits well enough our growing image of Looney Lou. For the audience, the tale serves two functions. It demonstrates both the human frailty (aren't we all afraid of being caught talking to ourselves?) and the whipcrack wisdom of the local successful man. At the same time, it puts down a nonentity, a stranger (who is "somebody"?), thus allowing the auditor to share in the triumph of his fellow townsman, with whom he identifies — at least while he is the auditor of these tales.

[5.] Jack Rust was the local village trucker who did general hauling of livestock and freight. He had one notoriously bad habit and that was playing the race horses (going to Avilion Race Track). One hot summer afternoon, Jack, dressed in his best clothes with a new straw sailor hat, went to the Avilion races. As he was watching the races in a huge crowd, a bird noosed on his hat. Jack said that it was damned funny to him how he could be in a crowd of 10,000 people and one bird to pick him out and noosy on his head.

This story is packed with purpose. It adds details to the social and economic structure of Williams Corners; it expresses a moral standard and shows embarrassment befalling the proud gambler; and it ends by inviting a consideration of the laws of probability (who better to question these laws than a horse-bettor?) and of inevitability. Nevertheless, in a burlesque spirit it is a funny story. (Incidentally, the intransitive verb "to noose" or "to noosy" I can find in no lexicon. It occurs in several of my texts, always with an animal as the subject. Its meaning is clear from the context. Could it be a rhyming formation from "loose" or a back-formation from "public nuisance"?)

The story's functions agree with its purposes. For the audience the first two sentences must be an exposition of William Corners as well as of Jack Rust. The contrast between Jack's garb and his ludicrous fate helps the audience to see as well as to enjoy the meaning of the story, and so does Jack's cry of "Why me?" Perhaps the audience does not see immediately the irony in that cry, but it is there. This is another story where part of the function, it seems to me, is to reassure the audience about the ways of the world. It is the sort of story with which the auditor may agree by saying, "That's the way things happen" or "That's life."

[6.] Every year Jack would have lost his money on the races when the time came around to buy his truck license and he would have to leave his truck in his yard until he figured out some way to raise $40.50 to buy his license. One year along in March, a man offered him $50 if he would move his household furnishings about 100 miles. Though he didn't have his license, he thought he would take the chance on not being picked up by the police and could buy his license, but as it happened he ran into a safety land block where the highway patrol were checking trucks for safety regulations. They checked Jack's brakes and no brakes; they checked his horn and no horn; they checked his lights and no lights. On informing Jack of his violation, Jack said, "What in the hell does a man need in brakes, lights, or horn if he doesn't even have any license?"

This tale is far less purposeful than the preceding one about the same character. Certainly it is more serious in its preachment against gambling — or, more precisely, against unsuccessful gambling. Otherwise it conveys a characterization of Jack Rust that makes him, rather unexpectedly, a simpleton in the mold of the classic wise fool. He is lacking not in logic but in common sense.

The function of this narrative is to evoke a sense of justice. It would be a perfectly complete but quite different story without the first sentence. When we know Jack is without a license because he gambled away his money, then his blurted-out self-incrimination is not funny stupidity alone, and the safety patrol becomes an agent of retribution.

[7.] Jack Rust hired Hank Schwartz to drive his truck over to the stockyards in Memphis and sell some horses for him. He told Hank he could eat all he wanted from the sale money since he knew Hank was a noted eater around the county and would probably get pretty hungry before he got back. Well, when he got back Jack asked him how much money he had left and Hank pulled out 15 cents. Jack took Hank over to the store and got 15 cents worth of chewing tobacco and told him to chew it all at one time if he had to keep his mouth that full.

This is a difficult tale to analyze. A tall tale, of course, it identifies and stereotypes one more denizen of Williams Corners (the big eater). Within the confines of this narrative there seems to be no justice, unless Jack Rust is penalized for his lack of wisdom in telling a big eater to eat all he wanted. If, however, the auditor knows or remembers the tales which characterizes Rust as an improvident gambler and a wise fool, then the loss and the resigned frustration in the last speech underlining that loss become meaningful.

For the auditor the tale functions as an exercise in recognition and fulfillment of expectation. The listener experienced in folk narrative will recognize the unwise promise and anticipate the catastrophe. The spending of the last fifteen cents is also recognizable as a parallel to the traditional situation in which the frustrated clown who has let fall all but one dish from his arms dashes that one to smithereens on top of the rubble at his feet. Does anyone, for an appreciation of the ludicrous image implied in the last sentence, need to be told that in the good old days fifteen cents bought more than a week's supply of chewing tobacco, which would fill a very big mouth indeed?

This is an interesting story for another reason. Possibly a real event lies somewhere behind the tale, but I doubt it. In all probability, no big eater ever ate in one day all the food that could be purchased with the income from the sale of a single horse, to say nothing of the income from the sale of a truckload of horses. The problem of suspending incredulity until the climax probably takes priority over other aspects of function and purpose in the tall tale, but for Mr. Fergus the story of Jack Rust and the big eater is just one more "true" story of Williams Corners — or at least he attempts to give that impression.

[8.] Every summer they'd have revivals with hell-fire and damnation preaching. If they got "It" [the Holy Ghost], they'd testify. One of the village rowdies, the father of Dr. Arnold Jolley who became president of a university up East, got up and testified: "I feel just like Joseph who slew 10,000 Philistines with the jaw-bone of a horse's ass."

Again the tale adds to the characterization of community life in the Williams Corners of the past and implies at least that there has been change in the religious patterns. In the completely gratuitous information about Dr. Jolley, the narrator is both alluding to the Horatio Alger ideal of success and boasting about a hometown boy. Dr. Jolley's success implies a virtue in the small town and especially in Williams Corners. The way in which the tale is worded suggests a superiority to "hell-fire and damnation" religion and a delight in the purposeful embarrassment of the sanctimonious by the rowdy's pretended ignorance.

Despite the connotation of the word "rowdy," I doubt that any serious condemnation of the senior Jolley's impish act is intended or understood. Rather, for the audience, the tale reinforces the traditional concepts that every small town has its bad boys (who are essentially good at heart) and that "boys will be boys." The auditor may well recognize that the confusion of words in Jolley's testimony is a traditional, even a hoary, joke, but this would not, and should not, hamper his belief in the anecdote, for the "harmless mischief" of village scamps usually involved (involves?) traditional verbal and nonverbal motifs (how many snipe hunts has a single community experienced in one generation?). The auditor would, I believe, admire the daring that such a testimony would require in a "rowdy" standing before the village elders. Certainly this function of the tale is supported by the auditor's probable wide experience with trickster motifs.

[9.] Rob Smith Jolley was as tight a man as you could find. The rope on his well was just about to wear in two so his wife sent him to the Corners to buy some new rope. When he got back, he had gotten just enough rope for the bucket to touch the water and the wife asked him why he hadn't gotten any more. He told her that they didn't make rope any longer.

The storyteller's purpose here is to commemorate and to stereotype another resident of Williams Corners (the village miser) and then to illustrate the stereotype.

The story allows the auditor to recognize a miser and to agree that his scrimping and his evasive falsehood are typical: that's what a miser would do.

[10.] Rob Jolley was absent-minded as well as being tight. One day they were all going to church and his little girl wasn't ready. Old Rob said, "Come on here, little girl, whatever your damn' name is."

Rather charming, this little story is meant to amplify the characterization of Rob Jolley and to illustrate absentmindedness, which like miserliness is a popular subject of folk amusement. The tale functions, I think, as it is supposed to. At the same time that he wonders how absentminded a man can be, the auditor probably is emotionally stirred by recognizing under Rob's rough and awkward summons a touch of parental affection.

[11.] Rob Jolley's son, Al, had taken one of their horses to Clifty, a little community not far from Williams Corners. Well, Rob came along the road and spotted the horse. He came running up the field and told Al that the horse would make a perfect match for the one they had at home. Well, the boys sold old Rob his own horse.

Another story of deception, this episode's main purpose is to indicate what fun there was in the old days. The disturbing dishonesty embedded in the tale is somewhat ameliorated by the fact that old Rob was eager to be deceived and that one of the deceivers was his own son. The tale functions much better, however, if the auditor knows that old Rob is both miserly and forgetful. This makes the tale more realistic and the deceit more justifiable. The auditor may feel that Rob deserves being deceived.

[12.] Al Jolley, Rob's son, was in the hospital and was in the room with a Catholic. The Catholic was praying with his prayer beads and Al was just watching. Finally Al said, "If those things are doing you any good, throw them over here to me and let me talk to them a while."

There are neither hospitals nor Catholics in Williams Corners. The nearest hospitals are not very near, and for one to be hospitalized implies that one is quite ill or has been seriously injured. The story, I think, is intended not to ridicule Catholicism but to ridicule Al's ignorance of Catholicism. The story functions well, for its hearer laughs at Al's ignorance and of course feels superior in that he recognizes that ignorance. The function is probably promoted by the auditor's remembrance that Al has already been identified as a trickster and by the auditor's experience of equating tricksters with wise fools.

[13.] One day I took Jerry Jolley to the dentist — he was getting too old to drive. So we went in and he wanted me to go with him in the office. So I did. The dentist squirmed around in his mouth and finally told him that he had a little old hole where his mouth should have been. The dentist was from Williams Corners too. Finally Dr. Higgins got his false teeth in and Jerry pulled out a little ol' tobacco pouch which had only a quarter in it. He asked me if he could borry five dollars and I told him he could; so he gave the dentist that and when we walked out of the office, he pulled out a bunch of bills bigger'n a hogshead and paid the money back to me. He said that he wasn't for sure the teeth would fit and he knew I wouldn't have $100.

This story is not completely coherent. The lapse of time necessary for the fabrication of the dentures is not indicated. More significant is the evident omission of Dr. Higgins's price for the dentures, $100, and of old Jerry's offer to pay for them on the installment plan. Minor purposes are served by introducing another member of the Jolley contingent of the Williams Corners community and by pointing out that the community's dental needs were cared for by a native son.

The function of the tale is clearer if the auditor remembers that miserliness has already been specified as a Jolley trait (in Rob), for the tale illustrates the wiles of a stingy, suspicious man who doesn't want to pay for (or even to reveal his ability to pay for) his dentures until he is sure they fit. Remembrance of other accounts of nonfitting dentures would enhance the auditor's appreciation of old Jerry's resourcefulness.

[14.] Dr. Wright was visiting one of his neighbors, Mr. Miller, who was a constant grunter. Dr. Wright asked him how he was feeling and Mr. Miller preceded [*sic*] to tell his ailments. Meanwhile Dr. Wright backed up against a peachtree and began to roll some of the peachtree gum up into little balls. He told Mr. Miller that he had just the cure for him right in his pocket, and he gave him some of the gum balls. The next week, the doctor went by to see him and asked him how he felt and Mr. Miller said, "Hilton, those pills did help me. I feel better already."

The cure effected by a placebo is a widespread traditional motif, used both seriously and comically. Again, this does not militate against the possible truth of this episode, particularly since it is a practical joke and these are usually traditional. If there is a purpose other than entertainment and — very lightly — recording local history, it is to show that imaginary ailments can be cured by the imagination.

The function of the tale is promoted both by the recognition of the hypochondriac in the "constant grunter," who deserves to be the butt of a practical joke, and by the appreciation of the double irony in the result of the joke. The listener is likely to agree that such are the ways of the world — and this is a function of the local legend.

[15.] My sister-in-law, Gloria Fergus, was down sick in bed one time. My brother and I went over to Dr. Wright's to get some medicine. On the way back I opened the bottle and it smelled just like hard cider; so we each had a snort and it tasted just like hard cider too. Anyway we gave it to Gloria and she was well in the next day or two. Later on, I asked Dr. Wright if that medicine wasn't just plain old hard cider and he just chuckled.

This narrative is based on another traditional humorous theme: the supposed curative power of intoxicants. Indeed, depending upon one's attitude toward hard cider — or upon the capacity of Dr. Wright's bottle — this tale may be merely a change rung upon the theme of the preceding one: the curative effect of a placebo. This tale may have one of two quite different purposes: it may be ridiculing the medicine of old times and thus implying the improvement in modern medicine, or — and more likely — it may be praising the ability to improvise and the effectiveness of home remedies.

The function of the tale depends upon the auditor's conception of Dr. Wright as a wise, unpretentious, humorous, and human family doctor — a conception that is strengthened by any carryover from the preceding tale.

[16.] Doctor Wright, the town Doctor, would drive his car real fast and when you asked him later on why he was driving so fast, he would say he was hurrying up to keep from running out of gas.

This bit of traditional humor is usually attached to some wise simpleton as an illustration of how little he knows about the ways of the motorcar. Certainly it does not have this purpose when associated with Dr. Wright. The association here probably springs from the realization that, in the rural community of yore, the doctor's was often the only car, and no car was out on the roads more than his. Any function of the tale would depend upon an impression, from other tales, of Dr. Wright as a man of whimsical humor who does not tell all that he knows. With that impression in effect, the tale would glorify the doctor's dry wit.

[17.] One night during the time when Jean and I were courting, I got home to Williams Corners around 11 or 12 one night and Dr. Wright's lights were on; so I went over to see what had happened. Well, this little ole nigger, Sam Lewis, had shot himself on the end of his finger and a bunch of boys were holding him while Dr. Wright was probing for the bullet. All you could hear was the scraping, and Dr. Wright was getting old and couldn't see too well. Finally, one of the boys got enough nerve to take a look, and come to find out, Dr. Wright was scraping that little ole nigger's bone. He's still living now though. It's a wonder, isn't it?

This painful tale requires some imaginative cooperation from the listener, who must realize the boys were holding Sam down because of the excruciation of having his finger probed without the benefit of anesthetic — an image that is made more painful by the further realization that the probing is unnecessary. The tale is meant to illustrate the necessarily improvisational techniques of old-time medicine and to point out that the patients survived even when the doctor was hampered by age and failing sight.

Again, the function depends upon carryover from the other Dr. Wright narratives. With carryover, the tale creates sympathy for an aging, failing doctor still devoted to his profession. Incidentally, contemporary listeners might well be antagonized by the racial attitide implicit here and elsewhere in these stories. It should be pointed out that the tone is not a key to Mr. Fergus's own racial posture either socially or professionally. Certainly, Mr. Fergus would never use the word "nigger" in conversation, formal or informal; yet, with perhaps unwitting realism, he uses it in his stories of the preintegration past, and so do many other storytellers.

[18.] One of the town merchants, he operated the general store, was noted for his stinginess, orneriness, and laziness. He was called Charley Polecat. Nevertheless he was petite [*sic*] in his dress. Being only about five feet tall, he presented a very striking appearance. He was also an atheist, but his favorite curse word was "By the eternal hell." The mail was thrown off from a speeding train in mail pouches in the early morning. Charley Polecat had been down the railroad to stake out his cow for some free grazing. He also was bringing back some blackberry briars that he had cut and was taking home for his wife to pull off the berries. As he was walking along the railroad rightaway [*sic*], which was also the street of Williams Corners, the train came roaring by and threw off the mail pouches and naturally they were carried a hundred yards or more by the wind. On this particular morning, they hit Charley on the legs and threw him several feet high. Charley was heard to yell over the roar of the train, "By the eternal hell, what happened?"

Almost architectonic, this tale quickly established Charley Polecat as fascinating, anomalous, and stereotypically evil. His evil traits are speedily illustrated: stingy (free grazing), ornery (the briars for his wife), and lazy (unwilling to pick his own blackberries). The introduction of the irrational oath is artfully early, a beautiful anticipation of the climactic sentence. Clearly a function is to commend and illustrate the justice that prevailed in the good old days. Who would be a better target for a flying mail pouch than a stingy, ornery, lazy atheist?

[19.] Susan, Charley Polecat's only daughter and pride and joy, was sent to the Memphis conservatory of music and Charley bought her a new piano. The boys around town carried it down to the house and put it down. Of course, Susan asked them what they'd like her to play for them — she was one of those long-haired musicians — and James Stetson said, "Cut down on *Red Wing*."

The significance of this slight narrative lies, of course, in the inappropriateness of requesting — and in slang, at that — a classical pianist to play a simple popular melody. The purpose of the story seemingly is to belittle the pretentiousness of Charley Polecat in sending his daughter to a conservatory. This is troublesome, for in Williams Corners there would ordinarily be nothing exceptionable in a merchant's ambition to send his daughter to a conservatory. Charley Polecat is, of course, a disrespectful nickname. Was he perhaps a "furriner," an immigrant with an unpronounceable name, who should not presume to be an equal with the old settlers?

[20.] Oliver Beck wasn't any real churchgoer and was absorbed in making a dollar. One morning he went to church and sat on the front row. Somebody asked him what the preacher preached about later and Oliver said, "I don't know, but they said he preached a good un."

Ordinarily this slight, wan story would be a rebuke of sacrilegious inattention. Occasionally it could be a comment upon the boredom of a sermon or of a church service. Here it is neither but seems to be a tentative admiration of Oliver's single-track devotion to the dollar and his utter imperturbability at having paid the preacher no heed whatsoever.

[21.] Oliver Beck was a horsetrader too. When he was trying to make a trade, he'd jerk his hand up and down and say, "Best one that ever shit on the ground, best one that ever shit on the ground."

Even slighter than the preceding one, this little anecdote further establishes Oliver as "a character" in the Williams Corners community, where he is rough, unselfconscious, so concerned about a possible profit that he is totally unaware of any impropriety.

[22.] Pa Fergus, my grandfather, used to bring home drummers [traveling salesmen] and my grandmother, Ma, would never know when he was going to bring them until she saw them coming up the road. One day she looked out and here came Pa with some drummers; so Ma jerked the cornbread out of the oven and it fell in the slop bucket; so Ma just wiped it off, put it in the oven to dry, and fed it to them.

Obviously a family legend (belonging to the family of the narrator), this tale is meant to keep fresh the memory of Pa and Ma — Pa, the hospitable, expansive male, eagerly curious (for drummers were glamorous exotics, frequently the purveyors of news, scandal, and scandalous stories) but hardly considerate, and Ma, the long-suffering, silent housewife.

For a non-Fergus listener, the functions are somewhat different from the purposes. The fact that the actors are Ferguses only adds to the picture of the corporate community some more interesting, stereotyped characters, a particular kind of husband and wife (incidentally, and perhaps significantly, from all the forty-one tales very little can be inferred about marital bliss and companionship in Williams Corners). The general auditor will, of course, recognize the stereotype of the often-put-upon wife and thus will be able to visualize the anger that causes the unusually violent awkwardness that leads to the fall of the cornbread. If the auditor is sympathetic toward downtrodden wives, he will sense the malicious but covert pleasure with which the cornbread is fed to the drummers (and Pa?) and perhaps conclude that the silent rebellious act affords a kind of relief and revenge.

[23.] Uncle Billy Rowe was a deacon in the church and one night they were having a meeting with the preacher. Uncle Billy was sitting there nodding and the preacher said, "Do you have anything to say for the Lord?" and Uncle Billy said,

"I make a motion we receive him," thinking the preacher was talking about receiving a new member.

Again a traditional motif appears: the embarrassed parishioner unwittingly reveals he has been sleeping by inappropriately answering the rhetorical question that has awakened him. The purpose here is not clear — the tale may be warning that he who sleeps in church is risking ridicule, or it may be commenting upon how soporific the church service was. The function is similarly unclear. The hearer may note that little in the wording implies any derogation of Uncle Billy. The tale may be simply preserving the account of something that happened in the community. The hearer may perhaps wonder if there is unwitting irony and a great truth in Uncle Billy's gaffe. Is the Lord received in every structure labeled His house?

[24.] Uncle Billy Rowe was driving his family home from a church meeting one summer afternoon and he made his daughter Belle get down and open up their gate. When Belle got the gate open, the old horse started running away with them. Billy started shouting to the top of his lungs, "Hold'er, Effie [his wife]. Dad gum'er, I've got her." That was the saying around Williams Corners for some time after that happened.

This is a typical legend; every folk community has narratives that explain the origin of peculiar local expressions, proverbial phrases, nicknames, however ephemeral. In this instance, the saying is no longer current, but once there was such a saying and this was its explanation.

For the hearer the tale suggests that Uncle Billy's excited assurance is ill-founded (for he has already been identified as something of a character) and that Effie will have at least as much as Billy to do with stopping the runaway mare. Thus the saying (and the story, of course) becomes an ironic and laughable comment upon the one who claims more than he deserves.

[25.] Old nigger Joe Randall was walking up the road one day saying: "She told me that she loved me and I couldn't say a word. Gosh, damn! What a fool."

Clearly intended to be funny, this little story ridicules the pretension of a black man who fancies himself subject to a romantic affair such as a white man might experience and who doesn't have the language appropriate to such a fantasy. Perhaps, too, this tiny episode and the next are supposed to present the black man as he was in the Williams Corners of long ago.

The modern hearer is likely to be troubled by the term "old nigger" and is not likely to see any other racial significance whatsoever. That same auditor might see in the narrative nothing but the pathos of inarticulate old age trying to express a sense of loss at missed romantic encounters.

[26.] Uncle Tulliver Morris, an ole nigger, died and he was very poor; so his friends got him a porpor [*sic*; pawpaw, an unlikely wood? poplar, a cheap wood? Perhaps it was originally a *pauper's* box.] box for his casket. One of his friends had an old Ford touring car and they put Uncle Tulliver on the car crosswise to take him to the cemetery. They turned a corner too sharp and Uncle Tulliver fell out of the car and out of the casket. The rest of the niggers thought the man driving the car was bedevilled and ran him out of town.

Certainly, again, this tale is meant to be funny at the expense of poverty, isolation, and superstition. The auditor is supposed to laugh at the frightened blacks who believe the driver must be possessed, and he is supposed to see the characters as the poor, artless, shuffling "good niggers" of long ago.

The corpse who leaves his coffin abruptly (or who seems to sit up), thus frightening the onlookers, is traditional narrative material. There is nothing intrinsically racial about the material, and I doubt that this tale functions with the modern hearer to do anything but create a grossly ludicrous or morbid incident.

[27.] Nat Rowe, an old bachelor, was going to the Christian Church for the first time in Williams Corners. He was just about ready to leave when he saw the sacrament being passed around; so when it got to him, he said, "No thanks, I'm going home to dinner."

As with the other narratives touching upon religion, the purpose is ambiguous. Besides creating laughter at the incongruous equation of the Sacrament and Sunday dinner, is the tale making fun of the ignorance of Nat Rowe? Is it laughing at the elders of the Christian Church (a specific Protestant sect) confronted with the naturalism of a simple man? Is it mocking the very concept of the bread of the Sacrament?

[28.] Uncle Jeff Montgomery and Sol Higgins were the town drunks but one night Uncle Jeff got the Holy Ghost at a revival meeting and tried to persuade Sol to get "It"; so he asked him if he wanted to go to heaven. Sol turned to the man next to him and said, "If I did want to go to heaven, I wouldn't want to go with that son of a bitch."

The incongruous behavior of drunkards at church — sometimes combined with the theme of falling asleep in church — is, of course, common in traditional narrative. Again there is ambiguity. Perhaps next to inducing laughter, the chief purpose is to question the validity of revival-meeting conversions, at least of some such conversions.

Sol's drunken bluntness must not only amuse the hearer, but impress him as basically more honest than Jeff's unthinking conversion. We must remember that in Williams Corners before radio, movies, and television, revival meetings were great and exciting events long anticipated, and everyone in Williams Corners knew stories of unlikely, instantaneous conversions and of almost equally instantaneous backslidings, sometimes even before the close of the revival. This knowledge would render more effective any function of a tale about revival conversions.

[29.] The people of Williams Corners made up money for L. D. Short to go off to a seminary to be a preacher and he went for a year and came back to Williams Corners to preach. He got up in the pulpit the first time and just fell over and fainted dead away. That was the last of his preaching and he was just wicked as could be for the rest of his days.

Unsatisfactory and ambiguous (again the subject is religion), this tale seems to lack some needed data: What was L. D. like before he went to the seminary? Why didn't his family send him to the seminary? Why did the community single him out? Why did he suffer so from stage fright? Perhaps the story is meant to condemn the community for trying to make a silk purse out of a sow's ear or to condemn L.D. for agreeing to become a silk purse. Perhaps the story is condemning in general the unworldliness, the impracticality, of organized religion.

However that may be, on the basis of the details supplied, the hearer is likely to sympathize with L.D. and to feel that his plight was harsh and undeserved.

[30.] Sammy Brown was walking up the street and didn't think anybody was around; so he let out a fart and Mrs. Ellie Rose, who was behind a bush, said, "Hello, Mr. Brown." Evidently she thought he had said something, let's hope.

Probably there is little purpose here other than to provoke laughter and perhaps a sense of superiority in the hearer. Possibly he is being warned never to assume he is safe. The story of Sammy Brown is rather similar to, and perhaps influenced by, one form of the very migratory legend "The Surpriser Surprised," a form in which a young lady at night steps into her boyfriend's car and resoundingly relieves herself while he is going around the car to get into the driver's seat and to announce that his parents are in the back seat.

[31.] Uncle Jack and Aunt Mamie Riley lived in an old house on a street beside the railroad track. They had worked hard all their lives. One day the house caught fire. The village bucket brigade was trying to save the house. Aunt Mamie came running out of the house when all of her furniture and belongings were nearly consumed. All she had in her hand was her old slop jar. She walked over to one of the neighbor women and said, "This is all I have and all I hope to have."

Simply human and pathetic, this little local legend is well constructed. The purpose is to show that Williams Corners had its sorrows, too. The use of the affectionate (and patronizing) "Uncle" and "Aunt," the poverty, the unfashionable neighborhood, the obvious merit of the Rileys, all anticipate and emphasize the catastrophe. The pathos is strongly stressed by the incongruous contrast between the homely object in Aunt Mamie's hands and the formal dignity of her words.

The function is promoted by the hearer's probable memory of other stories of fire and of the unlikely objects that the fire victims rescue. Perhaps, too, the hearer will sense an ironic symbolism between the little closing tableau and what life has in store for the Rileys.

[32.] Ronald Smith had all the family for a big family dinner. Mrs. Smith told Ron, the oldest, to say the blessing and all the time he was saying it he kept eying the liver and at the end he said, "Amen. Who in the hell burned the liver?"

Similar to so many family legends about what happened while the blessing was being asked at dinner, this little legend depends for its humor upon a realization of the incongruity in simultaneous consideration of the spiritual and the worldly, of the incongruity of the relative priority assigned to prayer and feast, and of the incongruity of switching in one breath from prayer to oath.

[33.] Uncle Shelton Wright used to love to drink his whiskey but he didn't want his wife to know about it. He'd send his neighbors to Louisville to get him two pints, and he'd keep one pint at home in the medicine cabinet and another one out in the barn. When he wanted a drink he would tell his wife he had the tizig [*sic*; cf. phthisic] and get a teaspoonful from the medicine cabinet and then go out to the barn and get a big snort.

Enjoyment of Uncle Shelton's story is increased if one remembers the whimsical adjustment to impertinent questions made by his brother, Dr. Hilton Wright. This is one of the few Williams Corners narratives that has anything to say about husband–wife relationships. Uncle Shelton is perhaps not henpecked, but certainly he prefers not to disillusion his wife. Depending upon point of view, a secondary purpose must be to show either (1) what extremes a man in the clutches of Demon Rum will go to or (2) how unnecessarily difficult it is for a man to enjoy a good drink. After all, two pints spread out hardly make a drunkard.

Certainly the function of presenting the good old days is enhanced by the use of the archaic word "tizig" (for tuberculosis), and the function of presenting the "drinking question" is much supported by the fact that the "dry-wet" issue is a very live political argument, frequently carried to the polls to this very day in Kentucky.

[34.] Noah Trotter was going to be drafted in the war, World War I; so he shot his trigger finger off. He went down to be examined and they asked him what happened and he said a steamboat ran over it. They sent him right on to France.

From a time when issues were clearly either evil or righteous, this little legend is meant to present and condemn draft-dodging. Noah's flippancy to the draft examiners is meant to evoke laughter, of course, but the concluding emphasis is upon the stark assurance that Noah was unable to evade military service or the war.

For the present-day hearer, complicated and delicate definitions of patriotism and draft responsibilities help to make this a story of the past.

[35.] Al Hindman, an ole bachelor, and Ock Schwartz, about half-crazy, lived close together. Ock told Al that the damned birds were about to pick his eyes out. Al walked to another corner and one of the neighbors told him that his heart had busted last night. A man Al knew all his life asked him where he was and he said he just went back home because he didn't know whether he was crazy or everybody else was.

Seemingly this tale is related to, or influenced by, a traditional motif, "Quest for the greatest of fools" (Thompson Motif H1312), one that usually occurs in tale genres other than the legend. Rather incoherent, the tale may be either premature and underdeveloped or half-forgotten and disintegrating. Perhaps the humor rests upon the literal interpretation of figurative expressions (in which case the story is poorly told) or upon the realization that the world is full of fools. Despite the appearance of two Williams Corners residents, the narrative lacks the impression of truth and reality conveyed by the others.

[36.] Vincent O'Brien was a spoiled rotten kid and his folks obeyed his every command. He was feeling sickly; so he went to the doctor and nothing really was wrong with him. Anyway he went home and told his parents that the doctor prescribed that he just sit under a shade tree and eat popcorn and drink lots of Pepsi Cola to get well. Sure enough, his parents believed him, and he spent the summer doing just that.

Every community has its spoiled brat, and this particularly pedestrian narrative presents the brat of Williams Corners and his doting, trusting parents. Its purpose is to condemn permissiveness and to warn doting parents that they will be imposed upon. The success with which it functions depends upon the hearer's recognition of the spoiled-brat stereotype and the vehemence of his desire to "shake such a kid."

[37.] The local rowdies would always pull exaggerated pranks and even do considerable damage at Hallowe'en time. Colonel Woods was one of the local rural carriers who carried the mail in a little enclosed United States Mail buggy. He also was a fancier of pacing horses and carts. Every Hallowe'en, the boys would take his cart and disassemble it and pull it up on the top of the old two-story school building where it was reassembled. They would also take his mail buggy and pull it out to someplace and hide it. One year Colonel decided he could stop this; so he took his shotgun and a flashlight and hid in his mail buggy. About midnight the boys came after his buggy and pulled it about a mile out of town. When they got to their destination, Colonel opened the window, flashed his light and aimed his shotgun and said, "Now, by thunder, you boys pull me right back home."

Again, every community has its legends of Hallowe'en pranks, though more commonly such legends recount the success rather than the failure of these pranks. One of the most common traditional pranks is the dismantling of a vehicle and its reassembling in some improbably high spot. If there is a purpose other than the nostalgic conjuring up of the past, it is the condemnation of carrying pranks too far. The Colonel's triumph seems to receive approval, perhaps to imply that one is justified in tricking tricksters. In general, the success of the narrative, I feel, depends upon the hundreds of other stories about Hallowe'en that the auditor has encountered — that, indeed, he may have participated in himself.

[38.] Snip Stark, the town bum, always had a bunch of dogs and he'd come down to Williams Corners around 2 or 3 o'clock every afternoon with a dog. One time some of the boys called the dog off and poured turpentine on his tail and that dog started noosing and noosed all over Snip.

This heartless little story is unfortunately very traditional, and both the account and the action accounted are (or, one hopes, *were*) common to most communities. I feel confident that the only purposes are historical and nostalgic. Although the sophisticated reader might assign a kind of pathos to the concern of the bum for his tortured dog, I doubt that the tale ever so functioned for its intended auditors.

[39.] When cars first came out you'd always get a book of directions and Mr. Bert Carrier got one. So he started it up and couldn't stop it; so he kept going around the square reading the directions to find out how to stop the thing. Finally he just headed into a tree because he couldn't read the directions and guide too.

Again the tale fits a common traditional mold. Communities usually cherish tales about the difficulties of adjusting to progress and its attendant new gadgets, and certainly the large majority of these tales concern difficulties created by the automobile. A community not far from Williams Corners proudly tells of its local Samson, who never conquered the problem of parallel parking and therefore lifted his car in and out of a parking space whenever he came to town. The single most common legend of this sort tells of the proud new owner of an automobile who drove it around a field or about his barn until it ran out of gas because he had not learned how to stop the vehicle before he embarked upon his first drive.

Although the tale laughs at Mr. Carrier's ineptness when confronted with that new contraption, the automobile, it also implies that automobiles were coming to Williams Corners — that the hometown was in step with progress. Of course, the tale succeeds with modern auditors by feeding their egos, since all of them naturally know how to bring a car to a halt.

[40.] Old Dunc Smith lived in the country down in the cave country, and his first trip to Jeffersonville, Indiana, he'd never seen a train or boat; so he got on the train at Williams Corners and rode to Louisville. He'd stick his head out of the window but when they'd get to a telephone pole he'd pull it back in 'cause he was afraid it would hit him. When he got to Louisville and got on the boat so many people got on he was sure it would sink; so he got out in the middle of the deck and sat there till they got across the river.

Less common but still traditional, this theme emphasizes the difference between the rural and the urban rather than between the ancient and the modern. Dunc's naïve fears are ludicrous, and are meant to be so, but he is presented as inexperienced rather than foolish, and I think our laughter is supposed to be tempered with sympathy for the old country boy.

[41.] A retired couple moved to Williams Corners who had raised a large family and the people were congratulating the old man. The old man said the only thing about it was that every night his wife had to warm some water and put it on his chest because he was so used to having babies wet on him that he couldn't go to sleep unless his chest was wet.

Like No. 35, this is not a typical legend. It is the only tale that has no named characters. Perhaps the "retired couple" is nameless because they are latecomers to Williams Corners. My guess is that this is a pleasant whimsy that has been localized. Perhaps its real purpose is to pose as just one more story that Mr. Fergus can tell his daughter about his hometown.

In summary then, and with the assumption that folk narration is a kind of cooperation in which narrator and auditor influence both the product and the process, I have attempted to determine the reason for narration in forty-one local legends as performed by one tale-teller. That part of the reason which is essentially due to the narrator I have called purpose, and that part which is essentially the auditor's I have called function. I have hoped that with tales as simple and trivial as these it might be possible to point to some of the factors in a very complex process. Actually, the character and the experience of both narrator and auditor, the content of the narration, and the particular degree of formality implicit in the particular performance, all interact and influence each other. For instance, these very tales might have been told very differently and have conveyed a different effect had they been performed by a teller whose adult life and career had kept him in Williams Corners.

It goes without saying that these little tales could be studied in many other ways: as a psychological insight into the narrator, as a comment upon one set of objectives for folk history, as a set of social standards.

Twenty of the tales express or imply some kind of appreciation, approving or disapproving, of what is called middle-class morality. Seven of those twenty permit an unexpectedly negative judgment of "good old-fashioned religion." Six of the tales afford interesting evidence about society's definition of eccentricity and the permissible attitudes toward eccentricity.

For this paper, however, the problem is purposes and functions. Putting aside the important and obvious purposes of entertaining (usually, but not always, synonymous with "amusing"), of holding the stage, of submerging one's identity and troubles in performance, of commanding an audience, however small, we can generalize the many specific purposes that have been enumerated for the separate narratives under two headings: nostalgic and didactic.

In the tales, the narrator, Mr. Fergus, can recreate that part of the past which is particularly meaningful and pleasant to him. He puts himself emphatically on one side of the universally recognized dichotomy, country mouse versus city mouse — "I'm a country boy myself." He establishes himself as belonging to a group and as having roots in a tradition. Having gone so far, Mr. Fergus then becomes didactic and shows what his hometown — and, by extension, the generic hometown — was like, what and who its citizens were, what its good points (and, very lightly, its bad points) were, and how it differs from the present. Perhaps because of the particular life history of the particular narrator, the comparison between the past and the present does not always favor the former.

If the purposes succeed, the functions usually correspond to or complement them, and that is reasonably true in these tales. Generally the functions can also be grouped under two headings: recognition and identification. The auditor recognizes — and, depending upon his experience, identifies with — the nostalgia of the narrator. He recognizes the stereotype characters and the cliché standards in the tales, and — this may be an important force — he is proud of his wisdom in doing so. He may or may not identify with the particular past which supplies the setting and the material for the narratives, but he certainly identifies with the need for tradition, for belonging to a recognizable community and society, for having roots.

At the risk of redundancy but in the fear that a point will be overlooked, I end with the reminder that the primary purpose of local legends, as of most other kinds of folktales, is the very act of performance and that the primary function is participation in creative communication.

Variation in Place-Names, Intonation, and Rhythm as an Expression of Varying Frames of Mind

ROBERT WILDHABER

When as a boy I spent vacations with my aunt in Chur, she would occasionally act out a little scene for me which dealt with the farm women from the nearby village of Maladers. In bad years, when they were asked where they came from, they would answer in a slow, whining voice, giving the place-name with an old dialectal pronunciation. If the year was a good one, however, they would answer in a cheerful, slightly impertinent voice, giving the name of their village with a "refined," urban pronunciation. My aunt would convey this to me by changes in voice, mimicry, and gesticulation, so that it entertained me greatly and made a strong impression on me. I later forgot the accompanying little verses, and have not been able to discover them despite many inquiries. In the past few years, however, I have come across similar examples from widely separated areas. Here I would like to lay out these examples, noting the problems connected with their written reproduction.

First of all, the use of dialect and dialectal forms of place-names is a significant factor in their effectiveness. This makes their written representation difficult and lessens their readability and the reader's appreciation of the associated elements of humor and mockery. These forms have yet to be given a folktale motif number. The form as a whole consists in the fact that, depending on the speaker's frame of mind, the place-name is altered and/or variously pronounced. This assumes that the inhabitants of the immediate or wider surroundings are aware of the discrepancy between dialect and standard forms and that the dialect form is associated with a mocking, even derisive, tone. It is necessary to cite the texts in full.

Evidence corresponding to the version from Maladers just mentioned

This paper is an expanded version of a paper published in German in *Miscellanea Prof. em. Dr. K. C. Peeters* (Antwerp: Drukkerijen C. Goværts, 1975), pp. 752–760.

comes from Swabia, Silesia, Lower Austria, the Vorarlberg, Hungary, and the Ardennes. According to Moser (1950:364; translation mine):

In Swabia we frequently encounter mockery of the various pronunciations of place-names, sometimes completely in dialect, at other times approaching the literary language. Thus, it is said of the inhabitants of Pforzen (Kaufbeuren) that in autumn, when the barns are full, their pronunciation of the name of their village, *Pforze'*, proudly resembles the literary pronunciation. In the spring, however, they are modest, using the dialectally lengthened *Pfoaza*. The people of Heiligenberg (Überlingen) say refinedly in the summer, while the visitors are still there, that they are *von Heiligenberg*; later, when the good times are over, this becomes *vo' Holge'berg*.

In this second example, reasons for the change are cited: it can perhaps best be explained in terms of the people's desire to express themselves understandably to foreign visitors.

In the following Silesian example, from Jätschau, not far from Glogau, there is still another mark of a change in mood, this time easily explained in terms of the leanness or fatness of people's bodies (Peuckert 1950:78–79; original emphasis, translation mine):

Before the harvest, *two* farmers from Jätschau normally could sit on *one chair*; but when the harvest is over, then *one* man from Jätschau always needs *two chairs*. When asked before the harvest where he was from, a Jätschau farmer would gloomily say: "*Vu Jiaätsch*" [from Jätschau]; but after the harvest he would answer merrily: "*Ich bin von Jätschau*" [I am from Jätschau].

In Lower Austria, the grape harvest is decisive (Lang-Reitstätter 1948:146; translation mine): "If one asks the people of Herrnbaumgarten where they are from during a poor wine year, they answer meekly: '*Von Bauert*.' But in a good year they throw out their chests and announce in High German: '*Von Herrnbaumgarten*.'" In the Vorarlberg the cherry harvest determines the pronunciation: "The people of Fraxern near Feldkirch take great pride in their many cherry trees. Before a good harvest they are *von Fraxern*; in a bad year for cherries they are only *voa Fraxara*." In the French Ardennes, likewise, the wine year sets the mood (Gueillot 1931:366, 373; translation mine): In the town of Senuc, "the inhabitants would say '*J'sons de S'nuc*' or '*J'sons de S'nun*,' depending on whether the grape harvest was good or bad." In the town of Vandy, "in years of good harvest, the native said proudly: '*Msiu, j'suis d'Vady*'; when the harvest was poor, sadly: '*Mon pauv' Messiu, ej'suis d'Vandy-la-Dolent*.'" In this last example, assuming that the author reproduces it correctly, it is notable that the correct place-name is used in a poor rather than in a good harvest year. Still another story about the different kinds of wine years is told by German settlers in southern Hungary, the so-called Donauschwaben (Cammann and Karasek 1976:373; translation mine). If one met them at a market or fair and asked them where they came from, they would answer differently according to the quality of the wine harvest. If it was good, they would give the proud answer "From Bácsalmás"; if it was bad, they would say rather dejectedly, "From Almás." Here again we have an official and a dialect form of their place-name.

Besides these examples, there are others that can be described either as a kind of null-grade or as poorly reported. First I shall cite a few texts in which the place-name is not changed, the change in mood being indicated through additions to it or altered intonation. For example, in the Ardennes (Guelliot 1931:338), the inhabitants say "'*Nous sommes de Liart: de Liart nous sommes*' when it is a good year for apples and '*Du pauvre Liart, mon bon Monsieur*' in the opposite case." A similar story is known in Norway (Ropeid 1975:194). If, in the spring, when provisions had become scanty, you asked a man from Tysvær where he lived he would answer, "Alas, in Tysvær, God forbid." If you asked him in autumn, when the crop had been good and the storerooms were full, he would answer proudly and confidently, "From Tysvær." (Ropeid does not give the Norwegian text.) Another story is told in Sussex, England (Simpson 1973:151–152):

> Amberley is a delightfully pretty village, but it is hemmed in by low-lying meadows of the Arun valley, which until recent times were flooded during much of the winter. Consequently . . . if you ask an Amberley man where he lives he will answer cheerfully in summer, "*Amberley, where would you?*", but in winter gloomily, "*Amberley, God knows!*"

A further story comes from Bavaria (Bronner 1911:40; translation mine), where it is said of the horseradish peddlers of Weisenheim that they are quite sharp-tongued in the summer:

> To the question "*Wo bischt de her?*" [Where are you from?] they answer roughly and gruffly, "*Vun Weiserem! Warum? Was witt?*" [From Weisenheim! Why? What do you want?] But when the lads travel around during the severe winter, knocking on door after door to sell their horseradish, they are subdued and, when asked where they are from, answer modestly: "*Vun Weiserem! Ach, kaafe se mer doch e Stang Meerrettich ab?*" [From Weisenheim! Oh, won't you please buy a bunch of horseradish from me?]

The setting is similar for a story from the Bern canton in Switzerland (Friedli 1922:43–44; translation mine):

> When a Lüscherzer was walking towards Bern at two o'clock in the morning with a container of fish on his back, and was asked where he came from, he answered in an almost tearful voice: "*Von Lüscherz, lieber, laider*" [From Lüscherz, unfortunately, my dear sir]. But when, on his way back from Bern over Mount Frienis, he received a coarsely baked hard roll at a cloister and, when he reached Aarberg, put it in a measure of red wine to soften, the answer was different: "*Vo Lüscherz, bi Gott! Worum? Bin ich der öppis schuldig? So säg's graad!*" [From Lüscherz, by God! Why? Do I owe you something? Out with it!].

In an additional example, the distinction is expressed only in the length or shortness of a vowel; moreover, the reason given for this change is unusual in that it attempts to explain the change in mood psychologically. The example comes from life on the sea (Wossidlo 1959:163; translation mine; also Neumann 1968a:88–89):

A traveler was leaving Rotterdam for the East Indies, a journey which at that time took a year. When asked where he was going, he answered: "*Nach de Bataavia*!" [To Batavia!]. The vowel is long here because he is afraid of the long journey. When he returned and was asked, "Man, where are you coming from?", he said in a loud voice: "*Von Batavia*!" [From Batavia!]. He says this quite sharply because he is a splendid fellow for having survived the long journey.

Psychologically very similar is the example of the Alpine herdsman, who spends the summer in the mountain pasture and is sad when this unconstrained life comes to an end. The report comes from Switzerland (Steinmüller 1802:117; translation mine; also Engelhardt 1812:112): "There is an old folk saying: When the shepherd is on his way to the Alpine mountain pasture and is asked, 'Where to?', he shouts, '*Ha, ha! auf Alp, auf Alp*' [Ha, ha! to the Alp], but when asked, on his return, 'Where from?', he says sadly and quietly: '*ab Alp*' [down from the Alp]."

Quite interesting also for its psychological basis is a bit of evidence from France. It deals with a shepherd who, when his herd is in poor condition, gives a completely different town of origin so as not to jeopardize the good reputation of his true home village (Poueigh 1952:135; translation mine):

"Where are you from, boy?", one asks a shepherd going by. If he is inclined to be vain about his flock, he loudly calls out the name of his village, all the more proudly if it is renowned as a stock-rearing center: "*De Bielle, ma fè*!" [From Bielle, indeed!], shouts the proud shepherd from Bielle. When sickness or accidents have reduced his flock and diminished his importance, the same Biellian, in response to the question, passes himself off as a native of Laruns, in order that his individual fall from grace does not reflect at all on the shared communal honor: "*De Laruns, se bous plats*!" [From Laruns, if you please!], he whimpers humbly, as a kind of apology.

A Swedish example introduces another variation. Here the awareness of the distinction remains, but the answers are attributed to two different persons. The thought is the same, but its expression seems to be a distortion of the full version. In this sense, this case is similar to place-name mockery (Linnarsson 1950:26; translation mine). The distinction is noted between the farmer from the plain, who sells his wares in the city, and the poor farmer from the forest region. The former, when asked what he has for sale in his sack, answers, in a strong and commanding voice, "*Råg å korn, puuh*!" [Rye and barley, by God!]; the latter answers in a plaintive and whining voice, "*Litte aska, gunås*" [A little ash, I'm sorry]. In a second Swedish example, the wealthy farmer answers, "*Arter å buner, puuh*!" [Peas and beans, by God!], but the poor farmer from the same place says, "*En skäppa havre, min goa harre*" [A bushel of oats, my good sir].

All the examples cited up to this point are of the same type; they would have to be classified together as a single motif. The difficulty in their written reproduction consists in the fact that one has to convey not only the exact sound values and the related implications and allusions, but also the accompanying mimicry and gestures. Musical notation alone would grasp only a part of this, and a photograph would be able to show only a moment in the flow of events. Since we are dealing with a histrionic performance, sound film would be the only accurate method of reproduction, unless one could develop a standard system for the representation of mimicry and gestures.

The examples just cited are alike in that they deal in some way with place-names. In other instances, varying frames of mind are indicated by changes in voice and speech rhythm. Perhaps the best-known example is Motif J1341.11 (Thompson 1955–1958; Baughman 1966): "Hired men sing of displeasure with food; change song when food is improved" (see also Aarne-Thompson Type 1567G, "Good food brings change in servants' song"). It deals with the hiring of seasonal workers during harvest-time or for some other farm work. In English and American versions, the story goes by the name of "The hungry mowers" or "The mean boss." Baughman cites English versions from Cumberland, Westmoreland, and York. He reproduces the Westmoreland text as typical: "Mowers sing very slowly, mow in tempo: '*Curds and whey, Iv-ve-ry day*.' After the food is improved they sing and work in tempo: '*Ham and eggs, mind thy legs!*'" The same version is given by Briggs (1970:125–126, with music) and by Briggs and Tongue (1965:139–140, with a listing of authorities). To the North American versions related by Baughman should be added a Negro story from Michigan (Dorson 1956:67–68, 213; 1967:156–157). Here we find not people speaking but a saw saying, "slow, thin, and reedy: '*So-o-oup, so-o-oup, so-o-oup*'"; when the workers receive a different type of food, the saw sings, "fast and snappy: '*Bread-meat-and-pudding-too, bread-meat-and-pudding-too*.'" The sickles of the harvest workers in Italian Friuli lament "two hundred, three hundred" until the workers have been fed; then they say "four hundred, five hundred!" (Percoto 1967:15–16).

Other texts point to the difference it makes whether a man works for himself or others, or whether or not he receives piece wages. Thus, an example from Scotland (Simpkins 1912:271) reads:

Our grandfathers used to illustrate the difference between time-workers and piece-workers thus: When a mason hewed by the day, his mell and chisel went slowly to the tune of *Auch-ter-much-ty* (speaking as slowly as possible), but when he was paid by piece they galloped on in rapid succession: *Cup'r-o'-Fife, Cup'r-o'-Fife, Cup'r-o'-Fife* (hurrying through the four syllables in a breath).

Besides the English-Scottish and American texts, Finnish versions are also known; according to Dorson (1956:213), "A Finnish proverb has the servant at the loom go fast when she does her own work, *ittellenittellenittellen* (for-me-for-me-for-me), and slowly when she works for her mistress, *ta-loo-hin, ta-loo-hin, ta-loo-hin* (for the house, for the house)." The Mecklenburg storyteller August Rust (Neumann 1968b:118–119) repeats a funny short anecdote in which neither the words nor the melody are changed, but the tempo is doubled. On the day of her husband's burial, the widow is asked to dance at the wake; when she declines, the request is repeated, with the promise to dance slowly to the words: "*Ick trür üm mien'n leeben Mann Martens, Mann Martens*" [I mourn for my dear husband Marten, husband Marten]. Thereupon she consents, but after a time the tempo and melody become more and more lively, until the couples have more than doubled the speed at which they turn in a circle.

In this connection, the oft-cited tones of mills and bells must also be mentioned. A few examples will suffice. The reasons given for the changes in tempo are interesting. It is natural that the slower or quicker clattering of the mill wheels should denote the sparse or plentiful flow of water (Bossler 1909:10; translation mine). Thus, in Hessen, "When there is little water: '*Ach, was seins für schlechte Zeiten*!' [Oh, what bad times we are having!]. When there is a lot of water, one hears: '*Alleweil giehts flott, alleweil giehts flott*!' [It is always going great!]." It seems that the German settlers have brought similar stories with them to Pennsylvania; a report from Lehigh County (Brendle and Troxell 1944:185) says:

Up country there was a grist mill that only ran after rain storms when the dam was full of water. Such mills are called thunderstorm mills. When the water was low, the revolving wheel creaked, "*God-help-me. God-help-me.*" But when the water was high the rapidly revolving wheel cried, "*I-can-help-myself. I-can-help-myself.*" In Pennsylvania German the two voices are: "*Gott helf mar*" and "*Kann mar selwer helfe*."

For the southern Tyrol, the quantity of grain to be ground is decisive (Mang 1946:30; translation mine): "in July, when there is only a little grain, the mills clatter quite slowly: '*Ja-ko-bi*,' but when they have the new harvest to grind, they busily say: '*Laurenzi*.'" The social sphere is touched upon when a stately mill in Austria calls "*Für ålle, für ålle*!" [For all!], whereas a small mill, kept in operation by a meager streamlet, murmurs in a tearful voice, "*Für mi und für mein Nachbarn, für mi und für mein Nachbarn*!" [For myself and my neighbors!] (Schmidt 1966:350;

translation mine). In the Bern canton, a mocking verse about "my" and "your" mill is sung by children at play (Friedli 1925:331; translation mine):

Mini Müli, mini Müli, mini Müli geit,
Dini Müli, dini Müli, dini Müli steit,
Mini Müli, mini Müli, macht fiins Mähl,
Dini Müli, dini Müli, Ho-bel-spään!

[My mill, my mill, my mill works,
Your mill, your mill, your mill stands still,
My mill, my mill, makes fine meal (flour),
Your mill, your mill, only wood-shavings!]

Related to these happy and lamenting mill voices, which express verbally two opposite situations, is the following text from Siebenbürgen (Haltrich 1885:157; translation mine):

When the wooden carts of the Szeklers, heavily laden with boards, moved at snail's pace through the streets, they sighed in protracted cries of pain (in Hungarian): *e-het-ném, i-hat-nám, e-het-ném, i-hat-nám* [I should like to eat, I should like to drink]. But if the owner had sold his boards and also had a bit to drink, he drove warbling through the street with his little horses, and the wheels sounded briskly and happily: *ettem, ittam, jól laktam! ettem, ittam, jól laktam*! [I have eaten, I have drunk, I have eaten my fill!].

Here may be added what people in Pennsylvania say about thieves and their wheelbarrows (Brendle and Troxell 1944:184–185):

A man went forth to steal and took his wheel-barrow along to haul back his plunder. The wheel of the barrow had not been greased for a long time and, as it slowly revolved, cried, "*It may be you'll be caught. It may be you'll be caught.*" The man was discovered and fled precipitously, and as the wheel revolved swiftly, it cried, "*I told you so. I told you so.*" The dialect forms in Pennsylvania German are: "*Wann du nett verwischt warscht*" and "*Ich hab dars gsât.*" The texts for two similar situations are: "*Not worthwhile*"-"*Dudd ke gud,*" "*Knew it would happen*"-"*Habt wisst ass so geht,*" and "*Going for turnips*"-"*Will Riewe hohle,*" "*Got-not-one*"-"*Kenni grickt.*"

A strikingly similar story comes from Saarland, western Germany (Burde-Schneidewind 1977:90, no. 148); here the wheels cry "*Riewestehle*" [Stealing turnips] and "*Ma han kä Riewe kritt*" [We haven't got any turnips].

Another story from Siebenbürgen relates to animal voices (Haltrich 1885:152–153; translation mine): "The fox, when heatedly pursued by hunters, only laughs and barks like a dog: '*Er bekut mich net, er bekut mich net*!' [You won't catch me!]. But if the hounds catch him, he wails: '*Ach jai, ech hu jo näst gedôn, näst gedôn.*' [But I haven't done anything!]."

I shall give only one example relating to bell tones, one that shows a clear connection with the texts mentioned above rather than belonging with the place-name mockeries (Bronner 1911:14): A pastor from a well-to-do wine-growing town in Bavaria was transferred to a parish in a poor region. The bishop visited him and asked him how he liked the new town. The pastor declared that the difference could be heard in the very ringing of the bells: in the old town, the bells had rung: "*Vi-num bo-num, vi-num bo-num*" [Good wine]; in the new town, however, they sounded only: "*Äppelwein! Grumbeer! Äppelwein! Grumbeer!*" [Apple wine! Potatoes!].

Here should be added a Bessarabian story which shows clearly that people are conscious of the differing pronunciation of vowels, in this case related to ethnic differences (Cammann 1967:310): A Swabian dog goes home from the butcher shop with a large bone in his mouth. A Kashube dog sees him and asks what he has in his mouth. The dog lays the bone on the ground and says "*Flaisch*" [meat]. Then the Kashube dog snaps the bone away from him. The Swabian dog seeks revenge. On the next day, he sees the Kashube dog with a bone in his mouth. When asked what he has there, the Kashube dog clamps his teeth even closer together and says, "*Fleesch*" [meat]. (For literature on idioms imitating dialectal peculiarities, see Taylor [1931:105; 1934:17].)

Finally, two more examples show how much speech melody can change a sentence (Landmann 1970:41–42; translation mine). A Jewish humorous definition runs: "What is consistency? *Heute* so, *morgen* so" [*Today* this way, *tomorrow* this way]. What is inconsistency? Heute *so*, morgen *so* [Today *this* way, tomorrow *that* way]." Even better is one of the delightfully human military jokes: *Sergeant*: "Conscript Katz, why should a soldier gladly die for his Kaiser?" *Katz*: "You're right! Why should he?"

Despite the difficulties in the recording of this type of text, further documents from other countries would be very useful. That there will be some is to be expected, since we are dealing here with a psychological phenomenon common to all humanity, one reflecting man's predilection for play and probably also his need for mockery.

REFERENCES

BAUGHMAN, ERNEST W.
1966 *Type and motif index of the folktales of England and North America.* The Hague: Mouton.

BOSSLER, A.
1909 Tierlaut- und Schalldeutung. *Hessische Blätter für Volkskunde* 8:1–17.

BRENDLE, THOMAS R., WILLIAM S. TROXELL
1944 *Pennsylvania German folktales, legends, once-upon-a-time stories, maxims, and sayings.* Norristown, Pa.: Pennsylvania German Society.

BRIGGS, KATHARINE M.
1970 *A dictionary of British folk-tales in the English language,* part A, *Folk narratives,* volume two. London: Routledge and Kegan Paul.

BRIGGS, KATHARINE M., RUTH L. TONGUE
1965 *Folktales of England*. Chicago: University of Chicago Press.
BRONNER, F. J.
1911 *Bayerisches Schelmen-Büchlein*. Diessen vor München: Jos. C. Huber.
BURDE-SCHNEIDEWIND, GISELA
1977 *Historische Volkssagen aus dem 13. bis 19. Jahrhundert*, volume four. Berlin: Akademie.
CAMMANN, ALFRED
1967 *Deutsche Volksmärchen aus Russland und Rumänien*. Göttingen: Otto Schwartz.
CAMMANN, ALFRED, ALFRED KARASEK
1976 *Donauschwaben erzählen*, volume one. Marburg: N. G. Elwert.
DORSON, RICHARD M.
1956 *Negro folktales in Michigan*. Cambridge: Harvard University Press.
1967 *American Negro folktales*. Greenwich, Conn.: Fawcett.
ENGELHARDT, KARL AUGUST
1812 *Feierabende des Vaters*. Pirna.
FRIEDLI, EMANUEL
1922 *Bärndütsch: Twann*. Bern: A. Francke.
1925 *Bärndütsch: Aarwangen*. Bern: A. Francke.
GUELLIOT, OCTAVE
1931 *Géographie traditionelle et populaire du département des Ardennes*. Paris: Emile Nourry.
HALTRICH, JOSEF
1885 *Zur Volkskunde der Siebenbürger Sachsen*. Vienna: Carl Græser.
LANDMANN, SALCIA
1970 *Der jüdische Witz* (eighth edition). Olten and Freiburg i Br.: Walter.
LANG-REITSTÄTTER, MARIA
1948 *Lachendes Oesterreich* (second edition). Salzburg: Oesterreicheischer Kulturverlag.
LINNARSSON, LINNAR
1950 *Bygd, by och gard*, volume two. Uppsala: Lundequistska Bokhandeln.
MANG, HERMANN
1946 "Vom Essen in unseren Tälern," in *St. Kassian-Kalendar (Brixen) für 1946*, 27–71.
MOSER, HUGO
1950 *Schwäbischer Volkshumor*. Stuttgart: W. Kohlhammer.
NEUMANN, SIEGFRIED
1968a *Plattdeutsche Schwänke: aus den Sammlungen Richard Wossidlos*. Rostock: Hinstorff.
1968b *Ein mecklenburgischer Volkserzähler: die Geschichten des August Rust*. Berlin: Akademie.
PERCOTO, CATERINA
1967 *Contes du Frioul*. Udine.
PEUCKERT, WILL ERICH
1950 *Schlesisch* (new edition). Munich: R. Piper.
POUEIGH, JEAN
1952 *Le folklore des Pays d'Oc: la tradition occitane*. Paris: Payot.
ROPEID, ANDREAS
1975 "Norwegische Nahrung," in *Ethnologische Nahrungsforschung/Ethnological food research*, 193–199. Helsinki: Suomen Muinaismuistoyhdistys.

SCHMIDT, LEOPOLD

1966 *Volkskunde von Niederösterreich*, volume one. Horn: Ferdinand Berger.

SIMPKINS, JOHN EWART

1912 *County folk-lore*, volume seven: *Examples of printed folk-lore concerning Fife*. Publications of the Folk-lore Society (London) 71.

SIMPSON, JACQUELINE

1973 *The folklore of Sussex*. London: B. T. Batsford.

STEINMÜLLER, JOHANN RUDOLF

1802 *Beschreibung der schweizerischen Alpen- und Landwirtschaft*, volume one, *Glarus*. Winterthur.

TAYLOR, ARCHER

1931 *The proverb*. Cambridge: Harvard University Press.

1934 *An index to "The proverb*." FF Communications 113.

THOMPSON, STITH

1955–1958 *Motif-index of folk literature* (second edition), six volumes. Bloomington: Indiana University Press.

WOSSIDLO, RICHARD

1959 *"Reise, Quartier, in Gottesnaam": das Seemannsleben auf den alten Segelschiffen im Munde alter Fahrensleute* (seventh edition). Rostock: Hinstorff.

Some Traditional Symbols in Slavonic Folk Poetry

V. K. SOKOLOVA

Associations between phenomena arising, like rituals and myths, out of ancient ideas formed the basis of many traditional symbols used in oral poetry. Later, though the sense of these symbols had been forgotten, they had become so firmly rooted in poetic phraseology that in some instances they continued in traditional use as artistic imagery. Moreover, in different genres, various functions and meanings might be accorded to them. The task of elucidating their origin and primary meaning is facilitated by the existence of rituals with which they are genetically connected. In their turn, the symbols contribute to a better understanding of ritual and the character of ancient ideas. Not only did the sense of traditional poetic imagery undergo change, however, but, out of the new situations, new images emerged and were molded into poetic formulae that sometimes bore a superficial resemblance to those based on ancient tradition. Further, although in actuality these images were essentially different, a coincidence such as this might evoke a certain interaction between them. For this reason, poetic imagery should be studied in its historical development and mutual relations. A problem of this complexity cannot be dealt with in sufficient depth within the scope of this study. My purpose here is to examine a few instances of poetic imagery in Slavonic, principally Russian, poetry associated with the death-marriage simile, which is found not only among Slavonic peoples, but also among others, and may be considered typical of a definite stage in the development of thought.[1]

Among Slavonic peoples, the association between death and marriage

[1] For example, an interesting and hitherto unknown custom of the Mordovians was described by L. S. Kavtaskin at an ethnography and folklore conference in Leningrad in 1971: at a girl's funeral, an imitation of her wedding was given with a friend in the role of the bride (see Shapovalova 1971:166).

may be seen clearly in the funeral customs with regard to young girls. A dead girl was dressed as a bride, and her friends, dressed as bridesmaids, accompanied her to the burying ground. In old Russian laments, the dead girl was spoken of as a white swan, the customary allusion to a bride. In northern Russian mourning laments for girls' burials, detailed descriptions are found of their wearing apparel. An illustration of this is the lament of the noted professional mourner I. A. Fedosova for her own daughter (Barsov 1872:116). As is pointed out by Chistov in his commentary on this lament (1960:101; translation mine), "These lines are of interest as a rare example of a peasant's description of a bride's attire in the mid-nineteenth century." The storyteller N. S. Bogdanova, who had also lost her daughter, complained bitterly that her poverty had necessitated burying the girl in the ordinary well-worn garments of a peasant woman. If she had had money, she would have buried her in bridal dress as custom required. Like Fedosova, she described the proper wedding clothes for burials (Shayzhin 1911:197).

In some parts of Russia, married women were also buried in their wedding gowns, carefully preserved for this occasion, but as a general rule it was obligatory for girls only. In northern Russia, a young man dressed as a bridegroom accompanied a girl's corpse to the burial. Apparently, the idea was that everyone's life experience must come full circle; if a girl had not yet been married, she had to pass through this stage after death. This is also the explanation offered by the Bulgarian scholar Angelova (1960:729–730). In her analysis of the Bulgarian girls' holiday known as Lazuravane, the purpose of which is to express good wishes for health, love, and domestic happiness, she notes that a young girl who dies before experiencing the happiness of love is arrayed as though for her wedding, and the wedding banner is carried in the cortege to the churchyard.

By constantly reminding people of this ancient association, ritual promoted its preservation, and it became deep-rooted in the people's consciousness and survived independent of ritual. For instance, in the interpretation of dreams, it was thought that to dream of a wedding or of seeing someone in wedding garments was an omen of that person's death. On the basis of this association, certain poetic images and symbols evolved and came into constant use in nonritual verse and in written literature. One illustration is the comparison between carnage and the marriage feast in "The lay of the host of Igor." The parallel between burial rites and nuptials has been employed in a different sense in the Christian symbolism of the idea of the brides of Christ — the Wise Virgins, awaiting the bridegroom.

In Slavonic nonritual poetry, certain images are common to both nuptial and burial poetry, and in some contexts marriage is a metaphor for death. In contrast, the metaphorical substitution of death for marriage seems to be out of the question, as is the inclusion of funeral elements in the wedding rites. Magical significance was ascribed to ritual movements and their accompanying words; consequently, a representation or a reminder of death had the power to invoke actual death.

Potebnya (1870:11) argued that the wedding was regarded as symbolic of battle and death because all three represented the Last Judgment, and perhaps for other reasons as well. The death-marriage simile existed, however, before the idea of divine judgment, of which not the slightest suggestion can be found in folk symbolism. It seems more likely that the basis for placing the two side by side was that marriage and death were both regarded as transitions to new circumstances — a new state and a new place. They marked a boundary between different stages in life. This idea gave rise to the image of passage or of crossing a river. In the mythology of some nations a river is crossed to enter the realm of the dead. The classic image is Charon ferrying the souls of the dead across the Styx. Norse mythology, as recorded in the *Edda*, also has its ship of the dead. No imagery of this type exists in Slavonic funerary poetry, nor is there any mention there of crossing a river; possibly these ideas disappeared with the advent of Christianity. The crossing of a river is found, however, as a symbol of marriage in the nuptial verse of almost all Slavonic peoples. A quantity of comparative material about this symbol is given in the work of Potebnya (1866), who specialized in the subject, but his explanation of its meaning is erroneous. Obviously, this is an allusion to the bride's crossing over to her husband's tribe or clan and the consequent change in her situation. It arose when marriage became patrilocal and exogamous. Later, as marriage among peasants remained patrilocal, the idea of crossing some boundary was taken to mean the bride's entering a new family — her husband's.

In bridal songs, the bride waits on the riverbank for someone to carry her across. Neither father, brother, nor anyone else but the bridegroom can do this, so he pushes off in his boat to cross the swift-flowing river (Gulyaev 1848:10). Again, there is mention of a bridge (perhaps only a log laid across a stream) by which the bridegroom helps the girl to reach the other side. In a Polish wedding song, the nearest relatives of the pair must cross a bridge. In a Serbian song of the same type, falcons join forces to convey Anna and Peter across the Dunai (Karadžić 1841:no. 11). In a song from Belozersk, a bride pleads with her father and mother not to give her in marriage and begs her brother to dig a ditch; he must not strengthen the bridge or push off in the boat — strangers must be prevented from crossing (Sokolov and Sokolov 1915:341).

River-crossing as a symbol of marriage occurs again in Ukrainian songs; the falcon begs the youth not to take aim at him, promising in return to bring the youth's bride across the Dunai when he marries (Golovatskiy 1878:60–68). The love-link image is used with identical or similar meaning in lyrical songs of a later period. A girl asks her lover to stretch out his arm to her across the stream or to make a bridge and cross over to her (Sobolevskiy 1897:275). A young man beckons to his love from the opposite bank; she replies that the bridge is too flimsy, so he says he will throw a stout log across it (Sobolevskiy 1899:139). In other Ukrainian songs, the youth offers to carry or convey the girl across and asks her to stretch out her arm. The sense of this image, as suggested in some songs, is asking the girl for her hand in marriage. One example tells of a girl who has lost her way in the woods; she reaches the riverside at last and asks the ferryman to take her across so that she can reach her home. His price for this is: "Marry me!" (Sobolevskiy 1896:168). As may be seen from these examples, the imagery of river-crossing in lyric songs is close to the ancient idea, although its mythological significance has long been forgotten.

The river as a barrier to be surmounted in order to reach a new stage and also as the boundary between different worlds became in folk poetry an allusion to the state of a frontier (which not infrequently it was). In Russian historical songs about escape from bondage, the captives must always cross a river before they can reach their own country. During the dangerous crossing, they are sometimes drowned. In one such song, two Russians who have escaped from captivity in Khiva are crossing the ice-bound River Ural when the ice breaks under one of them; the other cannot come to his aid because his arms are too short and the river is too deep (Otechestvennye zapiski 1848:141). In another version, a captive seeks a ford across the Dunai and, failing to find it, weeps bitterly; he will never again see his native Russia or his father and mother (Baranov 1913:6). In these and similar cases, the river, in addition to being symbolic, is also real — the River Ural, for instance. Generally speaking, in lyrical poetry river-crossing is a symbol of the uniting of lovers.

Of a totally different character are the images of the arduous journey and the alien unknown land encountered in various genres of ritual and nonritual folk poetry. In the majority of cases, they are perceived not as symbolic, but as faithful portrayals of unusual situations — their artistic synthesis. This gives them a comparatively stable character, but they vary and assume different shades of meaning depending on the concrete elements and on the genre and theme of the work.

The road and the unknown land are mentioned in funerary as well as nuptial poetry. The idea that the dead depart for a strange, faraway place is very ancient and persistent. From it arises a common expression still in use, "accompanying him on his last journey," a form which no longer retains the underlying significance of a life beyond the grave. This idea was a determining concept in the funeral rites of former times. In old Russian funeral laments, one of the stock phrases was the call to the dead to say where he was going and which road he was taking. His destination was never described in detail, but alluded to as a distant bourne reached after an arduous journey.

The bride's departure also occupies a prominent place in nuptial ritual and poetry, for it is associated with the symbol of transition, of being conveyed across some boundary. In this instance departure is presented as an actuality. Moreover, in peasant wedding songs of the late feudal period, attention was centered not upon the departure to a new place — which in those times was not likely to be very far — but upon the description of the bride's new life "among strangers." This theme occurs, for example, in the plaintive nuptial song about the lone swan left behind by the rest. A girl who has been promised in marriage pleads with her father not to give her to a stranger from an unknown part of the country. She asks her married sisters and aunts about what kind of a life they have among strangers; invariably they complain that their lives are wearisome and joyless. The betrothed declares that she knows this and has often heard from good folks about the wicked, who always seem to inhabit distant parts (Barsov 1872:78). The unfamiliar scene acquires the same meaning in the interpretation of the betrothed's dreams: gloomy woods denote the unfamiliar place, wild beasts are the alien folk, and the river signifies the tears shed by the bride among strangers (Shein 1898:no. 713). A great many similar examples exist, and, though the descriptions of unfamiliar scenes have features in common, the meanings differ. In nuptial poetry, the strangers and the strange place acquire a definite sense — the home and family of the future husband. The emphasis in these nuptial songs or epithalamia is chiefly upon the relations prevailing among the members of a large peasant family; these are truthfully and correctly described.

The "strange place," for which the same formula serves, has a different meaning in old Russian lyric songs; it is the destination of the peasant lad obliged to leave his home to earn a livelihood or to do military service. The "strangers" are either the masters for whom he must work or the officers under whom he serves. The imagery here assumes a social coloring, and the laborious and joyless life far from home is kept well in the foreground. It is in this meaning that these images found a place in the genre of rhyming couplets which developed in Russian folklore at the end of the nineteenth century and the beginning of the twentieth. The pictures evoked are traditional: a girl asks her mother to rise very early in the quiet morning so that she can listen to her daughter weeping in the strange household in her new place. The working girl compares her life among strangers to treading upon sharp knives and complains that they are all so hard to please.

The formalized description of these strange and unwelcoming places persisted to the extent of becoming a game. In the Perm' region, in earlier times, girls used to weave wreaths to hang on birch trees just before

Whitsuntide. One of the games they played, "The parting," was accompanied by songs about the strange and distant places where life was sad and full of care and girls shed tears of grief and longed for home (Shein 1898:no. 1234).

The typical description of strange places in Russian folk lyrics simply reflected the actual conditions of the peasants' lives. Although the wording in some ways coincided, it had no connection with the ancient ideas underlying ritual poetry's imagery of the long road and the unknown destination. By the turn of the century, these images had lost their original meanings of change of condition and clan in nuptial poetry as well; now they illustrated the real life of the peasant woman. Only in funeral ritual and laments has the earlier symbolic sense of the last long journey and the strange place been preserved.

These examples indicate that what appear to be the same image and similar formulae arose at different periods, possessed different senses, and were used in different situations connected with the departure from home and life in a strange place. Although the typical formula showed considerable synthetization — repetition of the notion of the dreariness of existence in a strange place — it could be supplemented and concretized in a variety of ways.

Despite the fundamental difference between realistic and mythological concepts of the long-road-and-unfamiliar-place imagery, certain associations were sensed in them. In one lament, the mourner Fedosova asked, on her sister's behalf, the deceased which road he was to take — the one that led to St. Petersburg, the one that led to the towpath for barges, or the one that led to the shops and warehouses — thus enumerating the only prospects open to the Olenetsk peasant in the nineteenth century (Barsov 1872:92).

The interest of the death-marriage metaphor of Slavonic lyric poetry lies not only in the fact that it established and perpetuated, almost to our own time, the ancient death-marriage simile, but also in its recurrence in similar situations and expressions in the folklore of almost all Slavonic peoples. The simile, once firmly rooted in the consciousness, produced typically similar artistic images.

In old Russian songs, the hero is a mortally wounded Cossack or a stagecoach driver taken ill and dying on the road, far from aid. Ukrainian songs also have their Cossack, the southern Slavs their *haiduk* or *yunak*. Sometimes, the hero is simply a young man who meets his death in a strange country. The situation is always the same: dying far from home, the hero bids someone (his comrade or his horse) to bear the news of his death to his parents or, more often, to his mother). This message is always worded in the same way: "Tell them I am married." By way of clarifying the sense of the metaphor, details are given: that he has taken the grave for a wife or that the ground, the damp earth, or a dug out is his bed.

Bulgarians generally use the term "black earth," "the black-earth girl," etc. Sometimes, the youth is drowned, that is, he has taken the river wave as his wife. In a Czech (Moravian) song, the heroine's father has promised her in marriage to a Turk. To escape this fate, she drowns herself in the Dunai, thus becoming the bride of the free, clean river (Sušil 1951:136).

The image may be developed further. In Russian songs, the mortally wounded Cossack says he has been wed by the swift bullet, his bride is the keen-edged saber, his bed is the bare ground, and so on (Sokolov and Sokolov 1915:481). In a Bulgarian historical song, Gotse Delchev sends the message that he has married for Macedonia's sake, his bride is the black earth, his sister-in-law his gun, his brother-in-law the bullet, his wife's parents the ravens (Vakarelski 1961:581). In the same way, the *haiduk*, as he is led to the gallows by the Turkish police, says he is going to his wedding, the rope will be his friend, the eagles his bride's parents, the crows his brothers-in-law, the jackdaws the matchmakers (Osinin 1961:284–285). A Moravian song tells of a drowning girl: her bridesmaids are the little fish, her betrothed's rich parents the carp. Supplementary details of this type, developing the image, do not make any essential changes in it; the sense and the functions remain the same.

In these songs, ancient symbolism is used with intention. The allegory, though comprehensible to everyone concerned, serves to soften the blow and prepare the mother for ill tidings. Thus the Russian soldier abroad, dying of wounds, sends his horse home, bidding him: "Say not, my good steed, that slain, I lie low! Say rather, my steed, that wedded I go!" (Kruglyashova 1967:151). In some Ukrainian songs, the dying Cossack makes the same request (Berezovs'kiy, Rodina, and Khomenko 1961: 105). In a Serbian *yunak* song, Andreash Kralevich, though mortally wounded by his brother Mark, begs him to conceal the truth from their mother and to say he has been delayed in the foreign land and cannot return because his love for a girl there is so strong (Kravtsov 1960:158). This message may be understood by the mother either metaphorically or literally. The latter is the case in a Bulgarian song in which the mother, when told that her son Nedka is betrothed to a girl from the black-soil land, orders her servants to prepare food and bake bread and sets out for the wedding; when she learns the truth, she dies (Osinin and Ognyanova 1962:479). This is an instance when the interpretation of the metaphor itself deepens the tragic mood of the song, but it is an exception. The meaning of the figure of speech is always plain. One version of the Serbo–Croatian ballad "Omer and Meirime" merges literal and figurative meanings. When the mother has obliged Omer, who loves Meirime, to marry another, he takes his own life on his wedding night. Meirime's sister tells her that her bridegroom has broken his vows and married another.

The figurative use of a poetic metaphor is possible in epic or lyrico-epic songs with a well-developed theme. Lyric songs, which, in the case of the Slavonic peoples, show a striking resemblance, consist, as a rule, of a single episode. The metaphor, expressed in the last wish of the dying hero, serves as the culmination and the conclusion of the song. The point is that the hero must inevitably die far from home, in an alien country, which in the context is understood in both real and symbolic sense as an unfriendly and distant place where the hero remains forever. Ancient symbols in this instance prove to be associated even in songs of much later times, thereby revealing the persistence of tradition. It is possible to trace a connection of this kind between ancient ideas and the associations stemming from them only when we are dealing with poetic allegory — symbol and metaphor. When the poetic image is employed literally, it is realistic in character and cannot be of use in illustrating ancient ideas.

REFERENCES

ANGELOVA, R.
1960 "Lazuravane v S. Boyanovo," in *Romanski: ezikovedski i etnografski izsledovaniya v pamet na Akademik Stoyan Romanski*. Sofia.

BARANOV, F. N.
1913 *Pesni Orenburgskikh kazakov s napevami*, volume two. Orenburg.

BARSOV, E. V., *compiler*
1872 *Prichitaniya severnogo kŕaya*, part one. Moscow.

BEREZOVS'KIY, I. P., M. S. RODINA, V. G. KHOMENKO, *compilers.*
1961 *Istorichni pisni*. Kiev.

CHISTOV, K. V., *editor*
1960 *Prichitaniya*. Leningrad.

GOLOVATSKIY, A. F., *compiler*
1878 *Narodnye pesni Galitskoy i Ugorskoy Rusi*, part two: *Obryadovye pesni*. Moscow.

GULYAEV, S. I.
1848 *Ocherki Yuzhnoy Sibiri*. St. Petersburg.

KARADŽIĆ, VUK STEF, *compiler*
1841 *Srpske narodne pjesme*, volume one. I Beču.

KRAVTSOV, N. I., *editor*
1960 *Serbskiy epos*, volume two. Moscow.

KRUGLYASHOVA, V. P., *editor*
1967 *Fol'klor na rodine D. N. Mamina-Sibiryaka v ural'skom gornozavodskom poselke Visim*. Sverdlovsk.

OSININ, DM., *editor*
1961 *B"lgarsko narodno tvorchestvo*, volume two: *Khayadushki pesni*. Sofia.

OSININ, DM., ELENA OGNYANOVA, *editors*
1962 *B"lgarsko narodno tvorchestvo*, volume seven: *Semeyino-bytovi pesni*. Sofia.

Otechestvennye zapiski
1848 *Otechestvennye zapiski*, volume eight: *Smes'*. St. Petersburg.

POTEBNYA, A. A.
1866 *Pereprava cherez vodu, kak predstavlenie braka*. Moscow.

1870 *O nekotorykh simvolakh v slavyanskoy narodnoy poezii*. Kharkov.

SHAPOVALOVA, G. G.
1971 Vtoraya nauchnaya konferentsiya "Etnografiya i Fol'klor." *Sovetskaya Etnografiya* no. 6:166.

SHAYZHIN, N. S.
1911 "Olonetskiy fol'klor: pokhoronnye prichitaniya voplenitsy N. S. Bogdanovoy," in *Pamyatnaya knizhka Olonetskoy gubernii na 1911 god*. Petrozavodsk.

SHEIN, P. V., *compiler*
1898 *Velikorus' v svoikh pesnyakh, obychayakh, verovaniyakh, skazaniyakh, legendakh i t.p.*, two volumes. St. Petersburg.

SOBOLEVSKIY, A. I., *compiler*
1896 *Velikorusskie narodnye pesni*, volume two. St. Petersburg.
1897 *Velikorusskie narodnye pesni*, volume three. St. Petersburg.
1899 *Velikorusskie narodnye pesni*, volume five. St. Petersburg.

SOKOLOV, BORIS, YURI SOKOLOV, *transcribers*
1915 *Skazki i pesni Belozerskogo kraya*. Moscow.

SUŠIL, F.
1951 *Moravské národní písně*. Prague.

VAKARELSKI, KHR., *editor*
1961 *B"lgarsko narodno tvorchestvo*, volume three: *Istoricheski pesni*. Sofia.

The Baltic Origin and Developmental Tendencies of Latvian Dance

HARRY SŪNA

Latvian dance offers reliable insight into the oldest genre of folk creative art — choreography, based on the primitive inclination to release one's feelings freely in unusual, rhythmic movements — and into one of its earliest branches, the Baltic. Pronounced primitive Baltic features persisted in Latvian choreography up to the beginning of the 19th century, their preservation fostered by the national isolation established by foreign oppressors. This heritage is now one of the most important sources for an understanding of the general regularities of the development of choreographic processes. Latvian choreographic folklore, together with the evidence of linguistics, archaeology, ethnography, and folklore of other kinds, permits an approach to a number of important questions.

Before considering the beginnings of Latvian dance, it seems worthwhile to have a closer look at the semantics and etymology of words denoting the process of dancing. An Indo-European stem, *dei-*, *doi-*,[1] underlies the ancient Latvian words *diet* [to dance, to leap, to dance and leap while singing] and *dīdīt* [to dance with somebody, to make somebody dance] and the Lithuanian words *daina* [a song, a dance song, a secular song] and *daināt* [to dance and sing simultaneously]. The ancient Latvian words *lēkt, rotāt, līgot, rakstīt, dižāt*, and *daudzināt*[2] are also sometimes used.

[1] Mancelius (1638); Langijs (1685:49–50); Mīlenbahs (1923–1932: vol. 1, pp. 477, 483; vol. 4, p. 81); Endzelīns and Hauzenberga (1934–1938: vol. 1, pp. 19, 79); Lautenbakh″ (1896:110); Zēvers (1927:14); Slaviūnas (1971:22); Duridanov (1969:94).

[2] Sirmais (1891); Vol'ter (1890:216); Jurjāns (1894–1921: vol. 1, pp. 5–6); Kasparsons (1937:20–21); Melngailis (1949:13); Endzelīns and Klaustiņš (1928–1932: vol. 1, 2293); Barons and Visendorfs (1894–1915:21167); Manuscripts of the Folklore Department, Institute of Language and Literature, Latvian Academy of Sciences 1954,2308; 1955,4007 and 4011; 1600,10170; 2000,816 and 756; 1107,209; 464,8591; 867,2154; 1400,703; 1965,1177; 1955,12253; 353,6328; Bb 30,581.

These words are indirect evidence that Baltic dancing has been accompanied by singing for a very long time. The same conclusion may also be drawn from the great number of Latvian dancing songs.

In the seventeenth century, the loanwords *dancis*, *dancot* [to dance], *dancināt*[3] penetrated into Latvian choreographic folklore, originally being used to denote some form of performance unknown to the Latvians (probably plot-related events and the closed position of two partners). The words *dancis*, *dancot*, *riņķa dancis* became especially widespread at the beginning of the nineteenth century, when international choreography rapidly penetrated into the everyday social life of Latvian peasants. The words *dejot* [to dance], *deja* appeared only later,[4] with the introduction of the international ballroom dance. In folksongs connected with the dance and in songs about dancing, for good reason we find almost exclusively *diet, dancot*, and their derivatives, only very rarely *dejot* or *rotaļās iet* [to sing and dance in a ring]. Although it is still impossible to determine in exactly what chronological succession these words (in particular, *diet* and *Hrotaļa*) entered the language, the rich material inherited from the past permits us to assume that some more ancient basic stratum is represented by the original name of dancing, *diet*.

Information on the history of Latvian choreography is to be found in written accounts, limited and often biased, published by foreigners in the sixteenth century.[5] It is easy to see from this evidence that Latvian choreographic and other creative art had been preserved intact since before the invasion of the German Crusaders in the thirteenth century and had acquired distinctive artistic form. Some kind of development was resumed after the restriction of serfdom in Vidzeme (1804) and especially after its abolition (in Kurzeme [1817], in Vidzeme [1819], in Latgale [1861]), when the Latvians were given a chance to broaden their contacts.

Rather reliable data on ancient Latvian creative arts (in particular, those of adornment) are presented by a wealth of archaeological material. The traditional association of adornment with dancing is reflected by the fact that *rotāt* means not only "to dance," but also "to decorate, to adorn."[6] The words *raksts, rakstīt* have two meanings as well ("adornment" and "dancing"). Thus the common ground for the two

[3] Mancelius (1638) gives both *diet* and *dancot*. Stender (1789a:34, 38) gives *dancat* [*tanzen*; to dance] and *diet* [*tanzen, hüpfen, frohlocken*; to dance, to jump, to rejoice]. It is significant that Langijs (1685) does not mention *dancis* or *dancot* at all. See Mīlenbahs (1923–1932:vol. 1, pp. 436–437), Endzelīns and Hauzenberga (1934–1938:vol. 1, p. 17).

[4] Mīlenbahs (1923–1932: vol. 1, p. 453).

[5] Russow (1848[1584]), Mannhardt (1936), Stribing (1606), Einhorn (1848[1636], 1848 [1649]).

[6] Langijs (1685:222); Mīlenbahs (1923–1932:vol. 1, p. 791; vol. 3, pp. 583–584); Endzelīns and Hauzenberga 1934–1938:vol. 2, p. 393): Jurjāns (1894–1921:vol. 2, p. 45); Melngailis (1949:13); Breidaks (1969); Barons and Visendorfs (1894–1915: 29229,5;21618; 27671,2; 33981); *Tautas dziesmas* (1936–1939: 54285); Manuscripts of the Folklore Department 2000,1237; 1954,4041.

meanings is emphasized.[7] It is important to know that dancers once arrayed themselves in elegant costumes. Having established the existence of certain parallels between various branches of creative art (adornment and dance) in a definite period of time, we can with more confidence date their common basic principles to a much earlier period.

Originally, the principle of equality ruled in the matter of adornment; men and women wore the same.[8] There is reason to believe that the most ancient Latvian dance form, in which males and females participated equally, making use of a common choreographic lexicon, is associated with this period. Later, adornments and decorations of different and richer patterns appeared. Perhaps, in conformity with the evolution of adornment, different types of dance also developed, based, as before, on the objective laws of the structure of choreographic processes of mixed content. By the first millennium A.D., there were not only different adornments for men and women (women having more), but also differences based on wealth.[9]

There is reason to believe that the choreographic creative art included, along with round dances, dances with a fixed number of dancers in a particular arrangement, mainly in twos and fours. The song accompaniment corresponded to the square structure of the choreographic setup; indirect evidence of this may be found in the first printed folk songs, from the seventeenth century.[10] With more confidence we may assert that the choral (collective) dance in which all the participants in a celebration, after having had a drink, danced around trees, as observed by the Jesuit J. Stribing in the Ludza and Rēzekne regions in 1606,[11] had been inherited from much earlier.

During the years of German domination, development ceased both in folk choreography and in adornment. The traditional form of adornment which had originated in earlier centuries was preserved, with concentration on its most characteristic elements. Thus, for instance, the details of *sakta* [brooches] and *villaine* [large woolen shawls] have a twelve-hundred-year-old tradition (for example, eight-century *villaine* from Kivti are comparable with nineteenth-century ones from Alsunga, Kuldīga, and Ventspils).[12] Just as in adornment the influence of Western

[7] Barons and Visendorfs (1894–1915:474; 474,2; 473; 475; 476; 477; 472; 5707,4; 7187; 7192; 18414; 28778,1; *Izglītības Ministrijas Mēnešraksts* (1927(7–8):3;1925(5): 513; Lasmane (1962:51); Manuscripts of the Folklore Department Archives 170, 1337 and 204; 1954,240; 200,1307; 1955,6393; 1673,154; 1502,2437; 94,1461; 527,26253; 1638,5002; 961,2963; 1673,154; 872,2143; 1719,3647; 1441, 51; 1400,24556; 2000,458 and 464; 2000,1370 and 1054; 1726,2455 and 733; 1730,77819; *Latviešu tautasdziesmas* (1955–1957:vol. 1, 4210, 4159; vol. 3, 4420); Jansons (1970:505,221; 477); Greble (1959:60); Jurjāns (1894–1921:vol. 3, p. 8); Riga Latvian Society vol. 16, p. 82.

[8] Vasks and Rozenberga (1971:3–4).

[9] Loze and Graudonis (1970), Urtāns (1970), Zariņa (1970).

[10] Menii (1632:43–47).

[11] Stribing (1606:441–443).

[12] Urtāns (1970:75).

European styles is expressed mainly in pattern and decorative details,[13] so also in folk choreography kindred patterned (plotless) processes and their choreographic means of expression were assimilated.

Although the rich records of Latvian folklore, amounting to more than 2,800,000 items (including more than 1,200,000 songs, more than 25,000 accounts of choreographic and game processes, and more than 28,000 entries of instrumental music, and in particular more than 100,000 dance tunes, dance songs, and songs on dancing) refer to the moment when they were recorded, all folklore compositions include material inherited from earlier times. Written materials, as well as archaeological and ethnographical data, have confirmed the antiquity of the view of life reflected in folklore and the veracity of that reflection.

The treasury of folklore clearly shows, firstly, that the Latvian people had their times for labor as well as their times for joyful dancing and feasting. Ancient Latvian songs criticized those who spent their time dancing at the expense of labor.[14] The fact that no process can be found in dance with a plot related to labor also testifies to the incompatibility of the choreographic creative art with labor.

Folklore data also show that the inclination to dance achieved its complete fulfillment in dancing with partners whether of the same or opposite sex and whether strangers or relatives (mother danced with her son and daughter, father with his son and daughter, brother with sister).[15] Although in most cases the partners were of the same age (as a rule, they were young), the young often danced with older people (in particular, at weddings).[16] Foreigners have considered this phenomenon characteristic of the Latvians.[17] It is not difficult to see in this kind of performance a primitive inclination of mankind toward dancing that has nothing in common with biological motives. The child, in its fondness for dancing, comes to obey other rules as well only after reaching a certain stage of development.

Folklore shows, further, that almost everyone must have been able to

[13] Vasks and Rozenberga (1971:3–4).

[14] *Latviešu tautasdziesmas* (1955–1957:vol. 3, 7628); Manuscripts of the Folklore Department Archives 1940,5842; 1722,8135; 2000,468 and 470; 740,24732; 1711,1517; 1954,1003; 57,727; 1975,3122; 1341,29766; 1341,29765; 1208,7556; 596,1585; 1377,1288;1730,44249; 1597,5189; 1043,233; 1975,3134; 935,13826; 1311,10958; 279,3789; 17,29888; 1730,2287 and 64015; 1368,1138; 1950,3893; 1532,1364; 1800,250; 321,7; 740,17306; 1730,66922; 1935,7909; 929,6823; 1414,444; 693,2750; 931,1610; 238,407; 1913,21; 1393,3065; 1148,2291; 166,3222.

[15] *Tautas dziesmas* (1936–1939:47179, 47254); Manuscripts of the Folklore Department Archives 1638,5425; 1955,12204; 459,577; 530,2371; 1955,12167 and 12230; 1705,2411; 1930,2629; 1207,4218; 1860,2448; 1225,32402; 929,67796; 97,305; 1955,4344; 910,5002; 1860,2448.

[16] Manuscripts of the Folklore Department Archives 1730,3454; 802,136; 90,420; 527,30484; 1238,1893; 880,2911; 72,13271; 1400,654; 72,11127; 303,242; 1930,2075; 1805,9371; 527,15474; 1840,626; 929,36577.

[17] Hupel (1777:134), Petri (1809:533–535), de Bray (1817:103–104).

perform his or her tribal dance. This is obvious in the case of weddings, in particular, where, if the bride came from another place, her relatives and those of the bridegroom danced in different ways.[18] No doubt this reflects ethnic differences between regions.

We can also conclude from the folklore that, regardless of the themes of songs accompanying dances, people took to singing under various pretexts. There are more than 300,000 variants of songs on the life of Latvian peasants whose meter corresponds to the choreographic rhythm (trochee and dactyl). Obviously, the choreographic rhythm is the basis of both the tune and the meter of the accompanying song. An insight into this situation is offered by the experience of the German priest G. F. Stender, who worked in Zemgale in the eighteenth century. Stender considered the Latvian choreographic creative art, which included songs with different texts and tunes but the same metric rhythm and lacking any plot, unforgivably primitive. To put an end to this "pitiful backwardness," he attempted to introduce German collective rounds and round dances illustrating the text of a song.[19] Though collective rounds were adopted, however, his efforts in the field of social-functional dance were unsuccessful.[20] Social-functional dance still does not involve any plot, and it is still the rhythmic basis for tunes and songs popular among the broad masses. Now as before, it has no dramatic character.

Dance is closely connected with festivities and feasts. Archaeologists have established the existence of festive traditions as far back as the third century A.D.[21] Folk choreography became more and more subject to the rules of ritual.

Latvian folk songs indicate that the gaiety of feasts reached its culmination in the wedding. If the young husband could not brew beer because of crop failure, the wedding was postponed. There is good reason that the expression *kāzas dzert* [literally, to drink wedding] has taken deep root in the people's vocabulary. It is significant that in folk songs the words *dzīrot, līksmot*, *diet*, and *dancot* [to feast, to dance] are often used with the same meaning. A deeper sense may also be seen in the fact that, in songs with a wedding plot, the events connected directly with dancing become central ones. It is emphasized in songs that those who did not dance were not invited to the wedding at all.[22] The most widespread dance song, not

[18] Manuscripts of the Folklore Department Archives 1935,1456; 1730,77069; 1400,412; 62,368; 214,573; 2000,1146 and 1149; 2000,1144; 880,3201; 1661;4832; 958,5495; 1326,34.

[19] Stender (1789b:49–89).

[20] The notion of *sadzīves horeogrāfija* (social-functional choreography) denotes all the dance-like behaviors existing in the social life of Latvian peasants, as distinct from those arising from the demands of a stage performance.

[21] Urtāns (1970:64).

[22] Barons and Visendorfs (1894–1915:2546); Endzelīns and Klaustiņš (1928–1932:vol. 1, 3764).

only at weddings, but also at other family and seasonal celebrations, was the one which told about the ability to dance. (There are hundreds of variants of such songs, for instance, "Māku diet, māku lēkt" [I can dance, I can leap], "Dieti, lēkti es mācēju" [I could dance and leap], "Es mācēju dieti vest" [I could dance], "Es mācēju danci vest" [I could dance], "Dancot māku, dziedāt māku" [I can dance, I can sing].

These songs are associated with earlier choreographic procedures. All the participants in the festivity, arranged in row and circle (*dārziņā*), take part in them. Later, on the basis of this type, processes arise in which an unlimited number of pairs in closed position dances in a circle. Of dances of this type, the most popular are "Līkumu dancis" [Winding Dance], "Garais dancis" [Long Dance], "Cimdu dancis" [Mitten Dance], and "Polis" [The Pole]. Besides, the repertoire of wedding dances includes other choreographic types. Processes may be performed by pairs in even numbers, by a particular number of pairs (two, three, four, or more), or by a particular number of participants (three, five, or nine). The borrowed circular dances with an unlimited number of pairs, as well as processes of the quadrille type,[23] are superimposed on ancient dances having an unlimited number of pairs or having two or four. A great many songs directly connected with this patterned way of dancing have been gathered.[24]

The Latvians celebrated weddings for several days (in this connection, the number three has been often mentioned). If we are to believe the biased old publications by foreigners, people would drink inordinately day in and day out, dance wildly, and sing indecently.[25] We have no evidence that the content of the indecent songs related to wedding traditions (and of songs of this type in general), and formerly connected with dancing, was reflected in dance movements. This suggests that erotic dances were alien to Latvian choreography. A friend of the Latvians, a German by birth, G. Merķelis, wrote in 1796 that it was at weddings that the earliest stage of Latvian culture — prehistoric primitivism — was most pronounced. He reported: "The Latvians at weddings dance and sing for several days running, accompanied by the sounds of strings and bagpipes."[26]

Dance occupied a special place in the baptism ceremony in Kurzeme. The choreographic process here was connected with the rocking of the *pāde* [godchild] while the godparents sang to it. The belief was that the appearance and the character of the godparents and in particular their skill at rocking the godchild determined all its future life. Only the most venerable people of the neighborhood could become godparents — those

[23] Jurjāns (1894–1921:vol. 4), Rinks and Ošs (1934–1936), Stumbris (1938–1940), Lasmane (1962), Sūna (1966a, 1970).
[24] Barons and Visendorfs (1894–1915:vol. 3, pp. 391–413).
[25] Einhorn (1848[1649]; 594).
[26] Merķelis (1953[1796]:44–45).

who were able to dance and rock the godchild well, dressed well, and had shapely figures and excellent manners. As a rule, several godparents were chosen. The first to rock the godchild was the most skillful of the godparents (if a boy was to be rocked, a godfather began it; if a girl, a godmother). Later the godchild was rocked by the others. Everybody rocked it in a different way, singing a wish for the child's future life. As the folklore materials show, the dance steps and the structure of the dance, as in other processes accompanied by songs, were originally subjected to the patterned choreographic schemes of string, circle, and row. The godparents (like the dancers in other celebrations) would dance in a string, not only indoors, but also outside where they would go winding across the yard and through the farmstead. In the course of time, the rocking of the godchild penetrated so far into the ethnographic field that it ceased to exist as a choreographic creative art, and gesticulation corresponding to the text of the song came to dominate. It is significant that soon afterward the ritual of rocking the godchild itself disappeared.[27]

In other regions (Zemgale, Vidzeme, Latgale), the godparents participate in patterned processes but as a rule do not rock the godchild. Sometimes the godparents are joined in their dance by the rest of the guests, dancing in the same way as in other family celebrations and festivities. It is no accident that in all regions it is the godparents who are invited to be *vedēji* [masters of ceremonies] at weddings.

In the choreographic processes connected with the funeral, tramping is a notable feature and one that shares some elements with wedding dances. Rather widespread in funerals are the so-called collective rounds of *vāķēšana* (the relatives of the deceased keeping watch over the corpse so that the spirit cannot leave it and enter someone still living). The word for collective rounds and round dance, *rotaļa*, is as a rule connected not only with choreography, but also with the round-game genre.[28] Lithuanian choreographologists use the word *rataliai* to denote processes belonging solely to the choreographic genre.[29] Some Latvian musical experts link *rotaļa* with the words *rotāt, rotāšana*.[30] The choreographic processes of *vāķēšana* have two forms. The first of them structurally has elements in common with the choreographic type most widespread in and most characteristic of Latvian creative art, a process in which an unlimited number of participants moves in a circle to the right or to the left,

[27] Barons and Visendorfs (1894–1915: vol. 1, pp. 171–195, 258–269); Riga Latvian Society vol. 2, pp. 52–54; vol. 19, pp. 154–156; Siliņa (1939:51–54); Vītoliņš (1970:11–16, 49–58); Greble (1959:86); *Izglītības Ministrijas Mēnešraksts* 1920(7):44; Endzelīns and Klaustiņš 1928–1932:vol. 1, 2362, 2329); Manuscripts of the Folklore Department Archives 1090,2; 1271,462; 1955,5787 and 4196; 1715,400.

[28] Sams and Tarziers (1890), Rūjienietis (1886), Barons and Visendorfs (1894–1915: vol. 5, pp. 195–242), Šēnfelde (1922), Melnalksnis (1931), Ošs, Rinks, and Slavietis (1937), Ķirkums (1937), Žeibe et al. (1958).

[29] Linigs, Slaviūnas, and Yakelaytis (1955:40–41), Morkūnienė (1970; 1971:2).

[30] Melngailis (1949:13), Jujāns (1894–1921:51; 1893).

around one or two participants in the center and which is connected with its song accompaniment only metrorhythmically. It is significant that a round dance of this type, "Kumeliņi, kumeliņi," frequently performed at all seasons, is also performed at funerals.[31] Sometimes the participants in the round dance proceed around the dead person too.[32] The earliest evidence of funeral ceremonies, in particular those of burial, provided by archaeological excavations, suggests that graves were marked by walking or dancing around them.[33] Attention should be paid to the parallel between the disposition of burials at the beginning of our era (a number of graves arranged around one central one) and the fact that in the second-to-fourth-century-A.D. cemetery of Rucavas Mazkatužu men, women, and children were buried in rows, while the Sēļi and Latgaļi in the third to ninth century buried their dead first in circles and later in rows. At Lejasbitēni and Boķi, the dead were buried in rows from the eighth or ninth century.[34]

The second *vāķēšana* form differs from the first not only in having a plot, which often penetrates into the round-game genre, but also in including a borrowed performance in which the action is not connected with the metrorhythm of the tune, but is subjected to the text (the participants illustrate the text of a song previously learned.[35]

An ancient way of dancing have nothing in common with illustration also forms the basis of seasonal traditions.

Dancing at the Līgo (summer-solstice) festival in 1584 is mentioned by B. Russow[36] and is described in the 1654 book of sermons by G. Mancelius. According to the latter, the participants in the festivity decorate the gate and then make a bonfire near it which they jump over, singing, all night long, as at some weddings.[37] There is evidence that formerly on the night of Līgo, the summer solstice, the dancing itself was very significant. Extolling Jānis, the host (an action similar in its meaning to the baptism dance), the participants in the festivity would go round the yard in a "circle dance." There is no doubt that the widespread songs of Līgo were connected with the earliest choreographic processes for mixed groups. People danced not only around a bonfire, but also around an oak. From the yard, the dance continued into the house.[38] This way of dancing has

[31] Sūna (1966a: 12–13, 15–22, 146–148, 150–159, 577–581).
[32] Siliņa (1939:78).
[33] Loze and Graudonis (1970:37).
[34] Loze and Graudonis (1970:45), Urtāns (1970:68).
[35] Sūna (1966a:606–607); Siliņa (1939:76–78); Jurjāns (1894–1921:vol. 4, p. 13); Riga Latvian Society vol. 19, p. 160.
[36] Russow (1848[1584]:58–62).
[37] Mancelius (1654:45–46).
[38] Barons and Visendorfs (1894–1915:32852, 32865, 32606, 32918); *Tautas dziesmas* (1936–1939:53976); Manuscripts of the Folklore Department Archives 1975,1870; 1995,516; 1390,126.

elements in common with the widespread funeral, wedding, and baptism processes, in which the participants danced around all the places in which the person in question had been or would be in the future. It is significant that the phrase *kā līgot nolīgotas*[39] was used not only with reference to the Līgo festival, but also with reference to weddings. Both of these festivities in their choreographic conception are characterized by the mischievous tradition of *apdziedāšanās* (humorous singing about each other). Merķelis viewed the *apdziedāšanās* of the Līgo evening as related to dance movements.[40]

The celebration of the winter solstice was so closely connected with dancing and leaping that it was referred to as a time of continuous dance. It is significant that almost all choreographic processes and those kindred to the game genre were often called *ziemsvētku rotaļa* [winter-solstice collective rounds and round dances].[41]

The unrestrained mirth of the dancing typical of Latvians at the winter solstice was described by P. Einhorn, the superintendent in chief of Kurzeme in 1636, who said critically that the Latvians celebrated Christmas indecently — the characteristic features of this festivity being gluttony, drunkenness, dancing, leaping and shouting.[42] Not without reason, folk songs refer to the participants in the Christmas celebration as *danča bērni* [dance children].[43]

An integral part of the dances held in winter, at Mārtiņi (November 10), at Bārbalas (December 4), during the winter solstice, and at the end of February at Vastlāvis (Shrovetide), was masking.[44] Especially in *ķekatas* [masking ceremony], unusualness of disguise was stressed. Just as the best dancer was the one who could give to everyday walking, running, and jumping steps the pronounced features of a dance, so the best participant in *ķekatas* was the one one who could give everyday dress an unusual look. The hightest esteem was reserved for the one who suc-

[39] Manuscripts of the Folklore Department Archives 2000,1530 and 1497; 2000,1536 and 1494; Barons and Visendorfs (1894–1915:16070); *Izglītības Ministrijas Mēnešraksts* 1936(9):239.

[40] Merķelis (1953[1796]:73).

[41] Barons and Visendorfs (1894–1915:vol. 5, p. 195), Sūna (1966a:586–611).

[42] Einhorn (1848[1636]:622–623).

[43] Barons and Visendorfs (1894–1915:33304, 33331); *Latviešu tautasdziesmas* (1955–1957:vol. 3, 6733); Manuscripts of the Folklore Department Archives 1400,2675.

[44] Einhorn (1848[1649]:585); Stender (1783:261); *Latviešu Avīzes* 1853(9):33; *Ancient Latvians* 1865(7):53; *Mājas Viesis* 1874(3):21–22; Vol'ter (1890:98–109); Jurjāns (1894–1921:vol. 2, pp. 25–35); Lerhis-Puškaitis (1903:306); Pētersons (1928); Šperliņš 1937:159–161); *Izglītības Ministrijas Mēnešraksts* 1927(11):382–384; 1937(4):618; Siliņa (1939:91–93; Riga Latvian Society vol. 19, pp. 157–159; Barons and Visendorfs (1894–1915:33309–33553); *Latvijas PSR Zinātņu Akadēmijas Vēstis* p. 165; Jansons (1933:141); Līdeks (1940:9, 16–34; 1942:60–61); Arājs (1957); Ozols (1955); Greble (1959:99–100); Manuscripts of the Folklore Department Archives 910,1245 and 1244; 1955,955; 1945,928 and 1025; 1040,6750 and 6511; 1731,6861; 1968,3112; Bb 43,1850; 1090,2; 1954,365–370; 1965,285; *Dienas Lapa*, Ethnographic Supplement, 1893(3): 141.

ceeded in disguising himself so well that even members of his own household could not recognize him.

The basis of these processes is choreographic action and traditional rituals. The choreography is based mainly on tramping, running, and jumping steps which have elements in common with the steps of dances performed at family celebrations and seasonal festivities. Leaps, in particular, are not only an integral part of the choreographic processes, but also connected with religious beliefs. In this connection, one of the most widespread designations for the mask procession is *ķekatās lēkt* [to leap in *ķekatas*].[45]

Although the German landowners and priests fought the *ķekatas* with all the means at their disposal, it continued to occupy an important place in the everyday life of peasants up to the beginning of the twentieth century. This tradition existed alongside those of family festivities (uninvited masked guests also came to weddings and baptisms).[46]

In the rhythmic leaping of *ķekatas*, the same choreographic action is expressed as in dances of the string type, in which the participants go winding through the house, across the yard, and from the garden to the fields. Besides, the *ķekatas* process has elements in common with similar processes in celebration of the summer solstice. All the participants in *ķekatas* (like the participants in the baptism dance) subject the action of their characters to a common choreographic idea. The conflicts between characters that occur in the genre of games or in collective rounds do not appear in these dances. In a choreographic process with mixed groups, the following pairs dance peaceably: a horse with a bear, a goat with a wolf, a hare with a fox, a poor peasant with death, the tall wife with her dwarfish husband. Even in cases in which the action of some character becomes more marked, no new choreographic type arises; rather, the choreographic lexicon is simply enriched. As is shown by a great number of folk songs, Latvians have tried to dance like a horse, a bear, a fox, a grouse, a wagtail, a bee. It is significant that even the processes of the few dances named after the characters of *ķekatas* — "Cūku dancis" [Pig Dance], "Sivēntiņu dancis" [Dance of Piglets], "Gailis" [The Cock], "Nabagu dancis" [Beggars' Dance] — are patterned. Thus, for instance, some variants of the popular dance "Danco, lāci!" [Dance, Bear!] have something in common with a quadrille-type process. It is no accident that

[45] Langijs (1685:112); *Konverzācijas vārdnīca* (1908:1702); Pētersons (1928:15); Mīlenbahs (1923–1932:vol. 2, p. 361); Endzelīns and Hauzenberga (1934–1938:vol. 1, p. 693); *Filologu Biedrības Raksti* 20:129–133; Barons and Visendorfs (1894–1915:33458, 33460, 33459); *Tautas dziesmas* (1936–1939:vol. 3, 54542, 54550, 54535); *Latviešu tautasdziesmas* (1955–1957:vol. 3, 6851, 6928, 6925); Manuscripts of the Folklore Department Archives 1818,19 and 33.

[46] Manuscripts of the Folklore Department Archives 1968, 3112; 1955,12087–12302; 1730,55222; 387,7586; Līdeks (1940:17–18); *Tautas dziesmas* (1936–1939:59996; 5969; 59275,9); Barons and Visendorfs (1894–1915:26134, 24127, 24146); *Filologu Biedrības Raksti* 7:70.

the participants in *ķekatas* also perform dances typical of other festivities and celebrations — "Līkumu dancis" [Winding Dance], "Garais dancis" [Long Dance], and "Krusta dancis" [Cross Dance].[47]

The development of choreographic types was slowest in family celebrations, in which only invited guests participated and, as in the case of baptism, were often chosen particularly carefully. Development was more rapid in seasonal festivities and most rapid in public-house dances.

Up to the seventeenth century, there were few public houses in the territory of Latvia.[48] However, in the eighteenth century Merķelis writes that Latvians have an unfortunate inclination toward carousing in public houses. In many folk songs, too, it is said that people danced (caroused) recklessly in public houses almost every Sunday.[49] When dance shifted from the tiny peasants' houses to the rather spacious public-house premises, it assumed quite different scope. In the public-house dance, the partners were inclined toward a freer interpretation of the traditional processes and more boldly adopted the new choreographic lexicon of town dances, which was submitted to the patterning characteristic of their ancestors' choreographic idea. As is shown by many records of choreographic folklore, particularly those of dance songs, this process was extremely complicated. Even such now typically Latvian processes as the quadrille-type dances and, particularly, circling (for instance, the round polka) originally encountered resistance.[50] The phenomenon of borrowing conflicted with the centuries-old principle of equality, of not forcing one's will upon others.

In the second half of the nineteenth century, dance left the public-house premises and went outdoors in the *zaļumballe* [open-air ball]. Dances were accompanied not only by rural instrumental ensembles, but also by brass bands. The musicians were more and more required to take into consideration the dominant way of dancing and the demands of the dancers. In the course of time, dance freed itself completely of the dictates of family celebrations and seasonal traditions.

There are common features in the choreographic development of

[47] Jurjāns (1894–1921:vol. 4, p. 35); Rinks and Ošs (1934–1936:vol. 3, p. 18); *Latviešu tautasdziesmas* (1955–1957:84); Sūna (1966a:437–439, 618–619); Manuscripts of the Folklore Department Archives 880,2225 and 2228; 1995,955; 1969,278.

[48] Mancelius (1654:107); Zēvers (1923); *Izglītības Ministrijas Mēnešraksts* 5:548–549.

[49] Merķelis (1953[1796]:84–153); Sūna (1966a:8); *Tautas dziesmas* (1936–1939:56666, 56390); Riga Latvian Society vol. 20, pp. 55, 71; *Latviešu tautasdziesmas* (1955–1957:vol. 3, 1225); Manuscripts of the Folklore Department Archives 910,4689; 1954,2367; 1305,1352; 1090,32; 1950,8231; 1699,106; 1730,20642; 1269,992; 1602,1685; 1730,76938; 1276,550; 668,1113; 1730,58446 and 45232; 796,17707; 17,29223.

[50] Barons and Visendorfs (1894–1915:24072); *Tautas dziesmas* (1936–1939:47217); Sūna (1970:129); Manuscripts of the Folklore Department Archives 170,2087; 828,5466; 353,2196; 668,5148 and 8974; 328,74.

older and younger strata of the social-functional dance of Latvian peasants. These features are typical both of the choreographic culture of Latvian everyday life in general and its separate types (folk choreography, old ballroom dance, modern ballroom dance) and of the different subgenres of folk choreography (dance, round dance, collective rounds).

As social-functional choreography was constrained either by the plot of the accompanying song, by didactic considerations, or by beliefs denying the equality of all participants in the choreographic process and subjecting the common choreographic idea to the cult of some other person or thing, it was modified to such an extent that a qualitatively different form — old ballroom dance — emerged. This, in the course of further development, was replaced by modern ballroom dance, in which the couple does not submit to a common picture of the dance, the woman partner becoming increasingly free of the man's movements in closed position. One must not overlook the fact that in the final stages of folk-dance development and at the beginning of old ballroom dancing, urban clothing replaced folk costume and ancient decoration in the peasants' social life.

The developmental tendencies of Latvian dance share some elements with those of the choreographic creative art of both kindred nations and other neighbors. Unfortunately, at present this problem cannot be strictly scientifically studied, for the choreographologists of different countries have neither a common research method and model for choreographic comparison nor the most basic prerequisite — a standard system of notation like that developed by musicians.[51] Since without comparison it is practically impossible to come to a clear conception of the processes of formation and development of the most characteristic choreographic types, we must try to compare verbal recordings of choreographic folklore with similar recordings made in neighboring nations and with more or less sound graphic choreographic notations from different countries and different times.

In the process of studying various systems of choreographic notation, differences have been found between the oldest and those of the twentieth century.[52] Since "choreography" originally meant the record of a dance (a fixed one), it is especially important to analyze the processes recorded in the course of these more than three centuries. Having investigated these processes, I have come to the conclusion that it is easier (and, simultaneously, most logical) to record only choreographic actions, not

[51] Sūna (1970; 1964:58–71; 1965a; 1971), Gumenyuk (1964).

[52] Arbeau (1967), Feuillet (1700), Laban (1956), Hutchinson (1954), Lisitsian (1940), Causley and Benesh (1967), Sūna (1965b, 1966b, 1966c), *Sistemul* (1965), Haskell (1960:60–75).

those which include movements of other genres (games, pantomime, acrobatics, sports).

The development of the dance is rooted mainly in the process of enrichment of the choreographic lexicon. As is shown by comparison of the dance of Latvians, Lithuanians, and others and by the evolution of systems of choreographic notation, the enrichment of the lexicon is closely connected with the development of the structure of the dance. This structure (which is marked in choreographic notations as the horizontal dimension of the process) may be similar for several nations. For instance, the dance "Zaglis" [Thief] has a similar figurative picture for Latvians, Estonians, Lithuanians, Germans, and others, while the choreographic lexicon (which is marked in choreographic notations as the vertical dimension of the process) differs. These different means of expression, based on the steps of the dance, are at the basis of the choreographic lexicon of every nation. It is no mere chance that the steps — the basis of the dance art — are reflected in choreographic notations in both dimensions.

Taking as a basis the logical laws of choreographic development, we can more safely consider the problem discussed by choreographologists most of all — the origins of choreographic creative art, and especially the question whether it is rooted in mythology. If choreographic creative art only appears simultaneously with traditions, then does it correspond to every ritual expressing family and seasonal traditions? In folk songs, the saying goes: "*Kādu godu svin, tādu dziesmu dzied*" [Every festivity has its own song].[53] It is significant, however, that there is no such saying about dancing. Further light might be thrown upon this problem by considering phenomena connected with certain widespread beliefs.

In Latvia, the attention of researchers has been attracted by beliefs connected with the number three, for neither family nor seasonal rituals seem to be able to do without it. Folklore also to some extent stresses this number. Of the subgenres of folk choreography, collective rounds show it most, the round dance less, and dance least of all. This fact is based on the objective laws associated with the very origin of the creative art. Not without reason, in those rare cases in which the ancient traditional square structure was subjected to the number three, alien to the choreography (during the quatrain participants would dance around the area three times), the basic structure of the choreographic type was destroyed. It is important to remember that the choreographic scheme corresponding to the demands of the number three did not take root. It is significant also that the most stable and widespread two-part choreographic

[53] Manuscripts of the Folklore Department Archives 1563,263; 1954,828; *Izglītības Ministrijas Mēnešraksts* 10:298.

type shares elements with the no less widespread patterned type.[54]

In the oldest Latvian mythological folk songs, the deities (Saule, Saules meitas, Dieva dēli, Pērkons, Laima, Ūsiņš, Tenis, Jumis, Veļu māte, Smilšu māte, etc.) are widely sung about as outstanding dancers. This shows clearly that the Latvians imparted to their most precious beings all the properties most important to themselves. No doubt, the art of dancing already existed at the time of composition of the folk songs, for one can give to others only what one possesses oneself. Furthermore, the dance served to express joy (not only the Sun, but also the severe, morose Veļu māte, dances joyfully).[55]

When investigating the origins of choreographic creative art, we cannot ignore so essential a feature as choreographic rhythm, which is based on the step pattern of primitive dancing, for to this day countless accompanying tunes and songs develop in accordance with the choreographic rhythm of social-funtional dance. In this connection, it is important to remember that the Lithuanian scientists Slavyūnas and Morkūnienė consider the so-called *sutartines dejas (Sutartinių šokiai)* — an especially distinctive genre in Lithuanian folk choreography, formerly performed only by women in groups of four, three, or two (depending on the number of voices required by the polyphonic melody) — to be the most ancient layer of Lithuanian choreographic folklore. Although they speak of the primitive syncretism of the *sutartine* song and the choreographic process and the complete harmony of their forms, only the metrorhythmic synchronism of the polyphonic melody of the *sutartine* song and that of the patterned development of other choreographic types is obvious.[56]

It seems sensible to recall here that in Latvian folk songs there are many lines devoted to the pattern of steps as well as to that most ancient accompanying instrument, the drum (when performing songs of Līgo, the drums are beaten by Jānis himself), and also to the fact that good dancers need no musician because *viņu kājas pašas bungas* [their feet themselves beat drums] and *mute* [voice] joins *raksts* [the rhythm of steps].[57] Latvian musical experts consider the so-called spoken-type songs, which sometimes become quite similar to rhythmic speech, to be extremely old, especially because the most ancient songs of *abdziedāšanās* were

[54] Dzērvītis and Ginters (1936), Karnups (1939), Slava (1966), *Latviešu tautas māksla* (1967), *Latviešu tautas tērpi* (1967), Ivanova and Madre (1968), Zariņa (1970).

[55] Ozols (1955:45–47); Kokare (1959:18); Barons and Visendorfs (1894–1915: 30213,2; 29199; 30875; 5007; 16095; 33747; 265,4–6; 32865,3; 26063,1; 33992; 33924; 27537–27540; 27799; *Tautas dziesmas* (1936–1939:54330, 50246, 49489, 49428); Endzelīns and Klaustiņš 1928–1932: vol. 9, 1227; vol. 10,3761: *Latviešu tautasdziesmas* (1955–1957:vol. 3, 7831, 6489, 6488, 6483); Vol'ter (1890:117); Manuscripts of the Folklore Department Archives 442,806; 1242,5690; 1730,39913; 548,9867; 1351,1512; 1926,422; 1400,2387; 935,8835; 1660,4293.

[56] Slaviūnas (1959, 1971), Morkūniene (1971:2–10).

[57] Barons and Visendorfs (1894–1915:33558); Manuscripts of the Folklore Department Archives 958,4104; 1259,100; 1400,7464; 1730,38934; 418,4251; 828,11872; 1276,550.

of this type, and, in all regions, the *trejdeksnis* [a percussion instrument with bronze pendants] was always an integral part of their syncretic performance.[58]

There is reason to believe that in ancient Baltic choreographic folk lore the rhythm of the patterned development had the decisive role. Dance rhythm is the basis of the ancient melodies and songs of other nations as well (as is particularly clearly seen in the creative art of African peoples).

Having investigated the developmental trends of Latvian dance and compared them to some extent with the choreographic evolution of other nations, we may conclude that types of social-functional dance change, die out, or are reshaped as certain of their essential features disappear or change. The Latvian traditional mixed-type patterned dances that have endured the test of the time are those that reflect relations of the partners based on the principle of equality.

REFERENCES

ARĀJS, K.
1957 "Senās latviešu gadskārtu ieražas," in *Latviešu tautasdziesmas*, volume one, 627–641.

ARBEAU, T.
1967 *Orchesography*. New York.

BARONS, K., H. VISENDORFS
1894–1915 *Latvju dainas*, five volumes. Jelgava (volume one), St. Petersburg (volumes two through five).

BREIDAKS, A.
1969 Latgaļu, sēļu un kuršu cilšu valodu sakari. *Latvijas PSR Zinātņu Akadēmijas Vēstis* 9:46–48.

CAUSLEY, M., R. BENESH
1967 *Benesh movement notation*. London.

DE BRAY, LE COMTE
1817 *Essay critique sur l'histoire de la Livonie*, volume three. Dorpat.

DURIDANOV, I.
1969 *Thrakisch-dakische studien: de thrakisch und dakisch-baltischen Sprachbeziehungen*. Sofia.

DZĒRVĪTIS, A., V. GINTERS
1936 *Ievads latviešu tautas tērpu vēsturē*. Riga.

EINHORN, P.
1848[1636] "Reformatio gentis Letticae in Ducatu Curlandiae," in *Scriptores rerum livonicarum*, volume two. Riga and Leipzig.
1848[1649] "Historia Lettica: Dorpat in Liefland," in *Scriptores rerum livonicarum*, volume two. Riga and Leipzig.

ENDZELĪNS, J., E. HAUZENBERGA
1934–1938 *Papildinājumi un labojumi K. Mīlenbaha Latviešu valodas vārdnīcai*, two volumes. Riga.

ENDZELĪNS, J., R. KLAUSTIŅŠ
1928–1932 *Latvju tautas dainas*, twelve volumes. Riga.

[58] Jurjāns (1894–1921:vol. 3, pp. 7–9).

FEUILLET, R.
1700 *Chorégraphie: on l'art de décrire la danse*. Paris.
GREBLE, V.
1959 Tautasdziesmas. *Latviešu Literatūras Vēsture* 1.
GUMENYUK, A. I.
1964 Zapis i printsipi klasifikatsiy narodnikh tantsiv. *Narodna Tvorchistv ta Etnografiya* 4:37–42.
HASKELL, A. L.
1960 *The story of dance*. London.
HUPEL, A. W.
1777 *Topographische Nachrichten von Lief- und Ehstland*, volume two. Riga.
HUTCHINSON, A.
1954 *Labanotation: The system for recording movement*. New York.
IVANOVA, G., I. MADRE
1968 *Jostu raksti*. Riga.
JANSONS, J. A.
1933 *Die lettischen Maskenumzüge*. Riga.
1970 *Dailes lokā*. Riga.
JURJĀNS, A.
1893 Latvju rotāšana. *Dienas Lapa*, Ethnographic Supplement, pp. 85–88.
1894–1921 *Latvju tautas mūzikas materiāli*, five volumes. Riga.
KARNUPS, A.
1939 *Novadu tērpi*. Jelgava.
KASPARSONS, K.
1937 Refrēni "līgo!" un "rūto!" *Filologu Biedrības Raksti* 17.
ĶIRKUMS, R.
1937 *Jaunākais rotaļnieks*. Cēsis.
KOKARE, E.
1959 Latviešu folklora. *Latviešu Literatūras Vēsture* 1.
Konverzācijas vārdnīca
1908 *Konverzācijas vārdnīca*, volume two. Riga.
LABAN, R.
1956 *Principles of dance and movement notation*. London.
LANGIJS, J.
1685 *Latviski-vāciska vārdnīca*. Riga.
LASMANE, M.
1962 *Latviešu tautas dejas*. Riga.
Latviešu tautasdziesmas
1955–1957 *Latviešu tautasdziesmas*, three volumes. Riga.
Latviešu tautas māksla
1967 *Latviešu tautas māksla*, volume three. Riga.
Latviešu tautas tērpi
1966 *Latvišu tautas tērpi*. Riga.
LAUTENBAKH, YA.
1896 *Ocherki iz" istorii literatury latyshskago narodnago tvorchestva*, volume one. Yur'yev.
LERHIS-PUŠKAITIS, A.
1903 *Latviešu tautas teikas un pasakas*, volume 7. Cēsis.
LĪDEKS, O.
1940 *Latviešu svētki*. Riga.
1942 *Latviešu svinamās dienas*. Riga.

LINGIS, YU., Z. SLAVIŪNAS, V. YAKELAYTIS
1955 *Litovskiye narodnye tantsy* (second edition, enlarged). Vilnius.
LISITSIAN, S.
1940 *Zapis' dvizheniya (kinetografiya)*. Moscow–Leningrad.
LOZE, I., J. GRAUDONIS
1970 Apbedīšanas tradīcijas Latvijā pirmatnējās kopienas laikā. *Arkehologija un Etnogrāfija* 9:31–59.
MANCELIUS, G.
1638 *Lettus*. Riga.
1654 *Lang-gewünschte Lettische Postill*. Riga.
MANNHARDT, W.
1936 Letto-Preussische Götterlehre. *Magazin der Lettisch-Literärischen Gesellschaft* 21:441–443.
MELNALKSNIS, A.
1931 *Rotaļas*. Riga.
MELNGAILIS, E.
1949 *Latviešu dancis*. Riga.
MENII, F.
1632 *Syntagma de origine livonorum*. Dorpat.
MERĶELIS, G.
1953[1796] *Latvieši*. Riga.
MĪLENBAHS, K.
1923–1932 *Latviešu valodas vārdnīca*, four volumes. Riga.
MORKŪNIENĖ, E.
1970 Lietuviu liaudies choreografijos klasifikacija. *Lietuvos TSR Mokslų Akademijos Darbai*, serija A, 1:163–181.
1971 *Cherty litovskoy narodnoy khoreografii tantsa XIX-nachala XX v.v.* Vilnius.
OŠS, J., J. RINKS, J. SLAVIETIS
1937 *Rotaļnieks*. Riga.
OZOLS, A.
1955 "Par latviešu tautasdziesmām," in *Latviešu tautasdziesmas*, volume 1, 3–50.
PĒTERSONS, K.
1928 Ķekatās iet (lekt). *Filologu Biedrības Raksti* 2:15–20.
PETRI, J. CH.
1809 *Neuestes Gemälde von Lief- und Ehstland unter Katharina II und Alexander I in historischer, statistischer, politischer und merkantilischer Ansicht*, volume one. Leipzig.
RINKS, J., J. OŠS
1934–1936 *Latvju tautas dejas*, four volumes. Riga.
RŪJIENIETIS, L.
1886 *Rotaļnieks*. Riga.
RUSSOW, B.
1848[1584] "Chronica der Provintz Lyfflandt," in *Scriptores rerum livonicarum*, volume two. Riga and Leipzig.
SAMS, V., K. TARZIERS
1890 *Rotaļas mājai un skolai*. Valmiera.
ŠĒNFELDE, A.
1922 *Rotaļu pūrs*. Riga.
SILIŅA, E.
1939 *Latviešu deja*. Riga.

SIRMAIS, J.
1891 No kurienes cēlušies vārdi "līgo" un "līgava"? *Dienas Lapa*, Ethnographic Supplement, p. 61.

Sistemul stenografic
1965 *Sistemul stenografic pentru notarea dansuribor "Gh. Baciu."* Bucharest.

SLAVA, M.
1966 *Latviešu tautas tērpi*. Riga.

SLAVIŪNAS, Z.
1959 *Sutartinēs*, volume three. Vilnius.
1971 *Tantsy-Sutartine, problemy ikh vozrasta, primeneniya*. Vilnius.

ŠPERLIŅŠ, J.
1937 *Senās suitu kāzas un ķekatas*. Riga.

STENDER, G. F.
1783 *Lettische Grammatik* (second edition).
1789a *Lettische Lexikon.*
1789b *Siņgu lustes*, volume two. Jelgava.

STUMBRIS, J.
1938–1940 *Dejosim latviski*, two volumes. Riga.

SŪNA, H.
1964 *Sistematizatsiya khoreograficheskogo fol'klora: metodicheskaya zapiska po arkhivnomu khraneniyu i sistematizatsii fol'klornykh materialov*. Vilnius.
1965a Daži tautas horeogrāfijas pētīšanas metodologijas jautājumi (abstract). Riga.
1965b Novaya sistema kinetografii zapisey khoreograficheskikh dvizheniy. *Latvijas PSR Zinātņu Akadēmijas Vēstis* 5:63–76.
1966a *Latviešu rotaļas un rotaļdejas*. Riga.
1966b Ein neues kinetographisches System. *Der Tantz* 3:17–23.
1966c Ein neues kinetographisches System. *Volkskunst* 3:41–47.
1970 "Zu einigen Parallelen in der lettischen und estnischen Volkschoreographie," in *Vzaimo svyazi baltov i pribaltiyskikh finnov*, 111–133. Riga.
1971 *Tendentsii razvitiya khoreograficheskogo tvorchestva baltov v bytovom i stsenicheskom latyshskom narodnom tantse*. Vilnius.

URTĀNS, V.
1970 Etniskās atšķirības apbedīšanas tradīcijās un kapu inventārā Latvijā 5.–9. gs. *Arkheologija un Etnografija* 9:61–85.

VASKS, A., V. ROZENBERGA
1971 *Latviešu tautas rotas lietas*. Riga.

VĪTOLIŅŠ, J.
1970 *Latviešu tautas mūzika*. Riga.

VOL'TER, Z. A.
1890 *Materialy dlya etnografii latyshskogo plemeni Vitebskoy gubernii*, volume one. St. Petersburg.

ZARIŅA, A.
1970 *Seno latgaļu apgērbs 7.—13. gs.* Riga.

ŽEIBE, A., M. LASMANE, V. ZĀLĪTE, M. RUDĀJA
1958 *Kustību rotaļas*. Riga.

ZĒVERS, J.
1923 Patapinātie vācu vārdi latviešu valodā. *Izglītbas Ministrijas Mēnešraksts* 5:548–549.
1927 Latviešu skola kultūrvēstures apgaismojumā. *Izglītības Ministrijas Mēnešraksts* 7–8:14.

Transformations of Chivalrous Literature in the Subject Matter of the Sicilian Marionette Theater

A. PASQUALINO

The Opra dei Pupi is the traditional Sicilian marionette theater. Its performances deal mainly with chivalrous subjects. Today, the remaining *opranti* (local jargon for the puppeteers, who occasionally also fashion and paint their own puppets, scenes, and backdrops) still zealously maintain the tradition, but the theaters themselves, once numerous and everywhere, are very few. In 1937, Palermo alone had twelve of them, and many others moved from place to place among the smaller towns and villages. Other, larger cities, such as Catania, Messina, Syracuse, Trapani, Caltanissetta, Licata, and Caltagirone, had a number of theaters each. Now only about ten remain, spread over the entire island. The puppets and theaters that have been abandoned with time have been bought by antique dealers, tourists, or foreign museums.

The Opra's success was tied to its natural audience, villagers and people from the poorest quarters of the cities, who followed the serialized plots every evening for months and months. In the past few years it has been losing this public to the amusements made possible by our consumer society and by mass communication — television, cinema, and billiards — and gaining a new public composed of tourists and middle-class people in search of local color. A show presented serially cannot hope to transmit its message to a single night's audience — tourists and Sicilians behaving like tourists in their own country, who, having once satisfied their curiosity, do not often return and rarely notice more than the superficial aspects of the show. This has had a negative effect on the character and quality of the shows, inducing many puppeteers to fabricate exhibitions for a single evening based upon spectacular effects (Vibaek 1972).

Without an intimate understanding of the sense of the events represented — so far from us in time and unreal, full of monsters, dragons, sirens, enchantments, and battles between Christians and Saracens — the

Opra seems a childish amusement to be viewed with curiosity and enjoyed as something exotic by adults on holiday. A deeper understanding of the Opra dei Pupi shows that for the Sicilian people it did not represent an escape, a world totally detached from everyday life. In its subject matter we can read the ideology of the poor, in an arc which extends from resignation to revolt.

It is difficult to pinpoint with certainty when and where the chivalrous subjects began to be performed regularly by marionettes, but it is fairly certain that the characteristics peculiar to the Sicilian Opra dei Pupi took form only in the first half of the last century. Neither Giuseppe Pitrè, the Sicilian ethnographer to whom we are indebted for the most extensive and most interesting available documentation, nor any other scholar has been able to prove that this theater form existed earlier or to fix the date of its beginnings (Pitrè 1885, 1889, 1913; Mazzoleni 1891; Lo Presti 1927; Toschi 1949; Cocchiara 1954; Li Gotti 1956, 1959).

According to some sources, puppets came to Sicily from Naples. Other sources, assembled by Pitrè and confirmed by the traditional stories preserved to this day in several families of puppeteers, say that what came from Naples were simple string marionettes, their transformation into armored puppets being the work of Gaetano Greco and Liberto Canino, owners of the first puppet theaters in Palermo. The Sicilian marionettes differ from others in the mechanics of their movement, and the shows are distinctive in their subject matter, their figurative style, the order and organization of their presentation, and their manner of speech (Pasqualino 1969a, 1972; Christensen 1972).

The most common themes of today's Opra's performances are the events in the legendary life of Charlemagne and his ancestors and descendants. The puppeteer's repertory also includes other chivalrous narratives, historical episodes such as *Ruggero the Norman's conquest of Sicily*, the *Sicilian vespers*, and the *History of Victor Emanuel and of Garibaldi*, a few Shakespearean subjects like *Romeo and Juliet* and *Macbeth*, the lives of bandits, such as *Antonio di Blasi alias Testalonga, Giuseppina the female brigand, Marziale the brigand assassin, Varsalona*, and *Pasquale Bruno* (a theme derived from the homonymous novel by A. Dumas [1904]), two different versions of the *Beati Paoli* (one from Linares's [1840] short story and one from Natoli's [1955] book), the lives of saints, such as *St. Rita of Cortona* and *St. Jennifer*, and other religious subjects, among them the *Passion* and the *Nativity* Pasqualino 1969b).

Often, at the end of a serious performance, a brief farce is staged in Sicilian dialect whose main characters are Nofriu, Virticchiu, Peppenninnu, the Neapolitan Testuzza, the baron, the doctor, Lisa, and Rusidda. The themes of these farces in the Palermo area come from the *vastasate*, comic shows that were extremely popular in Palermo toward the end of the eighteenth century and owe their name to their characters' profession: porters (*vastasi*). In fact, Nofriu (who is, of course, a porter), his wife Lisa, and the baron are characters in the *vastasate*, and the repertory of the puppeteers' farces includes *Lu Curtigghiu di li Raunisi*, identical in theme to the text of the only *vastasata*. In addition, the list of *vastasate* that we have includes many titles identical to those of the Opra's farces. It is interesting that this list also includes a story about bandits, *Testalonga and Guarnaccia* (Cocchiara 1926). In the Catania area, the protagonist of the farces is Peppenninnu, who still wears an eighteenth-century costume (in Palermo only the baron wears clothes from that period).

The marionette theater which uses themes inspired by the deeds of Charlemagne's paladins is not an exclusively Sicilian phenomenon. Around 1850, in fact, in Naples, Rome, and Modena there were marionette theaters telling of the feats of the Carolingian heroes; in Belgium, at Lièges, there is to this day a theater of this kind, brought there by the Tuscan puppeteer Conti in 1854 (Piron 1949, 1950, 1973; Legros 1961). The success of this theater form was, however, especially extensive and prolonged in Sicily and in the Sicillian colonies in Tunisia, Buenos Aires, and New York.

Whereas most of the themes mentioned above are brief and provide material for only one or two performances, the most popular chivalrous legends are long narratives presented in installments. Their immediate sources are to be found in recent publications. In fact, the remaining puppeteers and storytellers obtain their material from nineteenth-century or early twentieth-century books or from handwritten master scripts derived from the books. The more remote sources of these popular chivalrous traditions are represented by two genres of medieval French literature: the epic, that is, the chanson de geste, and the Arthurian novel.

The derivation of the Carolingian cycle (that in which the action takes place in the time of the Emperor Charlemagne) from the chansons de geste is the more direct. The chansons, which were originally passed on orally and sung, tell either of the wars between Christians and Saracens in the spirit of the Crusades or of the rebellion of the barons against the sovereign, a social evil which impeded the Holy Wars. Episodes of some of these poems — for example, Charlemagne's wars in southern Italy, narrated in *Aspremont*, a portion of the adventures of Rinaldo, narrated in *Renaud de Monteauban*, and Ganelon's treason at the battle of Roncesvalles narrated in the *Chanson de Roland* — are to be found with what seem minor changes in the Sicilian marionette theater.

Other legends have undergone drastic changes, and more recent narrative developments deriving in large part from the Arthurian novel have been inserted into them. This literary genre represents the ideals of behavior of thirteenth-century courtly society; in it amorous themes are more important than wars or politics. Feats undertaken by the heroes are in the nature of trials, often of a magical or miraculous character, required to win the love of a lady. Many later chansons de geste have, along with holy-war or feudal-discord themes, magical and amorous ones. In France, from the fourteenth century onward, the epic declined as the adventure novel assumed prominence with the middle class as well as the courtiers. It was at this time that the chansons began to be passed on in book form more than by word of mouth. Both in France and in other European countries, prose versions and cyclical compilations appeared. In Spain and in Italy, the French epic legends had a wide and enthusiastic following and they continued to develop there until the seventeenth century, by which time they had already been forgotten or held in rather low esteem for quite a while in France. In Spain this spread was manifest principally in the romancero, epic-lyrical ballads orally transmitted, and in the theater in Italy in poetry and novels. Slowly, the fusion of the motifs of the epic with those of the Arthurian novel, already begun in France, deepened. In Italy the rebel barons began to be described more favorably and the sovereign less so; in addition, the confrontation of villains and heroes as two families locked in eternal struggle against each other became a stable feature.

Three phases can be identified in the development of the chivalrous narrative in Italy. The first consists of the so-called Franco–Venetian literature, poems written from the thirteenth to the beginning of the fifteenth century in a hybrid, artificial language halfway between French and one of the northern Italian dialects. The second phase dates from the middle of the fourteenth century and comprises the Tuscan *cantari* (popular verse in ottava rima) and novels. Among these latter, *I reali di Francia* and *Guerrin Meschino*, by Andrea da Barberino, are notable for their wide diffusion among the peasant class. In these first two phases, as the middle class and the lower classes in the cities took over more and more of this literature from the aristocracy the texts assumed a rougher form and a more popular, often mocking character. Then, at the end of the fifteenth and beginning of the sixteenth century the chivalrous narratives were refined and made part of the dominant culture. This third phase includes *Morgante*, by Luigi Pulci, *Orlando innamorato*, by Matteo Maria Boiardo, and *Orlando furioso*, by Ludovico Ariosto, poems composed in the atmosphere of the Ferraran and Florentine courts. *Gerusalemme liberata*, by Torquato Tasso, while occupying a place of its own in the history of literature insofar as it indicated the transformation of taste which marked the end of the creation of chivalrous works, was grouped with these others in popular taste.

A long time after the production of chivalrous literature had been abandoned by the elite, the most famous of the poems and novels mentioned here and others far less well known continued to be among the first things read by youngsters and virtually the only literature of the lower classes. This was true not only in Italy, but also in France and in other European countries (Lançon 1926). In Italy, among the lower classes, this narrative material was primarily transmitted orally and semiorally. The Sicilian storytellers, the Neapolitan *Rinaldi*, and other professional narrators of chivalrous material are or were the direct heirs of the medieval jongleurs (Rajna 1878, Pitrè 1889, Croce 1936, Buttitta 1957–1959).

The Opra dei Pupi took advantage of the early-nineteenth-century vogue of the epic-chivalrous narrative, the result of a romantic interest in medieval culture. From the middle of the century to the first decades of the twentieth century there was also a great deal of editorial activity, beginning with the publication (between 1858 and 1860) and great success of the *Story of the French paladins*, by Giusto Lodico, reprinted in 1862, 1893, and repeatedly thereafter. It consisted of the compilation and partial fusion of the plots of a great number of novels and poems. Many works were published in its wake; some were more or less faithful reprints or reworkings of old novels or poems, and others, while naturally involving variation of the motifs and outlines characteristic of the traditional chivalrous genre, were conceived mainly in the imaginations of writers of popular literature who, besides dusting off old stories, had set themselves to inventing new ones.

The epic repertory of the Opra dei Pupi includes the following cycles:

1. *The deeds of Charlemagne*. This cycle begins with the ancient Trojans; the first part goes from the siege of Troy to the epoch of the Emperor Constantine and interweaves mythological and historical events from *Julius Caesar and Tarquin the Lion-hearted*, by Constantino Catanzaro, sometimes interposed with episodes from Crimi's *Alexander the Great*. These two works seem to be taken, at least in part, from ancient sources. Then follow the events narrated in *I reali di Francia*, which covers the generations from Constantine to Charlemagne. Then comes the feats of Charlemagne and his paladins, narrated in Lodico's *Story of the French paladins*. Following this come the lives of Charlemagne's descendants, recounted in *Guido santo*, written by the Catanese Emanuele Bruno and rewritten by Leggio, and in its sequels, also by Leggio. Among the latter, only the fifth volume, *Gerusalemme liberata*, has an obvious ancient model, being largely the prose translation of Tasso's work.

The heart of this long series of stories, from Constantine to the death of Guido Santo, and especially the history of Charlemagne, Orlando, and Rinaldo, has always been the most popular and has been shown so often that the puppeteers say: "Orlando and Rinaldo are always the ones that put the *pasta* in the pot." Another sequel to the *Story of the French paladins* is the serialized novel *Drusiano del Leone*, derived — or so it would seem — from the homonymous poem in octaves. This novel, at least in recent times, has had far less success and more limited distribution than *Guido santo*, but it is known to almost all the puppeteers and has been performed by some of them.

2. *The story of the Emperor Trabazio* and his children, narrated in the serial novel in two volumes, *Trabazio* and *Chiarimonte*, whose contents correspond to the Spanish novel *Espejo de príncipes y caualleros*.

3. *The Story of Guerrin alias the Meschino*, corresponding to the work by Andrea da Barberino, which for a few puppeteers is an old standard while others have never performed it.

4. *Uzeda the Catanese*.

5. *Erminio of the Golden Star and Gemma of the Flame*.

6. *Guido of Holy Cross* (with its sequels *Valentino and Germina* and *Orientale of the Stars*).

7. *Farismane and Siface*.

8. *Tramoro of Medina*.

9. *Belisario of Messina*.

10. *Calloandro*.

11. *Guelfo of Negroponte*.

Cycles 4 through 8 have had noteworthy success in the Catania and Syracuse areas and Cycle 9 in Messina. All of these are parts of serial novels of the same names and of recent origin. Cycle 10 comes from Marino's novel, reprinted in serial form. This and the last cycle are little known today and almost never performed, though they were a normal part of the repertory in the last century.

Since the publication of the Sicilian editions of the chivalrous narratives that are the direct source of the Opra's performances postdates the origin of this form of popular show, it would be interesting to pinpoint the chivalrous stories that supplied the material for the theater in its earliest form.

Of course, the derivation of several serialized versions of old works does not prove that their themes were well known at the popular level before their recent publication. Information about Sicilian editions of chivalrous works and their circulation before the first half of the nineteenth century is far from exhaustive, but we know that *I reali di Francia* and *Meschino* were reprinted dozens of times in Palermo and in Messina, that editions of these works came from Naples, Venice, and Milan, and that *Calloandro, Morgante, Orlando innamorato*, and *Orlando furioso* were easily obtainable all over Italy. We also know that Villabianca collected a story of Orlando and one of Meschino, works of blind balladeers, and Vico heard *Orlando furioso* and *Orlando innamorato* read by the Neopolitan *Rinaldi* in the eighteenth century.

The most significant dates for a picture of the chivalrous repertory at the beginning of the nineteenth century can de deduced from documents published by Pitrè (1885, 1889). Careful examination allows us to conclude that this repertory surely included *Calloandro, I reali di Francia*, an undefined story about Orlando and Rinaldo, and perhaps also *Drusiano del Leone, Meschino*, and *Trabazio*. In any case, all of these themes, together with *Gerusalemme liberata, Guelfo and Alfeo of Negroponte*, and *Alexander the Great II* (a story of Alexander which, like Crimi's work, also contained the adventures of Alexander's son), were to become part of the repertory by 1889 (Pasqualino 1969b).

It is not clear what relations there were between the stories of Orlando and Rinaldo that were already part of the repertory at the beginning of the century and Lodico's work, in which Orlando and Rinaldo are the main characters. It is probable, as Rajna suggested to Pitrè, that, in view of the huge success of Lodico, events or versions of traditional stories were forgotten or replaced (Bonomo 1951–1953).

The documentation which would have solved this problem was, unfortunately, not systematically collected. For quite a while there have been no theater owners or story-tellers, even illiterate ones, left who do not treat Lodico as Gospel. Nevertheless, the documents published by Pitrè (consisting of accounts of puppet theater performances and of the tales of storytellers and other informants, information about characters and stories performed, master scripts, and lists of posters belonging to the Opra) offer some interesting clues. Those that coincide with the *Story of the French paladins* of course tell us nothing about the preceding state of the tradition, because Pitrè collected his data after the publication of Lodico's work; those that do not coincide can be considered a sure indication of Carolingian traditions different from those collected and disseminated by Lodico. Since points of disagreement can be ascertained even from material such as Pitrè's, quantitatively modest and not collected with the intention of pointing out those differences, it is clear that there were many of them.

Two views are possible: that Lodico's contribution was considerable and that the differences between old and new versions were insignificant. While I take the latter view, I do not think enough data are available to exclude the former. Lodico's testimony in the preface to the first edition of the *Story of the French paladins* is ambiguous. Describing his method of working, he draws on the authority of written texts to prove the superiority of his book over the traditional stories (Lodico 1858–1860:3–4; translation mine):

> The description that I embark upon is not my original contribution, nor are its contents modern: it is that which has been told for centuries: in fact, who has not heard the clamour of the arms of Orlando and Rinaldo? And how many earn their living narrating the deeds of Orlando and Rinaldo? The gentle reader may ask me one question: whether or not they tell the truth? No, they know only as much of it

> as would provide a few days' entertainment, and this is not their fault but the fault of time scattering the sources, therefore, those who truly love this story will never be satisfied before they read my book, because no one shall forget that this chronicle is ancient but has never been complete nor reduced to a logical and progressive order, as it now is. My sole effort has been to reunite all the authors who have written of it, and those who illustrated these adventures with the genius of poetry, to omit that which was born of the poet's imagination and to describe what appears to be likely.

In other words, the storytellers' version was imprecise and incomplete, so he went back to the source books, reuniting all the works that tell of the deeds of his heroes and arranging them chronologically. He does not say, however, that the parts forgotten by the storytellers were numerous.

The importance of early written sources seems confirmed in the story of the puppet theater's birth handed down in the Canino family. I have heard this story told many times by Don Gaspare Canino of Alcamo, grandson of the early Palermo puppeteer. According to this story, the first presentation of *Orlando furioso* was a prose translation of Ariosto's verses. Then Greco and Canino, competing with each other for the public's favor, began to look for other stories, for example, *Lady Rovenza*. Lodico's book came later. Thus even the family tradition of a dynasty of puppeteers leads us back to the image of a popular chivalrous culture in rapport with the literature. In line with this point of view, it is easy to imagine that, prior to the publication of the *Story of the French paladins*, the repertory lacked the huge amounts of facts gathered by Lodico, consisting only of the outline plots of easily obtainable books. The deeds of Orlando and Rinaldo narrated in *Morgante, Orlando innamorato*, and *Orlando furioso* already comprise a long story. If the narratives of Bello's *Mambriano*, Tasso's *Rinaldo*, Dolce's *Orlandino*, and Brusantini's *Angelica innamorata* (poems to be found fairly frequently, even today in eighteenth- or nineteenth-century editions in the catalogues of antique bookstores) are added to these, we get a complete life of Charlemagne and his paladins.

Surprising as it may seem, however, even the plots of less popular poems which had not, to my knowledge, been recently reprinted were part of the Sicilian storytellers' repertory. Before the publication of Lodico's work, the storyteller Ferreri was already recounting one of the episodes from *La Trebisonda*, a poem whose last known edition was published in 1558. This information gives weight to the view that there were no great differences between old and new versions. Similarly Rajna tells us that the repertory of the *Rinaldi* included poems such as *Ancroia, L'innamoramento di Carlo Magno*, and *La Spagna* in addition to *Orlando innamorato* and *Orlando furioso*, insofar as the adventures of Charlemagne, Orlando, and Rinaldo are concerned (Rajna 1878). We also know from Pitrè that the Sicilian storytellers, like the *Rinaldi*, possessed chivalrous poems and novels in manuscript copies or publications (Pitrè 1885, 1889). Therefore, Lodico's contribution could have consisted mainly in an ordering of the traditional repertory aimed at grouping episodes together and eliminating incongruencies by excluding parts not consonant with the accepted ones. The most important difference between the cyclical repertory of the *Rinaldi* and Lodico's text is that the latter arranges and harmonizes its sources while the former, according to Rajna (1878:572–573; translation mine) is ordered without

> questioning the integrity of any of the works used to make up the system; each novel is read in its entirety without interposing, in whole or in part, other compositions. So the structure turns out to be slightly irregular and in many places the stones piled in rows do not meet, even approximately. . . . But the listeners make up for these partial abnormalities and lacks in continuity on their own for, in their minds, all the elements come together in a perfect unity.

Canino's story may reflect the state of the chivalrous culture of the Grecos and the Caninos more than it does the state of chivalrous culture among the storytellers of their time. According to that story, Greco began by showing the stories of Harlequin, Pulcinella and Colombina, and Canino, when, inspired by a chivalrous performance he saw in Greco's theater, he conceived the idea of making the first armored paladins and opening a theater, was a maker of player pianos by trade. Thus the two were apparently not members of the storytellers' circle. They may have tried to take advantage of the Carolingian stories' popularity by presenting the plot of *Orlando furioso*, learned through reading. Later, spurred on by success, they may have dramatized other stories, drawing upon such widely diffused books as *I reali di Francia, Meschino, Orlando innamorato*, and *Morgante*. The storytellers, in contrast, may have included in their repertory nearly all of the narrative material that Lodico eventually published.

The continuing popularity of the chivalrous narrative masks many changes, some evident, others subtle and hidden. Thus, while plot seems to remain the same, its meaning has changed over time. Even today, each puppeteer, while advocating faithfulness to tradition, gives the story his own personal form, which may be influenced by the opinions of his audience. On the other hand, certain of the repertory's narratives convey different messages to different audiences, either because of their intrinsic features or because of differences in understanding between one listener and another. The semiotic analysis of narrative offers a new methodology for the study of such ambiguities and changes of meaning. The problem is too complex to deal with here; I shall only mention certain aspects which will be studied separately later.

Students of narrative grammar maintain that every tale can be described as a syntagmatic sequence of *character actions* (Propp 1928; Greimas 1966, 1970). *Actions* and *characters* are units of semiotic analysis, the former comprising any process or variation relevant to the development of the story and the latter any entity which is relatively permanent in time but able to cause and/or undergo a change and constituted, aside from what it does or undergoes (its sphere of action), by the qualifications attributed to it. Characters and actions may be reduced to a small number of categories — *actants* and *functions*. This is the *surface narrative structure*.

A paradigmatic view of actions and characters, that is, the view that is obtained by setting out the semantic relations between these entities — relations of analogy, opposition, and correlation — allows one to expose the *deep narrative structure*, made up of abstract oppositions which establish classifications of the world and codes of behavior. The surface structure of the narrative is one of the discursive manifestations that can be generated, giving to the conceptual oppositions of the deep narrative structure the form of conflicts between human characters.

In order to clarify the problem I propose, I shall need to gather a large number of parallel textual analyses. Here I shall distinguish the various kinds of meaning changes and of ambiguity. Meaning changes can occur in one of the three phases of the process of communication — emission, transmission, and reception — each of which depends upon the preceding ones but not on the subsequent ones.

In the case of changes during emission, the sender (writer, storyteller, or puppeteer) changes the story. In the case of changes during transmission, the sender may let part of the story be lost or misunderstood. This second possibility is of course of little interest here. It is clear, however, that in both cases, the text of the story having changed, its sense may have changed. It must only be stressed that certain small variations in the surface structure (that is, in the actions and qualifications of the characters) suffice to change the meaning profoundly and to modify the functioning of the structure on all levels. The evolution in time of chivalrous literature offers many examples of the first kind of change. In the recent Sicilian popular phase, one can also find variations, suppressions, and important additions.

In the case of changes during reception, the sense of a text may change because of differences in *competence*. The receiver may be unable to comprehend the message as it has been emitted and transmitted and so reinterprets it in terms of his own sociocultural universe. It should be borne in mind that the acceptance of a theatrical show is freer than that of a text being read, especially when, as in the case of the Sicilian marionette theater, the spectators know the plot already and have their own ideas about it, so much so that they feel entitled to question whether the performance is historically accurate. Situations may consequently be evaluated in different ways. This may happen both to ordinary listeners and to the storyteller, the author of popular serial novels, or the puppeteer when they receive the traditional story: the change they produce when they become emitters may be due to a competence limitation at the time of reception of the previous version.

Ambiguity, for our purposes, is the possibility of giving two different descriptions of the deep structure of a story. True structural ambiguity raises difficult theoretical questions. One example of its occurrence in chivalrous literature and in some of the subjects of the Opra may be the struggle between the sovereign and the rebel barons.

Ambiguity due to the combination in a text of different and heterogeneous works which can be traced to contrasting world views occurs often in the *Story of the French paladins*: the different parts have not been modified enough to render their deep structures uniform. Only the evident factual contradictions between the various sources have been eliminated by dropping episodes or adding connecting links. In this case, concentration on different episodes may yield different evaluations. It is for this reason that the responses of spectators, encouraged by a questionnaire to express their opinions on the story, vary noticeably with what piece is being performed. The responses of puppeteers, on the other hand, do not depend upon the day's episode, but reflect a synchronic and integrated vision of the whole.

Multiple interpretations of the "same" story can be seen in two aspects of the *Story of the French paladins*: the conflict between sovereign and rebels and Angelica's relationships with her suitors.

At first glance, the conflict which is most evident in the Carolingian narrative is the one between the Christians and the Saracens. For the listeners of the chansons de geste, for whom the Crusades were a life experience, the Saracens were a real enemy. In the Sicilian popular versions, Christians and Saracens represent an abstract contraposition of good and evil analogous to that found in all types of adventurous escape literature. This opposition is duplicated in the opposition between converts and traitors, the former being the product of the transformation of foes into friends and the latter that of the opposite transformation (Pasqualino 1970, 1973a). The positive values, which characterize the first element of each pair (Christians, converts), are familiarity, fairness, and mercy; the negative values, which characterize the second element of each pair (Saracens, traitors), are alienness, unfairness, and cruelty. The symmetry of converts and traitors with Christians and Saracens is underlined by episodes in which a convert is slain by a traitor (example, the killing of Ruggero by Gano). The converts (often much-loved heroes) come to be identified with the heroes who are Christian from birth, but the traitors maintain a more distinct position with respect to the Saracens and assume great emotional importance. The fairness–unfairness opposition, which distinguishes them from the Christians, is fundamental in a world — such as that of the Southern lower classes — in which fairness is rare because, in order to survive, one is forced to step on one's neighbor, either directly or by influencing the holders of power.

Even more important than this conflict, however, is the conflict between sovereign and rebel vassals. The barons' behavior is determined by the opposition between obedience and rebellion, the sovereign's by the opposition between righteous authority and oppression (Pasqualino 1973b). The popular audience identifies this contrast with that between the powerful (policeman, boss, chief elector) and the poor. In the *Story of the French paladins*, this conflict is usually provoked by evil influence, insinuations, and slander on the part of traitors.

Many episodes could be cited to illustrate the Opra audience's hatred of the traitor. For example, it is Gano di Maganza's fault that Charlemagne persecutes Rinaldo, the most beloved of the heroes. The latter is poor and is often forced to steal in order to live; he saves the king many times, but his merits are often unacknowledged and he is frequently sent into exile and forced (like the emigrant) to wander far from home. This situation is particularly evident in an episode of the *Vantamento dei paladini* that derives from the anonymous fifteenth-century poem *La Trebisonda*, is included in the *Story of the French paladins*, and is performed in the puppet theater. Gano, in order to humiliate Rinaldo, who is poor, has induced Charlemagne to exhort all the paladins to boast of what they are prepared to offer the crown in case of war. When invited to speak, Rinaldo starts by declaring: "One must boast not of riches but of virtues, since to boast of riches is not worthy of a man." He then boasts of his deeds and of his victories, even over Charlemagne and Gano, humiliating them until the sovereign exiles him.

In the chansons de geste, rebellion is seen as a social evil which must be remedied by a sacrifice of pride on both sides, even if the rebel is more appealing than the sovereign. Judging from the *Story of the French paladins*, in the Sicily of yesterday and today the feeling for social order is less than it was in medieval France. In fact, the deterioration of the figure of Charlemagne is extreme in the Sicilian versions. The contrast between the rebel baron and the sovereign may even come to be identified with that between the hero and the traitor, that is, to play on the fairness–unfairness opposition. Even Orlando, who represents a mediator in that he sometimes sides with the sovereign and sometimes with Rinaldo, in seeking a reconciliation becomes involved in the discrediting of Charlemagne. On the other hand, part of what makes Rinaldo better liked than Orlando is that he is cunning, sagacious, and capable of deceit for the sake of winning. Thus while in Gano unfairness is condemned, in Rinaldo it is praised, and Orlando is often judged too fair — too loyal to Charlemagne, and therefore stupid.

What is more interesting is that such a process of sliding values, which produces an obvious transformation of the narrative structure, was accentuated in the aftermath of World War II, as Nino Canino, the puppeteer from Partinico, says with particular clarity in a tape recording among my archives:

Most [of the spectators] like Rinaldo because he is more astute, more agreeable. There are those who love Orlando, but now they are becoming convinced that Orlando represents deception in the sense that he cannot be humbled: so his prestige no longer exists; but Rinaldo is guileless. . . . Perhaps, I don't know, in the early days no one thought. . . . Orlando still has fans; but they are becoming convinced, because besides his arms he has the *Durlindana*, the invulnerable flesh. . . . Rinaldo is better liked in joking, in love, in misfortune, and everything; they describe him so well. There are those who say he doesn't exist, but anyhow. . . . [Q: And what character is the most hated by most of the spectators?] Gano di Maganza. [Q: And are there others who hate other characters?] Well, these days Charlemagne is getting to be disliked. I don't know, perhaps people were backward before, didn't understand: perhaps now they've opened their eyes, like children who read at first with their eyes closed, now they read with their eyes open. They already see that Charlemagne doesn't have real authority, they see him make first one mistake, then another, then the third, and still they [paladins] keep him with them [as their Emperor]: what does he represent? A useless person this Charlemagne. Or even better, they see him commit treachery, they find him out. . . . [Q: But tell me something, do you remember, from your childhood working with your grandfather in Termini Imerese, that more people respected Charlemagne?] I don't know, the thing is this; maybe they didn't notice then; but now, even the Earth has changed, been replenished, they already see that Charlemagne represents a worthless being. If they discover that this Gano commits treachery, I admit, they pardon him the first time out of respect because he is married to Charlemagne's sister, the second time out of respect for Baldovino [his son], another time because he is Charlemagne's brother-in-law; but he commits treachery constantly up to the end of Roncesvalles. . . .

Nonetheless, it is not to be supposed that these interpretations are universally accepted today. On the contrary, interviews with members of audiences still often yield conciliatory answers which absolve Charlemagne from any evil intention and consider his tragic mistakes excusable. There are also those who prefer Orlando to Rinaldo. This is not surprising, given that the present social situation cannot be considered prerevolutionary. The narrative carries with it opposing valuations; we can move from a reformist version (in which reconciliation with the sovereign is necessary) to a revolutionary one such as that lived through by Canino and his public.

In the nineteenth century, at the time the puppet theater probably had its beginnings and then its greatest success, the history of the Southern lower classes, and particularly the Sicilian lower classes, was one of continuous alternation between resignation and revolt. Seen from this point of view, the resurgence of 1860 can be considered an instrumentalization of the popular revolt by middle-class forces, which aimed at ends that were self-serving, extraneous, and incomprehensible to the peasants. The squads that helped Garibaldi were the same ones that, a few years later, were ready to begin the struggle again, this time against the Piedmontese.

The figure of Rinaldo, as just described, is an idealized equivalent of the Opra's more realistic bandits. Banditry is one of the main forms in which Southern lower-class rebellion is expressed, both in action and, through the idealization of the figure of the bandit, in the imagination. In the bandit narratives, nevertheless, noble actions and justifications or, rather, noble motives for less-then-noble actions alternate with episodes in which the protagonist's behavior is cruel or evil according to a moral code which the spectator shares with the middle class. From this a tragic contradiction, a positive-negative double standard for the protagonist, arises in which, even after many victories, he invariably succumbs to "justice." Rinaldo, on the other hand, is free to be right all the time and, though unable to prevent the paladins' defeat at Roncesvalles because of Gano di Maganza's treachery and Charlemagne's blindness, is destined to have his just revenge and ascend to Heaven as a saint. He is, therefore, a victorious instrument of fantasied revolt, free from a sense of guilt and from the contradictions associated both with the bandits of nineteenth-century popular narrative and with the rebel barons in the chansons de geste.

Similar complexity of interpretation may be seen in the love relationships of Angelica. In general, love relationships in chivalrous narratives have various functions. The beloved princess, usually Saracen, may serve, as in most fairy tales, only as the hero's final *reward*. Alternatively, brief affairs with Saracen princesses may serve as *trials*, either in that the foreigner's love represents temptation and victory consists in avoiding it or in that victory consists in the conquest and abandonment of the princess. These two semiotic values are combined and confused in the deeds of different heroes, particularly those of Rinaldo. His affairs with Princess Floriana of Media and with Caradina, the sorceress, come to mind; the first episode is from Tasso's *Rinaldo* and the second from Bello's *Mambriano*, and both are included in the *Story of the French paladins* and in the Opra's repertory. Often a hero is born of such a brief affair who is destined to search for his paternal family. In that case, the affair has a dual function, also serving to start off a new chapter by creating a situation of lack. These two situations — the affair as a reward and the affair as a trial — fit in perfectly with the Sicilian popular conception of love relationships. Finally, the search for the beloved one may serve as the springboard for action, as in fairy tales such as "Supernatural or enchanted husband (wife)."

In the sources, reciprocal attachments follow the highly formalized rules of courtly love, as in the case of Rinaldo's love for Clarice in Tasso's *Rinaldo* and in certain aspects of the story of Angelica, especially those derived from *Orlando innamorato*. In this case, the trial may consist of a choice between love and the duties of a knight or their reconciliation. In the Opra, however, as in fourteenth- and fifteenth-century popular poetry, courtly behavior is modified, furnishing us with a clear example of changes in meaning due to differences in sociocultural universe or limitations of competence.

For example, Agricane wages war on Angelica to force her to accept him as a husband, and Orlando comes to defend the fair princess, with whom he is hopelessly in love. Battling against each other, each of the men begins to admire and esteem his adversary. When night falls, they decide to rest on the spot, in the woods, and resume fighting there in the morning; while lying on the grass, they begin to talk. In Boiardo's poem, Orlando tries to convert Agricane to Christianity, but Agricane refuses to discuss theology. Turning the topic of conversation to love, they understand each other better, but when one of them tells the other that he is in love with Angelica and they discover that neither is willing to give her up at any price, they can no longer wait until morning, and they attack each other. In the Sicilian puppeteers' version, on the other hand, Agricane takes up the fight again in the middle of the night because he is angered by Orlando's insistence on discussing religion.

Orlando's relationship with Angelica in *Orlando innamorato* contrasts with the pattern of love as a reward. Indeed, Orlando is continually going through new trials without gaining Angelica's love. The same thing happens to other characters in the poem, to Angelica when she falls in love with Rinaldo, and to Rinaldo when he falls in love with Angelica; indeed, Sklovskiy (1968) proposes the following formula for this work: "When A loves B, B does not love A; if B loves A, A no longer loves B." Rinaldo is in love with Angelica, but he happens to drink water from a magical fountain and suddenly forgets his love. In the meantime, Angelica, who has quenched her thirst with water from another fountain with the opposite property, begins to show ardent love for Rinaldo, whom she has previously hated. Rinaldo flees from Angelica, who follows him from one place to another. Then, after having run all around the world in this fashion, Rinaldo and Angelica find themselves once again in the same woods with the magical fountains, they both drink the water again, and their roles reverse: Angelica begins to hate Rinaldo, while he begins to love her.

In its entirety, the story of Angelica arouses some of the most interesting differences in reaction between middle-class readers and the traditional Opra public. Chivalrous literature offers three works that deal with this character, each quite different from the others, all three of which were used as sources by Lodico and became part of the Opra's repertory: Boiardo's *Orlando innamorato*, Aristo's *Orlando furioso*, and Brusantini's *Angelica innamorata*.

In *Orlando innamorato*, the figure of Angelica is rather ambiguous: at the beginning she is presented as a schemer who comes to Paris to take the paladins prisoner by unfair strategy, using her beauty as bait. Soon she becomes a character with whom the reader identifies when she falls in love with Rinaldo, who hates her. Her behavior with respect to Orlando and other suitors is always scheming and cruel.

In *Orlando furioso*, Angelica is a figure whose interest lies mainly in her extraneousness to the world of knights and wars. This extraneousness shows itself in the rejection and flight of all the kings and nobles who had been in love with her and in her affair with Medoro, a poor soldier. The fair Angelica is always kind and humane, however, even towards the suitors who persecute her with their violent and untimely insistence. (Of course, what I say requires confirmation based on a careful study of the text, but this will certainly be the view of any modern reader with regard to this aspect of Ariosto's story; an agreeable and penetrating exposition of such a reading comes to us from Baldini [1940].) The significance of the event is quite different in the Sicilian marionette theater. In fact, the puppeteers and the public look upon Angelica with hostility verging on contempt when she chooses a poor soldier rather than a king or a paladin.

In *Angelica innamorata*, Brusantino's bizarre imagery puts Angelica in a magic garden where, as a result of the vindictive Alcina's spells and as a punishment for not having returned the love of so many illustrious suitors, she is forced to fall in love with all the knights who happen her way and to see them go away. Of course, all those who have been in love with Angelica come, one by one, to the place where she is made to wait. This cruel punishment is not appreciated by the modern middle-class reader, but it was appreciated by the people who made up the Opra's repertory and even seemed too soft to them. In the poem, Angelica, freed from the spell, ends up by conquering her persecutor. In the *Story of the French paladins* and the Opra, however, Angelica kills herself rather than be forced to marry the hated Ferraù. The choice of material made by Lodico and by the puppeteers seconds and confirms the disapproval of the Opra's almost exclusively masculine public for the freedom to choose in love, an action of which Angelica is judged guilty.

Although it is very difficult to determine in what proportion these different interpretations can be attributed to true structural ambiguity, to the combination of episodes derived from heterogeneous sources, or to differences in the competence of puppeteers and spectators, there is no doubt but the interweaving of these phenomena is part of the normal functioning and transformation of the narrative structure under conditions of semioral transmission. Interpretations taking such differing points of view demonstrate the wide range of possibilities for use of the *Story of the French paladins*. It is these possibilities which have made of it an efficient instrument for meditation on the world for the traditional public and enabled it to survive so long under changing sociohistorical conditions.

REFERENCES

BALDINI, A.

1940 "Patrocinio di Angelica," in *Beato fra le donne*, 17–53. Milan: Mondadori.

BONOMO, G.

1951–1953 Lettere di Pio Rajna a Giuseppe Pitrè. *Annali del Museo Pitrè* 2–4:1–34.

BUTTITTA, A.

1957–1959 Cantastorie in Sicilia: premessa e testi. *Annali del Museo Pitrè* 8–10:149–236.

CHRISTENSEN, C.

1972 *Mostra di cartelli dell'opra*. Palermo: Associazione per la conservazione delle tradizioni popolari.

COCCHIARA, G.

1926 *Le vastasate: contributo alla storia del teatro popolare*. Palermo: Sandron.

1954 I cartelloni dell'opra dei pupi. *Sicilia* 5:18–22.

CROCE, B.

1936 I "Rinaldi" o i cantastorie di Napoli. *Critica* 34:70–74.

DUMAS, ALEXANDRE (PÉRE)

1904 *Pasquale Bruno: Il bandito di Valdemone*. Florence.

GREIMAS, A. J.

1966 *Sémantique structurale. Paris: Larousse.*

1970 *Du sens*. Paris: Editions du Seuil.

LANÇON, R.

1926 *Le goût du moyen âge en France au XVIIIe siècle*. Paris/Brussels.

LEGROS, E.

1961 Le repertoire des théâtres de marionnettes liègeois. *Enquêtes du Musée de la Vie Walonne* 9:129–164.

LI GOTTI, E.

1956 *Sopravvivenza delle leggende carolingie in Sicilia*. Florence: Sansoni.

1959 *Il teatro dei pupi*. Florence: Sansoni.

LINARES, VINCENZO

1840 "I beati Paoli," in *Racconti popolari*. Palermo: Pedone Lauriel.

LODICO, GIUSTO

1858–1860 *Storia dei paladini di Francia cominciando da Milone conte d'Anglate sino alla morte di Rinaldo*. Palermo.

LO PRESTI, S.

1927 *I pupi*. Catania: Studio Editoriale Moderno.

MAZZOLENI, A.

1891 Gli ultimi echi della leggenda cavalleresca in Sicilia. *Atti e Rendiconti della Accademia di Scienze Lettere e Arti dei Zelanti e P. P. dello Studio di Acireale*, n.s. 3:45–69.

NATOLI, LUIGI (WILLIAM GALT)

1955 *I beati Paoli, grande romanzo storico siciliano*. Milan.

PASQUALINO, A.
1969a *L'opra dei pupi*. Palermo: Associazione per la conservazione delle tradizioni popolari.
1969b Il repertorio epico dell'opera dei pupi. *Uomo e Cultura* 2(3–4):59–106.
1970 Per un'analisi morfologica della letteratura cavalleresca: *I reali di Francia. Uomo e Cultura* 3(5–6):76–194.
1972 *Pupi siciliani*. Rome: Edizioni Regionali.
1973a "Conflicts and conceptual oppositions in the *Reali di Francia*." *Strutture e letteratura: Atti del simposium Strutture e generi della letteratura etnica, Palermo 5–10 aprile, 1970.* Palermo: Flaccovio.
1973b "Funzioni e attanti nello studio della narrativa popolare." *Ricerca scientifica e mondo popolare: Atti del convegno di studi demologici, Messina 19–21 gennaio 1970.* Palermo: Manfredi.

PIRON, M.
1949 Les marionnettes de Wallonie. I. Le "Bètième" de Mons. *Enquêtes du Musée de la Vie Walonne* 5(53–54):129–154.
1950 *Tchantshès et son évolution dans la tradition liègeoise*. Brussels: Académie Royale de Belgique.
1973 L'origine italienne du théâtre liégeois des marionnettes. *Enquêtes du Musée de la Vie Wallonne* 12.

PITRÈ, G.
1885 *Tradizioni cavalleresche in Sicilia*. Paris.
1889 "Le tradizioni cavalleresche popolari in Sicilia," in *Usi e costumi credenze e pregiudizi del popoli siciliano*, volume one, 123–341. Palermo: Pedone Lauriel.
1913 *La famiglia, la casa, la vita del popolo siciliano*. Palermo.

PROPP, V. IA.
1928 *Morfologia skazki*. Leningrad. (Translated 1966 by G. L. Bravo as *Morfologia della fiaba*. Turin: Einaudi.)

RAJNA, P.
1878 I Rinaldi o cantastorie di Napoli. *Nuova Antologia* 12:557–579.

SKLOVSKIY, V.
1968 "La struttura della novella e del romanzo," in *I formalisti russi*. Edited by T. Todorov, 205–231. Turin: Einaudi.

TOSCHI, P.
1949 "Il teatro dei pupi," in *Mediterranea: Almanacco di Sicilia*, 307–310. Palermo.

VIBAEK, J.
1972 Elogio dell'opra. *L'Ora* (Palermo), June 13.

Folklore Research in India

L. P. VIDYARTHI

Folklore in India has yet to establish its status as an independent discipline. Until recently, it was considered part of Indology. Bhagvat (1958a), in the course of a survey of Indian folklore, brings out this point very ably. Sengupta (1964) confirms this view and suggests that the term "folklore" was systematically used for the first time by W. J. Thomas in 1846.

Though sporadic publications of folk songs and folk tales, as examples of ancient oral literature, appeared in the *Journal of the Royal Asiatic Society of Bengal*, established in 1774, the output was very meager. In the first hundred years, only two dozen important articles on folklore could be counted. Interest in the study of folklore increased when *Indian Antiquary* was founded in Bombay in 1872 under the editorship of James Burgess, who recognized folklore as a special subject and gave particular attention to the study and publication of myths, folktales, folk songs, and popular traditions. The *Journal of the Anthropological Society of Bombay*, which started publication in 1886, gave maximum support to folklore. It encouraged a group of scholars such as S. C. Mitra and others to collect and publish folk songs and tales. In addition to these journals, a number of others concerned with historical and anthropological studies, such as the *Journal of the Mythic Society*, in Bangalore, the *Journal of the Bihar and Orissa Research Society*, in Patna, *Man in India*, in Ranchi, and *Folklore*, in London, also included valuable folklore materials.

In addition to the publication of folklore materials in these journals, some efforts were made to publish collections of folktales and songs. The history of the publication of folkloric collections goes back to 1868, when the first collection of Indian folktales, by Merry Frere, appeared, under the title *The old Deccan day*. It was followed in 1879 by the publication of a collection of Indian fairy tales by M. Stokes. In 1884, a collection of tales from the Punjab by Flora Steel and Sir R. C. Temple was published under the title *Wideawake stories*.

With this humble beginning, a tradition of folkloric studies was initiated, and literary scholars, Indologists, scholarship-oriented administrators and foreign missionaries, and anthropologists were attracted to the collection of folk songs and folktales from preliterate or semiliterate communities in different parts of India. While the collection of songs and tales has continued, in the last twenty years some analytic studies in this field have been also attempted. Among these, mention may be made of a number of doctoral dissertations on Bhojpuri, Maithili, Assamese, Marathi, and tribal folklore. Moreover, several analytical books have been published. An independent journal devoted exclusively to folklore materials has been appearing in Calcutta since 1950. Under the auspices of the Indian Folklore Association, annual folklore conferences have been organized in Bombay, Allahabad, and Calcutta during the last decade in which folklorists from different parts of India have attempted to strengthen the discipline. Shankar Sengupta, the editor of *Folklore*, recently and for the first time used the term "folklorology" to indicate the need for the scientific study of folkloric materials. The teaching of folklore is being instituted at the university level, along with anthropology and various modern Indian languages, and a trend toward the development of folklore as an advanced discipline of teaching and research is becoming apparent. A bibliography by Kirkland (1966) includes references to songs, tales, riddles, proverbs, and other such oral materials on South Asia.

The term folklore, derived from the German *Volkslehre* [people's customs], has been used differently in different countries and at different times. In anthropological usage, it has come to mean myths, legends, folktales, folk songs, proverbs, riddles and a variety of forms of artistic expression whose medium is the spoken word. Here, however, I shall confine myself to a review of studies of folktales and folk songs undertaken in India. For the sake of convenience, I shall take the state as the unit of study, attempting within each to consider the various language groups and to distinguish tribal and nontribal categories. In instances where a scholar has worked on both songs and tales, the categorizations may overlap. In the category of folktales, myths, legends, and fairy tales will be discussed collectively, though at appropriate places the characteristics of each will be brought out.

FOLKTALE STUDIES

Kashmir

The natural charm and beauty of the valley of Kashmir has been a source of inspiration for its natives which finds expression in a spontaneous outburst of songs and tales. Their leisurely life, their exposure to contact with other peoples, and their close association with nature have given them additional incentive to compose and maintain a rich oral tradition.

The folklore of Kashmir attracted the first attention of the foreign missionaries and scholarly administrators, who wrote about Kashmir folklore as early as the late nineteenth century. Leitner (1872) was the first scholar to write about Dardu legends, proverbs, fables, and riddles. On the basis of materials collected from the Gilgit region, he presents a fivefold classification of Dardu legends. This classification is of special significance as one of the earliest efforts to analyze legends in terms of sociological and historical variables. Leitner's categories are as follows: (1) *semons-yach*, or bard stories, dealing with the wedding of demons, the ability of demons to change coals into gold, etc.; (2) *barai peris*, or fairy stories, dealing first with the hunter and the castles of the fairies and secondly with fairies who punish their human lovers; (3) *dayals*, stories about wizards and witches; (4) historical legends of the origin of Gilgit; and (5) animal stories, including seven interesting legends relating to animals. In addition to these types of stories, given both in the original Gilgit Dardu text in English script and in an excellent English translation, Leitner presents seven riddles relating to the material culture of the local people.

Steel (1882) presents, accompanied by an analytical note by R. C. Temple, nine folktales which she describes as common stories in Kashmir. She fails to mention the area from which they were collected. She gives only the literal translation of the stories and does not attempt any content analysis.

With the assistance of the munshis and the local pandits, Knowles (1886, 1887) collected a few stories and published them under the title "Kashmiri tales." The stories of "Gulabi Shal" and "The four princes and the four princesses" are extremely interesting, though he fails to associate them with any region or any tribe or caste. By the end of the nineteenth century, the publication of these long papers had prepared the ground for a book (Knowles 1893) including sixty-four folktales of different varieties. As regards Knowles's sources of information and methods of collection, the following remarks from his preface are indicative:

> The vocation of missionary brings one into close and constant touch with the peoples, from whom, as I glide along in the boat, or walk by the way or squat in the hut or teach in the school, I have learnt many things. . . . My primary object in

collecting these tales was to obtain some knowledge of Kashmir. . . . My secondary object was to ascertain something of the thoughts and ways of the people.

Knowles does not attempt a typology of these folktales, as he notes overlapping contents and themes. The stories are presented in English, though there is profuse use of original terms with glossary and explanation.

Another clergyman of Gilgit, Gulam Mohammad, presents a vivid and searching analysis of the folklore of Gilgit (Mohammad 1905–1907). In this paper he gives historical, geographical, and ethnological details on Gilgit, opining that the Kramins were the original inhabitants of Gilgit and were conquered by the Yesh Kuns, Shins, and Ronos, in that order. He mentions the difficulties in collecting materials in the absence of written records and documents, saying that he had "to go from village to village and house to house" collecting the various details of his work. Mohammad describes the festivals of Shins-Bajuns and the songs associated with them; *ayi-boi* and *duma-nikha* ceremonies and their songs; marriage rituals and the associated songs; and the ceremonies of *seclo-ai-thathah, nagi-suchami, khurum* or *majari, danyals gan, wiyo*, and *yatheni*. In the sections that follow, Mohammad deals with omens about lunar and solar eclipses and the creation of the world; sacred stones, trees, and springs; the legends of Shri Badat, the man-eater, and several historical tales such as those of the Katchata family and *chile* ceremonies; and the murder of Wazir Thusha and six other historical legends and stories. Mohammad's work provides rich materials of ethnological and folkloric nature based on firsthand empirical study. It gives in most cases the original text along with a lucid translation. On the whole, it is a most valuable contribution to research in Kashmiri folklore.

In recent times, two books on Kashmiri folktales have been published: Dhar (1949) and Dhar (1963). The first, containing seven stories in English, is fascinating reading. Written in a simple style, the stories are especially intended for children. The other, in Hindi, provides a full-length study of Kashmiri folklore divided into four parts. The first part deals with the theoretical background and presents an introductory description of the economic, religious, and social aspects of the Kashmiri people. Parts two through four present folktales, folk songs, proverbs, riddles, and maxims, along with their scientific classification. Dhar's work is both a rich collection and a significant analysis of folkloric data and thus ranks as one of the finest books in Hindi on folkloric research. Another work in Hindi is by Chatta (1952). In a short introduction, Chatta attempts to highlight the significance of Kashmiri tales.

Punjab

Undivided Punjab also has a rich heritage of folktales. The attention of British scholars and missionaries was drawn to this fact as early as 1880, when Steel published one of three long papers on Punjabi folktales. In her first article she presented three stories in English: "Bopuluchi (or Bopu) the trickster," "The sparrow and the crow," and "The Lord of Death." The essence of the Punjabi text has been retained. In her second paper she published another long story, "The King and the crocodile," which according to her was common among Punjabi women. A third paper describes the theme of "Baingam Badshabzadi" or "Princess Aubegine."

This collection of folktales was followed by Swynnerton's collection of thirty different types of stories from the upper Punjab (Swynnerton 1892, 1928). He provides no interpretation for these stories, "leaving each of them to speak for itself." His interest finds its culmination in the publication of his voluminous collection (1884) *The adventures of the Punjabi hero Raja Rasalu and other folk tales of the Punjab*. The narration of Rasalu's early life, his first triumph, his return from exile, his interaction with other Rajas, etc., accounts for twelve chapters. In the remaining chapters, forty-five different types of short household stories are presented. In the introductory note, Swynnerton discusses the need for folkloric research. In an appendix, he also gives some Punjabi verses. The stories, however, are not classified, and they also lack the original texts. They were collected by Swynnerton with the help of other administrative officers and missionaries. Though he does not give any sociological analysis of these folktales, he does compare them with Greek mythology and legends. He finds a great resemblance, for example, between the stories of Rasalu and the tale of Phaedra and Hippolytus. The tale of Mirshikari, again, he finds reminiscent of some of the stories of classical antiquity.

With the opening of the twentieth century, such British administrative officers as Crooke, Temple, and Rose published papers on the folktales of the northwestern region. Crooke (1900), with the assistance of local officers, collected eighteen stories from the village of Ghazi, about fifty kilometers from Attock. These folktales were collected from the so-called The tribe, said to be descendants of Afghan soldiers. The tales are unclassified, and the original text is not given. Temple (1900) offers a motif index of Punjabi legends. In a paper with Rose (1909) he presents two legends, "The war of Aurangajeb with Guru Gobind Singh" and "The wedding of Rai Mornier and Princess Peahen," in both the original text and an Englsih translation. Rose (1909a) describes the legend of the war of Khan Khwas with his father Sher Shah Changatta, King of Delhi. She takes care to give the original text and the English translation side by side.

During the same period, McNair and Baslow (1908) published their significant book, *Oral traditions from the Indus*, which gave a fillip to folkloric research in Punjab. The book includes nineteen stories of different types collected from a remote village on the left bank of the Indus. The folktales are presented only in English and lack any type of interpretation or classification.

Among more recent publications, mention may be made of a paper by Elwin (1944a) on the legends of Rasalu Kuar and a book in Hindi by Shastri (1958). Elwin responds to the controversy raised regarding the legends of Rasalu and observes that this legend was first recorded by Abbott in 1854. Shastri's collection of folktales include twenty-two different folk stories of the Haryana open-air stage. The stories are presented in Hindi translation, and there is no trace of the original text.

Uttar Pradesh and Himachal Pradesh

The first to explore the folkloric material of Uttar Pradesh was Bennett, who as early as 1872 published a legend from Balarampur dealing with a great wrestler named Bhaban Mishra. It is presented in English without its original text. Steel (1884) published a paper entitled "Mirzapur folklore" and dealing mainly with omens. Crooke (1893) offers eight stories from the area near Mirzapur. These folktales, though collected from local informants, are represented only in English; however, the author has provided some footnotes on the local terms. In another paper, Crooke (1895) presents a legend, dealing with the region of Prithviraj Chauhan, as told by one Bhola Bhagat of Rohara, Binjore district. The legend is presented in English only, but local terms are mentioned here and there in footnotes.

The first Indian folklorist to write about the folklore of Uttar Pradesh was Mitra, who published a paper in 1896 on the different forms and names of the goddess Devi, or Kali, worshipped by thieves and robbers in North India. In another paper (1902), "On North Indian folktales of the rhea-sylvia and juniper-tree type," he presents as an example of the first type the story of "One Raja and two wives" and as an example of the second type the story of "The seven Chanepa brothers." This sort of classification is of some value, but Mitra fails to identify the folktales with any region or any community.

Among the early writings, mention may be made of a significant publication by Dracott (1906) on the folktales of the northwestern Himalayan region, including fifty-seven folktales collected from Pahari women. She observes that "Himalayan folklore with its beauty, wit and mysticism provides the most fascinating study. It is, however, sad to note that the day is fast approaching when the honest hill folk of north India will lose their fascinating tales under the influence of modern civilization." She presents the tales in English and leaves it to us to imagine the richness of the ancient hill culture reflected in them.

Gariola (1926) reports on the folklore of Garhwal. Assuming that the folklore of a country is largely molded by its environment, he describes the scenic beauty and religious orientation of the region. He also refers to the fact that Garhwal is hemmed in on all sides by other countries and peoples. On the north is the mysterious land of Tibet, the land of magic and black art, the Jadugiri vot, as it is called in the folklore of Garhwal. To the east is Kumaun, comprising the present districts of Almora, Naini Tal, and Nepal. To the west is Dehra Dun, or Mal, as it is called in the folklore, while to the south is Rohilkhand, the home of the much dreaded Rohilas. All these geographical, historical, and cultural factors have gone into the fabric of the folklore. Gariola classifies Garhwal folklore under the following main categories: (1) the legends of the Puranic gods and demons and their battles; in this category, the most popular legends are about the Pandavas and the early life of Lord Krishna; (2) legends of the ancient kings and heroes of Garhwal and its environs, locally called *bharwalis*; (3) tales and songs about fairies, ghosts, and village godlings; (4) ballads and love songs.

Another outstanding collection, published in 1935 under the title *Himalayan folklore*, was prepared by Oakley and Gariola. In the preface Gariola refers to the role of the local bards (*hurkias*), who were the chief sources of Himalayan folklore. He describes the historical heritage of the Himalayas and observes that the region's hills and glens were believed to be the homes of gods, demons, and fairies, and beautiful legends and myths were invented to describe their lives. The folklore of the Himalayas, apart from its myths, has reference to the medieval period and reflects the social and political conditions of those times. Gariola suggests classifying Himalayan folklore into seven categories: (1) legends of ancient heroes, (2) fairy tales, (3) ghost and demon tales, (4) bird-and-beast lore, (5) magical stories, (6) witty sayings, and (7) ballads and songs. He goes on to analyze the various aspects of historical, political, and religious experience that are reflected in the folklore. In the chapters that follow, legends of heroes, wit-and-wisdom tales, animal lore, bird lore, and ghost and demon lore are presented. This book is a landmark in the analysis and collection of folktales and legends of the Himalayas. The stories are given only in English.

Chaturvedy wrote three books in Hindi on the folktales of Bundelkhand. His first collection (1952) consists of seventeen folktales, mainly mythological, historical, and animal tales. In the preface, Basudeo Saran Agarwal emphasizes motifs as the building blocks of the folktale. Chaturvedy shows how the tales reflect Bundelkhandi culture. A second book by Chaturvedy (1957) includes nineteen Bundelkhandi folktales, the last accompanied by the original Bundeli text. In the introduction he refers to the linguistic characteristics of Bundeli and describes the attractive posture and physical gestures of the storytellers. Chaturvedy also edited a book (1955) which includes folktales from such languages as Bundeli, Chhattisgarhi, Awadhi, Magadhi, etc. All of these stories, except his own Bundeli story "Jal Kannya," have been reproduced from published sources. The book contains a long introduction bringing out the similarities and differences in the motifs of these stories.

As regards folkloric research on Braj, the contribution of Satyendra deserves special mention. His book *Braj ki lok kahanian*, published in 1947 and again in 1957, includes forty-one folk stories in Braj Bhasha. The themes of these stories range from birds and animals to the people of Braj. In another book of a general nature (1960), Satyendra examines the folkloric elements in Hindi literature of the medieval period. Since he specializes in the Braj dialect, he makes profuse references to it.

Folklore research in the Kumaun area has been pursued by Pandey. In his excellent collection of folk songs, folktales, proverbs, and riddles of Kumanun (1962), he compares these materials with those of Punjabi, Rajasthani, Braj, Bundeli, Awadhi, and Bhojpuri folklore. In his introduction, he offers a useful analysis of folklore.

Bihar

Bihar, the seat of an ancient culture, has four main cultural-linguistic zones: Maithili, Magahi, Bhojpuri, and tribal languages. From the point of view of folktales, very few studies have been undertaken in the first three regions; there are relatively better collections of the tribal folktales. The tribal materials will be discussed later.

Though there has been considerable work on the folk songs of Maithili, Bhojpuri, and Magahi, collections of their folktales remain almost nonexistent. Among the few collections of Maithili folktales is the work of Mishra (1951) who, while reviewing the folk literature of Mithila, refers to tales and legends in Maithili. Binod, (1960), in a book in Hindi, presents eighteen folktales of different types in Maithili and classifies them under fourteen different heads. The collection is devoid of any analysis of the motifs and the themes of the legends.

No full-fledged paper or book on Bhojpuri and Magahi folktales has yet appeared. Chaturvedy (1955), however, includes tales in Magahi, Bhojpuri, and Maithili. Both the original text in the respective dialect and the Hindi version are included in this book. Among Magahi folklore studies, special mention may be made of Aryani's (1965) doctoral dissertation, the first chapter of which is devoted to Magahi folktales. In her introduction, Aryani offers a critical analysis of the status of Magahi literature and presents a typology of folktales and songs. She also devotes a chapter to Magahi riddles and proverbs. From time to time, Magahi folktales are published in the Magahi monthly magazine *Vihan*, published in Patna.

Bhojpuri is very rich in folk songs, folktales, and ballads. The Rashtra Bhasha Parishad, under the supervision of Nalin Vilochan Sharma, took initial interest in the collection and publication of folk songs and tales in folk languages. Sharma edited a dictionary of folktales (1959a) which includes tales in Bhojpuri and other regional dialects of Bihar. In another publication (1959b), he collected twenty-two tales in various dialects of Bihar. The work of Vinod (1958) is also devoted to the general study of Bhojpuri folklore. Several chapters deal with Bhojpuri ballads and folktales, among them the ballads of Bihula and Vijaya Singh. The remaining portion of the book is devoted to a critical study of Bhojpuri folk songs. In eastern Uttar Pradesh, Upadhyaya has done considerable research on Bhojpuri folklore. His 1960 work includes the collection and analysis of Bhojpuri folktales. These tales, collected directly from village storytellers, maintain their originality and freshness. Another book, devoted exclusively to Bhojpuri ballads and tales, is that of Sinha (1957). It deals with the characteristics of Bhojpuri tales, classified as heroic, erotic, romantic, etc. Popular tales and ballads are given in an appendix of some 100 pages. In addition to these publications on Bhojpuri folktales, mention may be made of such periodicals as *Anjor*, in Patna, and *Purvaiya*, in Varanasi, which publish folkloric materials in Bhojpuri. *Anjor* has from time to time published bibliographies of Bhojpuri publications (see, e.g., Chaube 1969).

West Bengal

The collection and analysis of folktales in Bengal dates back to 1872, when Damant published five stories in the first volume of *Indian Antiquary*. These folktales were collected from Dinajpur in West Bengal and were published only in English. In another paper (1880), Damant presents three more stories from Dinajpur.

Mitra (1927–1928a) deals with the Tibetan folklore of the Darjeeling area. Mitra also reported on the worship of the godling Mahakala by the Rajbansis.

R. Tagore (n.d.) sees folk literature as the root of modern literature. In reviewing it, he discusses the theoretical characteristics of Bengal folk literature and opines that the *Mahabharata* and the *Ramayana* are treasure-houses of Indian folklore. A. Tagore's (n.d.) paper "Brata katha" deals with folk stories relating to religious fasts.

An outstanding work on Bengali folktales is that of Bhattacharya

(1954), a full-length survey of folkloric research in Bengal. In a long and learned introduction, he examines various definitions of folklore and observes that folklore is a kind of collective creation of the folk. Regarding the history of folklore, he compares it to a tree, with its roots deeply buried in the past, but continually putting forth new branches, leaves, and fruits. Folklore, according to him, is the connecting link between the old and the new. Some chapters of this book deal with legends and folktales, including a comparative analysis of Bengali folktales, tribal folktales, and European tales. Chapter eleven deals mainly with the theoretical background of myth — its origin, its relationship with psychology, and its difference from folktales — and presents a few myths prevalent in Bengal. Chapter eight is devoted to legends, their origin, history, and classification.Bhattacharya's work is commendable in that it combines the collection of myths and legends of Bengal with a general analysis of folklore.

Assam and NEFA

Assam is a land of mountains and malaria, earthquakes and floods, of the Kamakshya temple, and of fascinating tribes. The wildlife, the picturesque landscape, the crisscross of mountains and valleys all provide rich stimuli for folklore. The folktales of the tribals of Assam, NEFA, and Nagaland attracted the attention of early scholars, but it remained for Goswami (1960) to collect Assamese folktales and analyze them in a somewhat systematic manner. In the introduction to his book, he proposes to analyze Assamese folktales in the light of Thompson's motif index. He refers to oral tales as *sadhu katha* [wandering mendicants' stories], a term he sees as covering everything from myths to fables. He finds the application of Thompson's classification of folklore to Assamese materials rewarding. He offers a brief motif index of Assamese tales and ballads based on Thompson's index, classifying the materials, as Thompson does, under twenty-three heads. The book represents a scientific analsysis of Assamese folktales and ballads.

In an earlier (1949a) paper, Goswami collected folktales from tribal and nontribal ethnic groups of Assam, providing samples of Assamese, Garo, Khasi, Kachari, Pah, and Syntieg folktales.

Orissa

Orissa, like Bihar and Assam, is rich in both tribal and nontribal folklore. The eastern coastal region, composed of the deltaic plains of Mahanadi, Brahmni and Baitarani is characterized by nontribal Oriya folklore, the hilly western plateau by tribal folklore of very rich variety. The folklore research on Orissa includes very few publications on Oriya folktales. The tribal myths and tales of Orissa have attracted comparatively more attention.

The first published study of Oriya folktales is that of Dutta Gupta (1923). This book includes nineteen Oriya folktales in English. In the preface, G. E. Fawcus remarks that this collection will be helpful for administrators in understanding Oriya culture.

Das has written several articles both in Oriva and in English dealing with folk literature. Das (1953) refers to Munsi Abdul Mazid, Chandra Sekhar, Bahini Pati, Nilmani, Bidyaratna, and Gopal Chandra Praharaj, who collected Oriya folktales and published them in various journals. He calls attention especially to Praharaj's collection *Utkal kahani* and Raghaba Nand Das's *Praba-chans on cultivation*, published in 1919. Das comments on the declining interest of the Oriya people in the narration of folk stories. The younger generation, he says, knows fewer stories than he heard in his own childhood.

Madhya Pradesh

Madhya Pradesh, considered the heartland of India, is the meeting place of the boundaries of seven states — Uttar Pradesh, Bishar, Orissa, Andhra Pradesh, Maharashtra, Gujarat, and Rajasthan. Physiographically, as well, it presents great heterogeneity and is divided into five different parts: (1) Girdha Province, (2) Malwa Plateau, (3) Narmada Valley, (4) Satpura Mountains, and (5) Chhattisgarh. It is a treasure-house of tales, songs, and riddles, both tribal and the nontribal, being the land of the *ghotul* [youth dormitory], which is a breeding ground for folklore.

The collection of folklore in Madhya Pradesh and in the adjoining areas of western India started quite early; several publications of both songs and tales date back to the eighties of the nineteenth century. Among them are a series of five tales published by Wadia (1886) and several published by Venkataswami (1896–1903). Venkataswami's collection includes one on the goddess of smallpox, "The thousand-eyed mother." This story was told to him by one Chinta Poitty, an old man of Nawab Basti, Nagpur. He reproduces it in English. The story is not identified with any caste or tribe and is said to be popular in the "central provinces" in general. In this and successive articles he presents some twenty-five stories, all in English without any interpretation and without identification with any tribe or caste.

Dube (1968), in his *Barchan taringini*, published the story of Prince Chandrakanta and the Princess Halsabati. The story, told by an informant, is written in Hindi and marks the beginning of folkloric collection in Hindi in Madhya Pradesh. The book, however, lacks the original text as well as any interpretation of the folktales.

Gordon (1908) includes in his book *Indian folktales* several tales from the villages near Bilaspur. Along with the folktales he presents facts about the folk beliefs of the people relating to festivals and religion, birth, marriage, and burial rites, and snakes and other elements of their habitat. The book includes, among other things, seven tales and fifteen proverbs popular among the tribes and castes of the western portion of Bilaspur.

Rajasthan

The land of desert and oasis of the Rajput heroes of Indian history, though rich in folkloric materials, has not attracted the attention of serious scholars. While the land is famous for its bards (*charans*), the collection of songs and tales there remains in its infancy. Among the few efforts to collect folktales is the work of Sahal and Gore (1941), who edited a volume in Hindi entitled *Choubali*. The book, with a preface by Jainendra Kumar, includes four folktales and an introductory note by the editors. Named for the Queen of Rajasthan, it claims to present the most popular tales of the land. Currently, we have the work of Devilal Samar on the folk dramas and dance of Rajasthan. A detailed study of Rajasthan proverbs has been attempted by Jalpur (1958). His book, in Hindi, is a detailed, systematic, and analytical study. Gahlot (n.d.) has published a book on Rajasthani proverbs on agricultural themes.

All India

In addition to these collections and writings on folktales of the respective areas, there have been works on Indian folktales in general. Several scholars have undertaken work with somewhat broader objectives and attempted to provide some theoretical insight into folklore.

As early as 1879, Stokes took up an all-India theme, presenting in her book *Indian fairy tales* thirty folktales of India. Of these, twenty-five were told to her at Calcutta and Simla by two ayahs and the last five by her mother. Stokes does not give any interpretation of these tales, though they are of great significance from the point of view of diffusion of themes.

Sharpe (1939) presents fourteen stories of different types collected from different parts of India and attributed to the "Golden Age." Though many of the stories are here published for the first time, their original texts are not given.

Jacobs (1961) has edited a volume of thirty typical fairy tales selected from the published sources. As it is meant for the English-speaking world, the book is written in colloquial English without any reference to the language of the original text.

Thompson and Balys (1958) have done a great service by preparing a bibliography on the folktales of India. In the preface, they recognize India as a country of particular importance for the understanding of the history of folklore in Asia and Europe.

Among Indian scholars, Satyarthi (1951) has produced valuable work on folklore in Hindi. His main contribution, however, is in the sphere of folk songs and in fiction based on folktale themes.

Bhagvat (1958a) provides an inspiring work on Indian folktales that brings together the results of her own investigation of some important aspects of Indian folklore in the light of the modern methods in folklore studies. In a very systematic and scholarly manner, she first reviews the different schools and approaches in folklore studies in the West. She goes on to analyze the importance of folklore in Indian civilization and observes that Indian culture as represented in folklore has been of one and the same quality, texture, and strength since Vedic times. She reviews the history of Indian folklore, arguing that Temple was the first person to give a detailed classification of the motifs of Indian folktales and that no further work of this kind was done until Elwin attempted it in 1949. She examines the attitudes of Indians toward folktales and songs, their efforts at the preservation of lore, and their various efforts to give names to these tales and songs.

Bhagvat examines the concept of myth, suggesting *daivata katha* as its synonym in Hindi and rejecting *puran katha* because of its association with the popular class of Hindu literature *dharma katha*, appropriately termed "moral tales" by the Buddhists and Jains. She also recommends the use of Saunaka's term *pavitra katha* [sacred tales] because myths are associated with sacred themes.

Bhagvat devotes other chapters to the definitions and historical versions of fairy and supernatural tales and legends. Legends, *danta katha* (a term current in several Indian languages), she divides into two types: migratory and local. Another chapter is devoted to the fable, which she terms *kalpit katha*. She considers the fable, which aims to impart moral teachings, to be a product of a well-developed literary genius. There is no trace of fables in the Vedic literature; the earliest sources are the *Mahabharata* and the *Jatakas*. In these fables, animals are symbols of mankind, as opposed to the animals of fairy tales, which have supernatural power. She devotes a chapter to riddles, which she terms *prahelica* according to the Sanskrit text. She suggests several synonyms for riddles in different Indian languages and examines the importance of riddles in their cultural context. In general, Bhagvat has done a wonderful job in this theoretically oriented book, which goes a long way toward clarifying the terms and concepts, definitions and propositions, of the study of the folktales of India.

Another theoretically oriented publication is by Bodkar (1957), who presents an outline of the classification of animal tales in India. His research is based on the materials available in the Danish Folklore Archives and in the Royal Library in Copenhagen, supplemented by some publications borrowed from libraries in Sweden, Germany, and England. On the basis of this material, Bodkar has attempted to distinguish 750 types. The outline of his classification is as follows: (1) enmity between animals, (2) the wise (clever) animal, (3) escapes, (4) the unwise (foolish) animal, and (5) gratitude (helpfulness)/(ingratitude).

Agarwal (1949) discusses the different forms of folklore and its historical, philosophical, and literary uses. His book remains a work of a pioneering nature, since it was written when folklore research in India was in its infancy.

Upadhyaya (1957) deals with the methodology of the collection of folklore, the various methods for the classification of folklore, and the approaches to the analysis of folktales and ballads. He devotes careful attention to the origin and diffusion of tales and their classification. He goes on to analyze the cultural and religious background of folktales and, by way of conclusion, attempts to evaluate the importance of folkore to national life.

Sita's *Bharat ki lok kathaiyen* (1959) is an excellent collection of folktales classified in terms of festivals, rituals, and love themes. It includes popular proverbs from different parts of India. The book, with a long foreword by V. S. Agarwal and an introduction by the author, provides a critical appraisal of "diffusion" in the themes of folktales in India.

Pramar's *Bharatiya lok sahitya* (1954a) is a collection of twenty-one essays of prime importance both for their rich bibliographical materials on Indian folklore and for their significant themes. Some of these essays examine the themes of folklore critically and theoretically.

The mature thinking of Satyendra on folklore finds its expression in his book *Lok sahitya vijyan* (1962), which examines the theme in a critical, analytical, and comparative manner. This remains one of the most valuable contributions to the field of folklore in India and needs to be made available through translation to English-speaking readers. It is the first book written in Hindi to be used as a textbook for teaching folklore at the master's level. On the basis of his research in folklore, especially in Braj Bhasha, Satyendra presents the elements of folklore in broad perspective. His approaches to the interpretation of folklore materials from anthropological, sociological, psychological, and literary points of view are praiseworthy. For the first time in the Hindi literature, we find adequate discussion of classification, motif, and the uses of the study of folktales. A special chapter written by Savitri Sarin discusses the history of the definition, classification, and uses of folk songs, proverbs, riddles, etc.; in his interpretations he seems to be greatly influenced by foreign folklorists. The book includes a comprehensive bibliography of the work of Hindi scholars in folklore. It offers an integrated picture of folklore in general and Indian folklore studies in particular.

Prasad (1970) traces the various theories regarding the nature of folklore. He deals first with theories regarding myths. Reviewing the works of Western scholars in this field, he lends his support to the idea of Lévi-Strauss and Cassirer. Next he attempts to review other theories and forms of folklore in the Indian context. The publication of this book fills a gap in the Hindi literature insofar as the theoretical study of folklore is concerned.

STUDIES OF FOLK SONGS

Kashmir

Kashmiri songs, as Satyarthi has commented, deal with the common themes of life. The mother, for example, compares her son to her earring; human beings are compared to flowering trees and birds; girls threshing rice, boatmen plying the paddle, and laborers bending in their ceaseless toil all have their own favorite songs which they sing while at work. As has been illustrated by Satyarthi (1953–1954), these songs are a true expression of the Kashmiri mind.

Among the early scholars interested in the folk songs of Kashmir was Mohammad, whose *Festivals and folklore of Gilgit* (1905–1907) includes the different types of songs associated with festivals. Mohammad does not, however, emphasize or analyze these songs. Howell (1908), a member of the Indian Civil Serivce, with the assistance of local officers, collected folk songs of Chitral and the adjacent areas in their original language, Khowar. The collection includes one long song of war in praise of Mohammed and three other songs. The literal translation of these songs is given. However, they have not been identified with any tribe or caste.

Among recent studies of Kashmiri folk songs, the works of Somnath Dhar, Karan Singh, and Mohan Krishna Dhar deserve special mention. Dhar (1955–1956) the folk songs of the "Golden Valley of Kashmir" and traces Kashmiri folk songs to unknown bards of the tenth century. He says that folk songs are on the lips of every Kashmiri, young or old. Folk ballads are popular in the villages, where they are sung by wandering minstrels (*jiban bols*). Kashmiri songs, rich in theme, content, and form, have been classified by Dhar into opera and dancing songs, pastoral lore, romantic ballads, play songs, and semimystic songs. He illustrates these types of songs by giving their texts in English.

The work of Singh (1962), *Shadow and sunlight*, is a monumental piece of research on the folk songs of Kashmir. In a foreword, Rajendra Prasad welcomes this effort, believing, he says, that there is much in such songs which ought to be preserved. Singh went from door to door to collect these folk songs in the Dogra, in the southwestern part of Jammu and Kashmir. The Dogris, known for their gallantry and chivalry on the battlefield, are also rich in artistic and folkloric materials. Singh presents not only the texts of these songs, but also their tunes. This he thought necessary to enable people unfamiliar with the language to appreciate their rhythm and beauty. Singh has enriched his anthology by providing the original Dogri texts and their translation into both Hindi and English. In this collection of thirty-one folk songs, the majority reflect the theme of love. Given the adverse economic conditions and the struggle for existence, perhaps the theme of love continues to provide charm to their life.

A book in Hindi on the folklore of Kashmir has recently been published by Dhar (1963). The third part of this book deals with folk songs. According to Dhar, the folk songs of Kashmir can be divided into seven types: (1) general songs, (2) ritual songs, (3) seasonal and festival songs, (4) songs of specific castes, (5) work songs, (6) miscellaneous songs, and (7) ballads.

The forbidding mountainous land of Ladakh has a rich variety of songs. Franckeleh (1901) records different types of Ladakhi songs, classified in five different categories: (1) court songs, (2) dance songs and fairy-tale songs, (3) wedding songs, (4) drinking songs, and (5) pre-Buddhist hymns. The collection includes thirty songs in Romanized Ladakhi text with English translations.

Punjab

Punjab, the land of the five rivers and of heroes, is rich in folk songs. This heritage has attracted the attention of several British and Indian scholars from time to time. The first publications on the folk songs of Punjab date back to 1885, when Thornton published a paper in which he commented on the infinite variety of Punjabi songs. Every class, every tribe, even every form of occupation, he said, has its own group of songs. To support this statement, he presented in an appendix specimens of Sikh religious poetry, Punjabi *slokas*, songs of the canals, songs of the late Kabul war, etc. He reproduced here the songs published earlier by Temple (1882) and Steel (1882).

Rose (1909a) presents three Punjabi songs with very different themes.

The first is a *kafi* of Gulam Farid collected from Dehragazikhan, the second a song about a flower, and the third a wedding song from Multan. She finds these to be the most popular songs of Punjab and gives the original text with its meaning in English. In another paper (1909b) she gives three more songs, the first relating to love and the others to spinning. In addition to these popular songs, Rose presents a long ballad of the Sikh war (1909c), which she divides into two parts — the first dealing with the first Sikh war of 1845–1846 and the battle of Sobraon, near Firozpur, and the second with the siege of Multan and the second Sikh war of 1848–1849. This ballad, like most others, she sees as presenting "a confusion of history and a description of brave events." Rose also published a song related to Gaddi women and a Pahari love song (1909d).

Another early collection of folk songs of Punjab is Coldstream's book of work songs (1919). These eleven songs, published both in the original text and in English, were collected from Pallang (Palki) bearers on Pathankot and Dalhousie Roads in 1887. Each song, composed of couplets, was sung by the bearers at the head and the end of the line in turn.

Among recent scholars, Satyarthi has done painstaking research on the folk culture of Punjab. In a paper on the cycle of Punjabi folk songs (1945), he presents the songs under twenty-seven subheadings. Though these songs, presented in English, are based on Punjabi songs, there is no mention of the communities from which they were collected. Satyarthi established himself as an eminent folklorist with his excellent book *Meet my people*, published first in Lahore in 1946 and then, after some modification, in Hyderabad in 1951. In this anthology, Satyarthi brings together folk songs from different parts of India, including Punjab. While he has collected many of these songs from published sources, he includes Punjabi songs from his own collection. The book has an introductory note by Mulkraj Anand, who pays glowing tribute to Satyarthi for his valuable work in the field of folklore of Punjab and for bringing together the unique songs of minstrels and popular poets depicting the life of our people. In the introduction, Satyarthi briefly reviews folk-song studies, which have touched every corner of India during the last seventy-five years. He considers it a valuable service to bring to light the color, the fire, the sparkle of the "poetry of the earth." Many songs, in particular the songs about spinning, take us back to the folk poetry of Punjab. These songs call attention to the vigor of Punjabi women and their love of spinning. They depict everyday life and show that "the spinners seem to think little and dream much." In a chapter on war songs, Satyarthi presents the famous Landai songs of the Pathans. Every Pathan war song, as Satyarthi points out, is a lifelike etching and is associated with a gospel of sword and rifle. Satyarthi gives all these songs only in English, even though, of course, he has firsthand acquaintance with the original text.

In another long paper (1952–1953a) Satyarthi writes about Gaddi folk songs. Though the major concentration of the Gaddis is in Himachal Pradesh, he finds the Gaddi dialect akin to Punjabi and points out that the Gaddis originated in the Punjab. He comments that every phase of the Gaddi's daily life has its songs. The Gaddi dialect lends itself admirably to rhyming. Every Gaddi song has the beauty of simplicity and sincerity, and collectively the songs reflect the richness, charm, and flexibility of the dialect. Satyarthi goes on to present examples of love songs, songs about gardeners and bumblebees, marriage songs, birth songs, and the recent Congress Party songs. These typical folk songs, though few in number, express the essence of the Gaddi style of life.

In another article on folk songs of North India (1953–1954) Satyarthi makes a general survey of the folk songs especially of Kashmir, Punjab, PEPSU, Himachal Pradesh, Delhi, and Uttar Pradesh. He gives examples of spinning songs, love songs, and family songs popular in the Punjab and PEPSU. His intention is to stress the role of folk songs as the passionate expressions of the folk and the importance of folk songs in keeping alive the memory of the past.

Satyarthi has also published an anthology in Hindi under the title *Bajet awe dhol* (1952), a collection of folk songs from all over India made possible through the help of his friends. He devotes a long introduction to a review of publications in folklore. A preface by Girija Kumar Mathur observes that folk songs are the product of the collective consciousness and arise out of a general need of the people, reflecting history, social system, tension and conflict, nationalism, art, language, poetry, and music. The original text in Devanagari script is followed by a free translation into Hindi.

Singh (1951–1952), in a paper on the folk songs of Punjab, argues that folk songs crystallize and preserve either a memory of the past or a dream of the future. They constitute a running commentary by a people on itself and its environment. They preserve the wit and wisdom of generations that are gone forever. Singh goes on to analyze the forms, the theme, the style, and the content of Punjabi folk songs. He notes that most Punjabi folk songs are in form of dialogues and that this dramatization at once raises the pitch, the tempo, and the value of both sentiment and the artistic skill behind the expression of that sentiment. He presents the literal translation of two soldier songs and some other songs relating to marriage, games, crops, rain, and women.

A paper by Nath (1958) on the daughter in Kangra folk songs brings to light a recurring theme in folk songs and dramas from many parts of India, especially in the folk songs of the Kangra. Nath observes that the folk songs of any country reflect the primary impulses and feelings of the people. They are born of work, joy, and sorrow and are a more faithful record of their emotional life and reactions than any other form of expression. The folk songs of Punjab, particularly those of the Kangra

Hills, reflect the themes of the charm and self-denial of the married girl, separation from a sister or a daughter, and so on. The hill man's solicitude for his daughter begins even when she is a little girl. In a series of folk songs, he implores his wife to treat her generously, as she will be staying with them only for a limited time. Nath gives other types of folk songs that reflect the patterns of father–daughter and mother-in-law–daughter-in-law relationships.

A book in Hindi by Randwaba and Pravakar (n.d.) deals at length with the folk songs of Haryana. They collected popular folk songs from the different parts of Haryana and published them in five parts: (1) Thet Hariyana, (2) Vitmay Brajlhumi, (3) Yadavlhimi Ahirwal, (4) Mewal Lok Darshan, and (5) Bisnoi Samaj. In addition to the typical folk songs representing different aspects of life, the authors describe the geographical and ethnological setting of the folk life of Rohtak. Another book in Hindi on the folklore of Haryana is by Yadava (1960). In the first part of his book, Yadava describes some of the geographical and historical settings of this region. In the second part, he discusses the main features of the language in Haryana and compares it with the contiguous languages. The remaining chapters are devoted to folk songs, ballads, folk dramas, proverbs, riddles, etc. The book is a piece of meticulous research and hard labor. It fulfils its purpose of bringing out the rich heritage of Haryana in the field of folklore.

Uttar Pradesh, Himachal Pradesh, and Delhi

Studies of folk songs in Himachal Pradesh and Uttar Pradesh have been undertaken by several researchers. Among the earlier scholars was Fraser, who published songs from eastern Uttar Pradesh as early as 1883. His collection includes *kajari*, *thungri*, *gazari*, *jatsari*, *birha*, etc. In course of his introductory comments, Fraser observes that he has written down the songs exactly as he heard them. The English translation of these songs is also given.

After the casual efforts of Fraser, a systematic attempt at compiling the folklore material of northern India was undertaken by Crooke, who in his first publication (1894) collected the popular beliefs and folk customs of the people of Uttar Pradesh. This general publication was followed by several papers containing songs prevalent in the area. In an article published in 1925, Crooke presents the ballads of Raja Darshan Singh, a song about Amar Singh, and a ballad of Jagat Deo Thakur Panwar of Jarari. This collection, published in the original texts in Roman script, was recorded with the assistance of local schoolteachers. In the following year, Crooke published another long paper (1926) containing marriage songs from various districts in northern India. Among the collections, twenty-seven songs are Hindu and three Muslim. Crooke presents a complete set of Hindu songs from Mirzapur depicting the marriage ritual from beginning to end. The remaining songs, collected from Itwa and other districts, are connected with various aspects of marriage ceremonies. These songs were also collected with the help of schoolteachers, and both the original text and an English translation are given.

Another member of the Indian Civil Service, Shirreff, published a book on folk songs in 1936. It is evident from the introduction to this book that he collected these songs primarily during his tour as collector of Jaunpur in the winter of 1934–1935, particularly in the village of Koiripur. He gives the names and descriptions of the informants who gave him the ballads and songs and helped him to produce an accurate rendering of them. He presents fifteen types of songs in English, providing the original text in Devanagari in an appendix.

In addition to these collections of a general nature, special efforts have been made by various scholars to study the folk songs of specific languages in Uttar Pradesh. Among these languages, as we have seen, is Bhojpuri, spoken in Banaras, Ghazipur, Azamgarh, Ballia, Jaunpur, and some parts of Mirzapur and extending to the Uttar Pradesh districts of Shahabad, Saran, and Champaran and to portions of Muzaffarpur in Bihar. Bhojpuri folk songs have a long oral tradition behind them. They have survived the ravages of time and continue to provide examples of the earlier classical poetry of this area. Analysis of Bhojpuri folk songs should help us in understanding the development and milieu of Bhojpuri culture.

One of the earlier scholars to collect and write about Bhojpuri folk songs is Satyarthi, who published the vigorous Bhojpuri Ahir folk songs as early as 1942. Ahir folk songs, popularly termed *birha*, are about cattle and the lifeways of the Ahirs and are sung with deep sincerity and feeling. Though several examples of *birha* are cited, there is no trace of the original text. In another book, Satyarthi (1951) refers to *birha* as meaning "separation from the lover or the beloved." In Bhojpuri, however, the *bhira* is not necessarily a song of separation. In his article "Folk songs of North India" (1953–1954), Satyarthi also refers to the songs of Uttar Pradesh, which in his opinion are rich and vigorous. He makes special mention of several types of songs such as *janta* (songs of the grinding stones), *nirabani* (wedding songs, generally sung by the Chamar women), *sawan* (songs of the rainy season), *birha* (songs of separation, sung by males only), *sohar* (birth-rite songs), etc.

The study of Bhojpuri songs initiated by Satyarthi was followed up by Singh (1948), who published a comprehensive appraisal of Bhojpuri folk songs. The book is based on the analysis of thirty-four *sohar*, fifty *jatsar*, fifty-eight *jhumar*, five *kabrawala*, forty-two *bhajan*, fifteen *baramasa*, three *alchari*, two *khelsbana*, thirteen *devi*, thirty-three songs of marriage, five *purabi*, eight *kajari*, twelve *ropni* and *nirai*, thirteen *hindola*, eight songs on traveling, and twenty-three miscellaneous songs based on the verses of Vidyapati, Kabir Das, and Dharam Das. In the introduction, the author deals with the different aspects of Bhojpuri folklore, including questions of the classification of folk songs. A foreword is written by the noted Hindi scholar Shiva Pujan Sahay, who rates the book a pioneering work.

Tiwari (1949), another eminent Hindi scholar, published a paper dealing with Piria, a curious folk festival of Bhojpuri women. Tiwari presents two songs associated with Piria in both the original text and an English translation.

Another collection of folk songs is by Somdev (1949), who presents fourteen songs from the district of Gorakhpur. This work is confined to the collection of several types of songs, without any interpretation or even a brief introduction.

Since the fifties, a number of serious scholars have done monumental work in folklore research in Bhojpuri. Upadhyaya wrote a paper on Bhojpuri folklore and ballads (1950a) that brought to light, in particular, certain facts about the origin and characteristics of ballads. Firstly, a ballad is not associated with a single author; secondly, it never has an authoritative text as does a popular song; thirdly, its oral transmission is not accidental, but an inherent feature; fourthly, it is characterized by repetitive music and recitation. Upadhyaya goes on to give examples of three ballads — the ballads of Bihula or Bala Lakhindar, Viyaya Singha, and Lorika — which are popular in the Bhojpuri area and which illustrate the heroism and philanthropy of the ancient heroes. In this general survey, Upadhyaya presents a fivefold classification of Bhojpuri folk songs: (1) songs relating to various *snaskaras* [rites of passage], (2) songs relating to *bratas* [fasts], (3) songs of the various seasons, (4) songs sung by particular communities, and (5) action songs.

This long paper of Upadhyaya is followed by a full-fledged book (1956) which includes 271 Bhojpuri songs of different types. In addition to the lucid translation of these songs into Hindi, an interpretation in historical and geographical context is given. In the preface, Upadhyaya presents the theoretical background of folk songs in Indian and Western traditions, discusses the Bhojpuri language, and describes different types of folk songs in Bhojpuri in terms of their major themes. In the introductory note, he spells out the themes of the book, dividing it into three parts: (1) *Sadhan* [sources], (2) *Sidhyanta* [principles], and (3) *Sanskriti* [culture]. In the first part he discusses the difficulties in collecting folklore materials and offers certain methodological propositions emerging out of his experience. In the next part, he deals with several theoretical issues involved in the study of folklore, suggesting approaches to the study of folk songs, tales, legends, ballads, and riddles. In the last part, he points to the cultural implications of folklore and the cultural elements reflected in them. The book ends with an extensive bibliography of folklore studies in India, with special reference to different states and dialects. This is one of the most systematic studies of the folk songs of a particular area and sets an example for similar research elsewhere.

Tripathi (1952–1953), in his edited work *Gram sahitya*, deals in part with the folk songs of Uttar Pradesh. Songs collected from Prayag, Jaunpur, Pratapgarh, Raibareli, Mirzapur, Sultanpur, and other areas, mainly through correspondence, are presented in this part of the book. Among these are seventy-nine *sohar* songs, one *annapranshan* (first corn-eating ceremony) song, three *mundan* (first hair-cutting ceremony) songs, twenty *janeu* (sacred-thread ceremony) songs, and seventy-nine marriage songs. In presenting the songs of sacred-thread and marriage ceremonies, he quotes from the *Manu smriti* and other Sanskrit literature to bring out the link between the two. Tripathi has chosen to make a free translation into Hindi instead of a literal translation.

Mishra (1964) has made a valuable study, under the guidance of Udai Narayan Tiwari, of Bhojpuri folk literature in its cultural context. Basing his research on Bhojpuri folk songs, he examines the culture of Bhojpur as reflected in folk literature. He considers the expression in folk songs of natural beauty, of social, economic, political, and religious life, and of aesthetic sensibility (love of music, painting, sculpture). In Mishra's work we find almost the first effort on the part of scholar of Hindi to relate folk songs and other forms of folklore to the social and cultural aspects of the society. Folklore and culture are mutually interdependent, and Mishra's thesis is a pioneering piece of research on this relationship. In addition, Mishra has produced a series of papers on the cultural feature of Bhojpuri folk songs (see 1959). Giving Bhojpuri examples, he shows how folk songs both reflect and reinforce the cultural elements in the society.

Deva (1953) has made a sociological analysis of the folk songs of Bhojpuri and brought out the cultural and social structural elements reflected in them. Though his work is of great significance for anthropological and sociological studies, it is difficult to comment on it because it remains unpublished.

Next to Bhojpuri, the folk songs of the border areas of Garhwal and Kumaun — Almora, Naini Tal, Tarai — have been of special interest to several folklorists. Gariola (1926) presents folktales and folk songs of Garhwal, including songs about fairies, ghosts, and village godlings as well as ballads and love songs. He gives literal prose translations for the Garhwali songs. This sporadic work of Gariola was followed by a full-length study of Garhwali folk culture by Bhandari (1946) under the auspices of Ethnographic and Folk Culture Society of Lucknow. Bhandari visited this area for ethnographic fieldwork and in the course of his stay in various parts of Garhwal began the collection of traditional folk songs. As part of the general series on folk culture sponsored and edited by D. N. Majumdar, Bhandari published sixty folk songs in literal English translation only.

Another long paper dealing with Garhwal folk songs is that of Bhatt (1962), who describes the beauty and simplicity of Garhwal and adds that Garhwal has its own age-old customs, magnificent manners, geographical peculiarities, folklore, folk dances, and folk songs which, taken together, constitute the Garhwali style of life. He suggests dividing the folk songs of Garhwal into twelve types. He speaks very highly of the heroism, valor, and romanticism reflected in Garhwal ballads and songs.

The research of Babulkar (1964) on Garhwali folk songs deserves special mention. His book in Hindi aims at an analytical study of Garhwali folklore. The book deals with folk songs, ballads, folktales, proverbs, and riddles. It attempts a classification of Garhwali folk songs in the light of the author's rich collections. The various popular ballads of the area, such as "Surju Kunwar," "Barmi Kaul," and "Jagdeo Panwar," are fully recorded. Babulkar has succeeded in giving a holistic picture of the state of folklore in Garhwal.

Research in the field of folklore in Kumaun has been mainly conducted by Pandey, whose 1962 book *Kumaun ka lok sahitya* brings to light the rich heritage of folk songs, folktales, proverbs, and riddles of this area. He compares the folklore of this area with Punjabi, Rajasthani, Braj, Bundeli, Awadhi, and Bhojpuri folklore. In his introductory chapter, he deals with theoretical themes relating to folklore and suggests a classification of Kumaun folk songs. The book, with a preface by V. S. Agrawal, is excellent.

Pangtey (1948), under the inspiration of D. N. Majumdar, collected the Bhutia folklore of the Kumaun Himalayan region, particularly the border regions of Johar, in Almora district. The songs are classified in the following categories: (1) *saguna*, or auspicious songs, (2) *dhoska*, or ring-dance songs, and (3) *ritu git*, or seasonal songs. Pangtey later expanded this work into a book (1949), and here the greater variety of songs required the expansion of the classification from the original three categories to five: (1) *saguna*, sung on asupicious occasions such as marriage, childbirth, initiation, housewarming ceremonies, etc.; (2) *dhoska*, among them songs for the well-known dances *dandyala, chamfuli, dhoka*, and *dhuring*; (3) *fag* and *mangal git*, or songs of blessings, sung by professional singers and dancers such as *doms* and *hurkias*; (4) *Chanchuri*, sung by devotées on the way to the temple for *darsan* or on the way home; (5) *bhrag*, or legendary songs, dealing with the bravery of ancestors in connection with mountaineering; (6) *baira bhagnolas* and *ghora*, or ballads; and (7) seasonal songs. Pangtey presents thirty-one songs representing these seven groups in the original text in Devanagari script and in a literal translation into English. The book, though edited by an eminent anthropologist, fails to provide any interpretation of the songs. The author also confesses his inability to collect the "confidential songs" of the Bhutias.

Srivastava, who also conducted field research under the guidance of D. N. Majumdar in the Naini Tal–Tarai region, wrote a doctoral dissertation on the Tharu tribe and collected a few Tharu folk songs, among them songs dealing with the festival of Holi and such other occasions as *baghatana, barahmasa, chhalari, milan, khakarena*, and *barichkarai*. He presents these songs both in the original and in English translation (1949a, 1949b).

There have been some collections and interpretations of Bundelkhandi folk songs. According to the custom of this area, the region between the Jumna and the Narmada and between the Chambal and the Tamsa is known as Bundelkhand. The most complete and voluminous work on the folk songs of Bundelkhand is that of Sharma (1954). In the first chapter, Sharma deals with the aesthetic, emotional, and artistic side of folk literature. He classifies folk literature into *lok gaddya* [folk prose], *lok paddya* [folk poetry], *lok upachar sambandhi sahitya* [literature connected with folkways], and *lok maneranjan sambandhi i sahitya* [literature connected with folk recreation] and goes on to subdivide these classes. Sharma presents examples of birth-rite, marriage, and seasonal folk songs. He examines songs relating to the worship of Bhagawati and Sitalamai. He devotes a chapter to the folk songs of different castes, such as Kahar, Ahir, Nai, and Dhobi, with special reference to their musical instruments. He ends with a chapter on Bundelkhandi ballads. He gives the original text in Bundelkhandi and a prose translation in Devanagari script.

In a booklet entitled *Bundelkhand ke lok geet*, Verma (1957) observes that the folk songs of Bundelkhand are mirrors of the hills, rivers, forests, birds, and people of Bundelkhand. A few other scholars in Hindi have published on the folk songs of Bundelkhand, among them Sharma (1954), Chaturvedy (1950), and Chaturvedi (1950).

Braj folklore has been explored by Satyendra. In his book *Braj lok sahitya ka adhyayan* (1958) he deals mainly with the folk literature of Mathura, and in every chapter he brings out the literary elements of Braj folk songs. Another epoch-making book in folk literature, edited by Satyendra, is *Braj ka lok sahitya* (1953), in which he reproduces thirty-two birth songs and several marriage songs, thirty-one songs of *suman*, five songs about *abtar*, nineteen songs about *devis*, twenty-five songs about pilgrimages and fasts, eleven songs about girls and boys, thirteen songs about girls, five songs relating stories, twenty-two songs relating to Holi, twenty-five songs about games, and seven miscellaneous songs. His third book, *Madhya jugiya Hindi sahitya ka lok Tantrik adhyayan* (1960), is an admirable collection of the various types of Braj folk songs with a view to relating them, on the one hand, to ancient texts and, on the other, to the life and culture of the people. Like Tagore, he claims that folk literature is the root of modern literature.

In addition to the scholarly, comprehensive, and critical study of Braj folklore by Satyendra, the recent efforts of two scholars of Hindi literature deserve mention here. Gupta (1967) makes a study of Krishna tales as reflected in Braj and Bundelkhandi folk songs and compares these reflections with those of Sanskrit and Hindi literature. He examines these songs from poetic and cultural points of view and attempts to identify the motifs in them. In the second part of the book, he presents the songs.

Ganga Chandra Tripathi has made a comparative study of Awadhi, Braj, and Bhojpuri folk literature, but since this remains unpublished it is difficult to make a critical appraisal of his research findings. It will not, however, be out of place to comment that Tripathi has chosen a theme which attempts to integrate the knowledge of the folk literature of Uttar Pradesh and that such efforts are imperative in other areas where different varieties of folk literature exist.

Research in Awadhi folklore has been conducted by Pandey. In addition to his several papers, his book on Awadhi folk songs (1957) deserves special mention as a scholarly work of a high order. In his long introduction, Pandey presents a sociological analysis of Awadhi folk songs in relation to birth rites, marriage customs, family life, roles of women in society, etc. In the light of cultural elements reflected in Awadhi folk songs, he attempts to interpret many traditions and customs prevalent among Awadhi-speaking people. The sociological perspective has also figured prominently in the selection and classification of the folk songs presented. The songs given in these chapters are related to birth rites, the *chhati* ceremony, *annaprashan*, the hair-cutting ceremony, the sacred-thread ceremony, the marriage ceremony, and *piari* (the ceremonial presentation of clothes by a brother). Only in the last chapter are seasonal songs, love songs, etc., included. Pandey's work is of great significance and continues to be one of the few studies of folklore done from a sociological point of view.

Bihar

The folk songs of Bihar have been collected especially from the tribal belt of Chota Nagpur and Santal Parganas. There are three other cultural-linguistic zones: Magahi, Maithili, and Bhojpuri. Among Magahi folklorists, mention may be made of Prasad (1862), who gave impetus to folklore research in Bihar under the auspices of Rashtra Bhasha Parishad. In addition to inspiring a number of scholars in this field, he edited a volume entitled *Magahi sanskar geet* which was published by Rashtra Bhasha Parishad in 1962. This collection of ritualistic songs has been of immense use because of the analytical notes that accompany the text. The importance of the book is enhanced by a learned introduction.

The research of another scholar of Magahi folklore, Sampatti Aryani, deserves special mention. In one of her papers (1959), she brings out the democratic elements in Magahi folk songs. In her celebrated book on Magahi folk literature (1965), she deals systematically with the various categories of Magahi folk literature and its general features. In the chapters that follow, she discusses the folk songs, ballads, and folk dramas which characterize the Magahi language.

Another scholar, Ram Nandan, editor of the Magahi magazine *Bihan*, has published Magahi songs from time to time. The Bihar Magahi Mandal has also brought out a collection of Magahi folk songs, which, however, lacks any analysis of the songs in terms of their social and cultural content.

In Maithili, a collection made by Rakesh (1942) contains an explanatory note and a long introduction. Here, too, the social elements embodied in the songs have been lost sight of. Rakesh has classified the Maithili folk songs in seventeen categories, including *sohar*, *janeu*, *vivaho*, etc., and has translated them into Hindi.

Another unique collection, *Kosi geet*, contains forty-five Kosi folk songs. The compiler, Mullick (1947), has made a valuable contribution to the knowledge of folk songs by collecting Maithili songs about the River of Sorrow.

In addition to these publications, there are a few others. Grierson (1909) published a book on the Maithili language that included a few Maithili folk songs. Mishra (1951) produced a book on the folk literature of Maithili in which folk songs are discussed in terms of Maithili culture. Another book devoted exclusively to Maithili folk songs is that of Lal (1962), who offers an analytical appraisal of these songs.

A number of folklorists have worked on Bhojpuri folk songs in Bihar. Archer (1943a), with the assistance of Sankta Prasad, published a voluminous collection; written in Devanagari, the book includes 377 folk songs of various categories gathered mainly from women of a few Kayastha families of Shahabad district. In general, these folk songs cover the entire Bhojpuri area, but songs related to the sacred-thread ceremony are conspicuously absent. The songs have been classified into several categories, but the reader feels the necessity of some explanatory notes regarding their cultural usage.

The dissertations of Upadhyaya, Mishra, and Deva mentioned earlier also include Bhojpuri folk songs from Bihar. The collection of Singh and Tripathi, also mentioned earlier, analyze Bhojpuri songs from literary and cultural points of view. Choube (1956) has also published Bhojpuri songs.

In addition to these works, mention may be made of general publications on Bhojpuri by Vinod (1958), Tiwari (n.d.), and others. Vinod, in addition to making a critical appraisal of Bhojpuri folk literature, brings out the importance of cultural elements in folklore. Tiwari's work is of great linguistic and literary significance and remains an outstanding work on the Bhojpuri language. Upadhyaya (1950b) deserves special mention here for a comprehensive collection of Bhojpuri folk songs from the Bhojpuri regions of Bihar and Uttar Pradesh. The volume, however, lacks any interpretative or explanatory notes.

The outstanding pioneering efforts of Ram Naresh Tripathi in the collection of folk songs have been mentioned earlier. His contribution to knowledge of Bhojpuri folk songs from both Bihar and Uttar Pradesh is unique and immense.

On the whole, sufficient work has been done in Bhojpuri to permit integration of the research results in a more sophisticated analytical style.

Bengal

Bengali folk songs constitute a rich heritage, and several scholars have collected and analytically studied them. In a chapter entitled "Folk songs of Bengal" in his previously mentioned book, Satyarthi (1951) discusses the ecology of Bengal and then gives a short account of Bengali folk songs. He presents the songs only in English.

Bhattacharya, the eminent Bengali folklorist, deals in the second chapter of his book *Banglar lok sahitya* (1954) with the folk songs of Bengal. He classifies Bengal into four regions in terms of folk songs: west, north, northeast, and southeast. He points out that *patua* songs are more popular on the western borders of west Bengal, while *bhadu* and *tusu* songs are found in other portions of the western area, especially in Manbhum, Bankura, Birbhum, and Midnapur. Other forms of songs, such as *jhumar, jari*, and *gaj*, are popular in other areas. Bhattacharya presents several cradle songs, which are universal in nature. He compares Bengali cradle songs with those of Oriya, Telegu, and Oraon and brings out various common features. He also gives some data regarding the diffusion of folk songs and suggests that the richer elements of the tribal folk songs of Chota Nagpur have influenced the folk songs of Bengal especially in Birbhum and Mayman Singh districts.

Another scholar, Upendra Bhattacharya, presents a collection of 517 Baul folk songs from Bengal (1957). According to him, Baul is a kind of religious sect, and these songs go a long way toward explaining the origin and development of Baul spiritualism. As a student of comparative religion, Bhattacharya is interested in the Baul religion as expressed in folk songs.

Bhowmick (1957), Shasmal (1965), and others have collected and published folk songs along with their ethnographic research. The folk songs of the Lodha and those of the Bauri of Hooghly district have been studied by Bhowmick and Shasmal respectively. The Lodha folk songs are mostly of narrative type, with themes from the two great epics, the *Ramayana* and the *Mahabharata*. The other types of popular songs among the Lodha are *jhumar*, *bandana*, etc., in which the popular themes are the grace of the Lord Krishna and the welcome of the cow as the goddess Bhagvati. Shasmal deals mainly with *jhumar* songs of the Bauri, a scheduled caste of West Bengal.

Ghosal (1962) presents the rain songs of Bengal and the magical rites relating to them.

The journal *Folklore*, under the editorship of Shankar Sengupta, has published a number of folk songs and analytical papers on the subject over the past decade. Sengupta has also edited several books on folklore research in India (1963, 1964). Basu (1956), on the basis of his field collections, has published the songs of the Noluas of Bengal with a brief introduction.

Assam

Among the folklorists who have done work on Assamese folk songs and ballads, the name of Goswami figures prominently. In an early paper on Assamese ballads (1943), he offers a brief survey and narrates the ballads of Manikonwar and Fulkonwar. He goes on to establish the utility of ballads in historical reconstruction. He devotes another paper (1949–1950) to the several varieties of folk songs — ballads, marriage songs, lullabies, philosophical songs, boat songs, and so on. He goes on to present a number of Bihu songs sung on the occasion of the New Year's festival. Goswami brings out the fact that several Miri and Kachari tribal songs have found a place among the Bihu songs of the Assamese.

In his book on Bihu songs of Assam (1957), he presents a comprehensive collection of these songs and a detailed analysis. He also presents a general essay on folk songs in Assam in historical and sociological perspective. The translation includes 262 songs. In course of a long introduction, Goswami discusses the significance of the different types of Bihu songs. The New Year, with the germination of seeds, is marked by the Bohag Bihu, while the harvest season is associated with Magh Bihu. The period between the last day of Chait and first day of Baisakh is characterized by songs, dance, fairs, and social visits. Goswami also deals with the technical aspects of the songs, the dances associated with some of them, and the musical instruments. In one of the chapters he gives the translation of sixteen Miri and Kachari songs which are sung by Assamese

Hindus. Here he succeeds in bringing out the nature of the integration between the Assamese and these tribes insofar as it is reflected in the adoption of folk songs.

Goswami's book on ballads and tales of Assam (1960) analyzes the tales, songs, and dances along the lines suggested by Thompson and, under the influence of the writings of several social anthropologists including Franz Boas, attempts a sociological analysis of the folklore materials of Assam. Goswami defines a ballad as a simple, spirited poem in short stanzas narrating some popular story. He further refines the definition by suggesting that it is a short narrative poem adapted for singing, simple in plot and metrical structure, divided into stanzas, and characterized by complete impersonality as far as the author or singer is concerned. He examines the characteristics of Assamese ballads from many angles and classifies them into four divisions: (1) historical ballads, built around more or less authentic historical incidents or figures; (2) ballads of magic, in which the marvelous predominates and which use ancient and universal folklore themes; (3) realistic ballads, which are more or less transcriptions from life; and (4) satirical ballads, which caricature events or persons.

Another important book is *The red river and the blue hill*, by H. Barua (1954), which gives a penetrating and significant description of Assam's folk songs. Barua brings out the importance of community dancing and singing as the chief form of amusement in the countryside; with the approach of the Bihu festival in April, folk dances begin, and everyone is energized with new spirit. He goes on to describe the three Bihu festivals — Bohag, Magh, and Kati, which are celebrated at different periods of the year and are associated with different sets of folk songs. In general, he observes that the Bihu songs are often woven around themes of love and its different moods and youthful nature, and thus their compass is wide. They are characterized by sweetness, lucidity, and tender shades of suggestion and elocution.

In a short essay, B. K. Barua (1943) discusses the songs associated with Bihu festivals at the beginning of autumn and spring. Satyarthi (1951) also deals with Assamese folk songs, observing that they are rich in lullabies and marriage and Bihu songs. He gives examples of all these types of songs only in English; the original texts are omitted to simplify presentation.

Orissa

The study of folk songs in Orissa is just beginning. Most of the works in the field of folklore in Orissa are confined to the study of tales. The only reference to Orissan folk songs is found in Satyarthi's (1951) book, in a chapter entitled "Homage to Orissa." Here again he devotes his attention mainly to the ecology and history of Orissa, stressing the importance there of Buddhism; finally, he reproduces in English some folk songs from secondary sources. Adarshi (1960), in an essay in Hindi on cultural elements in the folk songs of forest-dwellers, refers to the folk songs of the borders of Orissa. He presents twelve songs in their original texts and in Hindi versions. Das (1953) has published a systematic study of Orissan folklore that deals, among other things, with Oriya folk songs. Being a mature folklorist, Das, in addition to the collection of songs, presents an analytical study of Oriya folklore.

Madhya Pradesh

The study of folk songs in Madhya Pradesh has been largely confined to tribal cultures. Dube (1947) presents songs collected from Chhattisgarh, including Raipur, Bilaspur, Durg, Balaghat, Bandora, and a number of districts of the adjacent states. Of these, the first three districts are the traditional home of the Chhattisgarhis, while the other two are on its fringes. Dube's collection includes 1,200 songs and a dozen ballads. While most of the songs are from the tribes such as the Gond, Baiga, Dindwar, Kamar, Bhuiya, Dharwar, and Korwa, other Chhattisgarhis are also included in this study. These songs, while given no formal ethnic classification, have been divided into general songs, dance songs, caste songs, songs for special occasions, tribal songs and legends. Dube's collection and its analytical introduction help us to visualize life in rural Chhattisgarh: a life of little love, a perpetual struggle marked by uncertainty and pessimism. He finds that the folk songs are fast disappearing and advises his fellow anthropologists to take up the cause of collection and analysis. He also cautions them to be sure, before undertaking fieldwork on folklore, that they are well-versed in the literature of the area, that they have patience and a knowledge of the language or dialect spoken in the region, and that they have the capacity to distinguish relevant material.

Singh (1953), in his edited volume, presents ninety-five folk songs of tribal and nontribal origin collected from Baghelkhand, classified in five categories: (1) *sohar*, (2) *bises geet*, (3) *lori*, (4) *basua*, and (5) marriage songs. The original texts in Bagheli are given along with their translations into Hindi.

Pramar, in his celebrated book *Bharatiya lok sahitya* (1954a), deals mainly with the themes of folklore in the light of materials collected from Madhya Pradesh. In a long introduction, he gives definitions and theoretical background. Then, in the course of a general survey, he devotes one chapter to the folklore of the Narmada Valley and another to the marriage songs of the Bhil and other criminal tribes. Pramar has also published on Malwai folk songs (1954b) and has devoted another book to the general analysis of Malwai folk literature (1954c). These works by Pramar bring out the rich heritage of Malwai folklore; I wish that there could have been some publications in English too to acquaint the scholars of the world with the wealth of folklore materials in this area.

Credit goes to Jain for an extensive study of folklore from the Vindhya region, resulting in the publication of collections of folktales (1953) and folk songs (1954). Jain's collections remain pioneering works in this area and are of immense significance because they are based on his rigorous fieldwork.

Rajasthan

Rajasthan is rich in folk songs, tribal and nontribal. The initiation of folk-song research in Rajasthan was made by Singh, Parikh, Swami, and Das (1940). In their collection *Rajasthan ke gram geet*, they give us songs related to love, water-fetching, beauty, separation and union of couples, etc. In another book, Parikh (1942) deals with every type of folk song from Rajasthan and compares these songs with those in Gujarati and Hindi. In making this comparison, he considers songs relating to festivals, marriage, family life, gods and goddesses, animals, flowers, moon, sun, etc., seasonal songs, songs about young girls, and songs about rain. All these songs appear in the original in Devanagari script and in a Hindi translation.

Satyarthi devotes a chapter of his 1951 book to Rajput war poetry. In it, he first describes Rajputana and then goes on to discuss the traditions of the bards as transmitters of war and genealogical poems from generation to generation. He describes the romanticism and heroism of the war poetry. He also refers to the high pitch at which these songs are sung and observes that they were sung to the great *manu rag*.

Then there are, in twelve volumes, the old Rajasthani songs compiled by various scholars including Das (1956). These volumes contain the rich heritage of Rajputana as reflected in its oral tradition. Another attempt in this field is that of Kaviraj (1957), published under the auspices of Rajasthan Vishwa Vidhyapith.

Another volume, edited by Daruka (1961), compiles all the Marwari songs. A collection of Marwari songs has also been made by Gupta (n.d.); the folk songs are presented with some explanatory notes.

A systematic study of Rajasthani folk songs has been attempted by Agrawal (1959). Her further works await publication.

Gujarat and Maharashtra

These two states are equally rich in folklore, and research has been conducted by Gujarati and Marathi scholars. Owing to inadequate acquaintance with folklore research in these and other South Indian states, it is impossible for me to review the literature on these linguistic groups. Among the publications on Gujarati folklore, these of Enthoven (1916) on the folklore of Bombay and Gujarat are well-known. The folklore materials have been translated into English. These two books, though in a sense out of date, continue to provide rich data on the folklore of this area. A volume edited by Krishnaswamy (1950) on Marathi songs under the auspices of the Madras Government Oriental Series deserves mention. A. R. Bhagwat has collected Maharashtrian folk songs and published them in the *Journal of the University of Baroda*. Folklore research in these and other South Indian states will be reviewed below.

RESEARCH ON TRIBAL FOLKTALES AND SONGS

The significance of tribal tales and songs needs to be understood in relation to ecological, social, and religious considerations. The tribal peoples have continued to live in the lap of nature, isolated from the so-called mainstream of the sophisticated puritanical, Brahminical culture of India. Because of their closer interactions with nature, on the one hand, and their isolation from the so-called civilized Brahminical way of life, on the other, the tribals have been able to maintain a traditional, closed situation for the preservation of the folklore resources of their respective cultures. Their social institutions of the youth dormitory, the village *akhra* [dancing ground], and the custom of free mixing of the sexes and indigenous drinking are all important in the development, maintenance, and transmission of tribal folklore. The combination of folk songs with folk dance, on the one hand, and their association with the numerous festivals and rituals have further contributed to the persistence of singing, dancing, and drumming.

The tribal folktales and songs are unique in terms of theme and motif and give a different feel to folklorists in a cross-cultural situation. While they reflect more faithfully the cultural elements and historical experiences of the tribals, they require more skill and caution in their recording and interpretation. They also call for more anthropological knowledge and training in fieldwork.

Though the anthropological study of tribal folklore is only beginning, several efforts by administrators, missionaries, travelers, writers, and ethnographers have been made to collect and, in some cases, interpret the tales and especially the songs of the tribals in different parts of India. I shall here review folklore studies in the predominantly tribal belts of northeastern India, comprising portions of Assam, NEFA, Nagaland, Manipur, and Tripura, and in the tribal belt of Middle India, comprising the states of Bihar, Orissa, and Madhya Pradesh, and then discuss some major studies of tribal folklore in other areas. The usual sequence of discussions — first tales and then songs — will be maintained in the first part of this review.

Tribal Folktale Studies

NORTHEASTERN INDIA. In the northeastern region, research on folktales dates back to 1875, when Damant published a Manipur story, "The two brothers." The story is presented in English, without any effort to give the original text. In another paper (1877), Damant narrates the story of Khamba and Thobi from Manipur. Here, also, he presents only the English translation of the story. Houghton, another British administrator, published a folktale of the Lushais in 1893. The story was originally collected by T. H. Lewivi and deals with Kungori.

These sporadic efforts at collection of tales in different parts of Assam, were followed by the publication of a full-length book on Kachari folktales by Anderson (1895). This collection was made in the course of a tour of six weeks in the Kachari villages of Mangaldai and includes fifteen Kachari stories of different types. A few specimens of Kachari folk songs are also given. The original texts are presented in Kachari in Roman script and followed by English and Assamese versions. In the course of his analysis, Anderson notes the impact of Assamese folktales on these Kachari tales and observes that in many cases the Kachari version is a word-for-word translation of the Assamese.

Still another British administrator, Cochrane (1911), posted to Burma and Bengal, brought to light a cosmological legend from Ahom, procured from a secondary source and presented in English.

Mitra has also collected myths and legends from the tribes of Assam. In one of his essays (n.d.a), he presents the plant myths of the Thado Kukis, and in others he presents the bird myths of the Lushai Kuki tribes. A Lushai folktale says that, whenever an eclipse occurs, a spirit called an *awk* is devouring the sun. The Lushai myth regarding the jungle babblers (n.d. b) illustrates to a remarkable degree an important trait of the mind of the primitive man: It is quite unconscious of the difference between man and beast. The Lushais appear to be possessed of a belief in the interchangeability of man and beast, for they have invented a myth to the effect that in the course of the darkness that followed an eclipse men readily metamorphosed into jungle babblers. Mitra, discussing another bird myth (n.d. c), describes the Lushais' conception of the evolution of the king crow.

Mitra (n.d. d) presents a Lhota Naga and Angami Naga folktale about the metamorphosis of a semidivine girl (a god's daughter) into an orange.

Rafy (1920) and Narayan (1942) have collected folktales of the Khasis. Rafy's collection includes thirty-two tales published in English. At this early stage, cultural interpretation of folktales was not in vogue, so Rafy gives us only the tales and leaves it to us to determine the cultural elements reflected in them. Narayan offers a brief analysis of Khasi folktales. He finds that the beliefs and traditions of the Khasis are handed down from generation to generation in the form of folklore of many kinds and on a variety of subjects. Some tales are about certain hills and rivers, while others explain natural phenomena like eclipses, thunder, lightning, the presence of spots and shadows on the moon, and the absence of moonlight during the day. Khasi tales describe how the peacock got his beautiful feathers, how doves began to coo, how the monkeys became grey, and so on. Narayan also presents certain cosmological tales regarding the origin of the earth and the world. He concludes by mentioning the tale of the "lost book," which explains why the Khasis have prescribed modes of worship and prayers handed down from one generation to another.

Goswami, in his essay "The folktales of Assam" (1949a), also deals with Khasi folklore and refers to the significant position of the snake (*thlen*) in Khasi folktales. In an article on Abor tales, Goswami (1949b) presents four stories of the Abor. The stories are given in English without any original text. In another paper (1954–1955), he presents a brief survey of Naga tales. He also narrates a story regarding the origin of the Naga tribe and brings out the fact that the Naga call themselves "Tengimie," the term "Naga" being from Indian sources. He also observes that, while the Naga do not worship the snake in the manner of the Khasis, it does occupy a significant place in their subconscious; he illustrates this with a tale. He points out that though the Assamese have certain animal tales centering on the monkey and the fox, the Kacharis and the Nagas have more animal tales.

The most recent and comprehensive work on the folktales of northeastern India is Elwin's book on the myths of the northeastern frontiers of India (1958). Elwin presents the cultural characteristics of NEFA and suggests it to be the home of bright colors, lovely weaving, dancing, singing, and enchanting people. He observes that myths are told on a variety of occasions, some being chanted during the dance as are the "Adi Abhanga" and the "Sherdukpen" tales. Certain myths are repeated in ceremonies and on occasions such as funerals, harvest, and thanksgiving, while others are told around the fire or in the youth dormitories. These NEFA stories, he says, are rich in poetic ideas, and the stories of the origin or creation of the world, the sky, and the heavenly bodies have an almost Miltonic grandeur of conception. Elwin goes on to emphasize that the people of NEFA have a strong sense of beauty and a love of bright colors and flowers. Among the motifs found in NEFA tales are those of a primeval ocean out of which the world was formed, an earthquake caused by the great animal on whose back the whole world rests, lightning as the pursuit of a girl by an unwanted lover, a land of women and of opium, the reincarnation of a girl whom no one had loved in her lifetime, the taboo against opening something during a journey, etc. In the first part of this book, Elwin presents tales of the origin of earth and heaven, of sun and moon, and of different tribes. In the second part, along with a short description of the traditions of different tribes, he presents other interesting stories collected from among them. Some of the tales were gathered by Elwin in the course of his ethnographic inquiries in various parts of NEFA, while others are reproduced from old books.

A recent publication on the folktales of the Garos is that of Rangamathu (1960). It presents eighty-nine folktales of different types. Rangamathu, himself a Garo, presents tales which he has collected from members of the illiterate and unsophisticated hill peoples of Assam. He gives the original texts along with translations and makes a case for more fieldwork in folklore, music, and tribal arts, which are in rapid transformation.

BIHAR. The collection of folklore from the tribes of Bihar was initiated during the nineteenth century by missionaries and British administrators, who took an interest in the folk literature of some of the tribes and collected folktales and folk songs. The collection of folktales, however, remains confined to some of the major tribes such as the Santal, the Munda, the Ho, and the Oraon. Research on folktales was extended by Mitra (1927–1928b, 1927–1928c, 1927–1928d, 1928a) to the Birhor tribe. Roy (1916), Trigunayat (1957), and, recently, the graduate students of the Department of Anthropology, Ranchi University (who have submitted field reports on various tribal communities of Chota Nagpur) are among the other Indians who have done research on the folktales of the tribes of Bihar.

The initiation of folktale research here dates back to 1875, when Cole published two folktales of the Santal. The first story deals with the sun and the second with the brothers Karan and Guju. These two folktales were collected by Cole from Taljhari, near Rajmahal, and are presented in English.

In 1891, Campbell published his work on Santal folktales. He classifies the tales into two categories: tales of purely Santal origin and tales borrowed from other sources. The first set deals mainly with mythical food, social customs and usages, cosmological myths, and religious beliefs and practices. The second set is based on Hindu themes with the modifications necessary to fit their cultural patterns and forms of thought and speech. These tales were collected by Campbell with the assistance of his local officers in the original text and later translated into English. Campbell claims that his translation is aimed at maintaining the interest and freshness of the Santali tales.

Campbell's enthusiasm for the collection and analysis of Santali folktales continued for some time, and in 1916 he published two more papers, one on cosmological myths and the other on social legends. In the first paper, Campbell records the Santal myths regarding the creation of the earth, fauna and flora, and the Santal themselves and the migration of the Santal from their original home to their present one. In the second paper, he presents four popular legends of the Santal. In both these papers he offers a very lucid English translation of the Santali text, along with notes on the tales that are of special interest for anthropologists.

Bompas, another scholarly administrator, presents a comprehensive collection of the folklore of the Santal (1909). In his long introduction, he describes the ethnological characteristics of the Santal. He reports that most of the stories and legends presented here were originally collected by P. O. Bodding of the Scandinavian mission, who was stationed in Santal Parganas for several years. The folktales have been classified into six groups; the first includes 109 folktales of a general nature, the second 14 animal and bird stories, the third 24 stories relating to Santal life, the fourth 12 stories dealing with god and man, the fifth 14 legends and their analysis, and the sixth 12 stories relating to witchcraft. Bompas has performed a valuable service by presenting this exhaustive collection. It only provides the English versions. Bompas claims to maintain the spirit of the Santal folktales intact in these translations, but he admits that in the course of translation some of the stories have been condensed.

The publication of Bodding's research is a milestone in folktale research in India. The stories presented in the first volume (1925a) include fifteen about jackals, nine about women, thirty-seven with humorous themes, six about ogres, five on *sugis*, six on the soul and the human body, two about animals born of women, and thirteen dealing with various other themes. Bodding collected these stories in Santali, which he knew very well. He discusses the cultural elements reflected in the folktales. Aryan derivations are especially conspicuous in articles of food and dress, implements, and methods of calculating time, as well as in trade and administration. Bodding's two further volumes of tales (1925b, 1927) deal with Santal ideals on disease and witchcraft respectively.

In recent times Doman Sahu Samir, who worked with Archer, has published a few tales in *Hor Sambad* (Deoghar) and several Hindi magazines.

Research on the folktales of the Munda was initiated by Roy (1912), who did pioneering research in the field of tribal ethnography and includes folktales in his first monograph on the Munda and their country. He also includes tales, myths, and legends in his later monographs on the Oraon (1915), Birhor (1925), and Kharias (1937). Roy used many of these oral sources in tracing the origin and migration of these tribes. In addition, he made a special study of the myths of the Munda (1916). He classifies Munda myths in two categories: myths regarding the principal deities and miscellaneous myths regarding the mythical adventures of men and gods. In other categories he presents animal stories dealing with beliefs about the minor spirits. Roy, with his rich ethnographic knowledge, presents these stories meaningfully, though they lack the original texts.

Bhaduri (1922) attempts to understand the astronomy of the Munda in relation to their star myths. He describes the legends woven around several star groups and relates them to Sing Bonga, the supreme God, and to the absence of stars in the daytime.

Mitra (1927–1928e) contributes a note on Mundari legends. His legend regarding the origin of the name of Ranchi is of special significance; he establishes that "Ranchi" was derived from a Mundari word *alachi* or *arachi* [stick]. He also refers to the origin of place-names like Pakhra, Doranda, and Hindpiri.

In the thirteen-volume *Encyclopaedia Mundarica* by Hoffmann (1950), certain folktales are offered by way of illustration. Hoffmann's interest in writing these volumes, he says, is to incorporate into them all that he has learned from the Mundas about their economic, social, moral, religious life and about their language, poetry, music, and dance.

Among the recent studies on the folktales of the Munda, mention may be made of Trigunayat's work on Mundari folktales. The first book (1957), in Hindi, narrates the story of Soso Bonga, which brings out the religious faith of the Mundas. The second book (1968) includes his collection of 167 Mundari folktales, given both in Mundari and in Hindi written in Devanagari script. It has a long and useful introduction on the theoretical aspects of Munda culture and Mundari folktales. It is divided into three parts: in the first are cosmological tales and myths, in the second legends, and in the third different types of tales. Trigunayat deserves appreciation for this valuable contribution to the store of tribal folklore, one of the few books devoted exclusively to the folktales of a particular tribe or community.

The folktales of the Oraon were collected by Hahn and edited by Grignard (1931). In his introductory note, Grignard presents a short account of Oraon customs dealing with village organization, family life, beliefs, and superstitions. Hahn collected these tales in the Kurukh language, and in this volume the original texts are given for the myths; the other forty-one tales appear only in English translation. This collection records most of the significant folktales of the Oraon and brings to light the cultural elements reflected in them. The literal translation and explanatory notes given here and there help us in understanding the themes and motifs of these tales.

There have been a few attempts to collect the folktales of the Ho tribe of Singhbhum, which belongs to the Mundari linguistic group. Among the earlier scholars special mention may be made of Haldar (1916–1917), who had intimate knowledge of the tribes of Chota Nagpur, in general, and Singhbhum, in particular, and published thirty Ho folktales. He gives the literal translation of the tales but does not present any analytical appraisal.

Mitra (1926) also published a Ho folktale which deals with the wicked Ho queen of Singhbhum. He considers it a very popular story among the Ho and presents it in a popular form in English. In another article (1928b), he follows up the study of this folktale with a comparative analysis involving a similar Santali tale from Bompas's (1909) collection. This comparison reflects the prevalence of similar type of folktales in tribes living in two different areas but belonging to the same linguistic group. It also shows that women eat certain fruits and observe certain taboos in order to procure children in these cultures.

A member of the Ho tribe himself, Deogam has done considerable works on the Ho songs and published a Ho folktale (1928). He presents this story first in the original text, in Roman script, and then in English. The story deals with a fox that killed goats.

Mitra also worked on the folktales of the Birhor. In one of his papers (1927–1928f) he presents the cosmological myth of the Birhor and compares it with Santali and American Indian folktales. In another paper (1927–1928d) he traces the element of cannibalism as reflected in Birhor folktales and observes that on the basis of these folktales one can suggest that they practiced cannibalism at some far-off time. This trait is established on the basis of "The story of the origin of *sabai* grass." Only the literal translation of this story is available; one might have expected Mitra to give the original text, especially when the motif is so vital.

The research students of the Department of Anthropology, under my guidance, have from time to time undertaken the collection of the folk songs, folktales, and riddles of the different tribes of Bihar. Such studies have been undertaken among the Maler, the Santal of Hazaribagh, the Ho of Singhbhum, and the Oraon and the Munda of Ranchi. In these collections, the songs, tales, and riddles are given both in the original and in their literal English translation. The materials are analyzed anthropologically to bring out the cultural elements in the folklore of the respective tribes. While detailed monographs on these tribes have yet to be published, a summary of these works has appeared (Vidyarthi and Chaubey 1973).

ORISSA. Like Bihar, Orissa has a considerable tribal population and a rich stock of tribal folklore. The first full-length publication on the folktales of the Orissa tribes is that of Dutta Gupta (1923). G. E. Fawcus wrote its preface, finding it a useful collection for both administrators and scholars of folk literature.

The most outstanding work on the tribal folktales of Orissa comes from Elwin (1954). His *Tribal myths of Orissa* is significant for tribal folklore research not only in Orissa, but in India as a whole. In addition to the detailed presentation of myths of various types, Elwin writes at length about the characteristics of folktales, which he regards as tribal "*Puranas.*" He agrees with Boas in considering folktales primarily and fundamentally works of primitive art. He examines the approach of Tylor, who considered myth primitive ethnology expressed in poetic forms. He also considers the Malinowskian approach to folktales and suggests that myth may play different parts in different cultures and fulfill different functions in the same culture. Elwin examines these concepts in the light of the tribal myths of Orissa. He goes on to establish the connections between myths and rituals and points out the function of myth in vitalizing and maintaining tribal customs.

Elwin presents the tribal myths in several parts: (1) tales regarding heaven and earth; (2) tales regarding the invisible world; (3) tales about the animal world; (4) tales about man himself; (5) tales regarding man's social institutions; and (6) tales about domestic life. In this voluminous collection, stories of different tribes and of different types are included, and, in general, it does seem, as Elwin says, that they function as tribal *Puranas*. The tribal myths of Orissa are simple; complex stories are very rare and generally appear to be borrowed. The genuine tribal tale consists of a single motif, though in some cases independent motifs seem to be put together almost haphazardly.

Elwin mentions several possible sources of diffusion. He emphasizes the role of the weekly bazaars, in which all the tribesmen except the wildest Kuttia Khond interact among themselves and with members of other communities. The creation myths, for example, follow a common pattern and are ultimately based on Puranic tradition. Elwin also observes that the stories of sun and moon are similar all over tribal India. The motifs about eclipses are also constant. Other common stories deal with the origin of the palm tree from hair or ornaments dropped by girls. The discovery of liquor by a god or by a hero who sees birds drinking occurs in the mythology of many tribes and provides an example of diffusion and borrowing.

Elwin refers to Hindu motifs which are fairly common. He warns, however, that sometimes a purely tribal character is given a Hindu name, and owing to this his character and venture have nothing whatsoever in common with his name. On the other hand, many Bondo and Gadaba stories have obviously come straight out of the *Ramayana*. The Hindu god Mahadevi is popular in tribal folklore, and Bhimsen, as a rain-god, also figures in it.

Elwin gives a detailed ethnographic account of the development of folklore. He refers to the dormitory clubs, which have great influence among tribes such as the Bondo, Didayis, Gadaba, Khond, and Muria. (Surprisingly, however, they are unknown among the Savara.) Many villages also have a common meeting place for the elders where, sitting on the ceremonial stones, they transmit to each other the rich heritage of folklore.

Das (1964) has surveyed the folklore literature of Orissa. He refers to some of the research on the folktales of the Koya, Khond, Praja, Gadaba, Juang, and others. He also mentions the work of Gopal Chandra Praharaj, Munsi Abdul Mazid, Chandra Shelkhar, Bahini Patti, and Nilmani, who have published folktales and songs in the regional languages.

MADHYA PRADESH. The tribes of Madhya Pradesh have been equally fortunate in the preservation of folktales and folk songs. Venkataswami published a series of articles on the folktales of Madhya Pradesh from 1899 to 1903. Though he does not mention the source of the collection, some of the stories have obviously tribal themes. Gordon (1908), in his book *Indian folktales*, includes legends of the tribes prevalent in the Bilaspur district of Madhya Pradesh.

Elwin started his contact with the tribes of Madhya Pradesh as a missionary, and his training in English literature inspired him initially to write novels and poems on the tribal themes. With this background, he then collected folktales of the tribals in Madhya Pradesh and published them in several articles and books. His first book, *Folktales of Mahakoshal* (1944b), contains tales from Mandala, Seoni, Balaghat, Bilaspur, Raipur, Rewa, Kawardna, and Saranghar in Bastar. These tales were collected from the original sources directly from the several tribes of Madhya Pradesh over a period of ten years' residence in the Maikal Hills and the Bastar states. They cover such tribes as Agaria, Ahir, Baiga, Brinjhwar, Dhanwar, Dhollens, Gond, Khuntis-Chokh, Kurukh Maria, Muria, Ojha, Panda, Pradhan, and Savara. Most stories collected in this volume have been taken directly from Eastern Hindi or Chhattisgarhi. The Bastar tales are told first in Gondi and then translated, generally by the people themselves, into Halbi or Chhattisgarhi and then into English. Regarding the translation, Elwin observes, "I have tried to read all the stories as if I were translating poetry, that there should be no extra words, no fresh images, no alien ideas." The name of the village and the tribe of the narrator is given for each story. In doing so, Elwin is quite conscious of the fact that the tales are generally the property of the area rather than of the tribe. In these tales Elwin discovers two major forms and styles. Some are straightforward narratives, recited with a wealth of gesture and expression but little variation. In others, certain parts of the dialogue are sung. Cumulative tales are told with great vigor and excitement, but these are rare. In Bastar, *ghotul* storytelling has become a fine art, and one is unlikely to forget the experience of listening to one of these tales, which are either in verse or in a sort of rhythmic prose and are chanted to a recognizable tune.

Another publication of Elwin's deals with the folklore of the Bastar clan-god (1943). He presents the story of the origin of the clan-gods of the Maria and Muria, which deals with Anga, Lingo-pen, and Tikanpal. Elwin also published legends of Rasalu and tales about witches.

In his unique book on the Muria and their *ghotul* (1947), Elwin describes the youth dormitory as an institution which is functionally related to every aspect of the Muria's life. He relates its origin to Lingo-pen, the Gond cult hero, who made a journey to earth with his brothers. The relationship between a man and his elder brother's wife is the central theme of the Lingo-pen legends. This relationship is more than a mere joking relationship; it is often one of deep romance. Elwin goes on to present several versions of the Lingo-pen legend popular among the Muria of Bastar and observes that its central theme is the founding of the *ghotul*. Sometimes, Elwin records, Gonds seem to identify Lingo-pen with Bhimsen or Bhimul, considering him a rain-god. According to another explanation, Lingo-pen is the liberator of the Gond gods. He is said to have divided the Gonds into clans and created a new god, Parsa-pen. Another Mandala story connects Lingo-pen with Lanjhi, a traditional home of the Muria. He is also associated with the discovery of fire and of liquor. However, to the Muria, as Elwin comments, perhaps the most significant thing about Lingo-pen is his establishment of the *ghotul* system. This is the greatest treasure he has given to mankind; neither the discovery of fire, the gift of liquor, nor the invention of music can compare with it. The Lingo-pen legend inspires the *ghotul* inmates to be chaste like Lingo-pen and to turn a joking relationship into one of avoidance as he did.

Elwin's most outstanding work in the field of folklore is *Myths of Middle India* (1949), which he himself calls a sort of aboriginal *Purana*. Like a Hindu *Purana*, this book abounds in fantastic stories, unusual and unreal names, and far-fetched analogies. Like a *Purana*, again, it reveals, without embarrassment or self-consciousness, theories of the origin of life on earth and of the sexual functions. The stories and myths included here are collected from Madhya Pradesh, Chhattisgarh, Orissa, and the adjacent areas of Chota Nagpur, Mirzapur, Rajputana, and other neighboring districts. In terms of tribes and castes, the stories come particularly from the Agaria, Bhuiya, Bison-horn Maria, Bondo, Dhanwar, Dhobi,

Gadaba, Gond, Juang, Khond, Kurukh, Lenjh, Saora, Muria, Raja Muria, Rajnengi Pradhan, Kol, Baiga, Ahir, Kahar, Panka, Korku, Kamar, Kewat, Takala Saora, Parkha, and Bharia. The comparative study of the folktales shows that the tribes have borrowed from the sub-Puranic and epic traditions. There are scores of subjects on which all the tribes have similar myths and legends. Ideas about the creation of the world have been largely standardized under Shaiva-Puranic influence. Myths of fire and death, however, receive fresh and original treatment from different tribes. Rice or millet play the same role in Gond, Juang, Gadaba, and Muria tales. Elwin also classifies the stories as of earlier and later traditions and finds the myths, whether Baiga, Bhuiya, Birhor, Chero, Gond, Munda, or Santal, reflecting both these traditions.

Griffith, in his Folklore of the Kols (1944), presents nineteen stories of different types. The Kols are the primitive tribes inhabiting three areas — the Central Area Agencies, Central Provinces, and United Provinces. The author does not mention the region from which he collected these stories. The Kols are proud of their music and songs and of their stories, which were not easy to collect. Like most primitive peoples, the Kols are unwilling to reveal them, and owing to this we know very little about them.

Fuchs (1960), in his monograph on the Gond and Bhuniya of eastern Mandala, describes the creation of man and the fertile soil as reflected in the story of Kichul Rajya. The origin of fire is related to Parvati and Gun Mahadevi, the salvation of mankind from fire and hunger to Janaki mata or Sita, the wife of Rama. He also refers to the division of the universe into three regions — Indralok, the place of the supreme God, Bhagwan; Sringar Dip, the residence of men and women; and Uttara Khand, the place of spirits (*bhuts*) and snakes. Fuchs fails, however, to present the full folktales related to these motifs.

Tribal Folk-Song Studies

The study of tribal folk songs of the Assam Hills and Nagaland was first attempted by ethnographers like Hutton, Mills, Gordon, Shekespear, and others who did monographic studies of the respective tribes. Among Indian scholars, H. Barua and P. D. Goswami also collected and wrote about the tribal songs along with Assamese songs. Among the scholars who did exclusive work, mention may be made of Brahma, who made a vast collection of the folk songs of the Bodo tribe of Assam (1960). The Bodo Cacharis, among the earliest settlers of Assam, built a powerful kingdom with its capital at Dimapur. Bodo folk songs reflect profound thought and imagination and are characterized by beautiful rhymes. Brahma observes that when one hears the spontaneous flow of songs from the mouths of unlettered Bodo women, one is bound to think that they possess an inborn capacity for composing songs and verses. The cornfields, the riverbanks, and the meadows are enveloped by the pleasant songs of the Bodo girls. They express their feelings and imaginations in their music. Folk songs of different types were collected from informants in Golpara (north Bank), Kamrup, and Darang districts. The book, divided into eight chapters, records Bodo songs of patriotism and valor, love and home, and prayer and philosophy, as well as a series of Bihu songs. Brahma presents these songs first in Bodo, then in Assamese and English.

Kabiraj (1962) has presented a series of Garo songs related to *jhum* cultivation and rain. He refers to four festivals in this connection: Agal Maka or Achiroka, Rangchugala, Jamogapa ahana, and Bangala.

Research on tribal folk songs in Bihar, as elsewhere, was initiated by British administrators and missionaries. Along with them, however, Indian scholars have also played a role. Mitchell (1879a) collected fourteen wedding songs of the Mundas with the help of a German priest. He gives the literal translation of these songs with an introductory note. In the same year, Mitchell also published Santali songs with translation and notes (1879b). Hoffmann (1907) writes about Mundari poetry, music, and dance, finding them full of vitality; he remarks that the three forms are closely interwoven and cannot be studied separately.

Among contemporary folklorists, mention may be made of Bhaiyaram Munda, Dulaichand Munda, Ramdayal Munda, L. N. Sahu, and Jagdish Trigunayat. The first three, all of the Mundari community, have published Mundari songs in the local magazine, *Adivasi*. Bhaiyaram Munda has published an article in *Vanyajati* and Dulaichand Munda has produced a field report on the folklore of the Santal. Ramdayal Munda has done some analytical work on Mundari folk songs and analyzed the Birsa rebellion as reflected in the songs. With Norman Zide, he has presented both the Mundari text and an English translation of a number of these songs (Munda and Zide 1969). Sahu has recorded nine Munda folk songs in English translation and discussed their poetic, imaginative, and visual qualities.

The most comprehensive compilation of Mundari folk songs has been attempted by Trigunayat (1957). The first part of the book is devoted to a general statement on the importance of the study of Adivasi folklore and on Mundari folk songs. The author points out the various motifs and themes of the Mundari folk songs — their love of nature and love of human beings, especially children. He goes on to examine the folk songs in terms of their literary qualities, in which he finds them very rich. A note on the Munda language is also given. The 357 folk songs presented here have been classified into eight categories: *jadurgeet* (123), *orejadur* (10), *gena* (42), *karma* (99), *jatga* (49), *japi* (8), *jatra* (9), and *arandi* (10).

These songs are presented both in Mundari and in Hindi, in Devanagari script. Trigunayat, being a poet in Hindi himself, has attempted to translate the Mundari folk songs in somewhat poetic form. Along with the folk songs, he presents the compositions of some Munda poets.

Among the analytical works on Munda songs, mention may be made of Bhaduri's (1942) paper assessing Hindu influence on Munda songs. Bhandari traces the influence of Hindu ideas on the language, customs, and manners of the Mundas of Tamar and Bundu Thana, in Ranchi district. He presents three Vaishnava love songs in Mundari to establish how Munda songs — their metaphors and themes of separation and love of nature — have been influenced by Vaishnava sentiment. In the course of a general analysis, he pushes their history back to the sixteenth century, when Sri Chaitanya passed through this area on his pilgrimage to Jagannath Puri and initiated Vaishnavism in this area.

Among the British administrators who did considerable collection of folk songs, especially from among the Oraon, the Santal, the Ho, and other tribes, the name of W. G. Archer will be written in gold letters. While posted to the subdivisions of Ranchi district in the years 1934–1937, Archer collected Oraon songs from the subdivision of Gumla and published them in 1940 under the title *The blue grove: the poetry of Oraon*. He collected these songs in Kurukh with the help of Oraon informants. This book includes 1,933 Oraon folk songs, grouped according to the classification of the Oraon themselves. This collection is supplemented by another publication, *The dove and the leopard: more Oraon poetry* (1948). This book includes 409 songs, among them the English translations of some of the songs collected and published earlier.

In addition to these excellent Oraon collections, Archer found vast potentialities for folklore research in Santal Parganas. Though Bompas (1909) and Bodding (1924a, 1924b) had already done research there, he noted that they were mainly interested in folktales while he directed his efforts toward folk songs. Archer made an intensive study of Santal songs, dances and riddles with the help of some local workers, including Doman Sahu Samir, from December 1942 to December 1946. While some of the songs were published in a book, in *Man in India*, and in the edited volume *Snow balls of Garhwal*, his full-length book on Santal folk songs has yet to see the light of day. Among his publications in article form, mention may be made of his nine Oraon poems on the Sarhul festival (1942a), twenty Oraon poems (1943b), twenty-five Santal festival songs (1944a), eleven Santal *sohrai* songs (1944b), three Santal rebellion songs (1945a) and sixteen Santal marriage songs (1946a).

Archer further contributed to folklore research as editor of *Man in India* after the death of S. C. Roy. When he accepted the editorship, he devoted an issue exclusively to folk poetry. This issue (vol. 23, no. 1, 1943) includes folk songs primarily from tribal areas. *Man in India* during his editorship continued to publish papers on tribal songs and tales. Moreover, he was a regular contributor on the theme of tribal folk songs (1942a, 1943b, 1943c, 1943d, 1943e, 1944a, 1944b, 1944c, 1945a, 1945b, 1946a, 1946b). His contribution to tribal folklore studies is unique and unsurpassed.

One of his associates for Santali collection, Doman Sahu Samir, who is the editor of a Santali weekly, *Hor Sambad*, has also published a number of papers in Hindi on Santali folk songs in various periodicals. Being a resident of a Santali village, Samir knows Santali almost as a mother tongue.

II. B. Murmu and Aditya Santhali have published Santali songs and broadcast many of them on All-India Radio. Murmu has presented nine different types of Santali folk songs in the original and in Hindi in *Vanyajati*, while Santhali has published several songs in the weekly *Adivasi*. Murmu has also compiled Santali songs in a book entitled *Dor sereng* (1963). The book includes a preface by Gouri Shankar Dalmiya and an introduction by L. N. Sudhangshu, a noted scholar of Hindi literature. The songs collected here have been translated into Hindi. The script used both for Santali and Hindi is Devanagari; Binova Bhave expresses appreciation for this in a note published with the book. Murmu has not attempted any classification of the songs. He simply presents them one after another along with their translations. In addition to the traditional themes of cosmology, social life, economic life, and religious beliefs and practices, some songs of recent origin touch on themes related to India's independence, Gandhi, Binova, national flags, etc. These recent songs reflect the awareness of the Santali villagers of current national developments.

Bahuguna (1960) discusses the basic features of Santal philosophy as reflected in nine folk songs. He also presents an explanatory note on cultural borrowing and diffusion.

The folk songs of the Maler of the Rajmahal Hills have been collected by Cole (1876), Mishra (1956), and Toppo (1959). Cole collected eight folk songs from the Pahari of the Rajmahal Hills. As he mentions in the introduction, he did this to fill a gap in Dalton's *The descriptive ethnology of Bengal* (1872), where he found no description of the dance or songs of the Pahari. Mishra includes four marriage songs in a description of the marriage ceremony of the Maler tribe. Toppo presents folk songs as well as tales and riddles of the Maler in both Malto and English. He also discusses the reflection of cultural elements in the folk songs and tales.

In the light of my field research among the Maler and the analysis of folklore collected from different tribes by my students, I have looked at folklore from an anthropological point of view (Vidyarthi 1962). I trace the development of folklore in tribal areas and present an anthropologically oriented definition of folklore. For me, folklore comprises all forms of oral literature which reflect, in the last analysis, the nature-man-spirit relationship in folk and tribal societies. At the level of the chief themes of tribal folk songs, sex and hunger dominate. I argue that the study of folklore is a great methodological tool for understanding the culture history and cultural patterns of a tribe.

After Dalton's collection of folk songs of the Ho (1872), Majumdar (1950) collected Ho songs to illustrate his ethnographic data. Archer (1942b) also published a collection of Ho songs. Ray (1949) presents fifteen songs of the Ho of Singhbhum. He fails to give us the original text, being content with presenting the English translation.

In his search for tribal myths in Orissa, Elwin did not pay any attention to the collection and interpretation of folk songs of the Orissan tribes; he only collected songs of the Juang and published them in a special number, on Juang, of *Man in India* (1948). Das (1953) and Mahapatra (1940, 1958, 1959) collected Orissan songs of nontribal nature but not tribal folk songs. In view of this, research on the tribal folk songs of Orissa has remained almost untouched. In a recent paper, Adarshi (1960) stresses the importance of folk-song studies of the tribes of Orissa. He presents twelve folk songs from the border of Orissa both in the original texts and in their Hindi translations.

Madhya Pradesh, however, has attracted several folklorists who have collected and written papers on tribal folk songs. Along with the collection of myths and legends of Madhya Pradesh, Elwin (1942) collected twelve Pradhan love songs from the Maikal hills. Though he obtained these songs from informants with the help of Shamrao Hivale, he presents only their English translations. In another publication (1944c), Elwin presents twenty-six folk songs collected from the Gond of Raipur and Bilaspur districts. In the same year, again with the assistance of Shamrao Hivale, Elwin published folk songs of the tribes of the Maikal Hills (1944). These songs are related to festivals, marriage, sex, and other themes of tribal life. They are presented only in English, with an introductory note. In addition to these publications, Elwin, in his monographs on the tribes of Madhya Pradesh, such as the Baiga (1939), the Bondo (1950), and the Muria (1947), includes their songs either in appendices or in the text. In his book on the Muria (1947) he deals extensively with Muria dance and songs.

Jungblut (1942) has published a number of magical songs of the Bhil of Jhabna. Working in the Bhili language, he collected these songs with extraordinary difficulty. The success of his meticulous work is due to the exceptional confidence the Bhil had in him. In the course of his fieldwork in 1939, William Koppers accompanied him and helped him in the analysis of these songs. Jungblut notes a strong influence of Hinduism on Bhil culture that is reflected in these magical songs. He notes that most of them are meant to cure the sick, while some are sung on special occasions.

He goes on to establish that the Lord song, a Bhil epic, is clearly derived from Hindu mythology. He also shows how these magical songs, related to tribal rituals, reflect Bhil cultural elements. Jungblut claims that this book offers almost a complete collection of witchcraft songs, and on the whole it is a very useful, meticulous, and authentic collection.

There are several other publications on the folk songs of the Bhil in both Hindi and English. Among the scholarly ones, mention may be made of a paper by Khanapurkar (1946). Pramar devotes Chapter fifteen of his book *Bharatiya lok sahitya* (1954a) to the folk songs of the Bhil and other criminal tribes.

Archer extended his interest in folklore to the Baiga tribe of Madhya Pradesh (1943c). He classifies Baiga folk songs into three categories: *dadaria* (a dance poem of two lines), dance songs for social occasions, and marriage songs. He presents a dozen songs of the first type and forty-five of the second. These songs bring out the human and natural themes and the imagery and symbols of the tribal poetry

The other scholar who has published exhaustively on the folk songs of Chhattisgarh is Dube (1947), who collected over 1,200 songs and a dozen ballads from the tribal areas of Raipur, Bilaspur, Durg, Balaghat, and Bandra and a number of adjoining areas of Madhya Pradesh. These songs, though not formally classified, are arranged under the categories of general songs, dance songs, caste songs, songs for special occasions, and tribal songs. Dube compares these songs with those found in the tribal area of Mirzapur. He also observes that the Gond and Baiga are advanced in folk poetry, while the Kamar and Bhuiya folk songs are fast disappearing.

Satyarthi (1951) devotes a chapter to Halbi poetry. He observes that Halbi has emerged as a lingua franca and is of great practical use for the local people. He presents a few examples of popular songs like "Leela Lija" as well as songs of the Maria rebellion.

Jain (1965) worked on the Agaria, Baiga, Bhuniya, and other Vindhyan tribes and wrote a book in Hindi on the folk songs of Madhya Pradesh. He records eighteen types of folk songs, the main ones being *karma, sua, saila, sajani, birha, rina, fag*, etc. These folk songs are associated with corresponding dances. Jain's collection is rich both in content and interpretation and may be considered as an excellent work on folk songs in Hindi.

The Tribal Research Institute of Chhindwara has done a valuable service by publishing five volumes in Hindi on the folk songs of the tribes of Madhya Pradesh. The first volume, produced by Dube (1963), includes the folk songs of Chhattisgarh. The collection is entitled *Tulsi ke birwa*, referring to the sacred *tulsi*, which is planted and worshipped in every household in that area. The book includes 167 typical songs divided into *bhojli* (17), *sua* (37), *raut* (18), *karma* (38), *holly* (12), *bibah* (16), *mata* (16), and *dadaria* (28). The book has an introduction by T. B. Naik, then Director of the Institute, who brings out the importance of each type of song to the people of Chhattisgarh. The themes of most of the songs are religious, social, seasonal, or recreational, and excepting for the last type of song they are meant for specific occasions or seasons. The *dadaria* is the most popular song of Chhattisgarh and is sung throughout the year and throughout the day in the villages. He points out that *dadaria* are short, like Bihari hymns, but quite impressive and effective.

The other four volumes published by the Institute deal with the ballads of the Pradhans of Madhya Pradesh (Gulab 1964). The Pradhans are the bards (*charans*) of the Gond tribe. They make extensive use of the stories of the *Mahabharata* and the *Ramayana*. These ballads are mainly in verse, but here and there prose versions are also found. In the first two of these volumes, Gulab has collected lyric ballads relating to the Kauravas and the Pandavas. If one reads these stories, one gets the impression that they were born and reared among the Pradhans and that the whole *Mahabharata* happened, as it were, in the land of the Pradhans and not in Kurukshetra. In the narration, the original story of the *Mahabharata* has been greatly modified, and the different characters seem to play somewhat modified roles. Though all the original characters find a place in the *Pandubani*, as the Pradhans call these lyric ballads, the roles of Bhim are overemphasized. The third volume of Pradhan ballads describes the themes of the *Ramayana*. Just as the story of the *Mahabharata* has been modified in the *Pandubani*, so the themes of the *Ramayana*, called *Ramayani* by the Pradhans, have undergone modification. The hero of the *Ramayani* is not Rama, but Lakshmana, and the whole cycle revolves round his activities. The fourth volume, entitled *Gondbani*, depicts the glories, heroism, bravery in war, and rich heritage of the Gond kings of Gondwamland. Through strenuous fieldwork, Gulab collected six long ballads about the six Gondi kings — "Raja Pemal Shah," "Raja Hirdeh Shah," "Hirakhan Chhatri Baihamani," "Pali Birwa," and "Raja Loh Gundi." These ballads describe the preparations for war, the use of weapons, battles, and the roles of spirits in generating power and inspiring the kings. At the sociological level, these ballads reflect the importance of folkways, rituals, the weekly markets, and supernatural power in the tribal style of life.

This collection illuminates the nature and extent of the integration of the tribes of Madhya Pradesh into the mainstream of Hindu culture. The Pradhans, basically bards and musicians, have played a significant role in the transmission of the themes of the epics to the major Gond tribes. All these materials are based on the field research of Seikh Gulab. In presenting these ballads, great care has been taken by the compiler to put them in their original form, in the regional language of the Parhans rendered in

Devanagari script. The editor of these volumes, T. B. Naik, has highlighted their significance in a series of introductions.

Avari (1957) has edited a volume in Marathi on the tribal songs of Maharashtra.

Folklore Studies among the Tribes of South India

Among the eminent scholars who have undertaken folklore research among the tribes of South India, mention may be made of M. B. Emeneau, G. L. Gover, P. C. Reddy, M. V. Ramana Rao, and S. R. Venkataraman. Before these scholars, sporadic collections of songs and tales were made by Iyer (1908) and Thurston (1943), who published songs and tales in the ethnographic handbooks and monographs referred to earlier.

Emeneau lived among the tribes of the Nilgiri Hills for about eight months in 1936–1938 and made an exhaustive study of the folklore of the Toda and the Kota. In his first publication of Kota texts (1944), he published thirty-seven myths and tales collected from a single informant, the best storyteller among the Kota. The myths and tales deal with the rearing of children, the cow, the creation of animal life, taboos, magic, reversals of fortune, change and fate, reward and punishment, etc. In the end, Emeneau examines the motifs and types of these stories.

Emeneau (1958) also collected 250 Toda songs on tape and recorded the techniques of singing them. He points out the striking feature of all Toda songs — their enigmatic and allusive character. He also observes that perhaps every Toda can and does compose songs. He discusses the importance of poetry in molding the Toda world view. He finds that the Toda in their poetry aim neither at universality nor at an expression of the individual poet's own psyche. For Toda, poetry is an enrichment of every fact of their experience, and it is an art that produces achievements which deserves respect and admiration.

In another paper (1943), Emeneau makes a comparative study of Toda and Kota tales and divides them into two groups, one influenced by North India and the other by South India. The style of Kota stories is one of oral composition, and all the stories of the past are characterized by a customary Kota formulaic style.

In a comparative study of Dravidian folktale motifs based on the analysis of three stories each from Kota, Toda, and Kurumba, Emeneau (1938) discovers an echo-word motif in the Dravidian tales. He also establishes a close connection between the South Indian stories and Sinhalese tales. Discussing the origin stories of the Toda and Kota (1943), he points out that most of the episodes of the stories are clear borrowings from the general Indian stock of folktales. He examines some parallel origin stories among Toda and Kota and from their similarities claims that there has been some diffusion. In view of this and other similarities in folk songs, he concludes that the Nilgiri communities in certain parts of their folktale materials should be considered a cultural area. In a recent publication (1965), Emeneau records Toda dream songs and discusses their contents and the relations of the dreamers to the persons and events dreamed about. These dream songs were collected from two members of the Toda community. The analysis reflects a particular Toda attitude toward the dead, since these dream songs are all sung about dead persons.

Smith (1948) makes a critical appraisal of the Kota texts of Emeneau and concludes that Kota folklore may not accurately be described as either primitive or preliterate. On the basis of the analysis of the folklore materials, he suggests that the Kota should be considered as a caste and not as a tribe.

Reddy (1948) presents a long Chenchu story which describes the origin of the Chenchu and their seven sects. This story was told to him by one Krishna Chenchu of Maharajugunta, in Markapur Taluk, Karnol district. The story, translated into English, deals with a dialogue in song form between the god Narasingham and a beautiful Chenchu girl. Reddy also records five love songs of the Yanadi. On the strength of these songs, he tries to establish a relationship between the Chenchu and the Yanadi.

Venkataraman (1956), a member of the Servants of India Society of Madras, in course of his social service activities came into intimate contact with the Koraga tribe. He collected three texts of folk songs with the help of a literate member of the Koraga community. The three songs, given both in the original text and in English translation, reflect three different themes. The first song appears to be of recent origin, as the rhyme and allegory are of modern type and the theme is the life of beggary of the Koraga. The second song reflects the practice of marrying one's aunt's daughter. The third song shows the influence of Hinduism on the animistic practices of the Koraga.

Satyarthi (1952–1953b) presents a set of Tamil, Telegu, and Malayalam songs. Among the tribal songs, he presents one Badaga and two Toda songs. In the first Toda song, the girl is depicted as a flower, while the boy is treated as a bee flying around her. The second song centers around the buffalo, a theme dear to the Toda. The Badaga song provides, with delicate sensitivity, a glimpse of the peacock. Satyarthi gives only the translation of these three songs, which he collected during his visits to the different linguistic areas of South India.

Ramana Rao (1956) presents an English translation of Savara love songs collected from the hills of Ganjam, Srikakulam, and Visakhapattam districts in the eastern Ghats. Some of these songs deal with the complaint of the neglected wife to her mother-in-law and father-in-law; others reflect other social dimensions of the family.

In an analytical paper on the folk songs of southern India, Gover (1959), a British folklorist, refers to the songs of the Badaga of the Nilgiri Hills. Drawing suitable examples from the songs, he finds similarity between Jewish and Badaga songs. This similarity is reflected in a Badaga song for the dead. Another song refers to the other world in which departed spirits dwell and illustrates the Badaga belief that the soul carries with it an image of its earthly body, capable of feeling pain and delight. Several other funeral songs of the Badaga are included. These songs provide examples of high morality and reflect the Badaga's pastoral traditions and musical genius.

S. S. Aiyar (1917) published a series of legends relating to festivals and rituals of the people of Kerala. Though he collected the legends and folktales of Malayali as early as 1917, he did not publish them till 1953. Achyutan (1954) collected Malayali folk songs and published them in the same language. T. S. V. Aiyar (1917) worked on the folktales of Kerala and published a few in the *Hindustan Review*. H. Gundart collected 1,000 proverbs as early as 1868.

Folklore research in Tamil Nadu has been undertaken by Ayyasvami and his team, who published a collection of songs in Tamil in 1960. Another collection of Tamil songs has been made by Annakamy (1959). In Hindi, collections of the folktales of Kerala and Tamil Nadu have been edited by Bhagvat (1958b, 1959). Tamil proverbs have been collected and translated into English by Taylor (1962). Tamil legends have been collected and published by Balasubrahmanyan (1940). In Telugu, a publication on folklore by Pantulu (1905) deserves special mention. This collection of Telegu folktales has been popular in Tamil Nadu and Andhra Pradesh and has witnessed several editions.

Among the publications of a general nature on the folklore of South India is that of Gover (1959) on the folk songs of southern India. This collection was first published in 1871 and includes songs of such South Indian languages as Telegu, Tamil, Malayalam, Kannada, Coorg, and Badaga. The fact that it is available in English in a second edition reflects its importance. Arnold Bake produced several reports in the 1930's on his research on the folk music and dance of South India.

The folktales and folk songs of the various dialects and languages of India have been here examined. In view of the difficulty of learning all these languages, I have had to depend in some cases on secondary sources of information in evaluating the literature. On account of this and the vastness of the subject, there are bound to be hundreds of omissions. However, the trends of development and the various approaches and areas of research in folklore have become sufficiently clear. It is evident that, except for a few works, folklore research in India continues to be descriptive. It is also evident that there is a need to preserve the vanishing folklore of tribal and rural areas by team research on the part of dedicated folklorists in the remotest corners of our country. While paying tribute to those folklorists who have initiated and encouraged research in folklore in India, it is our responsibility to undertake further research in this field at both the descriptive and the analytical level. Analytical work will require a team effort in which scholars in social anthropology, sociology, psychology, and literature all play a role. A systematic, scientific, and interdisciplinary approach to the study of Indian folklore in the context of the world literature in this field remains a Himalayan task.

REFERENCES

ACHYUTAN, A. NAMBUDRI
1954 *Anchu natoliphaffukal*. Pahlgat: Students' Fashion Home and Book Department

ADARSHI, B. P.
1960 Banbasi lok geet ome sun sanskrit bhabnayen. *Vanyajati* (Hindi section), April.

AGARWAL, V. S.
1949 *Prithibi putra*. New Delhi: Sasta Sahitya Mandal.

AGRAWAL, SWARNLATA
1959 "Rajasthani lok geet." Unpublished Ph.D. thesis, Rajasthan University, Jaipur, Rajasthan.

AIYAR, S. S.
1917 Festivals and legends of South India: a traditional story. *Hindustan Review* 40 (n.s. 199):115–119.
1953 Festivals and legends of South India. *March of India* 5(5):11–16.

AIYAR, T. S. VENKATARAM
1917 The land of the Keralas: a traditional story. *Hindustan Review* 40 (n.s. 199).

ANDERSON, J. D.
1895 *Kachari folktales and rhymes*. Shillong: Assam Secretariat Printing Office.

ANNAKAMY
1959 *Ettil ezhuttak kavithaiyal*. Gandhi Gram: The compiler.

ARCHER, W. G.
1940 *The blue grove: the poetry of Oraon*. London: George Allen and Unwin.
1942a Nine Oraon poems for the Sarhul festival; fourteen Oraon marriage poems. *Man in India* 22:198–220.
1942b *Ho surang*. Patna: Government Press.
1943a Bhojpuri village: songs collected in Kayastha households in Shahabad district, Bihar, in 1940–41. *Journal of the Bihar and Orissa Research Society* 24:Appendix, 1–15, 93–148.
1943b Twenty Oraon poems of the Ranchi district. *Man in India* 23:10–14.
1943c Baiga poetry. *Man in India* 23:47–60.
1943d An Indian riddle book. *Man in India* 23:267–315.
1943e Santal poetry. *Man in India* 23:98–105.

1944a More Santal songs. *Man in India* 24:141–144.
1944b Festival songs. *Man in India* 24:70–74.
1944c Comment. *Man in India* 24:207–209.
1944d The illegitimate child in Santal society. *Man in India* 24:154–169.
1945a Santal rebellion songs. *Man in India* 25:201.
1945b The Prible marriage. *Man in India* 25:29–42.
1946a "Santal marriage songs," in *Snow balls of Garhwal*. Edited by D. N. Majumdar, 5–8. Lucknow: Universal.
1946b Santal translation songs. *Man in India* 26:6–7.
1948 *The dove and the leopard: more Oraon poetry*. Calcutta: Longman's, Green.

ARYANI, SAMPATTI
1959 Magahi sangitome main jan chetana. *Samaj Traimasik* 4:599–615.
1965 *Magahi lok sahitya*. Delhi: Hindi Sahitya Sansar.

AVARI, G. J., *editor*
1957 *Adivasinchin lokageeten*. Nasik: Savodayakendra Pethdish.

AYYASVAMI, R.
1960 *Kulanlailukku natotippatalkal, kuzhandai kalukku, nadodip padalgal*. Madras: Pari Nilaiyan.

BABULKAR, MOHANLAL
1964 *Diwali lok sahitya ka bibechanatmak adhyayan*. Prayag: Hindi Sahitya Sammelan.

BAHUGUNA, K. P.
1960 Bharatiya sanskriti men santal ke den. *Vanyajati* (Hindi section), January.

BALASUBRAHMANYAN, S. R.
1940 Tirukkal ukkunrani. *Journal of Oriental Research* 14:310–317.

BARUA, B. K.
1943 Bihu songs. *Triveni Quarterly* 15:161–163.

BARUA, HEM
1954 *The red river and the blue hill*. Gauhati: Lawyers' Book Stall.

BASU, M. N.
1956 Songs of the Noluas of Bengal. *Folklore* 1(1):40–43.

BENNETT, W. C.
1872 Oudh folklore: a legend of Balarampur. *Indian Antiquary* 1:143.

BHADURI, M. B.
1922 Astronomy of the Mundas and their star myths. *Man in India* 2:68–77.
1942 "Hindu influence on Munda songs," in *Essays in anthropology presented to Rai Bahadur Sarat Chandra Ray*, 256–260. Lucknow: Maxwell.

BHAGVAT, D. N.
1958a *An outline of Indian folklore*. Bombay: Popular Book Depot.

BHAGVAT, D. N., *editor*
1958b *Sachitra keral ki lok kathen*. Delhi: Attaram.
1959 *Sachitra tamilnad ki lok kathen*. Delhi: Attaram.

BHANDARI, N. S.
1946 "Snow balls of Garhwal," in *Snow balls of Garhwal*. Edited by D. N. Majumdar, 20–87. Lucknow: Universal.

BHATT, H. D.
1962 Folk songs of Garhwal. *Folklore* 4(12).

BHATTACHARYA, A.
1954 *Banglar lok sahitya*. Calcutta: Calcutta Book House.

BHATTACHARYA, U.
1957 *Banglar baul aur baul gan*. Calcutta: Oriental Book Co.
BHOWMICK, P. K.
1957 Tusu festival and songs of Midnapur. *Folklore* 2.
BINOD, B. C.
1960 *Kar bhala hoga bhala (Maithili ki lok kathain)*. New Delhi: Sasta Sahitya Mandal.
BODDING, P. O.
1924a *A chapter of Santal folklore*. Kristiania: Brøggers.
1924b *Hor kahniko-santal*. Banagaria: Santhal Mission of the Northern Churches.
1925a *Santhal folktales*. London: Williams and Norgate.
1925b The Santhal and disease. *Memoirs of the Asiatic Society of Bengal* 10.
1927 Santhal witchcraft. *Memoirs of the Asiatic Society of Bengal* 11.
BODKAR, L.
1957 *Indian animal tales: a preliminary survey*. FF Communications 170.
BOMPAS, C. H.
1909 *Folklore of the Santhal Parganas*. London: David Nutt.
BRAHMA, M. M.
1960 *Folk songs of the Bodos*. Gauhati: University of Gauhati Publications Department.
CAMPBELL, A.
1891 *Santhal folk tales*. Pokharia: Santhal Mission Press.
1916a Santhal legends. *Journal of the Bihar and Orissa Research Society* 2:91–200.
1916b The tradition of the Santhals. *Journal of the Bihar and Orissa Research Society* 2:15–29.
CHATTA, NANDLAL
1952 *Kashmiri folk tales.*
CHATURVEDI, H. D.
1950 *Bundelkhand lok geet*. Allahabad: Indian Press and Publications.
CHATURVEDY, SIB SAHAY
1950 *Pasan nagari: Bundelkhand ki lok kahaniyan*. Delhi: Raj Kamal.
1952 *Pasan nagari: Bundelkhand ki lok sahitya*. Delhi: Raj Kamal.
1957 *Jaisi karni vaisi bharani (Bundelkhand ke lok kathayen)*. New Delhi: Sasta Sahitya Mandal.
CHATURVEDY, SIB SAHAY, *editor*
1955 *Hamari lok-kathayen*. New Delhi: Sasta Sahitya Mandal.
CHAUBE, GANESH
1969 Bhojpuri ke mudrit sahitya ki suchi. *Anjor* 9.
CHOUBE, RAMGARIB
1956 Bhojpuri ke pawas geet. *Sahitya* (Patna) 7(2):61–71.
COCHRANE, W. W.
1911 An Ahon (Shan) legend of creation from an old manuscript. *Journal of the Royal Asiatic Society of Great Britain and Ireland* 22:1132–1142.
COLDSTREAM, W.
1919 Labour songs of India. *Journal of the Royal Asiatic Society of Great Britain and Ireland* 30:43–46.
COLE, F. T.
1875 Santhali folklore. *Indian Antiquary* 4.
1876 The Rajmahal Hills men's songs. *Indian Antiquary* 5.
CROOKE, W.
1893 Folk tales of Hindustan. *Indian Antiquary* 22.

1894 *An introduction to the popular religion and folklore of northern India.* Allahabad: Government Press, North West Provinces and Oudh.
1895 A version of the Guga legend. *Indian Antiquary* 24.
1900 Folktales from the Indus Valley. *Indian Antiquary* 29.
1925 Songs and sayings about the great in northern India. *Indian Antiquary* 54.
1926 Marriage songs in northern India. *Indian Antiquary* 55.

DALTON, E. T.
1872 *The descriptive ethnology of Bengal.* Calcutta: Government Printing Press.

DAMANT, G. H.
1872 Bengali folklore. *Indian Antiquary* 1.
1875 The two brothers: a Manipuri story. *Indian Antiquary* 4.
1877 The story of Khamba and Thobi. *Indian Antiquary* 6.
1880 A legend from Dinajpur. *Indian Antiquary* 9.

DARUKA, BHAGWATI PRASAD
1961 *Mawari geet sangraha.* Calcutta: Bombay Pustak Bhandar.

DAS, K. B.
1953 *A study of Orissan folklore.* Santiniketan: Visvabharati.
1964 "A glimpse into the Oriya folk literature," in *Studies in Indian folk culture.* Edited by Shankar Sengupta and K. D. Uphadhyaya. Calcutta.

DAS, SANWAL
1956 *Prachin Rajasthani geet.* Udaipur.

DEOGAM, KANHU
1928 A Ho folk story. *Man in India* 8.

DEVA, INDRA
1953 "Sociological study of Bhojpuri folk song." Unpublished Ph.D. thesis, Lucknow University, Lucknow, U.P.

DHAR, MOHAN KRISHNA
1963 *Kashmir ka lok sahitya,* part three. Delhi: Attaram.

DHAR, SOMNATH
1949 *Kashmiri folk tales.* Bombay: Hind Kitab.
1955–1956 Kashmiri folklore. *March of India* 8.

DRACOTT, ALICE ELIZABETH
1906 *Simla village folk tales, or folk tales from the Himalayas.* London: Murray.

DUBE, AMRIT LAL
1963 *Tulsi ke birwa.* Chhindwara: Tribal Research and Training Institute.

DUBE, B.
1968 *Barchan taringini.* Bhopal.

DUBE, S. C.
1947 *Folk songs of Chhattisgarh.* Lucknow: Universal.

DUTTA GUPTA, U. N.
1923 *Folktales of Orissa.* Calcutta: Lahiri.

ELWIN, V.
1939 *The Baiga.* London: Murray.
1942 Twelve Pradhan love songs. *Man in India* 22.
1943 Folklore of the Bastar clan-gods. *Man in India* 23:97–104.
1944a The legend of Rasalu Kuar. *Man in India* 24:233–260.
1944b *Folktales of Mahakoshal.* London: Oxford University Press.
1944c Folk songs of Chhattisgarh. *Man in India* 24.
1947 *The Muria and their ghotul.* Bombay: Oxford University Press.
1948 Notes on the Juang. *Man in India* 28.

1949 *Myths of Middle India*. Madras: Oxford University Press.
1950 *Bondo highlander*. Bombay: Oxford University Press.
1954 *Tribal myths of Orissa*. Bombay: Oxford University Press.
1958 *Myths of the north-east frontiers of India*. Shillong: North East Frontier Agency.

ELWIN, V., SHAMRAO HIVALE
1944 *Folk songs of the Maikal Hills*. London: Oxford University Press.

EMENEAU, M.
1938 An echo-word motif in Dravidian folk-tales. *Journal of the American Oriental Society* 58:533–570.
1943 Studies in the folktales of India. 1. Some origin stories of Todas and Kotas. *Journal of the American Oriental Society* 63:158–168.
1944 *Kota texts*, part one. University of California Publications in Linguistics 2(1).
1958 Oral poets of South India: the Todas. *Journal of American Folklore* 71:312–324.
1965 Toda dream songs. *Journal of the American Oriental Society* 85:40–44.

ENTHOVEN, R. F.
1916 The folklore of Gujarat. *Indian Antiquary* 45:109–117.

FRANCKELEH, A. H.
1901 The spring myth of the Kasar saga. *Indian Antiquary* 30.

FRASER, HUGH
1883 Folklore from eastern Gorakhpur. *Journal of the Asiatic Society of Bengal* 52(1).

FUCHS, STEPHEN
1960 *The Gond and Bhuniya of eastern Mandala*. Bombay: Asia Publishing House.

GAHLOT, SUDHIR SINGH
n.d. *Rajasthani krishi kahavate*. Jodhpur.

GARIOLA, T. D.
1926 Folklore of Garhwal. *Visva-Bharati Quarterly* 4, April.

GHOSAL, SAMIR
1962 Folk cults and magical rites relating to rain in Bengal. *Folklore* 3(12).

GORDON, E. M.
1908 *Indian folktales*. London: Kegan Paul, Trench, Trubner.

GOSWAMI, P. D.
1943 Assamese ballads. *Triveni Quarterly* 15.
1949a The folk tales of Assam. *Eastern Anthropologist* 2(4).
1949b Abor tales. *Man in India* 29.
1949–1950 The Bihu songs of Assam. *Eastern Anthropologist* 3:57–100.
1954–1955 Naga tales. *Eastern Anthropologist* 8(2).
1957 *Bihu songs of Assam*. Gauhati: Lawyers' Book Stall.
1960 *Ballads and tales of Assam*. Gauhati: University of Gauhati Press.

GOVER, CHARLES E.
1959 *The folk songs of southern India* (second edition). Tirunelveli: Southern Indian Saiva Siddhanta Works Publishing Society. (Originally published in 1871).

GRIERSON, GEORGE
1909 *An introduction to the Maithili language*. Calcutta: Baptist Mission Press.

GRIFFITH, W. G.
1944 Folklore of the Kols. *Man in India* 24.

GRIGNARD, A
1931 *Hahn's Oraon folklore in the original: a critical text with translation and notes.* Patna: Superintendent of Government Printing, Bihar and Orissa.

GULAB, SEIKH
1964 *Pradhan geet katha*, four volumes. Edited by T. N. Naik. Chhindwara: Tribal Research and Training Institute.

GUPTA, OMPRAKASH
n.d. *Marwari geet sangraha*. Delhi: Garg.

GUPTA, SALIGRAM
1967 *Braj aur Bundelkhand lok geets me krishna katha*. Agra: Vinod Putak Mandir.

HALDAR, SUKUMAR
1916–1917 Ho folklore. *Journal of the Bihar and Orissa Research society* 1, 2, 4.

HOFFMANN, J. S.
1907 Mundari poetry, music, and dance. *Memoirs of the Asiatic Society of Bengal*, 2:85–120.
1950 *Encyclopaedia Mundarica*, thirteen volumes. Patna: Superintendent of Government Printing, Bihar.

HOUGHTON, BERNARD
1893 A folktale of the Lushais. *Indian Antiquary* 22.

HOWELL, E. B.
1908 Some songs of Chitral. *Memoirs of the Asiatic Society of Bengal* 4:381–389.

IYER, L. K. ANANTA KRISHNA
1908 *Cochin tribes and castes*, two volumes. London: Higginbotham.

JACOBS, J.
1961 *Indian fairy tales*. Bombay: Wilco.

JAIN, CHANDRA
1953 *Bindhya Pradesh ke lok geet*. Delhi.
1954 *Bindhya Pradesh ki lok kathayen*. Delhi.
1965 *Madhya Pradesh ki adibasiso ke lok geet*. Jabalpur: Mishra Bandhu Karyalaya.
n.d. *Bundelkhand ke lok kabi*. Delhi.

JALPUR, KANAIYALAL SAHGAL
1958 *Rajasthani kahavater: Ek adhayayan*. Jodhpur.

JUNGBLUT, L.
1942 Magic songs of the Bhils of Jhabna State. *Internationales Archiv für Ethnographie* 43.

KABIRAJ, S. N.
1962 *Jhum* cultivation of the Garos and rain. *Folklore* 3(22).

KAVIRAJ, MOHAN SINGH
1957 *Prachin Rajasthani geet*. Udaipur: Rajasthan Vishwa Vidhyapith.

KHANAPURKAR, D. P.
1946 "The folk songs of the Dagni Bhils," in *Snow balls of Garhwal*. Edited by D. N. Majumdar, 9–17. Lucknow: Universal.

KIRKLAND, EDWIN CAPERS
1966 *A bibliography of South Asian folklore*. Indiana University Folklore Series 21. The Hague: Mouton.

KNOWLES, J. H.
1886 Kashmiri tales. *Indian Antiquary* 15.
1887 Kashmir story. *Indian Antiquary* 16.

1893 *Folk tales of Kashmir*. London: Kegan Paul, Trench, Trubner.

KRISHNASWAMY, M. RAO, *editor*
1950 *Lok geet*. Tanjore Saraswati Mahal Series 17, Madras Government Oriental Series 52.

LAL, TEJNARAIN
1962 *Maithili lok geeton ka adhyayan*. Agra: Vinod Pustak Mandir.

LEITNER, G. H.
1872 Dardu legends, proverbs, fables, and riddles. *Indian Antiquary* 1.

MAHAPATRA, CHAKRADHAR
1940 *Bohunka sukha dukha*. Bhubaneswar: Geetika.
1958 *Oriya gramyageeti*. Bhubaneswar: Sahitya Academic.
1959 *Utkal gamuli gita*. Cuttack: Surama Mahanti.

MAJUMDAR, D. N.
1950 *The affairs of a tribe: a study in tribal dynamics*. Lucknow: Universal.

MC NAIR, J. F. A., T. L. BASLOW
1908 *Oral traditions from the Indus*. Brighton.

MISHRA, JAYAKANT
1951 *Introduction to the folk literature of Maithili*. Allahabad: University of Allahabad Department of English.

MISHRA, N. S. P.
1956 Saoria pahariya bibah padhati. *Vanyajati* (Hindi section), October.

MISHRA, SHRIDHAR
1959 Elements of culture in Bhojpuri folk songs. *Hindu Review* 4(2).
1964 "Bhojpuri folk songs." Unpublished Ph.D. thesis, University of Bihar, Patna, Bihar.

MITCHELL, J. M.
1879a Specimens of wedding songs of the Munda Kolhs from the German of the Rev. Th. Jellenghana. *Indian Anthropologist* 4.
1879b Santali songs with translation and notes. *Indian Anthropologist* 4.

MITRA, S. C.
1896 North Indian folklore about thieves and robbers. *Journal of the Asiatic Society of Bengal* 64(1).
1902 On North Indian folk tales of the rhea-sylvia and juniper tree type. *Journal of the Asiatic Society of Bengal* 71(3).
1926 On a Ho folktale of Wicked Queen type. *Journal of the Bihar and Orissa Research Society* 12.
1927–1928a Tibetan folklore from Kalimpong in the district of Darjeeling in the eastern Himalayas. *Journal of the Anthropological Society of Bombay* 14.
1927–1928b A note on human sacrifice among the Birhors of Chotanagpur. *Journal of the Anthropological Society of Bombay* 14.
1927–1928c On a Birhor folktale of the Wicked Queen type. *Journal of the Anthropological Society of Bombay* 14.
1927–1928d A note on the prevalence of cannibalism among the Birhors of Chotanagpur. *Journal of the Anthropological Society of Bombay* 14.
1927–1928e Notes on the Mundari legends and customs connected with the origin of the names of Ranchi and some of its suburbs. *Journal of the Anthropological Society of Bombay* 14.
1927–1928f On the cosmological myth of the Birhors and its Santhali and American Indian parallels. *Journal of the Anthropological Society of Bombay* 14.
1928a Notes on a Birhor legend about Ravan's abduction of Sita. *Journal of the Bihar and Orissa Research Society* 14.

1928b Further notes on a Ho folktale of the Wicked Queen type. *Journal of the Bihar and Orissa Research Society* 14.
n.d.a *On a Thado Kuki folktale about the metamorphosis of a sorcerer into a plantain tree or banana tree*. Studies on Bird Myths 23.
n.d.b *On a Lushai Kuki axiological myth about the jungle babbler*. Studies on Bird Myths 25.
n.d.c *On a Lushai Kuki axiological myth about the king crow*. Studies on Bird Myths 24.
n.d.d *An Angami Naga (and Lhota Naga) folktale about the metamorphosis of a semi-divine girl into an orange fruit*. Studies on Plant Myths 26.

MOHAMMAD, GULAM
1905–1907 *Festivals and folklore of Gilgit*. Memoirs of the Asiatic Society of Bengal 1.

MULLICK, BRAJESHWAR
1947 *Kosi geet*. Bihar: Panchgaslia Saharae.

MUNDA, R. D., NORMAN ZIDE
1969 Revolutionary Birsa and Mundari folk songs. *Journal of Social Research* 12(2).

MURMU, B.
1954 Lok geet. *Vanyajati* (Hindi section).
1963 *Dor sereng, santal pahariya seva mandal*. Deoghar: Baidyanath.

NARAYAN, J. S.
1942 Khasi folklore. *New Review* 16.

NATH, KIDAR
1958 Daughter in Kangra folk songs. *March of India* 10.

OAKLEY, E. S., T. D. GARIOLA
1935 *Himalayan folklore*. Allahabad: Superintendent of Printing and Stationery.

PANDEY, INDU PRAKASH
1957 *Awadhi, lok geet aur parampra*. Allahabad: Ram Margalal.
1959 *Awadh ki lok kathayen*. Bombay: Shiva.

PANDEY, TRILOCHAN
1962 *Kumaun ka lok sahitya*. Agra: Almora Book Depot.

PANGTEY, K. S.
1948 The folk songs of Bhotiyas and Kumaons. *Eastern Anthropologist* 1(4).
1949 *Lonely furrows of the borderland*. Lucknow: Universal.

PANTULU, G. A. SUBRAMANIAN
1905 Folklore of the Telugus. 1. Friendship. 2. Arrogance defeated. *Indian Antiquary* 34:87–90, 122–124.

PARIKH, S. K.
1942 *Rajasthani lok geet*. Prayag: Hindi Sahitya Sammelan.

PRAMAR, SHYAM
1952 *Malwai lok geet*. Indore.
1954a *Bharatiya lok sahitya*. Delhi: Raj Kamal.
1954b *Malwa ki lok kathayen*. Delhi.
1954c *Malawi aur uska sahitya*. Delhi.

PRASAD, BISWANATH, *editor*
1962 *Magahi sanskar geet*. Patna: Rashtra Bhasha Parishad.

PRASAD, DINESHWAR
1970 *Lok sahitya aur Sanskriti*. Allahabad: Lok Bharati.

RAFY, K. V.
1920 *Folk tales of the Khasis*. London: Macmillan.

RAKESH, R. E. S.
1942 *Maithili lok geet*. Prayag: Hindi Sahitya Sammelan.
RAMANA RAO, M. V.
1956 Savaras and their songs. *March of India* 8(2).
RANDWABA, M. S., D. S. PRAHAKAR
n.d. *Hariyana ke lok geet*. Delhi: Attaram.
RANGAMATHU, DEWAN SINGH
1960 *The folk tales of the Garo*. Gauhati: University of Gauhati Department of Publications.
RAY, G. S.
1949 A few songs of the *adivasis* of Kolhan. *Man in India* 20.
REDDY, P. C.
1948 Chenchu and the Hor divine bridegroom. *Eastern Anthropologist* 1(4).
ROSE, H. A.
1909a The legend of Khan Khwas and Sher Shah the Changatta (Mughal) at Delhi. *Indian Antiquary* 38.
1909b A triplet of Punjabi songs. *Indian Antiquary* 38.
1909c Three songs from Punjab. *Indian Antiquary* 38.
1909d A ballad of the Sikh wars. *Indian Antiquary* 38.
1909e The song of Sindhu Bir. *Indian Antiquary* 38.
ROY, S. C.
1912 *The Mundas and their country*. Calcutta: City Book House.
1915 *The Oraons of Chotanagpur*. Ranchi: The author.
1916 The divine myths of the Mundas. *Journal of the Bihar and Orissa Researcher Society* 2.
1925 *The Birhor*. Ranchi: Man in India Office.
1937 *The Kharias*, two volumes. Ranchi: Man in India Office.
SAHAL, K. L., P. P. GORE, *editors*
1941 *Choubali*. New Delhi: Sasta Sahitya Mandal.
SATYARTHI, DEVENDRA
1942 Bhojpuri Ahir folk songs. *New Review* 15.
1945 A cycle of Punjabi folk songs. *Man in India* 25.
1951 *Meet my people: Indian folk poetry*. Hyderabad: Chatana. (Originally published in 1946.)
1952 *Bajet awe dhol.* New Delhi: Asia.
1952–1953a Gaddi folk songs. *March of India* 5.
1952–1953b Folk songs of South India. *March of India* 5.
1953–1954 Folk songs of North India. *March of India* 6.
SATYENDRA
1957 *Braj ki lok kahanian*. Mathura: Braj Sahitya Mandal. (Originally published in 1947.)
1958 *Braj lok sahitya ka adhyayan*. Agra: Sahityaratan Bhandar.
1960 *Madhya jugiya Hindi sahitya ka lok Tantrik adhyayan*. Agra.
1962 *Lok sahitya vijyan*. Delhi: Shivalal Agrawal.
SATYENDRA, *editor*
1953 *Braj ka lok sahitya*. Mathura: Braj Sahitya Mandal.
SENGUPTA, SHANKAR, *editor*
1963 *Folklorists of Bengal*. Calcutta: Indian Publications.
1964 *Folklore researchers in India: Reception Committee of the All-India Folklore Conference, 1963*. Calcutta: Indian Publications.
SHARMA, HARI PRASAD
1954 *Bundelkhand lok geet*. Allahabad: Rai Saheb Ramdayal Agrawalla.

SHARMA, N. V., *editor*
1959a *Lok katha kosh*. Patna: Rashtra Bhasha Parishad.
1959b *Lok katha parichaya*. Patna: Rashtra Bhasha Parishad.
SHARPE, E.
1939 *Indian tales*. London.
SHASMAL, K. C.
1965 *Jhumar* and *khemta* songs of the Bauris of Hooghly District, West Bengal. *Folklore* 6.
SHASTRI, RAJA RAM
1958 *Hariyana lok manchha ki kahanian*.
SHIRREFF, A. G.
1936 *Hindi folk songs*. Allahabad: Hindi Mandir.
SINGH, D. S. P.
1948 *Bhojpuri lok geet me karun ras*. Prayag: Hindi Sahitya.
SINGH, KARAN
1962 *Shadow and sunlight: An anthology of Dogra-Pahari songs.*
SINGH, L. P., *editor*
1953 *Bhageli lok geet.*
SINGH, MOHAN
1951–1952 Folk songs of Punjab. *March of India* 4.
SINGH, M., S. K. PARIKH, T. SWAMI, S. DAS
1940 *Rajasthan ke gram geet*. Agra: Prasad.
SINHA, SATYAVRATA
1957 *Bhojpuri lok gatha*. Allahabad: Hindustan Academy.
SITA
1959 *Bharat ki lok kathaiyen*. Delhi: National Publishing House.
SMITH, M. W.
1948 Kota texts: a review of the primitive in India. *Journal of American Folklore* 61:283–297.
SOMDEV
1949 Some folk songs of Gorakhpur district. *Eastern Anthropologist* 2(4).
SRIVASTAVA, S. K.
1949a The Diwali among the Tharus. *Man in India* 29.
1949b Spring festival among the Tharus. *Eastern Anthropologist* 2(1).
STEEL, F. A.
1880 Folklore in Punjab. *Indian Antiquary* 9.
1881 Folklore in Punjab. *Indian Antiquary* 10.
1882 Folklore from Kashmir. *Indian Antiquary* 11.
1883 Folklore in Punjab. *Indian Antiquary* 12.
1884 Mirzapur folklore. *Indian Antiquary* 13.
STOKES, M.
1879 *Indian fairy tales*. Calcutta.
SWYNNERTON, C.
1884 *The adventures of the Punjabi hero Raja Rasalu, and other folk tales of the Punjab*. London.
1892 *Folktales from the upper Indus*. London: Elliot Stock.
1928 *Romantic tales from the Punjab*. London: Oxford University Press.
TAGORE, R.
n.d. *Lok sahitya*.
TAGORE, A.
n.d.

TAYLOR, WILLIAM, *translator*
1962 *The proverbs or sententious sayings of Athivira-Ramen in Oriental historical manuscripts*, volume two.
TEMPLE, R. C.
1882 Folklore in the Punjab. *Indian Antiquary* 11.
1900 The legends of Punjab. *Indian Antiquary* 29.
TEMPLE, R. C., H. A. ROSE
1909 Legends from the Punjab. *Indian Antiquary* 38.
THOMPSON, S., J. BALYS
1958 *The oral tales of India*. Bloomington: Indiana University Press.
THORNTON, T. H.
1885 The vernacular literature and folklore of Punjab. *Journal of the Royal Asiatic Society of Great Britain and Ireland* 17.
THURSTON, EDGAR
1943 Songs of mourning, probably from Chingleput district. *Man in India* 12:37–38.
TIWARI, U. N.
1949 Piria. *Man in India* 29.
n.d. *Bhojpuri bhasa aur uska sahitya*. Patna: Rashtra Bhasha Parishad.
TOPPO, EDMUND
1959 "Maler folklore." Unpublished M.A. thesis, Ranchi University, Ranchi, Bihar.
TRIGUNAYAT, JAGDISH
1957 *Bansari baj rahi*. Patna: Rashtra Bhasha Parishad.
TRIPATHI, RAM NARESH, *editor*
1952–1953 *Gram sahitya*, three volumes. Allahabad: Hindi Mandir; Delhi: Attaram.
UPADHYAYA, K. D.
1950a Bhojpuri folklore and ballads. *Eastern Anthropologist* 3, 4.
1950b *Bhojpuri gram geet*. Allahabad: Hindi Sahitya Sammelan.
1956 *Bhojpuri lok geet*. Prayag: Hindi Sahitya Sammelan.
1957 *Lok sahitya ki Bhumika*. Allahabad: Sahitya Bhaban.
1960 *Bhojpuri lok sahitya ka adhyayan*. Varanasi: Hindi Pracharak.
VENKATARAMAN, S. R.
1956 Three Koraga folk songs. *Vanyajati*, April.
VENKATASWAMI, M. N.
1896–1903 Folklore in the Central Provinces of India. *Indian Antiquary* 25, 26, 28, 30–32.
VERMA, B. L.
1957 *Bundelkhand ke lok geet*. Jhansi: Mayur.
VIDYARTHI, L. P.
1962 *The Maler: Nature-man-spirit complex*. Calcutta: Bookland.
VIDYARTHI, L. P., C. CHAUBEY, *editors*
1973 *Bihar in folklore studies*. Calcutta: Indian Publications.
VINOD, BAIJNATH
1958 *Bhojpuri lok sahitya: ek adhyayan*. Patna: Gyanpith.
WADIA, D. H. P.
1886 Folklore in western India. *Indian Antiquary* 15
YADAVA, SHANKAR LAL
1960 *Hariyana Pradesh ka lok sahitya*. Allahabad.

Biographical Notes

SATO APO. No biographical data available.

SORY CAMARA (1940) studied psychology, sociology and ethnology at the University of Bordeaux where he obtained a *doctorat de 3è cycle*. He continued his studies at the University of Paris V (Sorbonne) where he recently obtained a Ph.D in Ethnology. His research centers on the Mandenka — a West African people who at present are dispersed over Guinea, Mali, Senegal and some other countries. At the University of Bordeaux II, where he is a Maître de Conférences d'Ethnologie, he teaches theoretical, psychological, and medical ethnology. In addition he teaches at the Institut Culturel Africain de Lomé (Togo, West Africa). Among his published works are: *L'Univers dramatique et imaginaire des relations familiales chez les Mandenka* (1973); *L'Histoire pour les Mandenka* (1973); *The concept of heterogeneity and change among the Mandenka* (1975); *Différences et interactions culturelles* (1976); *Gens de la parole* (1976); *Paroles de nuit ou l'univers imaginaire des relations familiales chez les Mandenka* (1977).

ALAN DUNDES received his B.A. (1955) and M.A.T. (1958) from Yale and his Ph.D. (1962), in folklore, from Indiana University. Since 1968 he has been Professor of Anthropology and Folklore at the University of California, Berkeley. He is a fellow of both the American Folklore Society and the American Anthropological Association. Previous publications include: *The morphology of North American Indian folktales* (1964); *The study of folklore* (1965); *Every man his way* (1968); *Mother wit from the laughing barrel* (1973); and *Analytic essays in folklore* (1975).

BENGT K. HOLBEK (1929–) is a lecturer at the Folklore Institute of the University of Copenhagen. He was educated there (M.A. in folklore 1962), and was Archivist at the Danish Folklore Archives (1962–70) and Director of the Nordic Institute for Folklore (1928–72) before becoming a teacher. He has published studies of fables, proverbs, fabulous beings, jokes, etc., and is currently investigating tales of magic with a view to developing a new method for interpretation.

WM. HUGH JANSEN (1914–) is Professor of English and Folklore at the University of Kentucky, Lexington, Kentucky, U.S.A. Educated at Indiana University (Ph.D. under Dr. Stith Thompson) and Wesleyan University (Connecticut), he has been a Fellow of the Ford Foundation, of the National Endowment of the Humanities, and of the Fulbright Commission and is currently a Delegate Member of the American Council of Learned Societies. He was a pioneer in establishing the Esoteric-Exoteric (S-X) factor, in using implicit stereotypes in a folkloric item to characterize the cultural context of the item, and in quantifying performance expectation inherent in different folkloric genres. The author of *Abraham Oregon Smith* and numerous folkloric articles, he was also the editor of some fifteen volumes in both the *Memoirs* and the *Bibliographical Series* of the American Folklore Society.

ANTONIO PASQUALINO (1931–) is working as a surgeon in Palermo. Since 1965 he has been the Chairman of the *Associazione per la conservazione delle tradizioni popolari* [Association for the Preservation of the Popular Traditions]. This society has created the *Museo internazionale delle marionette* [International Marionette Museum]. He is Vicedirector of the anthropological review *Uomo e Cultura* [Man and Culture] and has been Vicepresident of the *Associazione italiana di studi semiotici* [Italian Association for Semiotic Studies].

In the field of human sciences his more significant works are: *Il repertorio epico dell'opera dei pupi* (1969) [The epic repertory of the Sicilian marionette theater]; *Funzioni e attanti nello studio della narrativa popolare* (1970) [Functions and actants in the study of popular narrative]; *Per un analisi morfologica della letteratura cavalleresca. I reali di Francia* (1970) [For a morphological analysis of chivalrous literature]; *Codici gestuali nel teatro dei pupi* (1975) [Gesture codes in the Sicilian marionette theater]; and *L'opera dei pupi* (1977) [The Sicilian marionette theater].

JUHA PENTIKÄINEN (1940–) is Professor of Comparative Religion at the University of Helsinki. He received his M.A. from the University of Helsinki in 1963 and a Ph.D. in Folkloristics and Comparative Religion from the University of Turku in 1968. He has been Visiting Professor of

Anthropology at the University of California in Berkeley in 1972, of Folklore at Indiana University, Bloomington, in 1972, and of Folklore at the University of Texas, Austin, in 1977. He is primarily concerned with the methodology of cultural anthropology; folkloristics and comparative religion (religious tradition, world view analysis, structuralism, depth research). His regional specialities include Arctic and Nordic peoples, especially minorities. Recent publications include *The Nordic dead-child tradition* (1968); *Kulttuuriantropologia* (with Lauri Honko, 1970); *Marina Takalon uskonto* (1971); *Uskonto ja yhteisö* (1976); *Lappische mythologie* (1978); *Oral repertoire and world view* (1978).

HAROLD SCHEUB. No biographical data available.

VERA K. SOKOLOVA (1908–), Doctor of Philological Sciences, is now Head of the folklore group of the Institute of Ethnography in Moscow (The Academy of Sciences of the USSR). Her publications include: *Russian historical songs of XVI—XVIII centuries* (1960), *Russian historical legends* (1970), articles on the history of Russian folklore (in *The essays of history of Russian ethnography, folk-lore and anthropology* (1956), and also articles in other books and periodicals (*Sovetskaja Etnografija*, for example).

HARRY SŪNA (1923–) works as a choreographer, and has been a Candidate of Science in Choreographology, a Merited Worker of Culture of the Latvian S.S.R., a researcher in the Folklore Division of the Language and Literature Institute of the Academy of Sciences of the Latvian S.S.R., Latvian dance class director in the Choreography Department of the Latvian State Conservatory, and General Director responsible for dance at the Latvian Song and Dance Festivals from 1960 to 1977. He completed his graduate work in the Department of Choreography of the Moscow State Theatre Arts Institute. He has choreographed dances for choreography ensembles, ballets, and opera as well as theater performances. Twenty-seven of his dance compositions have been published in Riga, Moscow, and Tallinn. He is the author of the following book: *Latvian collective rounds and round dances* (1966). Among his important articles are: "People's choreography at festivals of song and dance in Soviet Latvia" (1964); "The systematization of choreographical folklore (1967); "New system of cinetography — notation of choreographic movements" (1965); "The new cinetographical system of H. Sūna" (1966); "Folk choreography and choreographical culture in Latvia" (1969); "Some parallels between Latvian and Estonian folk choregraphy" (1970); "Ancient Latvian choreographic ceremonies associated with the festival of masks" (1974); and "The basic problems of origin and development of Latvian dance" (1976).

FRANCIS LEE UTLEY (1907–1974) was Professor of English in the Department of English, Ohio State University, Columbus. Among his publications are *Dictionary of the history of ideas* (1971) and *Studies in biblical and Jewish folklore* (1960).

LALIT P. VIDYARTHI (1931–) received his doctorate from the University of Chicago and is now Professor and Chairman of the Department of Anthropology at the University of Ranchi, India. Currently (1974–1978) he is the President of the International Union of Anthropological and Ethnological Sciences and of the Xth International Congress of Anthropological and Ethnological Sciences to be held in India in 1978. Dr. Vidyarthi is the President of the Indian Anthropological Association, a Founder Member of the Indian Council of Social Sciences Research, Chairman of the Task Force on Development of Tribal Areas of the Planning Commission, and a member of the Central Council on Tribal Research, Institute of the Ministry of Home Affairs, Government of India. He is Founder Editor of the *Journal of Social Research*, the *Indian Anthropologist*, and the *Research Journal of Ranchi University*. His numerous publications include books and articles as well as many volumes which he has edited. His major fields of research are the tribal culture of India; the Andaman and Nicobar Islands; urban-industrial, political, and action anthropology; Indian civilization; the history of Indian culture; folklore; and village studies.

ROBERT WILDHABER (1902–) was the former Director of the Swiss Museum for European Folklife in Basel, Switzerland. He studied at the Universities of Basel, Zurich, Heidelberg, London, and Perugia. He was a visiting professor at three American universities; he also arranged folk-art exhibitions in the U.S.A. for the Smithsonian Traveling Service. He is the editor of *International Folklore and Folklife Bibliography*, of the periodical *Schweizenisches Archiv fuer Volkskunde*, of the book *Schweizer Volksmaerchen*, and author of many folklore and ethnographic articles in Festschriften and periodicals.

Index of Names

Index of Subjects